Jack Benny and the Golden Age of
American Radio Comedy

Jack Benny and the Golden Age of American Radio Comedy

Kathryn H. Fuller-Seeley

UNIVERSITY OF CALIFORNIA PRESS

University of California Press, one of the most distinguished university presses in the United States, enriches lives around the world by advancing scholarship in the humanities, social sciences, and natural sciences. Its activities are supported by the UC Press Foundation and by philanthropic contributions from individuals and institutions. For more information, visit www.ucpress.edu.

University of California Press
Oakland, California

© 2017 by The Regents of the University of California

Library of Congress Cataloging-in-Publication Data

Names: Fuller-Seeley, Kathryn, author.
Title: Jack Benny and the golden age of American radio comedy / Kathryn H. Fuller-Seeley.
Description: Oakland, California: University of California Press, [2017] | Includes bibliographical references and index. |
Identifiers: LCCN 2017019382 (print) | LCCN 2017021349 (ebook) | ISBN 9780520967946 () | ISBN 9780520295056 (pbk.: alk. paper) | ISBN 9780520295049 (cloth: alk. paper)
Subjects: LCSH: Benny, Jack, 1894-1974. | Jack Benny program (Radio program) | Radio comedies—United States—History and criticism.
Classification: LCC PN2287.B4325 (ebook) | LCC PN2287.B4325 F85 2017 (print) | DDC 791.4/0924—dc23
LC record available at https://lccn.loc.gov/2017019382

[Manufactured in the United States of America / Printed in China]

26 25 24 23 22 21 20 19 18 17
10 9 8 7 6 5 4 3 2 1

CONTENTS

List of Illustrations vii
Acknowledgments xi

Introduction 1

1 · Becoming Benny: The Development of Jack Benny's Character-Focused Comedy for Radio 21

2 · "What Are You Laughing at, Mary?" Mary Livingstone's Comic Voice 53

3 · Masculine Gender Identity in Jack Benny's Humor 86

4 · Eddie Anderson, Rochester, and Race in 1930s Radio and Film 120

5 · Rochester and the Revenge of Uncle Tom in the 1940s and 1950s 154

6 · The Commercial Imperative: Jack Benny, Advertising, and Radio Sponsors 188

7 · Jack Benny's Intermedia Juggling of Radio and Film 223

8 · Benny at War with the Radio Critics 250

9 · Jack Benny's Turn Towards Television 281

Conclusion 309

Notes 319
Bibliography 357
Index 367

ILLUSTRATIONS

1. Benny and cast members Mary Livingstone, Phil Harris, Dennis Day, Eddie Anderson, and Don Wilson broadcasting. *Fortune*, April 1939. Author's collection. *4*

2. Jack Benny and his wife and co-star Mary Livingstone on cover of *Radio Mirror*, April 1935. Author's collection. *12*

3. Bandleader George Olsen and vocalist Ethel Shutta, the original draws for the Canada Dry Ginger Ale radio program, *New Movie Magazine*, September 1932. Author's collection. *28*

4. Jack Benny working closely with his current young script writers, Bill Morrow and Ed Beloin, while former Benny show writer Harry Conn is depicted working solo, *Radio Mirror*, November 1938. Author's collection. *45*

5. Mary Livingstone in an advertisement for Philco radios, *Saturday Evening Post*, December 1935. Author's collection. *66*

6. Mary Livingstone is given the glamorous cover girl treatment as befits one of radio's most popular stars. *Radio Guide*, October 19, 1935. Author's collection. *70*

7. Fred Allen and Jack Benny cleverly extended their feud long after its 1937 beginnings. Here in 1943, Fred reacts to the supposed rotten smell of Jack's poor jokes. *Tune In*, May 1943. Author's collection. *93*

8 and 9. The humor of Jack Benny's 1941 film adaptation of the old farce *Charley's Aunt* was promoted by local theaters as the surprise of a man dressed in women's clothing. Colonial Theater (location unknown) souvenir, 1941. Author's collection. *104*

10. Even before Benny performed his Gracie Allen routine on television, fan magazines were obsessed with reporting the details with which Benny transformed himself for private stage performance with women's clothing and makeup. *Radio Best*, October 1949, 34–35. Author's collection. *112*

11. The new celebrity scandal magazines seized on images of Jack Benny in makeup for his Gracie Allen impersonation as headline-worthy outré sexual behavior to exploit. *Uncensored*, November 1955. Author's collection. *117*

12. A rare appearance of Eddie Anderson as Rochester in a print advertisement for Jack Benny's radio sponsor's product, Jell-O. *Life*, circa Winter 1942, unknown date. Author's collection. *139*

13. By the 1940s, Eddie Anderson had become the most prominent African American star in Hollywood, and tourists sent home postcards of his elegant home. Circa 1942. Author's collection. *151*

14. Eddie Anderson and Jack Benny parlayed their radio popularity into film successes. *Movie Radio Guide*, December 20, 1941. Author's collection. *158*

15. The pairing of Jack Benny and Eddie Anderson on the cover of *Look* magazine, one of the first nationally prominent representations of black celebrity and interracial equality. *Look*, May 1950. Author's collection. *182*

16. Unlike previous sponsors' unease with Jack Benny's thorough mixture of impertinent mentions of the product into his comedy, Jell-O was pleased to promote his ratings and product sales success. Plymouth Theater program, Boston, November 26, 1934. Author's collection. *204*

17. Jack Benny and Mary Livingstone are transformed into cartoon characters happily consuming the playful product in this popular Jell-O giveaway recipe booklet, 1937. Author's collection. *207*

18. Young and Rubicam, the advertising agency for the Jell-O program, not only made the Benny program highest in the ratings but also brought awards for commercial writing and sold the product at extraordinary rates. Young and Rubicam ad, *Fortune*, February 1937, 121. Author's collection. *211*

19. Fan magazines were anxious to give their readers the inside scoop on what a live broadcast of a popular radio show like Benny's looked like,

so they could imagine joining in with the studio audience. *Radioland*, March 1935, 8. Author's collection. ***234***

20. Jack Benny created invaluable intermedia marketing synergy by playing up the radio cast's experiences on the set at Paramount producing their film *Buck Benny Rides Again*. *Movie Radio Guide*, February 1940. Author's collection. ***242***

21. The Sportsmen Quartet, who could only hum in response to Jack Benny's questions, sang parodies of popular songs that turned into delightfully nonsensical Lucky Strike cigarette commercials. *Radio Best*, March 1948, 10. Author's collection. ***269***

22. The studio audience's view of Jack Benny's live radio broadcast, featuring, left to right, Eddie Anderson, the Sportsmen Quartet (Bill Days, Mac Smith, Marty Sperzel, Gurney Bell), Don Wilson, Phil Harris, producer Hilliard Marks, Jack Benny, Mary Livingstone, musical arranger Mahlon Merrick (seated behind Mary), and Dennis Day. Mel Blanc is at far right. *Radio Mirror*, November 1948, 34. Author's collection. ***279***

23. The American Tobacco Company marketers achieved a brand promotional trifecta in this print ad, combining grinning caricatures of their stable of radio and TV stars, awkward product placement and brash ad slogans into an over-the-top holiday sales pitch. *LIFE* Magazine, December 1950. Author's collection. ***286***

24. Local television program guides promoted Jack Benny's first TV program as a special event in October 1950. *TV Forecast*, Chicago, October 28, 1950. Author's collection. ***295***

25. This joke magazine reflects the inseparable nature of Jack and Rochester's bond, and Rochester's fearless criticism of the Boss's failings. *1000 Jokes*, March 1956. Author's collection. ***303***

26. The biggest star in radio, when radio was the most prominent mass medium in the United States. *Radio Stars*, February 1938. Author's collection. ***310***

27. Jack Benny attempted to build the market for fans to purchase recordings of his best radio comedy routines so that they could collect and savor examples of his humor when was not broadcasting live on air. *The Jack Benny Album*, 1947. Author's collection. ***314***

28. The Top Ten series of record album releases were early, unsuccessful attempts to provide consumers with permanent copies of ephemeral live broadcasts. *The Jack Benny Album*, 1947. Author's collection. ***316***

ACKNOWLEDGEMENTS

I first became interested in Jack Benny as a twelve-year-old Ohio kid in the early 1970s, who loved watching old movies on TV. I prevailed upon my Grandma B. and my Mom to get me for Christmas several books in the Time-Life history of pop culture series *This Fabulous Century*. The 1930s volume fascinated me with its pictures of glamorous movie actresses, the 1939 World's Fair, Orson Welles performing his *War of the Worlds* broadcast, and especially a photo of two insane-looking men in suits, Jack Benny and Fred Allen, being restrained from attacking each other by their wives, with dialogue from their radio feud printed beneath it. I didn't know much about Benny, other than I had seen some of his guest appearances on TV programs like Ed Sullivan, *Laugh-In*, and *The Lucy Show*. I had never lived in a town where TV reruns of Benny's program were shown, but I had seen the 1959 Warner Bros. cartoon, "The Mouse that Jack Built," several times on Saturday mornings. I wanted to learn more about Jack Benny's radio program. So I wrote away for one of the Old Time Radio recording catalogs advertised in the revived *Liberty Magazine*. I remember paying $7.00 of my hard-earned babysitting wages to acquire each cassette tape containing two episodes of Benny's early 1950s radio programs. I listened to a dozen tapes over and over on a small player, coercing my little brothers JK and John to join me. (I am sure it has made them the marvelous fellows they have grown up to be.)

Fast forward forty-five years. Now $7.00 on eBay can buy 750+ Jack Benny radio broadcast recordings, digitized into .mp3 format and downloaded to a single DVD. For free I can access websites like www.archive.org to find episodes, or I can subscribe to Benny podcasts or OTR satellite radio channels. These are excellent times to be a fan of Jack Benny's radio program. To contribute to online resources for enjoyment of Benny's radio comedy, I have created a companion website for this book (www.jackbennyradio.com) where you will find links to radio episodes discussed in each chapter, plus additional photographs, scripts, and memorabilia. I hope you will check it out.

My graduate school training was in social and cultural history, and I have done a lot of research on the history of US film exhibition and moviegoing practices. But it has long been my dream to write about Benny's radio comedy, for despite his importance he has not yet been given his full due in academic scholarship. I am grateful to Michele Hilmes, Susan Douglas, Alan Havig, Arthur Wertheim, James Baughman, and other media historians whose pioneering publications have anchored Jack Benny's place in broadcasting studies. Previously, Joan Benny, Mary Livingstone, Irving Fein, Milt Josefsberg, and the Museum of Television and Radio told Benny's story in biographies published in the 1970s, 1980s, and early 1990s.

A Fellowship for University Teachers awarded by the National Endowment for the Humanities in 2013 gave me the time and support to write the manuscript, for which I am extremely grateful.

Helpful archivists assisted me in utilizing Jack Benny's archives at the American Heritage Center, University of Wyoming, and the Center supported me with a travel grant to do my initial research there; I am also grateful for the help I received at the State Historical Society of Wisconsin and the Margaret Herrick Library of the Academy of Motion Picture Arts and Sciences, as well as the UCLA Library Special Collections.

Laura Liebowitz, founder and president of the International Jack Benny Fan Club (www.jackbenny.org and on Facebook), and the club's incredibly knowledgeable and talented members have been a constant source of wonderment. Thanks Laura, Jim, Graeme, Linda, Don, John, Ellen, Matt, Darrel, Ben, Keith, Garth, Brad, Barry, Paula, Emily, R.C., Bill, Jon, Scott, Ira, Shelley, Jeff, Ellen, Martin, Jay, and all the IJBFC members, for your help, advice, encouragement, comradery, and terrific sense of humor.

Thank you to the wonderful colleagues who have read drafts of the chapters and encouraged me through the years I have been working on this project: David Weinstein, Eric Smoodin, Cynthia Meyers, Tom Doherty, Richard Butsch, Alan Havig, Michele Hilmes, Rob King, Colin Tait, Bill Kirkpatrick, Jennifer Hyland Wang, Brendan O'Neill, Nora Patterson, Shawn VanCour, Andrew Bottomley, Nick Marx, Ben Schwartz, Kyle Barnett, Richard Butsch, and Dana Polan, plus the Radio Studies Special Interest Group at SCMS, and media historians everywhere. At the University of California Press, thank you for the wise guidance of Raina Polivka and

Zuha Khan, and the hard work of production editors Nicholle Robertson and Kate Warne.

Many thanks to my colleagues at the University of Texas at Austin, including Alisa Perren, Tom Schatz, Caroline Frick, Suzanne Scott, Mary Beltran, Charles Ramirez Berg, Cindy McCreery, Paul Steckler, Jeff Miekle, Bert Herigstad, Elana Wakeman, A. J. Bunyard, Mona Syed, Rachel Walker, Char Burke, Gloria Holder and Michelle Monk. Thanks also to the many undergraduate and graduate students who have responded enthusiastically when I talk about Jack Benny, radio history, and comedy studies.

Thanks to the wonderful friends who have read chapter drafts, helped me find radio ephemera, toured historical Benny sites, and been fantastic supporters: Dick Simon, Bonnie Konowitch, Martha Kearsley, J. K. Helgesen, John Helgesen, Art and Kay Seidenberg, John Whiting, Penny Campbell, Karan Sheldon, Don O'Keefe, and Dave Bowers.

I am especially grateful for my dear family, who have always supported my research passions. My father-in-law Harry Seeley Jr. patiently read drafts of chapters and has been eternally encouraging. Kendall Seeley is generous with her encouragement and willingness to help. Kenny Seeley is always my best audience and editor, and he never complains about having to eat the Jell-O I feel compelled to make when I have been listening to 1930s Benny radio episodes.

Introduction

Jack Benny's most famous radio gag was first performed on March 28, 1948:

> Jack is walking down a neighborhood street at night. We hear him softly humming and his shoes contentedly tapping down the sidewalk. (He's carrying Ronald Colman's Oscar statuette, which he has borrowed to take home to show to Rochester, but that's another story....)
>
> Suddenly, a menacing male voice leaps out of the quiet, growling at Jack, "Hey buddy...this is a stick up!...Your money...or your life!"
>
> Silence. All we hear is seconds of silence...and the nervous tittering of the studio audience. Silence, or "dead air" was a risky proposition in commercial network radio broadcasting. It may have given listeners the impression that someone was thinking, but it often left listeners falling into a void of ether nothingness and loosened the grip of the advertisers over their attention.
>
> Breaking into the tense stillness, the robber repeats his demand, "Didn't you hear me?! I said...Your money...or...your life!"
>
> Again the silence, stretching, stretching, but this time accompanied by the growing laughter of the studio audience, chortling at the absurdity of Benny's continuing delay, each second compounding the hilarious suspense....
>
> "I'm thinking it over!" Benny finally cries.

The studio audience exploded into roars of laughter, releasing a pent-up emotional response of relief and disbelief that swept across the auditorium. Their reaction was shared by millions of radio listeners in homes across the nation. Their beloved, fallible "Fall Guy" had faced a dire situation and responded in a hilarious, typically self-centered way. But this wasn't simply a joke, and not quite a full comic routine; it was an exchange distilling an essential aspect of a continuing character, a moment that drew on more than fifteen years of writers' and performer labor as well as fifteen years of audience familiarity with Jack's infamously parsimonious character.

The "Your Money or Your Life" gag, so long in the making, was subsequently replayed by critics, fans and Benny himself for the rest of his radio and television career, and since then in every article discussing his lasting legacy in American entertainment. The genius of Jack Benny's humor is that it rarely stemmed from jokes with standard set ups and punch lines. It stemmed from character, embedded in a narrative, in countless stories of a foolish man's humiliation, enriched by the actors' voices, tone, and timing, with radio comedy's richness captivating the ears and imaginations of its listeners.

. . .

Radio was the most powerful and pervasive mass medium in United States from the late 1920s to the early 1950s, as its simple and inexpensive technological reach and its intense consolidation through commercial networks (NBC Red and Blue, CBS, Mutual) amplified the live messages of its most prominent speakers broadcast to an audience of unprecedented size. Thirty million or more Americans, gathered in small groups around receiving sets in their living rooms, stores, workplaces, and cars, simultaneously became a national audience. The charismatic political leaders, demagogues, crooners, and comics heard over the radio in this era had a tremendous impact on popular culture. Comedians were network radio's most popular performers, and Jack Benny was the most successful of them all. His voice was as familiar to listeners as President Franklin Roosevelt's. Jack Benny, in twenty-three years of weekly radio broadcasts, indelibly shaped American humor, and became one of the most influential entertainers of the twentieth century.

Born on Valentine's Day, February 14, 1894, in Chicago, Benjamin Kubelsky was the eldest child of Eastern European Jewish immigrant Meyer Kubelsky and his wife Sara. Benny Kubelsky was raised in the gritty northern Illinois manufacturing town of Waukegan, where Meyer was a moderately successful saloon operator and then haberdasher. Benny and his younger sister Florence had comfortable childhoods, merging their small Jewish community with a diverse array of assimilated and ethnic cousins and schoolmates. He wanted to title his autobiography "I Always Had Shoes."[1] From an early age, his parents hoped he would become a renowned concert violinist; Benny Kubelsky was a reluctant student of either textbooks or rigorous music lessons, however, and by age sixteen he abandoned school and took a job playing fiddle in the pit orchestra of Waukegan's Barrison Theater. Eventually he formed a duet with a local matronly pianist Cora Salisbury and started touring small-time Midwestern vaudeville, then partnered with young piano player Lyman Woods. World War I intervened, and Benny Kubelsky was drafted into the Navy. At the Great Lakes Training Center he took the comic stage role of a disorderly orderly in a camp production, and he found he enjoyed making people laugh. In the 1920s, he embarked on a vaudeville career, playing the violin much less and joking more often. Kubelsky encountered difficulty with his stage name, as his real name sounded too much like famous violinist Jan Kubelik. So he tried the moniker "Ben K. Benny," but the more well-known violinist-comic-bandleader Ben Bernie objected. Thus Benny Kubelsky styled himself "Jack Benny."[2]

As we will learn in subsequent chapters, Jack Benny became a moderately successful vaudeville solo comic performer in the 1920s, developing a style of breezy, informal, urban, but assimilated Anglo-type humor that drew from the suave "master of ceremonies" role model of star Frank Fay—but with self-deprecating tones that were all his own. In 1927 he married Sadye Marks, a twenty-one-year-old nonperformer he had met through the wife of a friend also playing the western vaudeville circuit. Soon Sadye was taking the occasional role of the flighty young flapper with whom Jack bantered in his stage routines. Benny appeared at the famed Palace Theater in New York, as the master of ceremonies in MGM's first talkie film *The Hollywood Revue of 1929*, and on Broadway in the risqué show Earl Carroll's *Vanities*. In the crunch of the Depression in 1932, with vaudeville and Broadway revues fading and film roles unsatisfactory, Jack Benny decided to try his hand at radio comedy.

Jack Benny's radio show, as it developed over the years on the air between 1932 and 1955, commercially sponsored most famously by Jell-O gelatin mix and Lucky Strike cigarettes, was a half-hour weekly comedy variety program that featured a group of quirky comic characters, led by Jack, who put on a radio program. Jack engaged in repartee around the microphones with the bandleader, singer, and announcer, and with chief-heckler/companion Mary Livingstone (Sadye Marks, who soon adopted this professional name as her own). The cast eventually coalesced around key regulars—announcer Don Wilson who joined in 1934, bandleader Phil Harris (1936), and singers Kenny Baker (1937) and Dennis Day (1939). When not fulfilling their purported duties, they joined Jack in studio adventures (enacting movie parodies and murder mysteries and kidding the sponsor's product). Other times their

FIGURE 1. The ad agency for Jack Benny's program during the Jell-O years, Young & Rubicam, touted to business leaders in ads like this the show's outstanding ability to integrate commercials with comedy, winning both high ratings and increased product sales. Benny and cast members Mary Livingstone, Phil Harris, Dennis Day, Eddie Anderson, and Don Wilson are shown in midbroadcast. *Fortune*, April 1939. Author's collection.

adventures occurred at Benny's house (staffed beginning in 1938 by Eddie Anderson portraying Rochester, Jack's impertinent valet) or out on the streets of Hollywood. The show's narrative world in the post–World War II years included additions such as infuriating department store floorwalker Mr. Nelson, hapless violin teacher Professor Le Blanc, long-suffering movie star neighbors Ronald and Benita Colman, the race track tout, Benny's underground money vault, and Jack's ancient, wheezing Maxwell jalopy.

The centerpiece of the comedy was vain, miserly "Fall Guy" Jack, whom his cast and his world constantly conspired to insult and frustrate. Jack Benny's radio character suffered all the indignities of the powerless patriarch in modern society—fractious workplace family, battles with obnoxious sales clerks, guff from his butler, and the withering disrespect of his sponsor, every woman he met, and Hollywood society. As the years rolled by, Jack's ever-more-absurd schemes to avoid spending money collapsed like his dignity, week after week, as his inflated ego was punctured by fate, abetted by his unruly radio cast.

Jack Benny was a comic genius, an absolute master of comic timing, an innovative creator, a dedicated craftsman, and a meticulous program producer. A canny entrepreneur, Benny became one of the pioneering "showrunner" producer/writer/performers in broadcasting history. His modern style of radio humor did much to spawn a wide variety of comedy formats and genres popular today. In vaudeville, he helped pioneer a kind of standup comedy that did not rely on props, costumes, gags, or circus-like physical slapstick. In radio, Benny and his writers pioneered the character-focused situation comedy, the genre that's remained at the heart of television's broadcast schedule. His informal monologues and easy repartee with comic assistant "stooges" were direct ancestors of the late night television talk show.

Benny skillfully leveraged vaudeville and broadcasting stardom across media forms into film and advertising prominence, and he innovated the "intermedia" integration of those rival industries into his radio show. He overcame difficult challenges thrown up by his sponsors to gain greater creative control of his program. His humorous commercials sardonically skewered American cultural foibles, slyly broke down listeners' reluctance to purchase his sponsors' products, and made his audiences actually enjoy listening to the advertising.

Benny and his writers utilized what radio historian Susan Douglas calls "linguistic slapstick," incorporating layers of aural humor into the program to engage listeners' imaginations.[3] The Benny show created a narrative space of disordered gender roles, a world turned upside down where sharp-tongued women brashly wounded the inflated egos of middle-class men like Benny who were "unmanly," cuckolded by their murderous wives in satirical sketches, disdained by Hollywood movie stars, and sneered at by supercilious department store clerks. Family audiences on Sunday evenings found that radio's invisibility, the laughter shared with studio audiences, and the familiar characters of the sitcom format made even Benny's most envelope-edge-pushing situations of gender blurring, racial integration, or racial stereotyping more acceptable fare when they might otherwise have been too controversial to depict visually. The socially conscious humor of Benny's radio program intrinsically drew on what radio historian Michele Hilmes terms the "disruptions caused by a disembodied medium in an insistently embodied (raced, classed, gendered) world."[4]

A caveat: Jack Benny, his writers, and the cast created their humor more than half a century ago, a time when cultural norms accepted vast amounts of racism, sexism, homophobia, and xenophobia. Benny's radio humor was a product of its time and place and will be subject to critical examination throughout this study. But at the same time, Benny and his writers, despite all their failings and omissions, could also sometimes show a flexible acceptance of social and cultural difference, creating a space to disrupt these widely held attitudes toward race and gender, taking the side of the marginalized against traditional patriarchal culture.

Jack Benny guided his radio program through challenges and successes throughout the 1930s, through wartime malaise and postwar triumph of rejuvenated appeal. In this time he also appeared in a number of films and in 1940 was an unexpected box office star when teamed with his radio comic foil, Eddie Anderson. Benny also weathered the personal crisis of a widely publicized scandal over supposed jewelry smuggling that could have ended his career. During wartime, Benny embarked on summer adventures with USO tours to military camps near the front lines in Africa, Europe, and in the Pacific. But soon after revitalizing his radio show in 1946, television loomed on the horizon, and Benny struggled with sponsors, the limits of the new media, and exacting newspaper critics, in the process of adapting his aural humor to the visual, which he finally began in October 1950. Benny remained the top comedian in radio through 1955, by which time network audiences had completely dwindled. Well established in television by that point, Jack Benny continued his highly rated TV comedy show for a total of fifteen years, until it was cancelled in 1965. Benny spent his seventh decade busy with regular television specials, frequent performances in Las Vegas and Lake Tahoe, and with giving scores of charity symphony concerts to benefit musical organizations around the nation. Benny worked right up until his death from pancreatic cancer on December 25, 1974, and TV specials and newspaper headlines mourned the loss of a national treasure.

This is not meant to be a full biography of Jack Benny, but rather a multifaceted examination of his radio career, his greatest achievement. I use close analysis of the entertainment industry trade press, primary research sources, and original scripts and program broadcasts to explore the impacts of performer, media industry, texts, and audiences on each other, which created the cultural meaning of Benny's radio program for midcentury America. It persists as classic comedy to entertain us today. I hope that this book encourages you to listen to the wealth of available Benny radio recordings. To that end, I have created a companion website (www.jackbennyradio.com) containing audio clips, original scripts, memorabilia, and further information on internet sources that explore Benny's humor. Jack Benny's radio comedy remains fresh today; its light-hearted, self-reflexive impertinence and sense of camaraderie invites us all to become part of Benny's gang.

CONSTRUCTING COMEDY ON THE RADIO

As were Jack Benny's earliest Canada Dry radio performances in May 1932, comedy over the airwaves could be produced as if it was just vaudeville with the lights turned off. Removing the physical comedy and visual cues to the audience, however, created major challenges for performers steeped in theatrical traditions, like Ed Wynn and Eddie Cantor, who had been dependent on creating reactions with their outlandish costumes and punching up their jokes with mugging and facial expressions, body movements, use of props, pratfalls, and other kinds of physical shtick.[5]

The radio comedian's primary tool was his voice. "Rough or smooth, high or low, a good radio voice must have personality, with all the intangibles and seeming contradictions the word implies," *New York Times* radio critic John Hutchens once commented. "At its best, it is really distinctive to the point where you would recognize it if you had not heard it for months or even years."[6] The comic's voice needed to be clear and understandable as it passed through technologically limited microphones, out into the ether, and back in through tinny radio speakers, and to be heard over the static or reception difficulties in listeners' living rooms.[7] Franklin Roosevelt, like Jack Benny, had a radio kind of voice. Hutchens called FDR's voice "warm and confidential, dignified but informal, unhurried; even though he reads his speeches, it seemed conversational, that he was talking to individuals."[8] Jack Benny's Midwestern twang (which represented "honesty and common sense" to Hutchens) transferred well from vaudeville to the radio. He'd used relatively few visual cues on the stage, dressed in a tuxedo or modern suit, and moved smoothly and quietly, and his only props were a violin he rarely played and a cigar he rarely smoked.

Benny was widely acknowledged to have the best sense of comic timing in the radio industry, a concept he struggled to explain: "I talk very slowly and I talk like I am talking to you... I might hesitate... I might think. Everybody has a feeling... that I am addressing him or her individually." His informal style often came across to the audience as if he was ad-libbing, when in fact, Benny and his cast were presenting scripted dialogue, carefully edited by Benny to have the best rhythm and flow.[9]

Benny and his first scriptwriter writer Harry Conn, like other early creators of radio humor, soon began moving from monologues to experimenting with the inventive possibilities listeners could bring to the production, and began to expand fictional spaces in which the show's dialogue and sketches took place, helping their programs create what would become radio's biggest asset as "theater of the mind."[10] Through vocal inflections, whispers, sobs, laughter, snideness, singing, or bellowing, talented radio actors could express a world of emotion, and could unleash the listener's imagination. From the mid-1940s onward, Mel Blanc would voice scores of different human and animal characters on Benny's program, even the sputtering engine of Benny's decrepit Maxwell automobile.

With no visual cues to tell a crowded scene of actors apart, the number of people speaking in a radio sketch needed to be limited to no more than three or four speaking, and no two could sound too similar. In the early 1930s, Conn believed that ethnic American voices were inherently funny. Without the costumes to help create an immediately recognizable stereotype, Conn thought that ethnic comedians filling small roles on the Benny program should lay on the accents thickly. When Phil Harris joined the Benny program in fall 1936, his voice and Jack's were said to sound too much alike, so Phil adopted a broad Southern accent for his on-air character. When Eddie Anderson joined the program the first time in 1937 in a role as a train porter, it was similarly because Benny and the writers sought an unusual voice.

New voices needed to be introduced by name, and names repeatedly mentioned to keep characters in the audience's imagination. Benny's radio show thus had a lot of identifying dialogue ("Say, Jack, I'm opening the door... What's in your hand, Don?... Oh, here comes Mary") that would have to be excised once the show moved to television. As Erik Barnouw discussed in his textbook on radio writing, when a person on the radio was not speaking for more than a few seconds, the audience would forget his or her presence. Barnouw complimented the Benny program for using Mary Livingstone's voice to turn this liability into a humorous surprise, such as when Jack and another character would trade a long series of boastful comments, and then Mary would leap into the crescendo of the exchange with a sharp putdown.[11]

Radio writer Art Hanley's guide to comedy writing for broadcasting instructed students to use dialogue to paint descriptive word pictures of settings and characters.[12] "Keep all speeches short and to the point," Hanley counseled, "Use action words, color words, natural words; mention specific places and tangibles such as the furniture in the room.[13] The Benny program baldly violated some of Hanley's cardinal rules, such as "Don't write in bit parts of one or two lines for extra voices unless there's very good reason. They tend to confuse the listener and complication the action." Benny often spent up to $1,000 in salary just to have Frank Nelson suddenly pop into a scene to drive Jack crazy with a withering "Yeeeeeessss?" Hanley, however, approved of another Benny program staple, the running gag, as a "short cut to effective comedy," a bit repeated three or four times, "often enough to become familiar and excite humorous association and humorous anticipation at another hearing."[14]

Hanley taught writers that on radio, a joke's punch line must be placed at the end of a line, for fear that studio audience laughter would muddle or "walk over" what home listeners were able to hear.[15] Managing talk and silence, and leaving time for audience laughter were major tasks in writing the Benny radio program. The program was performed live in front of studio audiences usually numbering 300–400 people. Studio audience laughter was a kind of currency for network comedy programs. Benny's writers and ad agency program producers "graded" the strength and duration produced by each laugh during each episode.[16] Sponsors demanded to hear as many laughs as possible on their programs, and annual renewals hung in the balance.[17] Benny's writers had to properly estimate the timing of the "spread," the space left between actors' jokes for audience laughter, usually two or three seconds. Extraordinarily big jokes might produce audience laughter of 6, 8, or 12 seconds (several extraordinary Benny studio audience laughs have been clocked at over 20 seconds).[18] With live radio shows scripted down to the last second, failing to account for audience laughter could run afoul of the all-important closing commercial or make a show run overlong (both verboten, back in the day); it sent Benny's writers and ad agency producers with slashing blue pencils to remove jokes to have the show end up on time.

Most radio comedians did not labor alone to create their own scripts (Fred Allen being a famous exception). Jack Benny needed writers to craft the enormous amount of new material required for each week's program, up to thirty-nine episodes per season. While Benny wasn't a quick comic writer, he made tremendous contributions to the show as one of the keenest and most obsessive script editors in the business, as a 1945 magazine article noted:

> There is one area in which Benny feels confident and secure. He knows better than any other man in the world what will be funny on the Jack Benny program. More exactly, he knows what will NOT be funny. "I can't always tell when a line is good," he says, "but brother, I can tell when it's lousy." By the slow and painful process of eliminating the lousy, Benny builds a good script.... Perfectionist Benny will work for half an hour over a single line, polishing it as lovingly as a poet would a couplet. He knows the speech rhythms of all his players and reshapes each line to fit these idiosyncrasies.[19]

Hanley cautioned the comedy writer of performers, "You supply the meat, he the dressing." Writers' material could only be as funny as the actors who performed their lines. A radio actor needed a spontaneous ability to "read around" the dialogue, giving a loose reading to the line to make it sound like idle patter. Hanley warned that a poor performer could "muff your lines, pace his reading badly, hog the spotlight when he doesn't belong, throw in ad-libs that don't fit, stop being funny and jump laughs" noting that it was imperative that actors have the patience to wait for the studio audience's laugh, but then to be able to jump in quickly with topper gags.[20]

Radio comedians and their writers crafted "linguistic slapstick" to produce humor over the air that paralleled the raucous physical and visual shenanigans with which their film compatriots entertained movie audiences.[21] The easiest and most direct way to play with language was with puns, simple wordplay drawing its humor from the incongruity of mixing up similar sounding words with different meanings. While humor theorists consider puns the lowest form of humor, the more unexpected or incongruous a pun was, while slyly making a new kind of sense out of nonsense, the more surprisingly humorous a pun could be. The "rule of threes" helped structure jokes and exchanges; the first two attempts to do something straightforwardly set up a pattern that the unusual occurrence the third time comically destroyed.[22] Other humor tailor-made for radio was funny-sounding words.[23] Humorists note that the sound of the letter K in all its permutations, and B, D, G, P, and T make words sound amusing, while others have suggested sprinkling specific, colorful words into jokes to make them punchier and more memorable.[24]

Benny and his writers were able to create seemingly endless streams of humor, not by reworking stock gags from joke books, but by creating characters with odd traits and quirky personalities who made their comedy by interacting with each other. The comic persona of "Jack," honed over the first years of the show, was the tent pole of the show's humor. A 1938 *Scribner's* article claimed Jack was

> a character aimed dead-center at the universal tendency to howl at the self-confident man who makes a fool of himself. Jack isn't the wise guy who tells all the jokes on his show nor the brightie [*sic*] who has all the funny lines. He's on the other end of the gun. He is the target of most of the jokes, most of the comic situations. You laugh at him, but you also sympathize with him because, almost inevitably, his best-laid plans blow up in his face. He's the pleasant oaf, strutting down the street, superbly sure that he's making a tremendous impression. When he steps on a banana peel, and lands on his backside, you guffaw at him, but you pity him a little, too.[25]

Humor theorists have found incongruity to be the basis of most comedy—audiences laugh at things that do not fit logical patterns, that are exaggerated, absurd, out of place, and which cross up our expectations. Henri Bergson found humor in the incongruity of people acting like machines, being too literal minded to bend with the flexibility life demands. Sigmund Freud found underlying subconscious desires about sex, death, and humiliation at work in jokes. Thomas Hobbes was especially interested in the laughter of the sudden superiority of a victor over a foe.[26] Pomposity brought down to the common level through pratfalls or insults is always funny, as have been the endless battles between supposedly loving husbands and wives. Yet for all the incongruities, insults, and humiliations that the Jack Benny character faced, for him and his cast-mates to remain popular with audiences the comedy managed also to include sympathetic aspects for the characters to remain beloved by fans. Benny's radio program ultimately balanced insults and sympathy, disdain for Jack and everyone's feeling of superiority to him, with a lasting, familiar connection.

FIGURE 2. Jack Benny, and radio fan magazines, came to prominence together. He and his co-star Mary Livingstone (his chief heckler on radio and wife in real life) were frequently promoted in publications geared to the growing number of fans, who sought to learn about their personal lives as well—such as news about the Benny's adopted daughter Joan. *Radio Mirror*, April 1935. Author's collection.

Benny's favorite comic writer, Stephen Leacock, a Canadian humorist and economics professor at McGill University,[27] outlined a progression of humor that moved from the simple slapstick of children and delight in physical incongruities and play, to the word-play of puns, through jokes, parody, and satire, to what he considered the deeper level of humor, the development of comic characters. The highest form of humor, he thought, past puns and jokes and incongruity and vivid characters, "is the incongruity of life itself, the contrast between the fretting cares and the petty sorrows of the day and the long mystery of tomorrow. Here laughter and tears become one, and humor becomes the contemplation and interpretation of our life."[28] Benny's comedy took this to heart, in the way that the sixteen-year development of Jack's "schmo" character on radio could lead him to debate how to face a question like "Your money or your life?" Leacock, like Benny, found that, ultimately, humor is about life itself, "from the angers and troubles of childhood to the fates and follies of all mankind."[29]

SOURCES

To begin my exploration of Jack Benny's broadcasting comedy and career, I started with the radio programs. Benny performed 922 half-hour episodes live over the airwaves between 1932 and 1955. Absence of recordings and lack of access to them has always been the greatest challenge to American radio scholarship. Listeners interested in Jack Benny are fortunate, in that approximately 750 full or partial recordings of Benny's programs exist. In the past, it was an onerous task to find, collect, or listen to those nearly 400 hours of shows, an endeavor that involved great expense or many years of trading tapes with other fans or searching for nostalgic broadcasts of "Old Time Radio" (OTR) programs. Today, digital recording technology and internet availability are revolutionizing public access to old broadcasts, and Benny's radio programs can be inexpensively purchased on CDs and DVDs, and accessed freely through websites like www.archive.org and the International Jack Benny Fan Club, www.jackbenny.org, and can be listened to through a wide variety of electronic devices. With access to so many episodes, choosing only a few to study could not fully reveal the insights into character development and construction of humor of Benny's show as it evolved over twenty-three years on the air, so I have listened to them all, repeatedly, over several years while on long cross-country car trips or daily commutes.

Original program scripts provide additional insight, and all of Benny's scripts exist in university archives, although they are usually only "as broadcast" copies. Few preliminary drafts of Benny's weekly radio script treatments survive for us to trace the writers' and editors' work as each episode was constructed. Some of Benny's own working copies of his final scripts, however, reveal his editorial efforts, as they contain extratextual markings. Benny polished the dialogue and language of his lines up to the moment of broadcast, to perfect the timing, emphasis, and laugh-getting potential of each line.

Benny donated a nearly complete set of his radio program scripts to UCLA. This collection also includes scripts for the approximately 170 episodes (broadcast 1932–1936) for which there are no recordings. Reading these early scripts, unheard for over eighty years, unveiled the process of experimentation, trial, and error that Benny and scriptwriter Harry Conn used in constructing the comedic form of the program and developing the program's characters. Other partial collections are housed at the American Heritage Center and the Library of Congress. Lucky Strike–era radio and TV scripts are available in digital form at www.tobaccodocuments.com.

Following Jack Benny's career in the entertainment trade press enabled me to better understand Benny's role as radio producer and intermedia performer who moved across the rival media forms of vaudeville, film, and broadcasting. The ability to search articles and reviews in digitized versions of *Variety*, *Billboard*, *Sponsor*, and other publications at www.mediahistoryproject.org shed light on the challenges and problems Benny faced throughout his show business career. Regrettably, Benny's archives contain almost no correspondence with radio network executives, sponsors, or the advertising agency workers who actually co-produced Benny's programs. The details of contract negotiations, fan mail, complaints from the public, negotiations with NBC and CBS's Continuity Acceptance departments over script details, and the entries to the "Why I Can't Stand Jack Benny" contest all are long gone. The NBC papers at the Wisconsin State Historical Society and Library of Congress contain some scattered but very intriguing examples from early in Benny's radio career of how network executives developed program formats, were involved in hiring performers, and had to run interference between anxious, demanding, interfering sponsors and anxious, demanding, interfering talent.

Jack Benny and Mary Livingstone assembled an extensive series of personal scrapbooks and clippings files containing reviews and articles published in newspapers, magazines, and fan periodicals throughout their careers. Benny's scrapbooks are housed at the American Heritage Center at the University of Wyoming. They offer fascinating insight into what material evidence Jack and Mary sought to preserve and remember about their careers, including both favorable and unfavorable theatrical notices and reviews. While Eddie Anderson did not leave archival materials behind, the African American press frequently discussed Anderson's career and role as Rochester.

Material culled from these historical newspapers greatly increased my understanding of the support and criticism he faced in both the black and white communities in the 1930s and 1940s.

Resources at the Margaret Herrick Library of the Academy of Motion Picture Arts and Sciences gave me insights into how the light musical/variety films in which Benny appeared in the 1930s and 1940s proceeded through the Production Code's vetting. Director Mark Sandrich's scrapbooks invaluably documented the production and promotion of Benny's three most radio-flavored films (and huge box office successes) at Paramount in the 1939–1941 period. Studio advertising press books for the films demonstrated how the studio bumbled its way through creating intermedia links to promote the films to the American public.

My project benefits from the work of many scholars writing about radio broadcasting history, comedy, celebrity studies, gender and racial identity, cultural history, and media industry studies, which I will address in the following chapters. I am grateful that several biographical accounts were published in the years after Benny's death by his manager Irving Fein, scriptwriter Milt Josefsberg, and wife Mary Livingstone. In 1990 Joan Benny published a wonderful volume that combined her own memories with an autobiographical account written by her father in the 1960s.[30] The full flowering of research into American radio history, examining entwined development of the industry, its creators, programs, technology, audiences, and cultural impact, began with the outstanding analysis of Michele Hilmes in *Radio Voices* (1997) and Susan Douglas in *Listening In* (1999). Both see Benny as a defining figure representing some of the highest achievements in the history of American commercial network radio. Their critical insights have set high standards for scholars to build on, as the fields of twentieth-century media industry studies and broadcasting history and sound studies have continued to expand.

THE CHAPTERS

The first half of this book takes a cultural history approach to the origination of Jack Benny's radio comedy, examining how Jack Benny and his writers developed comic characters for himself, Mary Livingstone, and Rochester, and continuing, flexible narratives through a process of trial and error. The first chapter explores how Jack Benny adapted his vaudeville style of humor, as a self-deprecating, Midwestern-flavored "Broadway Romeo," to radio, beginning in May 1932. Discovering that live weekly broadcasting was a ferocious devourer of new material, Benny hurriedly hired vaudeville gagster Harry Conn to write the program with him. Partners Benny and Conn began expanding the narrative possibilities of the radio format from monologues to dialogues, which pulled in the bandleader, announcer, and singer; they opened out the narrative world of the show by having speakers figuratively move away from the microphone to fictional adventures. Benny and Conn developed a program that was refreshingly self-referential, with the cast blending fiction and reality by performing as a group of workers putting on a radio show. They irreverently broke the fourth wall of theatrical performance, acknowledging their audiences and making fun of the advertisements and their roles on the program. Most significantly, in 1934 they reshaped Jack's character to become an increasingly more fallible character, the "Fall Guy," the butt of everyone's jokes. Jack became egotistical and vain, penurious and mistake-prone. Constantly making social faux pas, he became more frequently criticized, humbled, and insulted by his cast of radio show employees. Tensions in Benny and Conn's creative partnership over how they shared authorship boiled over in March 1936. Conn quit and struggled to find success, while Benny hired new writers who helped him take his show, now sponsored by Jell-O, to new heights of popularity.

The second chapter examines the strength of the "Unruly Woman" comic voice on the Benny program, in the character of Mary Livingstone (Benny's off-stage wife Sadye Marks). Mary's character exhibited an extraordinary level of independence and biting wit that made her the equal of strong-willed Hollywood film heroines. In her initial appearances on the radio program in 1932, Mary began as an addlepated girl, but her character soon combined the genial nonsense of a Gracie Allen with sharper, mocking tones. In satirical skits, Mary adopted an imitation of Mae West (which eventually morphed into a "tough girl" voice) to represent a confident sexuality. Using her distinctive laughter to leap into conversations and disrupt Jack's egotistical pretensions, Mary became an impertinent, sharp-tongued companion and chief heckler who joined by the other brash waitresses and steamroller-driving mothers who emerged victorious in the show's battle of the sexes.

Chapter Three explores how, over twenty-five years, Benny's radio character played with the construction of gender identity, questioning rigid ideas about heterosexual masculinity that punctured the pretensions of patriarchal culture. Jack enacted a variety of masculinities from demanding boss, to the boisterous rivalry of the Benny Allen feud, to the unmanly character mocked for his vanity, his age, his toupees, his cheapness, and especially his lack of sexual prowess, to dead-fish-kissing asexuality, to queerness. Jack's masculine Jewish identity was also expressed with subtlety. The ways in which critics interpreted Benny's slippery character kept changing during the shifting cultural climates of the Depression, wartime, and postwar years, while Jack's playful gender blurring remained much the same. Benny played the cross-dressing lead role in a 1941 film version of *Charley's Aunt*, and critics found the source of its humor in the titillation of the sharp boundaries of male and female being crossed in slapstick manner. Benny incorporated skits about donning his Charley's Aunt costume to dance with soldiers into his wartime-era radio programs, inviting laughter that mingled titillation with confusion. In the late 1940s Benny devised a skit with George Burns in which he impersonated Gracie Allen, with uncanny accuracy of dress and performance. When Benny showcased his Gracie routine in TV episodes in 1952 and 1954, loud critical reaction showed the power of visuality and growing tensions in American culture over appropriate gendered behavior and fear of alternative sexual expression.

Chapters Four and Five discuss the career of Eddie Anderson, whose success was deeply entwined with and dependent on Benny's. Anderson performed the role of Jack's African American valet Rochester Van Jones on the radio program from 1938 to 1955 (and would continue on television). As the most frequently featured black actor in American radio, film, and TV, Anderson's radio and film career (neglected by media historians) provides a notable case study of the struggles and achievements of an African American performer moving between media industries in the first half of the twentieth century. Rochester's character was central to the construction of race on American radio. Made "safe" for white audiences to enjoy because of his servant role, Anderson as Rochester entered millions of homes every week. Although Rochester was an intelligent, sassy butler, Benny's writers often saddled the character with racist stereotypes, enabling many radio reviewers to describe him as shiftless, superstitious, and content with low pay and a tyrannical boss. The radio show was obsessed with making references to his black skin, emphasizing his difference yet uniqueness.

Audiences in the black community struggled with Anderson's identity as a famous radio celebrity, some delighted and proud to see an African American become so prominent in mainstream white network radio. Anderson's 1940 surprise success in several movies co-starring with Benny brought even more renown. During the racial tensions of World War II, more African American critics began to speak out against the crushing limitations of servant roles on the expression of a more complex black culture. Eddie Anderson as Rochester found himself very much caught in the middle—between widespread success, then growing racist backlash from conservative whites on the one hand, and growing disdain from black liberal critics on the other. Debates in the African American press and film and radio trade journals chart Anderson's story from the peak of his mainstream stardom in white culture early during World War II, to the resistance and criticism he and his character increasingly faced as wartime optimism and ideals of racial integration into popular film and society started drawing backlash from both white and black critics. From the mid-1940s into the 1950s, Rochester became Benny's most constant companion. Increasingly, however, the tensions of the civil rights movement complicated Rochester's position, as Anderson faced hostile responses not only from racist Southern whites for his "too-familiar" film roles but also increasing criticism from the black community.

The second half of the book analyzes the continuing development of Jack Benny's radio show from the perspectives of media industry studies. Chapter Six examines Benny's achievements as a canny creator of advertising messages and media producer. It explores his battles with sponsors over creative control of his program, and his famous integration of sponsors' products into his comedy, from conservative Canada Dry in 1932, to Jell-O (too successful, forcing the sponsor to end it), to Lucky Strike in 1944 (the most hucksterish of all sponsors, feared in the advertising industry and loathed by cultural critics). Benny brilliantly sent up his sponsors' products with ironically humorous commercials that turned the commodities into absurdities and soothed the incursions of consumer culture into listeners' everyday lives.

Chapter Seven argues that Jack Benny was among the most innovative and successful intermedia performers in mid-twentieth-century American entertainment. He conquered not only radio but also film, advertising, and live performance, simultaneously. Despite Hollywood's disdain for radio, and numerous barriers to collaboration and integration of separate media, Jack Benny (like Bing Crosby and Bob Hope) succeeded in the strategic intermedia incorporation of elements of radio, film, and sponsor's products into his live broadcasting performances. Benny's publicity helped make Los Angeles the capital of American radio production, and promoted Southern

California as a tourist destination. His innovative incorporation of parodies of popular films helped domesticate the brittle glamour of Hollywood films and stars and entwine the two media in listeners' minds. Several of Benny's popular radio-themed Hollywood movies, produced from 1939 to 1942, pushed intermedia collaboration at the box office, but stirred up a hornet's nest of criticism from appalled New York film critics, who complained (just as would TV critics a decade later) that radio's focus on aural humor compromised the cinematic form.

Chapter Eight examines Benny's wartime creative crisis and the role he played in radio broadcasting's larger postwar aesthetic turmoil. Starting in 1945, a new generation of outspoken newspaper and magazine journalists including John Crosby, Jack Gould, and Gilbert Seldes and others began to blast critical commentary at the inadequacies of radio programming, laying much of the blame for radio's stultifying sameness on the comedians—from the bland staleness of their formats to their overdependence on corrosive insult humor, to the conservative domination of sponsors over the weekly schedule. Their favorite target for scorn was Jack Benny, as the quintessential symbol of the American system of commercial broadcasting. The critics' invective stung, but also spurred Benny and his writers to develop innovations in characters, situations, and themes, reclaiming the ratings leadership and earning acclaim of those who call the postwar years Benny's "golden era" of radio humor, all of this occurring in the shadow of coming changes in broadcasting.

Chapter Nine analyzes how Benny struggled to meet the creative challenges that television brought to his career. While Milton Berle's fame in the new medium skyrocketed in 1948–1949, Benny was initially quite reluctant to make the leap. TV critics' insistence on a new visually oriented comedy confused and discomfited Benny, who hesitated to move his fantastical comedy elements such as the subterranean vault and wheezing Maxwell, which depended for their humor on the listener's imagination, to the new medium. Through trial and error and in the face of criticism from TV reviewers, Benny eventually followed his own path of adaptation to television. He reduced some favorite radio routines but blended in aspects of his old vaudeville act, and especially found new ways to connect directly with television audiences, as he moved from occasional video appearances in 1950–1951 to a regular TV schedule and the eventual ending of his radio series in 1955. The book concludes by considering the legacy of aural humor and radio themes that remained interwoven into Benny's television performances.

ONE

Becoming Benny

**THE DEVELOPMENT OF JACK BENNY'S
CHARACTER-FOCUSED COMEDY FOR RADIO**

Anticipation mixed with anxiety in the small, glass-enclosed broadcasting studio installed in the old roof garden situated atop Broadway's New Amsterdam Theater on Monday night, May 2, 1932. Beginning at 9:30 P.M. EST, the inaugural episode of Canada Dry Ginger Ale's half-hour radio program aired live, carried over a network of NBC Blue radio stations covering the eastern United States. The only audience members were representatives from the show's sponsor, advertising agency, and network. The program's concept and cast had been assembled for Canada Dry by NBC executive Bertha Brainard as a new direction in sponsorship for the company, which had previously underwritten a dramatic (and violent) adventure series set in the Canadian Rockies.[1] Canada Dry's advertising agency N. W. Ayer & Son billed the new show as "30 minutes of music and quips" featuring six numbers played by New York bandleader George Olsen and his orchestra and sung by his spouse, Ziegfeld Follies star Ethel Shutta. Already widely familiar to radio listeners, they were considered to be the main attraction of the show.[2] The music would be interspersed with brief monologue segments performed by thirty-eight-year-old vaudeville veteran Jack Benny, who was introduced as "that suave comedian, dry humorist and famous master of ceremonies."[3] In his first performance for Canada Dry, Benny told a series of jokes drawn from his well-honed stage routine, offering informal and genially self-deprecating comments on personal experiences, such as his Hollywood adventures and the mediocrity of his girlfriend, who posed for the "before" in "before and after" photos. By the conclusion of his fourth biweekly episode, Benny queasily realized he had used up nearly every monologue he had perfected over fifteen years in vaudeville, and more broadcasts lay ahead of him.

The new Canada Dry show joined a rapidly increasing number of variety-comedy programs on primetime network radio. While music had been the dominant program form of the previous five years, the entertainment trade press noted that comedy was growing as a less expensive option for sponsors weary of paying for high-priced orchestras and temperamental crooners. New shows in the 1932 season featured not only newcomer Jack Benny but also other vaudevillians such as George Burns and Gracie Allen, George Jessel, Fred Allen, and Jack Pearl. Most, like Benny, were serving as "emcees" (short for M.C. or master of ceremonies) for programs that mixed music, comedy, and advertising messages. The new entrants joined such already-popular variety programs as those hosted by Rudy Vallee for Fleischmann's Yeast, Ed Wynn for Texaco, and Eddie Cantor for Chase and Sanborn Coffee.[4]

The burgeoning popularity and financial success of commercial network radio was the one bright spot in an American economy sliding ever further into the Great Depression. The unemployment rate was nearly 25 percent, banks were closing left and right, and major industries had ground to a standstill. The entertainment world was hit especially hard. The majority of Broadway theaters were shuttered, major league baseball teams were playing in stadiums emptied of spectators, and vacation resorts appeared abandoned. Even the movie studios and picture palaces, which with the tremendous popularity of "talkies" had seemed immune to the economic crisis, now experienced a devastating downturn in business.[5] The advertising business (also tremendously hard-hit) found that clients who promoted their products on radio programs (especially inexpensive consumer goods like tobacco, soap, and coffee) were seeing enormous sales gains.[6] The speed and extent to which previously unknown performers like Freeman Gosden and Charles Correll had become nationally famous as "Amos 'n' Andy" astonished entertainment veterans like Benny (the duo hadn't paid their dues by honing their act for years in theaters in the hinterlands).[7] The gloating of the Pepsodent company, whose toothpaste's previous meager sales skyrocketed when it began sponsoring the *Amos 'n' Andy* program in 1929 was impossible to ignore. The pull of this growing entertainment medium, coupled with the push of steeply declining opportunities on Broadway and in vaudeville due to the Depression, propelled the apprehensive Benny to try his hand in radio.[8]

Facing the daunting challenge of filling radio's unprecedented, ferocious demand for new content, Jack Benny initially struggled, but ultimately thrived in the new medium by developing new approaches to comedy. Benny and scriptwriter Harry Conn began to craft a personality-based radio variety program, drawing on Benny's vaudeville style and exploring new (to them) comic constructions of what contemporary critics termed *character comedy* and comedy *situations*. Experimenting as the program progressed from week to week, Benny and Conn expanded the narrative world of the show. They began developing comic identities for the major performers (orchestra leader, vocalist, and announcer) who stood around the microphone. Framing the group as workers putting on a radio show, Benny and Conn developed a personality for each of them that blended reality and fiction. The cast became a stable of recognizable, quirky-yet-likeable continuing characters who could bounce off each other in informal exchanges in the studio or interact in situations from visiting the zoo or having dinner at a cast member's home to performing a parody of a popular new film. This variety greatly reduced Benny and Conn's reliance on pat monologues and standard joke telling. What they developed was a forerunner of the situation comedy, a genre that would become much more prominent only fifteen years later in radio and television broadcasting in response to changing industrial practices and cultural norms.[9]

The duo could have created comic content for the program while leaving the emcee as the star, a dominant figure who was fed straight lines by subordinates, or by making him a pleasantly bland father figure who rode herd over his workplace family. Instead, over a three-to-four-year period, Benny and Conn gradually transformed the Jack Benny persona. Writer and performer transitioned the role from the vaudeville character of a suave but self-deprecating monologist (called by vaudeville critics the "sleekly bored joker") to that of a vainglorious, hapless Fall Guy, a "negative exemplar," in historian Steven Mintz's terms, roundly (and ritually) roasted by his stable of zany stooges.[10] Benny and Conn turned the humor around. Benny the emcee became the butt, not the mouthpiece, of the acerbic comic lines. The "Jack Benny" character of radio fame was their greatest creation. Even when their partnership unraveled in 1936, they had solidified Benny's place as the premiere comedian in American radio broadcasting.

BENNY'S EARLY VAUDEVILLE PERSONA

Jack Benny had already spent more than twenty years developing a vaudeville identity that brought him, if not immense stardom, solid success as a musician who had transitioned into a humorist who held a violin in one hand and a cigar in the other as he joked. Working as a "single" who occasionally interacted with an assistant or other acts on the bill, Benny joined the expanding group of informal, modern vaudeville hipsters whom we would know later as stand-up comics. Benny's twist to the genre involved creating a "middling" personality who was neither young nor old, wealthy nor poor. He was not loud or buffoonish, and he related to a homogenizing American audience as much more Anglo-American than Jewish or ethnic.[11] He was a Midwestern variant of what vaudeville historians term "the Voice of the City."[12] *Variety* critic Robert Landry later asserted that Jack Benny's stage manner had always seemed "big time," even as it was perfected in local theater orchestras, military camp shows, and small-time vaudeville in the 1910s and early 1920s:[13]

> [Benny's] style was subdued, his delivery one of the first examples of modern "throw away." He was poised, unhurried, seemingly effortless. . . . He was not an ad libber, in the general sense. He prepared his stuff ahead but changed it frequently, infused it with topical allusions. But he sounded ad lib.

Landry acknowledged that Benny's appeal was nevertheless somewhat limited, because his act "demanded too much attention and quiet" to thrive either in noisy metropolitan night clubs or among the rough and tumble milieu of vaudeville comics in the hinterlands.

Reviews of Benny's routine in the early 1920s commended the "reserve, poise and personality" of the monologist.[14] "Jack Benny with his slow, easy patter, gets his crowd before he is well under way," commented a typical critic, who also mentioned the mediocrity of Benny's jokes.[15] When he appeared in 1925 at New York's Palace Theater, vaudeville's pinnacle, *Billboard* praised Benny's "droll delivery," but also labelled his routine as being "a cross between the Frank Fay and Ben Bernie styles."[16] Initially, as Ben K. Benny (his early stage name), in his act Jack Benny had superficially resembled deep-voiced bandleader Ben Bernie, who grasped a fiddle and embellished the punch lines of his jokes with the catchphrase "yowza yowza!"[17] Bernie pressured the younger Benny to further modify his stage name to widen the perceived differences between them.[18] The comparisons with Frank Fay continued, however, as Jack Benny unabashedly modeled his act on that of the well-known Irish-American comic. When Benny returned to the Palace in April 1926, *Variety* complimented his "excellent material and delivery" and his witty interplay with other performers: "Stanley and Birns [the next act] came out early and asked to tell a story in Benny's spot. Benny's comments on the story were real funny. It was likeable nonsense and a yell when Benny stopped

[them] as he recognized it as a stag story."[19] Benny regularly reenacted this routine with a female assistant whispering the salacious story in his ear, so that he could flirtatiously dance between polite and sexually suggestive humor. When he incorporated it into a 1928 Vitaphone talkie short, a reviewer snarkily noted its similarities to a Frank Fay routine—"They can fight out who did it first."[20]

Frank Fay's urbane manner made him one of the most prominent and highest-paid performers in vaudeville.[21] He was one of the first to enact the emcee role at the Palace and the nation's other top theaters. Emcees had existed previously in minstrel shows (where they were called *interlocutors*) and in British music halls (where they were called *comperes*), but Fay was said to have coined the term used in American vaudeville.[22] The emcee role was an outgrowth of Fay's innovative monologue act. Fay was one of the first stage comedians to eschew outlandish costumes, makeup, props, and broad physical shtick. The debonair redheaded, blue-eyed Fay dressed with impeccable, aristocratic style and moved with a feminine grace. His timing and delivery were judged "masterly."[23] He was a "boastful big city boulevardier" with a breezy delivery and relatively restrained, soft-spoken demeanor that covered a rapier wit. "Faysie" had a devastating ability to ad lib insults that could destroy any heckler in the audience. A *Life Magazine* profile described "his cockiness and his conceit, ... the gentle smile, the quizzical lift of the eyebrows, the sweet voice and then the dirty crack."[24] Fay did not depend on strings of one-liners, but was a storyteller whose collection of whimsical and digressive tales were peopled with everyday individuals such as a family that obsessively saved string. Fay also sang stanzas of current songs like "Tea for Two," stopping to dissect the absurdities of the lyrics along the way. He was elegant, suave, and superior—and made sure the audience knew it, through his wicked repartee and stinging quips, perfecting what a critic called "an odd combination of humor and elegance."[25] Fay's act was widely admired and copied by other comics, but offstage he was reviled for his bigotry, his alcoholism, and his massive ego (he called himself "Frank Fay, the World's Greatest Comedian"). Fellow comic Fred Allen once cracked, "The last time I saw Fay, he was walking down Lover's Lane holding his own hand."[26]

Vaudeville acts had traditionally followed each other on stage in quick succession, identified in printed programs and by title cards placed on an easel at the side of the stage. But as attendance began to dwindle, vaudeville managers began to add an extra attraction—a headliner such as Fay, Jack Benny, Julius Tannen, or George Jessel to present the show. The lead comic would appear not only in his own spot, but also throughout the bill, introducing the acts, interacting with (or interrupting) other performers, ad libbing patter between the spots, and filling time if there were delays in the show. Some critics complained that this restructuring slowed the pace of the program, but the emcee's performance made the disparate parts of the program seem more interconnected. Benny approached the emcee role with a collaborative spirit, whereas Fay took the opportunity to turn the spotlight on himself and dominate the entire proceedings. Benny did borrow Fay's quiet charm, elegant manner, and womanly walk, but, lacking his quick and inventive tongue, replaced Fay's arrogance and ad-libbed putdowns with carefully crafted lines that sounded off-the-cuff, and included a subtle self-deprecation. "Benny's opening line, which he used for years, was celebrated," recalled vaudeville historian Maurice Zolotow. "He would casually lope toward the center of the stage, tuck his violin under his arm, brush his hair back with his left hand, and inquire of the maestro, 'How is the show?' 'Fine up to now,' the maestro would reply. 'I'll fix *that*!' Benny would say."[27]

Jack Benny rivaled Fay as one of the most frequent emcees at the Palace between 1927 and 1931.[28] "Benny knows the Palace and its audiences there as few others do, knowing what else they like besides actor and show biz gags," noted a reviewer, who also voiced the concern mentioned by other critics, that Benny struggled to find enough new material to last through repeated viewings.[29] In Chicago, "Jack Benny, who had acted as M.C. throughout the bill, was refreshingly humorous in his easy, graceful way, his chatter and violin playing both going over big."[30] Vaudeville appeared increasingly unstable, however, so Benny experimented with other media. He appeared on Broadway in the 1927 Shubert Brothers' revue *The Great Temptations*, but felt that the predominance of "blue" humor did not complement his style.[31] He also tried his hand at the movies, riding the wave of talent from vaudeville and the stage flowing to Hollywood with the coming of talkies. However, after playing a prominent role as the emcee of MGM's *Hollywood Revue of 1929*, his subsequent film roles (and reviews of his performances) were lackluster. Nevertheless, Benny kept trying to play up his film connections.

In 1930 and 1931, Benny moved his act between films, vaudeville venues, and cavernous picture palaces, which began adding live stage acts to their movie shows to shore up attendance. Entertainment forms were converging, but Benny did not seem to fit comfortably into any of them. Playing the Palace, Benny asked to be billed as "the cinemaster of ceremonies."[32] Skeptical critics expressed concern that Benny's work was too quiet and low-key to take command of 5,000-seat auditoriums. Although he did moderately well, devising some punchy additions to enlarge the scale of his act (Zouave soldiers, Japanese acrobats, comeuppance from the abrupt start of the film program onscreen), a reviewer of his show at New York's Capital Theater was still unconvinced. "Benny is still the suave and clever emcee working all through the show to keep it pieced together effectively. His suaveness, then, tends to slowness, which hardly helps a presentation in a 'deluxer.' The type of entertainment that goes is that which is served speedily and peppily."[33] Benny was at a career crossroads, as he wandered among various venues and media forms, trying to find the most advantageous platform for his particular skills. Worsening economic conditions of the early 1930s made the search more nerve wracking.

In 1932, radio and advertising executives like NBC's Brainard, scanning the horizon for talent that might best adapt to broadcasting's needs, considered Jack Benny, although they were not initially very enthusiastic about him. Neither network brass nor sponsor's agencies were certain what styles and types of performers would work on the radio—many preferred the loud brashness and quickness of other comics and the stentorian tones of tuxedoed announcers. NBC had actually approached literary humorist Irvin S. Cobb prior to contacting Benny, but Cobb's salary demands were too high. Executives probably noted the affinities Benny's stage act had with aural presentation—Benny produced most of his humor through low-key language and smooth, superbly timed delivery of his lines. He was not a primarily physical or visual comedian getting laughs through broad facial expressions, costume, or slapstick body movements. Benny engaged in quiet, intimate joking, confiding in the audience as if it were a small group, similar to the methods of the "crooning" singers like Bing Crosby and Rudy Vallee who were becoming popular through radio appearances. On the other hand, Benny's droll stare at the stage audience, with hand to his cheek, which silently communicated his frustration and won viewers' sympathy, would be lost on radio listeners. It would only reemerge in the early 1950s to embellish his comedy routines on television.

CHALLENGES OF THE INITIAL *CANADA DRY PROGRAM*

As Benny began the twice-weekly broadcasts of Canada Dry's new musical comedy radio show in May 1932, it seemed that not only he, but the sponsor,

FIGURE 3. "Bandleader George Olsen and vocalist Ethel Shutta were the original draws for the Canada Dry Ginger Ale radio program. Jack Benny successfully coached them both into becoming fine comedy dialogue readers." *New Movie Magazine*, September 1932, 60. Accessed from Media History Digital Library   http://archive.org/stream/newmoviemagazin06weir#page/n311/mode/2up

ad agency, and network were almost shockingly naïve about how much labor Benny's role might entail. The orchestra and vocalist had large musical catalogs from which they could draw new tunes to perform, but if Benny was to do more than introduce the title of the next song, he was going to need fresh material every episode. Apparently no provisions were in the original plans for the program to hire writers. The executives must have assumed Benny ad-libbed or wrote his own humorous asides. As a popular emcee, Benny had experience in creating short gags and exchanges with vaudeville performers, but he was used to repeating similar patter for different audiences the whole week of the engagement, either getting new performers to work with or a new city to play in the following week. No one involved with the *Canada Dry Program* had entirely thought through how a twice-weekly show with the same performers and the same audience might work.

The first live episode demonstrated the promise and the drawback of the concept. In seven short monologues interspersed between the songs, Benny presented himself as a suave, urban, and thoroughly Americanized fellow who was witty and personable, a wisecracker who was self-centered but who self-deprecatingly understood that his attempts at boastful egotism would end in mild humiliation. Benny exchanged a little banter with orchestra leader George Olsen and singer Ethel Shutta as he introduced them. Nervous awkwardness of the new endeavor was apparent in Benny's doing most of the talking and their very brief responses to standard vaudeville jokes, such as ribbing the age of Olsen's automobile. Benny worked from a script; he wanted a written structure to guide him to make sure he was organized and that the jokes could be carefully pored over and crafted into polished gems.[34] He delivered his lines, though, in such an easy, nonchalant manner that listeners may have thought he was speaking off-the-cuff. Studies of Benny's career usually point out the assertive way that, even in this first episode, he wove the middle-of-the-program advertising messages into his monologues, entwining a playful (and fairly unusual) mocking tone toward the product in the same way he told self-deprecating stories about himself. Benny's introductory monologue was probably drawn from when he played at the Palace, but with the added twist of a backhanded plugging of the sponsor's product:[35]

> Ladies and gentlemen, this is Jack Benny talking, and making my first appearance on the air professionally. By that I mean, I am finally getting paid, which will be a great relief to my creditors. I really don't know why I am here. I'm supposed to be a sort of master of ceremonies and tell you all about the things that will happen, which would happen anyway. I must introduce the different artists, who could easily introduce themselves, and also talk about Canada Dry made to order by the glass, which is a waste of time, as you know all about it. You drink it, like it, and don't want to hear about it. So ladies and gentlemen, a master of ceremonies is really a fellow who is unemployed and gets paid for it.

In the second and third episodes of the *Canada Dry Program*, with a dash of desperation, Benny provided brief descriptions of his fellow radio performers that again drew on standard vaudeville insult-humor patter—George Olsen was penurious, Ethel Shutta lied about her age, the boys in the band were drunkards, and announcer Ed Thorgerson resembled a Hollywood playboy with slicked-back hair and a thin mustache. (It "looked like he'd swallowed all of Mickey Mouse but the tail,"[36] Benny quipped.) But the others were given few lines to speak. Benny appealed to his unseen listeners directly, asking if there was anybody out there and reintroduced himself halfway through the show. In the second week, he opened the program with "Hello somebody. This is Jack Benny talking. There will be a slight pause while you say 'what of it?' After all, I know your feelings, folks, I used to listen in myself."[37] He closed with, "That was our last number of our fourth program on the 11th of May. Are you still conscious? Hmm...?"

Variety's reviewer in May 1932 sensed Benny's nervousness, but tried to be encouraging, noting "there's no reason why a clever, intimate comedian of Benny's type shouldn't hit over the air. Essentially he has everything it takes, from an excellent speaking voice to the right kind of delivery." Nevertheless, the reviewer was unenthusiastic about the integration Benny was trying to bring to the separate elements of music, comedy, and advertising in the show, recommending that Olsen "should leave all the talking to Benny." The comic advertising was also disturbing: "Plug angle was considerably overdone here, with Benny handling it throughout. He pulled some pretty obvious puns, such as "drinking Canada Dry".... Right now the subtle spotting of the plug should be handled with silk gloves."[38] *Billboard*'s review of the new program noted that Benny's nonchalant style of humor and delivery was different from what other comics were offering on air. "A taste for his style has to be acquired," cautioned the reviewer, who also noticed the reliance on old vaudeville patter—"On this particular program he rang in some of his old material, but no doubt new to radio fans."[39]

Years later, Jack Benny confessed his panic: "In vaudeville you had one show and that was it. You changed it whenever you felt like it. And in this, when you realized that every week you needed a new show, this got a little bit frightening."[40] In another interview, he recalled: "I didn't have any idea how important it was to have good material, and how hard it was to get. The first show was a cinch—I used about half of all the gags I knew. The second show consumed all the rest, and I faced the third absolutely dry."[41]

Established performers appearing on the airwaves similarly expressed terror at the speed with which the live broadcasts to huge audiences consumed a career's worth of material in just a few hours. "The scourge of the amusement field is radio," warned *Variety*. "Radio is devouring too much music, eating up the stage too cannibalistically and burning out all talent too fast, so that it may undo itself about as rapidly as it made itself prominent in its relation to the masses."[42] Ed Wynn complained that "the gags used in four half-hour programs would provide enough material for a full-length Broadway play."[43] While *Variety* acknowledged that radio had made nationally known stars of niche performers like Wynn and Jack Pearl, as well as previous unknowns like Gosden and Correll, it cautioned:

> The very biggest on the ether today soon become boresome simply because it's not showmanly to dish up a new act 52 times a year. Comics used to be able to test out their new routines in smaller towns like Plainfield and Union City, now can kill their careers with a bad routine in front of 20 to 50 million listeners in one night.[44]

Performers and program producers struggled to adapt old business models to this new mode of communication. The radio networks had consolidated the breadth of the vaudeville system into just a few broadcast outlets to serve a nationwide audience. The networks demanded that broadcasts be live each week. Program producers could not use previously recorded performances or reruns, options that might have made the search for fresh material, the pressure to perform at peak ability, and the chase for high ratings less fearsome.

During his years in vaudeville, Benny had regularly enhanced his routine by purchasing jokes and routines from gag writers such as Al Boasberg, Dave Freedman, Sid Silvers, and Harry Conn.[45] He turned to them now.[46] In the 1920s, Burns and Allen had paid Boasberg a continuous 10 percent of their $1,750 weekly vaudeville salary in exchange for his creation of individual routines, such as "Lamb Chops," which they performed for years. The duo asked him to write material for their weekly radio broadcasts on the *Robert Burns Cigar Program*, but Boasberg balked at how much more work was involved in creating the seven to eight minutes of new material they required each week, for only 10 percent of their $1,000 radio salary. Boasberg quit and moved to Hollywood to take film-writing jobs.[47] Burns and Allen and their radio producers soon assembled a staff of five writers to churn out all the necessary material. Dave Freedman devised an alternate method to address radio comics' endless need for material (Eddie Cantor was one of his major clients). Freedman hired a staff of young assistants who combed through every source of humor in the library—joke books, magazine articles, and nineteenth-century literature—to cull every possible jest, quip, and comic exchange. They organized these jokes into vast files on every conceivable topic that Freedman could then dip into, rearrange a few particulars, and assemble into scripts churned out for a half-dozen different radio comedy shows each week.[48]

By the end of the second week, Benny sought out Harry Conn, a tap-dancing former vaudevillian who had turned to full-time writing, penning routines for dozens of comedians and for Mae West's Broadway shows in the 1920s.[49] In the spring of 1932, Conn was working on the Burns and Allen staff. Benny decided to rely solely on Conn, paying Conn's salary out of his own pocket. The two quickly became partners, working closely together week in and out to create, edit, and perfect the dialogue. To Conn's chagrin, the radio network would not allow writers to get on-air credit, however, so Benny always remained the focus of public and critical acclaim.[50] Benny was as financially generous with Conn as he was dependent on him, paying Conn one of the highest salaries earned by a radio writer.[51]

By the end of the third week on the air, with Conn on board, the *Canada Dry Program* scripts started to become more adventurous. George Olsen now was given more straight lines as he and Benny engaged in conversation. Everyone else in the studio—from orchestra members and Conn to Benny's personal assistant Harry Baldwin—was pulled to the mike to voice fictional guests in brief one-time appearances. Benny and Conn began experimenting with creating a richer fictional world for the program, creating sketch routines that briefly moved away from the microphone. On May 23, 1932, they finessed the problem of segueing by endowing announcer Ed Thorgerson with a magical ability to tune an on-air radio into conversation made by the characters at a soda fountain located in the building's lobby. At midshow, Thorgerson asked where Jack was, and band member Bob Rice responded that he'd just left:

ED: but who's going to take charge of the program?

BOB: I don't know.

ED: I think I'll tune in the soda fountain and see what's going on there. (ad lib tuning noises, and FADE OUT)

(FADE IN: Scene at soda fountain. Sound effects: clink of glasses, fizzes of charged water, babble of voices requesting drinks, etc.)

ALLEN: And I'll have a chocolate malted milk.

ETHEL: Make mine a made to order Canada Dry.

FRAN: There you are—and what will you have, sir? (band member Fran Frey played the soda jerk)

JACK: Give me two nickels—I want to telephone.

FRAN: Say, this is a soda fountain.

JACK: I'll have a glass of Canada Dry Ginger Ale, made to order, by the glass at all soda fountains.

FRAN: Do you know the chorus, Mister?

JACK: Oh I see—now just give me a glass of Canada Dry.

FRAN: Would you like a little flavor in it, sir, say, a little cherry?

JACK: No—no—just plain Canada Dry.

FRAN: How about putting some ice cream in it? It's swell with ice cream.

JACK: Yes, I imagine it is very good. But if you don't mind, I'll have just the plain Canada Dry—see?

FRAN: Would you like toast with it?

JACK: NO!! Say, were you ever a barber?

FRAN: Who wants to know?

JACK: Jack Benny

FRAN: Are YOU Jack Benny?

JACK: Yes—yes.

FRAN: The Jack Benny who broadcasts for Canada Dry?

JACK: Yes.

FRAN: Every Monday and Wednesday?

JACK: Yes.

FRAN: And if you ask ME if I was ever a barber. Gee THAT's hot.

JACK: Will you *please* give me a glass of—(Ethel enters and interrupts)

ETHEL: Oh Jack!

JACK: Hello, Ethel.

ETHEL: You'd better hurry back. George is getting ready to play a number.

JACK: Come on, let's have a drink first.

ETHEL: No thanks, I don't want . . .

JACK: Come on, Ethel—I'll pay for mine. (Ethel laughs at this)

JACK: Aw, I'm only kiddin.' Come on, Ethel, I'll buy them. Hey! Give us two Canada Drys. And make mine large.

FRAN: Okay... say, do you want a piece of cake with it?

JACK: Come here—lean over a minute. (sound effect, crash of plate) And NOW give us two glasses of Canada Dry.

(sound effect: fizzes of charged water)

ETHEL: What's he doing?

JACK: That's the way you make it—first put just the right amount of syrup in—then add the charged water—and there you are! Well, here it is, Ethel—-good luck!

ETHEL AND BENNY: (singing) How Canada Dry I am... How Canada Dry I am... (both start to laugh)

(Fade In: piano music, opening bars of the song "Tender Child")

ETHEL: What's that?

JACK: Say, that's George beginning to play the next number.

ETHEL: Gee, I'd better run back—I have to sing it with Fran.

The show staff created sound effects of glasses clinking and ginger ale fizzing. The scene may have only lasted two minutes, but when Benny "returned" to the studio after the next song, he jokingly assumed that he had to explain to the audience what they had done: "Well folks, this is Jack Benny back at the studio. Well, to tell you the truth, we never even left here. Olsen's bass drum was the counter. And the fizz you heard was one of the boys sneezing."

Subsequent episodes contained a three- to five-minute sketch occurring in a fictional place away from the immediacy of the studio space. Some involved Jack traveling to a special event and reporting on it (essentially performing a monologue). Jack "attended" the Dempsey-Sharkey prize fight at Madison Square Garden, and parodied radio sports coverage, giving play-by-play action. Another time, Jack and George Olsen were arrested for speeding and broadcast the program from jail, and on July 6 the cast visited the zoo and gathered testimonials from the animals about how much they enjoyed drinking Canada Dry. Meanwhile, Jack continued to rib George Olsen about being a spendthrift. Back at the soda fountain, George offered to treat Jack to a glass of ginger ale, but had forgotten his wallet, so Jack ended up picking up the check for the entire orchestra's order.

A PERIOD OF EXPERIMENTATION WITH TOPICS AND CHARACTERS

Benny and Conn strove to avoid a rigid formula in constructing the radio program's humorous segments, devising a mixture of comic monologues, repartee, pun tossing, and fictional adventures between the musical numbers. Some of their experimental ideas were solidly successful, while some were problematic and abandoned as unworkable. Others ended perhaps at the behest of their sponsor. Topical humor that satirized current radio programming fads was one of their first experiments. On May 9, Jack announced the beginning of a write-in contest, in which listeners would submit testimonials to the deliciousness of Canada Dry Ginger Ale. Benny's radio show was followed by a musical program for San Felipe cigars, which was then currently conducting a jingle-writing competition with prizes valued at $70,000. Advertising agencies who created the radio programming loved these contests, for they generated thousands of listener responses that agencies could use to demonstrate the radio program's popularity and justify the hefty expense of radio sponsorship to their clients. The Federal Radio Commission and NBC worked to eliminate contests, however, as they added a tawdry, hucksterish element to a network broadcasting that was trying to seem more culturally elevated.[52] Benny's increasingly absurd contest rules exposed the crassness of these gimmicks and made his sponsor seem insincere and foolish.[53] Radio reviewers praised Benny for his clever parodies, calling them a delightful new twist in radio humor.[54] On May 11, Benny announced his latest contest wrinkle:

> Walk up to your favorite soda fountain, order a glass of Canada Dry Ginger Ale made to order by the glass and sip it through a straw—of course this is optional. You can either sip it through a straw or drink it right out loud. But if you DO happen to sip it through a straw, save it. Don't go a losin' it. Why? Send it to your Canada Dry cleaners to be pressed. Then, on one side of the straw write us why you like Canada Dry made to order by the glass, and on the other side, write the "Star Spangled Banner." Mail your straws to us at your earliest convenience, as the straw hat season opens next week. We will not tell you what the prize is yet, but keep a scallion in mind.[55]

In the first months of the program, Benny and Conn dipped a toe into political satire. The upcoming presidential election must have been a topic difficult for radio jokesters to avoid, as the candidates' sloganeering filled the newspapers. Conn and Benny brought a touch of cynical humor and an absurdity to their political skits, weaving Roosevelt and Hoover's names into Benny's monologues similarly to the way they talked about Clark Gable and Greta Garbo. In early June, Benny made a mild joke about ex-servicemen descending on Washington in the Bonus March, and at least one newspaper critic took him to task for making fun of a serious subject.[56] On June 20, at midshow, Benny announced, "Ladies and gentlemen, we have been singing and joking tonight, but we realize our mistake, your minds are at present concentrated on the political situation. What you want is *politics*, not hokum, so *politics* you'll get." After a barrage of digressive jokes and puns, and a song (Olsen's band performed a tune entitled "Everything's' Going to be Okay, America"), Benny introduced "The Canada Dry candidate for president, Trafalgar Bee-Fuddle... The man who broke his umbrella and is neither wet nor dry. He is a friend of the farmer, and is also a friend of the traveling salesman and the farmer's daughter. He is a soldier, a scholar and a citizen, and has proved his worth at Leavenworth."

> BEE FUDDLE—(between bouts of coughing) If I am nominated at this convention for the highest honor that can ever be bestowed up on an American Citizen, I will... erm, I will... that is, er... er... I will be FOR the people... BY the people, OF the people... WITH the people... ON the people... and IN SPITE of the people....
>
> [Bee-Fuddle's hysteria escalates, and then a pistol shot was heard, followed by silence]
>
> JACK—Ladies and gentlemen, there is nothing to worry about... the LATE Trafalgar Bee-Fuddle will not run for President, but no matter who's elected, Canada Dry Ginger Ale will be sold by the glass, at all soda fountains, TO the people... BY the people... and FOR the people. And it's darned good... several people told me.

On October 19, Jack performed one of his prize fighting play-by-play monologues, this time a bout between "Battling Herbert Hoover and Fighting Franklin Roosevelt"

> Hoover has trained faithfully in Washington, skipping the rope, balancing the budget, and doing some roadwork in Iowa and Cleveland... Roosevelt has trained in Albany and has done his roadwork in eighteen different states. We haven't seen a fight like this in four years.... (gong) They both meet in the center of the ring. Hoover steps in with a light Rhode Island... and Roosevelt counters with a hard Smash-achusetts to the jaw. Herbert comes back and flings a Michigan, and Franklin blocks with Oregon.... They are

now both throwing Iowas at each other.... So far it is a pretty even fight. There they go, dancing around, taking their time, but looking for an opening. Ah, Franklin now comes in and hooks a light Delaware to the ear. Herb now counters with a Nebraska, and Frank drops one knee to the Kansas, I mean canvas ... and is up again from the Floor-ida ... brushing off his pants-sylvania (Gong) and the bell sends them both to their corners.

Benny and Conn also experimented in those first months on the radio with ways to add additional voices. On May 25, Benny interviewed the janitor of the building, Mr. Philander Kvetch, played by band member Bobby Moore, who only responded to questions in gurgles of baby talk. On June 1, Kvetch briefly returned, speaking in a heavy German accent. This time the part was probably played by Harry Conn. On June 15, Conn was an Italian-American tough guy attending the boxing match. On July 13, Jack talked to a group of Scottish gentlemen who would be judging the latest Canada Dry contest; all the Scots were played by Conn (including a Scottish terrier who simply woofed). Ethnic characters were a favorite staple in Conn's bag of comedy writing tricks; although use of foreign accents was a creaky throwback to earlier vaudeville days of Gallagher and Sheen, or an insensitive burlesquing of immigrants, it's probable that Conn saw the ethnic-accented caricature of American voices to be a bit of "verbal slapstick" or unexpected aural comedy costuming for the airwaves. Despite Conn's favoring of ethnic voices, he rarely appeared on-air as a performer again. The Benny show instead hired a range of ex-vaudeville comics as "dialect specialists" to play occasional small parts.

In the show's second month, Jack began to talk about hiring an assistant to handle all the mail the program was receiving in response to the outrageous Canada Dry contests. This search continued over the next month, as Jack acquired first an inefficient male secretary, then an incompetent female secretary named Garbo.[57] The next chapter details how Benny's wife Sadye Marks Benny (his sometime assistant on the vaudeville stage) became incorporated into the radio program, as a young woman named "Mary Livingstone," a fan of the program from the small town of Plainfield, New Jersey. She assumed the role of Jack's lackadaisical part-time secretary on the radio show, and soon became a central character.

Along with adding Mary to the show came Benny and Conn's brief experiment with a serialized narrative. Several comic radio shows had ongoing plots for their characters. *Amos 'n' Andy* had a fifteen-minute comic-melodramatic plot that played out five nights per week. Eddie Cantor had experimented with a fictional narrative on his show (with mixed results, a few critics complaining about too much plot). Fred Allen placed his character into a constantly changing series of situations (running a night court, operating a department store) which introduced new characters every episode. Ed Wynn parodied opera librettos, a different one each time.[58] Conn and Benny aimed for a continual mixture of different show formats—a situation or sketch one week, a parody of a film or standing around the microphone another. Still, the pair toyed with a romantic comedy subplot. Episodes in September and October 1932 played out Jack and Mary's flirtations and comic misunderstandings, and climaxed with a scene of them espousing their love for one another. Benny and Conn had written themselves into a corner. Would the show now be dominated by a love story? Where would the comic conflicts arise? They quickly decided to move in another direction, however, backing away from romantic complications, or a continuing plot. Mary returned to flirting with the bandmates and ribbing Jack's small foibles.

SPONSOR UPHEAVALS AND COMEDY POLISHING

After several months of twice-a-week programs, Benny and Conn began to garner critical notice for their experimentations with advertising and comedy situations. *Variety* reported in August, "Jack Benny was in good form on last week's program, having evolved sundry effective gags for plugging Canada Dry. In line with the recent trend toward a humorous plug for the sponsor, he is sugar-coating and making palatable what is usually a boresome interlude in the best of programs."[59] In October, it commented, "Jack Benny is improving on his Canada Dry humor. Benny has built up a unique style of comedy, especially with those puns which, however, are not injudiciously primed for strong returns."[60]

Just when Benny and Conn thought they had achieved a solid, successful mixture of comedy and music, with distinct characters, situations and parody sketches, their program was upended. In October 1932 Canada Dry and its ad agency abruptly declared their displeasure with many aspects of the program.[61] N. W. Ayer & Sons found what it considered to be a more propitious broadcasting time at CBS, where a larger number of stations (27) were available to carry the half-hour program, on Thursdays at 8:15 P.M. and Sundays at 10:00 P.M. However, Benny's bandleader George Olsen, his orchestra, and Ethel Shutta were all under contract to NBC and couldn't move. The sponsor and ad agency and new network also changed the intimate set-up of Benny's rooftop recording studio into a broadcast performance emanating from a cavernous stage before a large studio audience. Even worse, they hired an additional actor/writer (Sid Silvers) to improve what they thought was Benny's flat comedy.

Benny and George Olsen stormed into Bertha Brainard's office at NBC on October 7.[62] Brainard reported that "Mr. Benny expressed himself as decidedly unhappy and uncertain about the future success of the program." He objected to the change in orchestras, the additional writers, different broadcast set up. Benny certainly did not want Silvers added to the program, but his lawyer had informed him that he had to give it a chance. The lawyer also reminded him of the cancellation clause he could toss at the sponsor, if need be. Brainard continued,

> I told Mr. Benny and Mr. Olsen how very unhappy we were at the loss of such a splendid program, which was building weekly, and that the feeling was that it was a gamble as to its popularity when Mr. Olsen left the program. Mr. Olsen told Mr. Benny that if anything should come up which left Mr. Benny free, we at the NBC would no doubt agree to combining the Benny-Olsen combination again, and continuing it on the air perhaps sustaining, if a client were not immediately available. Mr. Benny left saying that he was glad to know the door was wide open, and that we gave him a much clearer picture of how he might proceed. His statement was "Now I can use a black-jack," meaning, I assume that unless things are decidedly as he wants them, he will give his notice, and offer his services to NBC.[63]

Benny and Conn were saddled with Sid Silvers and had to start over from scratch—teaching a new bandleader, singer, and announcer how to become comedians, and fighting off the intrusions of Silvers, who turned the show into the continuing story of a befuddled Broadway producer and his smart-aleck assistant (played by Sid). Silvers filled the scripts with zippy one liners instead of dialogue, made himself a comic equal to Jack, and left little room for Mary. There were no more parodies of movies or informal real-life exchanges around the microphone, and the Canada Dry ads were much less integrated.[64] Although Benny, Conn, and Livingstone held no personal animus against Silvers (they would work with him in later years in film and Friars Club performances), within a few weeks the three staged a showdown with the sponsor, demanding that Silvers be removed and creative control of the program be returned to them, or they would quit.

By December 8, Benny, Livingstone, and Conn emerged victorious from the debacle. Sid Silvers was gone and the show returned to its previous style.

In his opening monologue, Jack welcomed listeners back: "You know, I tell a joke and Ted Weems plays, I tell a joke and Andrea Marsh sings and I tell another joke and you laugh, and if you don't I hear about it." Although critics had praised him, one writing that Benny's "air appearance [has] brought forward much of the present style of radio humor,"[65] exasperated Canada Dry executives judged radio sponsorship too troublesome, cancelled Benny's show in January 1933, and withdrew from broadcast advertising.

Jack Benny went through a stressful period as the producer and star of his comedy program over the next twenty-four months, as he was picked up and dropped by several sponsors. The story of his management struggles is told in chapter 6. Despite the many challenges of persevering through changes in cast members, sponsors, advertising agencies, networks, and broadcast nights and times, Benny's radio audiences followed him and stuck with him. The program's steadily rising ratings were one indication that Benny and Harry Conn had developed a winning comedy formula, drawing from the strong framework they had created in 1932. When the program returned to the air, sponsored by the Chevrolet automobile manufacturing company in March 1933, Jack was the program's acknowledged main focus, and it was billed as a comedy program that contained music. Mary assumed a much more prominent role on the program as Jack's companion, the only female character on the show, and the program's main "stooge."

Political humor played a significant part in episodes that month, as Benny and his troupe joked regularly about Franklin D. Roosevelt's inauguration, the bank holiday, and other aspects of the New Deal initiatives Roosevelt rolled out in his first hundred days. On March 17, while doing his radio columnist skit as "The Earth Galloper," Jack announced that banks were reopening, three of them in Hollywood (Tallulah Bankhead, Douglas Fairbanks, and George Bancroft).[66] In another episode, Mary compared Frances Perkins's appointment to the cabinet with her own time spent in a steam (weight-reducing) cabinet. This all was the lightest kind of topical humor, neither supporting nor criticizing the New Deal, reducing political news to the foolishness with which they portrayed Hollywood celebrity gossip. But nevertheless, by the end of their first month broadcasting for Chevrolet, every reference to politics was removed from the program. Given Chevrolet's financial difficulties, its problems with labor unrest, and its upcoming negotiations with Roosevelt's National Recovery Administration, company executives and ad agency staff were probably very nervous about their sponsored radio show raising anyone's hackles.

Critical acclaim for the show continued to grow. The *Ottawa Citizen*'s reviewer complimented Benny for the quality of humor he created with his cast of characters—"Jack has the knack of making everyone on his program real and human, instead of just a lot of radio voices."[67] That summer, when Chevrolet put the radio show on hiatus (retreating from national advertising when their revenues lagged so badly) Benny and Mary Livingstone returned to the stage in a personal appearance tour, and vaudeville critics remarked on Benny's new level of radio-fueled stardom: "[His] popularity was never so frankly confessed by the public prior to his radio career. What the air did for Benny was to make him a household character," a Chicago reviewer noted.[68]

By spring 1934, despite the continuing turmoil of changing cast and broadcast times, and rancorous relationships with sponsors, the humorous content of the Benny show remained rich; the show's narrative formula and characterizations were evolving into the forms Benny would rely on for the rest of his career. Harry Conn concentrated even further on developing the personas of the cast's other performers as quirky, individual characters. Bandleader Don Bestor was a highbrow; tenor Frank Parker was a sophisticated young smart aleck. Mary was boisterous but not very bright. Jack was making fewer of the jokes, and more often it was the stooges who got the laugh lines, by ribbing Benny.[69] More than ever, Benny became the poor "shmo," the unlucky fellow to whom humiliating things always seemed to happen.[70] On the May 11, 1934, show, to make a peace offering after they'd had an argument at the show's opening, Don Wilson invited Jack out to his mother's home in the Bronx for the weekend. Jack suffered numerous misadventures on their journey, getting robbed three times and gladly handing over his money in each instance. The thief even awarded Benny a card identifying him as a frequent customer. When the pair finally arrived at the Wilson home, there was no food, no spare bed, and no luck for the hapless Jack.

Benny's character began to shift further from being just the likeable, self-deprecating but professional emcee of the program to develop more personality quirks and flaws (cheapness, boastfulness, his poor violin-playing skills, his vanity, his advancing age, and his lack of masculinity). The list steadily grew longer as the Jack character lost most of that assured "Broadway Romeo" suavity he'd demonstrated during his vaudeville career, and was now depicted as inept at interacting with the opposite sex. His patriarchal authority as star of the show was more frequently challenged by his mocking radio employees. While standard joke book-style insults about cheapness and stupidity were still bandied about by the entire cast, the jabs were refurbished so that charges were now often made by others, egged on by Mary, and aimed at Jack.

A significant turning point for the Benny character occurred in a skit about Jack's Hollywood screen test, on the June 8, 1934, program. Benny had taken his radio cast out to California, as he was appearing in *Transatlantic Merry Go Round*, a film about criminal intrigue set on an ocean liner, produced by Edward Small at RKO. As Benny had done since the beginning of his radio show, he entwined references to his moviemaking work and personal details of his life into his scripts, blurring the lines between fictional and real Jack Benny personas. Conn and Benny drew on his self-deprecating traits and pushed them further, now enacting professional incompetence. Conn created a skit in which Jack was at the film studio, where he has been compelled to submit to a screen test to secure the role of romantic leading man. As scripted, Mr. Kane the director was trying to complete the test, and a nervous Benny was making that difficult:

KANE: Now for the first line, say "Ah Christina, your royal highness, thou are ravishing this evening, Would'st that thou favor me with thy presence at luncheon forthwith!"

JACK: I've been waiting for a Jimmy Cagney part like this.

[Jack's first stumbling attempt to read his line is, "Oh, Christina. . . . er . . . er . . . ah Christina . . . er . . . er . . . can you cash a check?]

KANE: Now Mr. Benny, I think we better rehearse this first. . . . you walk up to Miss Hill and say "Christina, I love you."

JACK: I see, OK. [SFX heavy clomp of footsteps]

KANE: Not so heavy on the walk!

[Don Wilson the announcer interjects a reference to sponsor General Tire]

DON: Jack, I think he means the Silent Safety Tread!

JACK: You would, Don. . . .

KANE: Yes, that's it. Now come on, read your line.

JACK: All right . . . [very flatly].Christina, I love you.

KANE: How do you expect her to believe that? Come on, put some passion into it . . . try it again.

JACK: Christina, I love you!!!! [pants] ... How's that, Mary?

MARY: I still like Robert Montgomery.

KANE: Aw, a little more fire now.... Ask Christina for her hand in marriage.

JACK: Will you marry me?

BEVERLY HILL: I should say not!

JACK: Now what do I do?

KANE: Register surprise!

JACK: Why Christina, I'm surprised at you!

BEVERLY HILL: I never want to see you again!

KANE: Register grief!

JACK: Gee whiz, gee whiz....

KANE: For heaven's sake, is that grief?

JACK: That's grief where I come from.

KANE: Where do you come from?

JACK: Waukegan.

KANE: That IS grief!

JACK: Oh yeah? Cut!

KANE: Wait a minute, that's my line ... cut!

The scene devolved into further humiliation for Jack as the director called Don Wilson over to demonstrate appropriately virile histrionic skills. Wilson passionately extolled the virtues of General Tire's blowout-proof tires to the heroine, while Jack fumed on the sidelines.

After another sponsor switch, to General Foods' Jell-O product, and several worrisome months of low product sales, the stars of both the business and humor sides of the production aligned for Benny in late 1934. His sponsor was happy, and Benny's program topped the ratings charts. Journalist O. O. McIntyre lauded the show: "Benny's humor has the dry crackle of sun-burned twigs. Never explosive, he bungles along, firing the arrows of contempt at himself. He brought to the business of being a comic a combined restraint, a suavity that was something entirely different, and it clicked."[71] *Radio Guide* agreed, noting: "Comedian Benny learned long ago that the way to make people laugh without straining is to create a comical situation—not to redress old jokes in party clothes and rely on studio applause to get them over. Jack also learned that the public loves to see the headman made the fall guy."[72]

THE TROUBLE WITH HARRY CONN

As the fall 1935 radio season opened, the collaboration between Jack Benny and Harry Conn appeared to be golden—the show was ranked number one in the ratings, and accolades showered down upon the pair. They were considered the closest creative team of performers and writers on the air after Don Quinn and Jim Jordan of *Fibber McGee and Molly* and Gosden and Correll of *Amos 'n' Andy*.[73] *Variety*'s review of the *Jell-O Program* in late September was lavish in its praise of the show's writing and performance:

> Harry Conn, who authors this program, seemingly has struck upon the happiest formula yet found for commercial comedy on the air.... Conn's method is to first establish his characters, then build his laugh directly through or with the character itself.... Where Conn also shines is in the blending of his writing style with the delivery of Jack Benny. No better example of perfect actor-writer mating is to be found in show business. Conn writes the way Benny talks, and vice versa.[74]

Strain between the collaborators began building, however, due in no small part to the constant effort it took the two to keep their popular show on the air. An indignant Harry Conn saw Jack Benny reap all benefits and salary of stardom, while Conn labored behind the scenes. Scriptwriters for all major radio programs were frustrated by their meager status. A 1935 *Variety* story asserted, "Writers 2% of Budget; Sponsors rate scribes low."[75] NBC until very recently had refused to give writers on-air credit for their work, *Variety* reported, the network claiming that sponsors did not want precious airtime given over to lengthy film-like credit sequences. Screenwriters in Hollywood earned salaries equal to about 10–15 percent of the budgets of pictures they were contracted to write. Radio writers, on the other hand, earned a pittance, often only between $50–200 per week for a show that cost thousands of dollars. Conn was the highest-paid writer in radio, the article acknowledged. Now Harry Conn's ego swelled while his resentment grew. He enmeshed Benny in an increasingly bitter struggle over the question of who was responsible for the radio program's success—was it Conn's authorship of the script or Benny's sense of timing and performance?

FIGURE 4. Fan magazine *Radio Mirror* shows Jack Benny working closely with his current young script writers, Bill Morrow and Ed Beloin, while former Benny show writer Harry Conn is depicted working solo, more important than the comics he supplied with dialog. *Radio Mirror*, November 1938, 41. Author's collection.

While Jack Benny rarely detailed his creative input into the radio program, his contributions to the show's writing and production were enormous. Benny's role was far more than just a dialogue reader. While Benny acknowledged that he was no ad-libber, and that he was not quick to invent a steady stream of comic situations or one liners to fill the weekly scripts, he was a superb editor of comic dialogue. He possessed a keen sense of language, rhythm, and timing, and he constantly tinkered with scripted lines for himself and the cast right up until the moment of live broadcast. He condensed and sharpened the jokes, their build-up and responses, eliminating unnecessary words and polishing the lines as if they were song lyrics to compliment a tune. Benny's other major contribution was in the performance of the script. He was brilliant at adding emotional and comic emphasis to line readings with his tremendous sense of timing, and he could coach it out of other performers and nonprofessionals. Benny conducted his rehearsals and broadcasts like a symphony maestro without a baton—with looks, nods, and fingers pointed at the performers to key their lines and to direct the sound effects engineers.

Harry Conn considered himself the creative force of the radio program, the person who invented the original characters, skits, and dialogue for the show. He gave little credit to that alchemy of talent and public appeal that made Jack Benny a star. In 1935, Conn began a public relations campaign in newspapers and magazines, giving interviews about his contributions to the *Jell-O Program*, reframing the group project to emphasize his lead role as writer and insinuating that Benny and his cast merely read his scripts.[76] One story, published in the *Los Angeles Times*,[77] was accompanied with a large photo of Conn perched confidently at the typewriter, and Benny looking on from behind like an underling. Another in the *Boston Globe*[78] featured "Sad Faced Harry Conn, Radio's Little Known Mogul of Mirth": "Radio's no.1 wit is a man who has never appeared before the microphone. . . . Meet Harry W. Conn, Jack Benny's ghost writer. . . ." Conn was famously known to joke about Benny's lack of spontaneous creative ability, claiming that "Jack Benny couldn't ad lib a belch after a Hungarian dinner."[79] His flippant pronouncements about Mary Livingstone's acting skills also danced on the edge of being insults. "Conn calls Mary Livingstone (Mrs. Benny) an 'indifferent comedienne'" one interview noted, continuing, "He has written a Mother's Day poem for her to intone today. 'I don't care how I write them,' he said, 'and she doesn't care how she reads them. So between us, we get a laugh.'"

For the Fall 1935 season, Conn demanded a significantly larger share of the Benny empire—not only a doubled weekly radio salary (from $750 raised to $1,400), and extra money for polishing the dialogue in Benny's films ($1,200 per week when they worked at MGM), but also 5 percent of the income earned from Benny's live stage show appearances, and 5 percent of Benny's film earnings. Conn further demanded a royalty of 5 percent of Benny's subsequent radio earnings for five years after the contract, whenever Conn's material was used. Benny's later manager, Irving Fein, recalled that this contract (to which Benny acquiesced) made Conn feel only more entitled, and provoked even more rude and arrogant behavior. "One incident which helped bring much friction to the surface occurred when Mary Benny came in one day with her first mink coat, and Harry Conn's wife said 'If not for my husband, you wouldn't be wearing that mink coat.'" Benny must have felt increasingly squeezed between his dependence on Conn to continue to provide the material that made their program a hit, and frustration with a partner seeming to overstep his bounds. A more cynical performer might have brought in additional writers to spread the responsibility and maintain managerial control; but Benny was loyal to his tight circle of friends and business associates.

Perhaps these behind-the-mike tensions impacted the quality of the *Jell-O Program*, for in early 1936, radio critics began finding fault with the show.

Larry Wolters of the *Chicago Tribune* claimed that the scripts had grown considerably weaker, laying the problems to continuing cast turnover (popular tenor Frank Parker left and several band leaders had come and gone).[80] Benny acknowledged only that "his scriptwriter had a barren period" and Wolters added, "Jack admitted that criticism of his efforts this year has been widespread and he is bending every effort to restore the old sparkle of his program."[81]

Amid this turmoil, Benny, Conn, and the radio cast embarked from Los Angeles in February 1936 on a grueling twelve-week road tour, making personal appearances at theaters across the Midwest and East, while performing the *Jell-O Program* each Sunday. Conn had fallen back into the habit of relying on ethnic dialect to provide the humor in many of the program's sketches, disguising a lack of witty dialogue with unexpected voices. One week the cast performed a Northwest Mounted Police sketch that involved Greek and Irish characters played by dialect comic Benny Rubin. Another week, it was a zoo tour in which cast members encountered zookeepers played in Jewish and Irish accents. Other skits, however, such as Jack, Don, Mary, and Kenny switching roles and personalities to break up the monotony of the program opener, were sharp. The frustrations of travel added to the general show malaise. In Cleveland, Jack became so ill that the group had to cancel its week's appearance onstage. In March, the Benny troupe bounced between Pittsburgh; New York; Washington, DC; and Baltimore.

As Benny placed an acknowledgement in *Variety* of winning the *New York World Telegraph*'s popularity poll for the second consecutive year, Conn countered with a boastful announcement, printed on the same page:[82]

> Writer of First Run Material
> HARRY W. CONN
> Now Serving fourth year writing the radio programs for
> Jack (indifferent) Benny and
> Mary (careless) Livingstone
> And My public, please forgive me
> I'm responsible for writing Mary's Poems
> And also
> "The Chicken Sisters"
> Fifteen minutes of Torso Vibrating Laughs
> Now appearing in Mr. Benny's State show
> State, NY, this week (March 6)
> Fox, Washington, next week (March 13)
> Written by HARRY W. CONN Staged by JACK BENNY

Benny said nothing publically about Conn's presumptuousness. March was contract renewal time for the next broadcast year, and Conn chose this moment to make his most daring demand yet, presenting Benny with his contract requirements, as the Benny troupe pulled into Baltimore for a week of shows at the Loew's Century Theater. Conn requested a 50 percent share of Benny's salary. "Jack told him that it was ridiculous and refused to discuss such a contract," recalled Irving Fein. "Jack was ready to give him a handsome raise, but Conn refused...."[83] Holding firm in his demands, Harry Conn and his wife immediately disappeared.

As it became later and later in the week, Jack Benny fumed in his Baltimore hotel room between stage appearances, with no Conn-provided script for Sunday's live radio broadcast in his hands. Finally, Benny was forced to plunge in and hurriedly write a script. He called his friend, radio comic Phil Baker, who lent him two writers, Sam Perrin and Arthur Phillips.[84] Benny's vaudeville friends Jesse Block and Eve Sully attended the Baltimore broadcast and came up from the audience to join Jack and Mary on stage. Benny resurrected one of the program's oldest melodrama parodies from 1932, "Why Nell Left Home."[85] While the episode was not spectacular, it was adequate.

Late the following Tuesday night, with still no word from Conn (who had decamped to Atlantic City and then to Miami), Benny's frustration poured out in a torrent of words in a four-page telegram, sent to Conn at his Miami hotel. The telegram's text reveals a rare example of Benny at his most emotional. It is also one of the few times he detailed the labor he put into the production of his program.[86] After rebutting Conn's complaints that Benny did not publically acknowledge the writer's contributions to the program, Benny dismissed Conn's assertions that Benny's fame was completely the product of Conn's scriptwriting:

> You have also told many people, including my father, that you made me the star that I am today. That is fine talk, particularly to my father. You cannot make me a star or anybody else in show business—all you can do is help and that is what you have been getting paid for. I am not the only star in show business. Phil Baker is a star, Freddie Allen is a star, Burns and Allen are stars, Eddie Cantor is a star, and you have never written for them. I have paid you more money than any two authors would get from an actor all out of proportion to my radio salary. Every move I have made, whether it is pictures, stage or radio, you were included. Can you name one radio writer whom the public knows as well as they know you. As far as making me a star is concerned, I was a star long before you and I ever became associated. While I am on the subject, let me mention the very latest ad you took out in Variety two weeks ago which at least

twenty people have mentioned to me as being most humiliating and in the worst of taste. In your future ads please state that you are writing the Jell-O program and leave the names of Jack Benny and Mary Livingstone out of them.

Finally, Benny made a case for the importance of his own authorial contributions to show scripts, and ultimately drew the line between performer and employee:

> I have sat up for hours, constructing, editing and helping on all material for which I have never taken the credit.... This past season has been the most miserable I have ever spent in show business. I have given you every protection an author could possibly get insofar as writing—no matter what the expense.
>
> After the expiration of this present radio contract you are free to do as you please, as I do not think that either of us could stand the strain longer. However, as this contract with me has 13 more weeks to go, I would like to have the scripts as per our contract, delivered to me not later than Thursday night of each week. From then on I will be glad to work on them alone. Everything contained in this wire has been on my mind and in my heart for the past year and I am glad it is out.

Scrambling to create episode scripts, once in New York, Benny called in favors from his friends to help secure writing talent—Goodman Ace contributed, along with gag writers Hugh Wedlock, Howard Snyder, and Al Boasberg. His producers at the Young & Rubicam agency, Tom Harrington and Pat Weaver, also pitched in.[87] Benny got some of his confidence back in a lively, funny program on April 5. Fred Allen had offered Benny the use of one of his assistants, Ed Beloin. Beloin's familiarity with Allen's material may have generated the script idea, for the topic of Benny's show was a parody of Allen's *Town Hall Tonight*. The episode sparkled with wry humor, and its spot-on burlesque of Allen's show presaged the Benny-Allen feud that would commence eight months later. Beloin, Bill Morrow, a young radio writer from Chicago, and the experienced Al Boasberg emerged as Benny's new team of writers.[88]

Benny's third show without Conn was nightmarishly difficult. He and the cast were back on the road in Cleveland to make up for the earlier missed stage appearances. Benny decided to proceed with an attempt at parodying Eugene O'Neill's current hit Broadway drama *Ah, Wilderness*. Benny and Conn had garnered big publicity when they had asked O'Neill's permission earlier in the year to do the take-off, as the author had turned down requests from several other comics. The script in Benny's files shows many last-minute edits, deletions, additions in shorthand, and dialogue lines crossed out of the muddled skit. Right before the parody skit began, the audience heard a loud "click" sound, and when Benny asked "What was that noise?" Mary curtly replied, "O'Neill just turned his radio off." After several more weeks of travel, the cast finally returned to Los Angeles in late May, to fine tune a new system of collaboration in the last four weeks of the broadcasting season.

Harry Conn was still under contract to Benny through the end of June. He submitted the required scripts in a desultory and often last-minute manner, along with providing (unwanted) advice on Benny's management of performances on the *Jell-O Program*. Conn repeatedly remonstrated Benny for pacing the program too quickly. On June 9 he wrote Benny, "Last week's show played very good, but I think you are letting your people run with lines. By doing that, they make you rush, and you are at your best in a slower tempo. I have mentioned this before and repeat it as I know I am right."[89] Perhaps this was the kind of give-and-take bantering they used to have as partners, but surely Benny did not wish to be addressed as the performer who knew less about both management and performing. Conn also provided several ideas for film parodies, which would have been challenging assignments for the new writers; comic twists on Shakespeare's *Midsummer Night's Dream* sketch (based on the recent Warner Bros. adaptation); and the controversial Broadway drama *The Children's Hour*. "Mary has to play her lines as the BRAT... and you will have to do a janitor with *Strange Interlude* cracks to be in it. Kenny [Baker] and [bandleader Johnny] Green [could] do a few of the girls as it is a seminary and you explain you're short of girls. I think it's a great bit if no one rushes, it needs a good rehearsal."[90] Benny and his new writers did not take him up on the suggestions. After a summer of rest, they created a rejuvenated *Jell-O Program* with more sparkling wit than the previous year, and rode back to the top of the ratings.

When Conn soon afterward secured a lucrative scriptwriting deal with the Ruthrauff and Ryan advertising agency, the news made the front page of *Variety*. Everyone in the radio industry wanted to see what the talented writer would do next. Conn landed a contract to write the scripts for veteran radio comic Joe Penner for the *Cocomalt Program*, earning $1,300 per week, as much as the fading star. Conn cheekily published an open letter to Benny in *Variety*, publicizing the end of their four-year association and patting himself on the back for "providing the material that kept the Jack Benny program up there on top for so long."[91]

Just ten weeks into the Fall 1936 season, however, Cocomalt fired Conn.[92] *Variety* noted with wry amusement that Conn's replacement, Don Prindle, formerly a $40 per week scripter at a Seattle radio station, would now write

Penner's program for $250 a week.[93] Conn's downward slide was swift. In January 1937, Ruthrauff and Ryan placed Conn as a writer on Al Jolson's radio show to build up a major role for actor Sid Silvers (the *Canada Dry Program* interloper in Fall 1932).[94] But six weeks later, both Silvers and Conn were terminated.[95]

In November 1937, Harry Conn announced he was to write and star in his own comedy, *Earaches of 1938*, broadcast as a sustaining (unsponsored) program on CBS.[96] The show was scheduled at a terrible time, opposite the popular Charlie McCarthy–Edgar Bergen program.[97] The situation-comedy narrative that Conn devised was a copy of the *Jell-O Program*, with a group of zany characters (an emcee portrayed by Conn, exchanging insulting banter with a band leader, announcer, and some comic stooges), attempting to broadcast a radio program.[98] Reviewers snidely noted Conn's nervous performance, and faulted Conn for not creating a unique comic character for himself, yet admitted that the show had promise.[99] *Earaches* did not succeed in securing a sponsor, however, and the program was cancelled after thirteen weeks.

In 1939, after burning his bridges in radio, Conn launched a lawsuit for breach of contract against Jack Benny, seeking $60,000 as his percentage of Benny's ongoing earnings from use of material and characters drawn from Conn's original radio scripts.[100] The lawsuit spent a year in the courts until finally it was settled by an arbitration board. Benny paid Conn $10,000, and both retained the right to use material from the 226 scripts Conn wrote, although Benny was careful to insist that Conn couldn't reuse entire episodes, mention Jell-O, or use any of the names of the characters he had originated (particularly, that of Mary Livingstone).[101] Afterwards Conn faded into obscurity, and little is known about the rest of his career, other than that he had serious health problems and that he occasionally wrote to Benny to sell him comedy material or to borrow money. Conn was last spotted by New York newspaper columnist Dorothy Kilgallen in November 1958, working as a backstage doorman at Broadway's Playhouse Theater, where Jack Benny was embarrassed to have accidentally encountered him.[102]

. . .

When the *Jell-O Program* returned to the air in October 1936, firmly anchored in Hollywood and with yet another new bandleader (Phil Harris), Jack Benny's program solidified its place as the most popular comedy show on American radio. In the four years since his tentative start, vaudevillian

Benny had learned a great deal about radio and conquered many of its particular challenges—from his fortuitous choice of writer Harry Conn through the pair's experimentation and innovation in development of quirky, individual continuing characters, humor built not through stings of one line jokes but in a workplace-anchored situation comedy, and flippant commercials, to Benny and Conn's development of Jack's Fall Guy persona who was the butt of incessant insults and mishaps. Along the way, Benny and Conn briefly experimented with romantic plot devices and political humor, and they had struggled to gain creative control over the program's format from meddling sponsors. They became radio's brightest fun makers, until the pressures of production deadlines, creative spark, and public fame and fortune destroyed their partnership. Harry Conn deserves half the credit for turning Benny the vaudevillian into Jack Benny the radio star. Unfortunately, his ego and insecurities damaged his subsequent career and blunted his legacy. The fact that the vast majority of the radio episodes Benny and Conn created together from 1932 to 1936 have not been available to circulate in recorded form has prevented fans then and now from being able to assess their accomplishments. Now that efforts are being made to make the scripts and reenactments of these long-lost episodes public, this early period, which fans have considered the least important of Jack Benny's radio career, will receive more appreciation for the sparkling comedy it produced and groundwork these shows laid for the future of Benny's show.

Along with Benny and Harry Conn, the third pillar supporting the creativity and innovations of the Benny program's early years was his wife, Sadye Marks Benny, popularly known as Mary Livingstone. The next chapter explores the evolution of Mary's character and its development as the lynchpin of the success of Jack's Fall Guy character. It also examines Sadye Marks's reluctant journey along the way to becoming a prominent and influential (if now largely forgotten) radio star.

TWO

"What Are You Laughing at, Mary?"

MARY LIVINGSTONE'S COMIC VOICE

Mary Livingstone's boisterous laughter and forthright puncturing of Jack Benny's vanity were the cornerstones of one of the most unusual characters in American radio comedy. Chief "stooge" (or comic foil for the main character) of the Benny radio program, taking her amusement at Jack's expense, she occupied the rare position of an attractive, unmarried female who had full equality with the fellows in Benny's gang. Jack's long-suffering neighbors on the show, actress Benita Colman and her movie star husband Ronald, called Mary the only "normal one" among Benny's troupe of zanies.[1] Mary was the first character on the Benny radio program that did not have a defined duty on the show (neither bandleader, singer, nor announcer). Serving vaguely as Jack's secretary, she haphazardly performed a few tasks, impertinently disobeyed his requests, prattled like a mild version of Gracie Allen, and read letters from her hapless family back in Plainfield, New Jersey. Mary mainly functioned as Jack's sometimes cynical, sometimes silly, heckling friend. After five years on the air, when the *Jell-O Program*'s writers had the Kenny Baker character voice the addlepated aspects of the show's humor, Mary's character became smarter and more sophisticated, and she began to critique Jack's foibles with increasing tartness.

Key to Mary Livingstone's character on Benny's radio program was her independence—with only hints of paid employment, she lived alone and in comfort, and could say whatever she pleased, whenever she wanted. Rare among female characters in primetime radio, Mary was never dependent on men—she did not need a husband, father, or even a steady boyfriend. She was never desperate for romance or lacking because she was not in a relationship (unlike other radio characters such as the tart-tongued Connie Brooks of *Our Miss Brooks* or man-hungry Vera Vague on Bob Hope's *Pepsodent Program*).[2]

Mary was never criticized by other characters for her laughter, her critical barbs or her looks (unlike married women such as Sapphire on *Amos 'n' Andy* or Jane Bickerson on *The Bickersons*).[3] Jack's only punishment of Mary was to tease her about her salad days selling hosiery at the May Company department store, and to threaten, not very convincingly, to send her back there.

The Mary Livingstone character was as independent as any of the feisty Hollywood film heroines of the 1930s and 1940s—Barbara Stanwyck, Claudette Colbert, Carole Lombard, or Rosalind Russell. (Perhaps not coincidentally, these actresses were Mary's friends in private life.) As "unruly women," using media historian Kathleen Rowe's term, they were unafraid to make spectacles of themselves. These transgressive, confident female characters became the center of attention and unsettled social hierarchies by disrupting, redirecting, and transforming the humor usually made at women's expense, using the power of female laughter to "challenge the social and symbolic systems that would keep women in their place."[4] In some ways surpassing the freedom of the unruly women of Hollywood film, Mary's character had even more avenues for disruption; since the Benny weekly half hour radio program was not a romantic comedy whose plot must be resolved within ninety minutes, Mary's character never needed to seek a "resolution" to her status, never had to fall in love, wed, or get her comeuppance from a leading man—no Cary Grant or William Powell ever tamed or domesticated her.

This chapter explores the centrality of Mary Livingstone to the narrative world of the Benny radio program, and the development of her comic character during the early years of the show. Mary's voice was an important ingredient of her performance, and this chapter examines how the radio program's comedy utilized her laughter, her heckling of Benny, and her parodies of transgressive female characters to insert a feminist-inflected accent into the male-dominated world of radio comedy. Mary and other unruly, outspoken minor female characters on Benny's show played formative roles in shaping the gender dynamics of the program's narrative world. The similarities and differences between Mary's character and that of Mae West on the one hand, and Gracie Allen on the other, allowed Mary to add even more dimensions to her part. Mary mastered a Mae West impersonation in early 1933 and for two decades used it in Benny's radio show skits to give voice to tough, independent women who cuckolded their husbands and shot their lovers, and always got away with it.

Despite her importance to the Benny radio program, Mary Livingstone's gradual retirement in the early 1950s and Jack's subsequent years of television broadcasts without her have caused her place in the history of radio comedy to have largely been forgotten. To compound this neglect, away from the microphone, Mary Benny was a sharp-tongued, aloof person not remembered fondly by Benny's friends and colleagues.[5] She was insecure and jealous of anyone close to her husband, especially other women.[6] The crippling stage- and mike-fright from which Mary suffered began to cause her to faint after the broadcasts; the condition increasingly worsened over the years. Eventually, it drove her to avoid the public spotlight.

In the 1930s, however, Mary Livingstone the radio performer was popular with critics and the radio-listening public. She was known as a feisty, wise-cracking dame with a lilting laugh, and she was regularly singled out for accolades. Her witty bantering with Jack was key to the show's popularity, as every story about Benny's program pointed out. A 1936 *Delineator* essay maintained that Mary and Gracie Allen were the two most popular radio comediennes. Mary's radio persona was judged to be "cute," a bit dashing with a deadpan voice, and a "pleasant girl you'd meet anywhere except in the theatrical profession."[7] A 1938 *New York Times* survey of women in radio ranked Mary among the highest rated and best paid of all the on-air comediennes.[8]

Mary Livingstone's persona on Benny's show contained complexities and contradictions. Even after she evolved from a dizzy girl into a smart-alecky, tough dame, when reading her poems or her letters from home Mary reverted to the role of the unsophisticated kid from Plainfield, New Jersey. She could act like a lovesick teenaged movie fan mooning over Robert Taylor, or wrangle dinner invitations from men she met on the train like a brash single woman, but the audience knew that in reality she was Jack Benny's wife. Perhaps that made her flirtations with other men and put-downs of Jack even more amusing to radio listeners. By having Mary's character *not* wed to Jack on the show, she could slip in and out of the role of the spouse who could completely deflate the pretensions of her husband, and always have the last laugh at his expense.

Benny's comedy took pleasure in turning accepted male-female relationships upside down—the women were dominant in marriages, independent and strong, while the men in their lives were lazy, drunken louts. While Benny's shows did not criticize or denigrate Mary Livingstone or the glamorous film actresses who made guest appearances, the other female characters at the margins of the show were burlesques of traditional femininity—Dennis's mother was a pipefitter, husband-hungry Babe (Mary's sister) drove a steamroller, Gertrude and Mabel the switchboard operators and Gladys

Zybisco (Jack's sometimes date) were bedraggled drudges, and Mary's mother and Dennis's mother regularly pummeled their weakling husbands. The war between the sexes played out constantly on the program (as it did on so many other radio shows), but here the women nearly always triumphed over the men (and over Benny most of all).

SADYE MARKS BECOMES MARY LIVINGSTONE

Although she had peripheral connections to show business while growing up, young Sadye Marcowitz (the family changed its name to Marks several years after Sadye was born) apparently never harbored ambitions of becoming an entertainer, even though she was naturally talented as a singer. Although for publicity's sake she usually shaved a few years off her age, records show that she was born in Seattle, Washington, on June 25, 1905, the second child of David Marcowitz, a fruit importer who had immigrated from Romania, and his second-generation immigrant wife Esther Wagner Marcowitz.[9] Sadye was raised in a middle-class West Coast Jewish household in Vancouver, British Columbia, with her older sister Babe (née Ethel) and younger brother Hilliard.[10] Sadye had regular contact with vaudeville performers throughout her youth. When the Marks family lived in Vancouver, her parents liked to entertain visiting Jewish actors. She recalled that "they derived particular pleasure out of opening their home to show business performers appearing in town at the Orpheum, our local vaudeville house. Friday night suppers were frequently gay and interesting affairs, as the country's top stars had an opportunity to relax." In 1921, Zeppo Marx (the Marx Brothers were no relation) invited Jack Benny to join him at a Passover meal at the Marks home in Vancouver while the performers were appearing in town. The twenty-seven-year-old Benny gave the teenager little notice.[11]

Completing high school after the family moved to Los Angeles, Sadye worked in the hosiery department of the May Company store in downtown Los Angeles, close to the city's theaters and movie houses. Describing herself in her autobiography as shy, she never spoke of career ambition other than marriage. In the mid-1920s, Sadye's older sister Babe married a vaudevillian, violinist Al Bernovici. This gave Sadye further exposure to the world of entertainment.[12] Sadye met Jack Benny again in 1926, when Babe reintroduced them. Benny was then touring the West Coast Orpheum vaudeville circuit on the same bill with Bernovici. Jack had had plenty of romantic experience by this point in his life, having pursued a romance with older vaudeville star Nora Bayes, and having been engaged on and off for several years to singer Mary Kelly (introduced to Jack by her roommate Gracie Allen). Jack quickly became romantically interested in Sadye, but she was engaged to someone else.[13] Benny persevered, visiting her several times when she was at work at the May Company store. Six months later, he persuaded Sadye to marry him. She hurriedly took the train to Chicago, and they were wed on January 14, 1927. *Variety* announced the nuptials and noted that Benny's new wife was a nonprofessional.[14]

Sadye found herself the young wife of an itinerant theatrical entertainer and watched his performances from backstage. While she liked the traveling, she was jealous of the scantily clad chorus girls with whom Jack associated. Several months before they were married, Jack's role in the elaborate Shubert Brothers' stage revue *The Great Temptations* had ended and he had returned to vaudeville bookings. His routine varied between acting as emcee, performing a solo routine, and doing a skit paired with a young female assistant performing a "Dumb Dora" role, as a dimwitted but pretty young woman who exchanged light banter with him.

Benny had used other assistants in the past, but now (supposedly to save money) he asked Sadye if she might try it. Sadye joined Jack as his on-stage "stooge," or comic foil, and although she was a reluctant and nervous performer, managers reported that audiences were pleased with the results.[15] Benny family lore maintains that Jack rehired the original actress when they played Los Angeles, but after several performances the theater manager stated that the reviews weren't as good as when Sadye was on stage, so the girl was sacked and Sadye got the job permanently. Even though she probably had no professional vocal training, Sadye soon was also singing two numbers in Jack's act.[16] Her voice was pleasantly medium-ranged, without so much of the warbling popularized by other female singers of the era.

Adopting the stage name "Marie Marsh," Sadye performed together with Jack in occasional vaudeville bookings between 1927 and 1931. They also appeared together in a brief 1928 Warner Bros. talkie short, *Bright Moments*, in which she billed herself as "Marie Marlo."[17] Even though Sadye's stage appearances were successful, she did not request equal billing in the act, unlike their friends Burns and Allen, or Block and Sully. When Benny took roles in films, or on Broadway in *Earl Carroll's Vanities* in 1931, Sadye apparently was content to remain behind the scenes. When Benny decided to appear on radio, his original contract with Canada Dry was for a solo act.

This intriguing reluctance to promote herself publically as Jack's partner foreshadowed the way Sadye downplayed the early moments of her radio career. Throughout her life, Sadye adamantly maintained that her entrance onto the Canada Dry Program was unintentional, and that it was just as unplanned and happenstance that she might become a radio actress as it had been when she'd become a vaudeville performer. Sadye's determination to cast herself as a reluctant star and self-effacing spouse is unusual in an American show business star culture that fostered and promoted stories of unique talents, Cinderella stories, large egos, and preordained destinies. Over the years, Sadye's story of her entrance into the Benny program toggled back and forth between her late incorporation into the show in order to pad out a short script, or as a last-minute substitute due to Benny's inability to find a suitable actress to play a small part. Either way, the Mary Livingstone role is set out as a one-time occurrence. As a 1935 newspaper profile of the Bennys' radio origins recounted:

> One night Jack's script ran short. He had to fill in for a couple of minutes and an idea flashed through his mind. He waved to George Olsen to start a number, walked over to where Mary was sitting and brought her over to the microphone with him. He signaled to the engineer to fade the music out and started an impromptu bit of dialog with her. They succeeded in ending the broadcast without any "dead air." Within two weeks Jack had received so many requests that Mary be made a regular part of the show that there was nothing to do but get Harry Conn, his writer, to bring her into scripts regularly. In spite of herself, Mary Livingstone became a radio star.[18]

In a 1965 interview, Sadye/Mary claimed:

> One day they had a bit on the show for a girl from Plainfield, New Jersey, who was supposed to come on and read a silly poem. They auditioned a lot of girls and by the afternoon they still hadn't found one to satisfy them. The director asked me if I would try. So that night I read the poem on the show and the next thing I knew so many letters came in they wanted me to do another one, which I did. Before I knew it, I was on steady as Mary Livingstone, the girl from Plainfield.[19]

Such self-generated stories explain that it was Sadye's delightful laughter (induced by her nervousness, Sadye suggested) that provoked the welcome, if unexpected, audience response. This unanticipated success purportedly kept Sadye on the show in a onetime role that transformed into a major character on the show.

Evidence uncovered by examining the original *Canada Dry Program* scripts provides an alternative story to this myth of Sadye the accidental radio star. Harry Conn and Jack Benny developed several narrative threads into the show's loosely sketched plot that can be seen as laying the groundwork for the introduction of a continuing character to serve as Jack's assistant. As the first chapter related, very soon after Benny began broadcasting his twice-a-week comedy and music program in May 1932, he and Conn realized that the program needed additional characters to involve Benny in witty repartee. Given Benny's pressing into service of the band leader, vocalist, musicians, Conn, and Jack's personal assistant Harry Baldwin, it's easy to imagine that other people in the studio, such as Sadye, might be called upon to perform. On the second show (May 6) Jack announced the beginning of contests that would result in listener entries that would need to be processed. On the May 23 program, Jack asked Ethel to take a letter as he dictated a response to a listener query. On June 15, Jack announced that he had placed an advertisement in the "help wanted" section of the newspaper for a secretary. A young woman named "Garbo" answered the ad (played by Blanche Stewart with a Swedish accent); when Jack tried to dictate a letter to her, she was quickly found to be incompetent, and Jack fired her. On the June 27 *Canada Dry Program*, Jack announced that he had hired a male secretary; this character, too, disappeared after one episode.[20]

They dropped the topic, but four weeks later, Benny and Conn picked up that narrative thread again, and on Wednesday, July 27, 1932, the Mary Livingstone character appeared on the show. Blanche Stewart had already taken several small nonrecurring roles on the *Canada Dry Program*, and Jack could have chosen her to fill the role. Stewart remained with the Benny program for many years, performing bit parts and serving as Mary Livingstone's understudy. Nevertheless, it was Sadye who took the role and not Blanche. Although copies of their contracts with Canada Dry no longer exist, Benny might have negotiated a paid acting position for his wife that started with this episode, the first after his thirteenth week show renewal.

For many years the July 27 script was considered lost, as there is no copy of it in Benny's personal papers. Jack and Mary were sentimental about their performing past. Perhaps they stored it separately from the other documents in Benny's script collection. Eventually they misplaced it. With no other evidence, critics and historians have tended to accept the Bennys' version of Mary's origin story. A copy of the script was finally located, however, on microfilm in the NBC Masterfile script collection at the Library of Congress.

From it, we can examine how the particular narrative elements introduced into the show on this one episode would have long-lasting consequences.

The July 27 *Canada Dry Program* episode opened with Jack, announcer du jour Jimmy Wallingford, George Olsen, and Ethel Shutta congratulating each other on completion of the first thirteen weeks of twice-a-week broadcasting and the sponsor's renewal of the show.[21] Jack made a joke about being a "hay and feed man"—he said "Hey!" to a girl and then had to feed her. At this point the Mary Livingstone character simply joined the dialogue with no introduction, commenting on Jack's "hay" joke after Wallington groaned at it. The script indicated

SADYE: (laughing) Oh, I think that's *awfully* funny.

Wallingford immediately shushed her, saying "Pardon me, Miss . . . but the guests are not allowed to make comments during our program." Sadye responded that she thought Jack was the "cutest thing." Jack tried to continue the show, and Wallingford said to him, "Jack, don't mind that little girl interrupting, but she's been coming up here to see you two or three times, and seems to be kinda anxious to meet you." Jack tried "forcefully" as the script directed, to return to the business of running his show, but also kept whispering to Wallingford "Who is she?" "Do you know her?" "Is that HER standing over there?" "Oooh . . . Jimmy, she's a cutie, isn't she?" After a musical number from the orchestra, Jack and Wallingford read out congratulatory telegrams from listeners that incorporated spoofing mentions of ginger ale. One wire from a listener in Scotland read "Up here in Scotland we're all drinking Canada Dry by the GLASS-gow" and Sadye jumped in to say "Oh, I think that's SWELL!" Wallingford attempted to quiet her but she continued making little asides and laughingly remarked, "When you drink Canada Dry, where does the GLASS GO? That's the funniest joke, I must tell it to my mother." Jack interrupted her with "That isn't what I said, Miss . . . I said, they're all drinking it by the glass-go." Jack asked her to sit down until the program was concluded, and she continued to pester him, asking if she must call him Mr. Benny or could she call him Jack. He responded "Jack," and she retorted, "Thanks, Mr. Benny." Jack then inquired as to her name:

SADYE: My name's Mary Kurtizinger Livingstone. . . . but just *Mary* to you.

JACK: I'm awfully glad of that . . . these are only half-hour programs, you know. Say, by the way, *where* do you live?

SADYE: (quickly) Oh, I live in Plainfield . . . you get on a bus, then you get off at the one stop-light . . . Walk three blocks to your left . . . Then you cut through the cemetery and over the hill . . . then up the road until you see a little red house . . . and you go right through the field, and *THERE YOU ARE*!

JACK: There *YOU* are . . . not *ME*. . . . Well, it was sweet of you to come up here, Mary. Now why don't you sit down quietly and listen to the rest of our program?

SADYE: All right, Jack.

In the episode's final skit, set at a testimonial dinner for Canada Dry Ginger Ale, Jack pompously intoned a speech about the product's virtues that drove away all the guests except Mary. She announced that she was going home, and Jack asked her to come up to the program again sometime. She suggested Monday night, and he said "Err . . . oh, all right." Sadye departed, saying, "I thought you were SWELL . . . good-bye, Jack." Benny ended the program with a hint that Mary intrigued him: "That was the last Mary. . . . I mean, the last number of the 26th program on the 27th of July."

As opposed to the version of the story the Bennys crafted to explain Sadye's unintentional radio debut, the original script shows that the Mary character was involved throughout the program, not just in a few lines tagged on at the end. Conn seemed to have created a fleshed-out Mary Livingstone character in one episode, as Mary exhibited aspects of her character's personality and biographical details that would remain remarkably stable over the years, such as her hometown, the importance of her mother, her jumping into conversations, her scatterbrained dialogue, and her flirtatious, contentious relationship with Jack. Above all, in the first show, Sadye brought Mary Livingstone that attention-getting laugh.

The Mary Livingstone character was central to the following episode, broadcast August 1.[22] Mary was not there in person, however. Ethel read out a letter Mary had sent to Jack, who had been fidgeting that the young fan had not reappeared—

Dear Jack: You probably don't remember me, but I'm the girl who came up to the studio Wednesday night. Remember me . . . Mary? I'm sorry I can't be with you tonight, but you see I have been very busy helping mother with the dishes as she has a sore thumb. I am still laughing at that joke you told Wednesday about when you drink Canada Dry by the glass, where does the glass go? I told it to my mother but she didn't laugh. And father doesn't seem to like you, either. But I think you're swell. Well must close now as I have a lot of work to do. I am studying shorthand and stenography. Will be up to see you on Wednesday night. Good bye. (It's signed) Mary Livingstone, From Plainfield. Oh PS, I think you're swell.

Mary returned in person on August 3, laughing and pronouncing that everything she encountered was "swell."[23] Sadye was then absent for two weeks, (one source suggests she was ill), but she returned on the August 17 program, when Jack hired Mary to be his personal secretary. Subsequently, Mary appeared in every episode.[24]

In September, Benny and Conn introduced a romantic subplot into the shows. Jack ceased joking about his "girlfriend in Newark" and began to flirt with Mary, and the growing romance became a major element of the narrative. There were complications and misunderstandings as Mary asked Ethel for romantic advice, members of the band flirted with Mary, and she overheard Jack flirting with Ethel. In the October 17 episode, Mary and Jack impetuously professed their love for one another.[25]

As the previous chapter discussed, this experiment by Benny and Conn was one of the narrative avenues that they quickly abandoned. The imposition of too much romantic story line would seriously hamper the informal, joking atmosphere they had been building, so they abruptly ended its story line. Mary Livingstone remained Jack's boisterous, incompetent secretary—she forgot to put paper in the typewriter, asked Jack for definitions of words she did not understand, and hampered his efforts to get correspondence completed. Mary also began flirting with the other members of George Olsen's band and allowed them to escort her home, while Jack stood by and quietly fumed in frustration.[26] There was much more humor to be mined from unresolved affection than in true love. Milt Josefsberg, one of Benny's later writers, noted that Mary's ill-defined role on the radio program "was a complete contradiction of the most basic rule in creating comedy programs. For a running character to sustain as a regular member of a successful series, she, or he, must have a clearly-defined function in relationship to the star."[27] Breaking the narrative rules with this unruly, unattached woman was another of the Benny show's many innovations.

At this point, Sadye Marks adopted "Mary Livingstone" as her professional stage name. Sadye might have continued to use "Marie Marsh," but several actresses in New York and Hollywood had similar-sounding names.

By mid-October, Benny's radio scripts, which had previously cued her as "Sadye," began calling her "Mary" as well.[28]

During the first seven months of the Canada Dry radio show in 1932, Mary Livingstone's character played the naïve second banana to Ethel Shutta, the sophisticated singer who had appeared in Eddie Cantor's *Whoopee* and in the Ziegfeld Follies. Ethel's character on the show was an independent-minded married woman in her thirties who brooked no nonsense from men. Ethel and Jack bantered and flirted with each other in dialogue, and she played the original "unruly woman" roles in the program's film parodies. Ethel imitated Greta Garbo as the ballerina Gruskinskaya in the *Canada Dry Program* send-up of the hit film *Grand Hotel*, with Jack playing the suave Baron. On October 24, the Benny gang performed a sketch titled "The Murder of Mr. X," in which Ethel imitated new movie sensation Mae West with a cue in the script calling for a "very breezily" rendered line of "You said it, Big Boy" and sexy humming of "Harlem Moon." In another episode, Ethel played a socialite pushing her hapless husband (played by Olsen) out the door of their apartment so that she could invite in her lover (played by Jack). Cool-headed Ethel then commanded Benny and a succession of other suitors to hide behind the curtains when the cuckolded husband inevitably returned for his missing hat. Mary played no role in these skits.

On October 26, 1932, the cast performed the sketch "Why Girls Leave Home," a burlesque of the old "ten-twent-thirt" theatrical melodramas about a poor girl's virtue being threatened by the lasciviousness of an evil landlord. In this skit it was Mary, and not Ethel, who took the lead role. Mary played the part of a fourteen-year-old girl who was sole support of her family, industriously scrubbing floors and operating a sewing machine. Jack was her elderly father. George Olsen played the malevolent landlord who arrived to demand an enormous rent payment. Mary pled permission to go to the Big City to find work. Just as the landlord returned to kick the old father out into the street, Mary melodramatically returned home. Jack inquired how she got the rent money, and Mary loudly proclaimed she worked very hard and saved and "was a *GOOD GIRL*" (emphasis in the script). Jack announced that her morality did not matter: "What's the difference, Nellie? The home is ours!" The skit's humor lay for listeners in the cynical knowledge that innocent virtue of Victorian times was in short supply for the working girl in Depression times.

One other contribution Mary's character made to the program in Fall 1932 was her first Labor Day poem. Ridiculous stanzas, recited in a sing-songy voice, would become a longstanding Mary Livingstone trademark. While the early poems helped reinforce Mary's "Dumb Dora" persona, their continuation through her transition to a harder character served to soften the bitter edges of her sharp-tongued criticisms of Jack by reminding listeners that she still had a playful side. The initial Labor Day poem Conn wrote for Mary was notable for a morbid tone that subsequent doggerel avoided. Directions in the script instructed Mary to sniffle while reading it:

> As thru life we wander—often even as we go
> Troubles—worry—care endure as yet
> Something listens in our ear as oft it was—and STILL
> Isn't it the truth is what you get?
> When the night begins each morning or afternoon we feel,
> That those times are not just what they used to be
> Labor Day! Oh Labor Day....
> It just seems to reveal
> That a rolling stone is not your friend at all,
> Old pal of mine...
> ... ISN'T THAT SAD?[29]

Conn soon reconceptualized the manner in which these bits of doggerel contributed to Mary's developing character. Subsequent poems would be much lighter in tone. Mary recited these odes to holidays like a schoolgirl, such as this example from February 1934:

> Dear old Winter, Dear old Winter,
> With your ice and snow,
> Drafty echoes in the valley
> Hidey-hidey-ho.
> Dear old Winter, Dear old Winter
> Brrrrrrrrrrrrrr![30]

Mary's poems added bit of human frailty to her sometimes acid wit; the verses were filled with bad puns and sophomoric wordplay. They provoked lots of audience laughter, and Jack began to intersperse commentary between her lines that questioned her odd rhyming. Her poetry was one of the few ways that Jack could find fault in Mary, but even then his criticisms carried an air of affectionate tolerance.

MARY BECOMES CHIEF STOOGE

As a consequence of the upheavals to the cast, broadcast time, and network that sponsor Canada Dry heaped on Benny, Conn, and their program in late October 1932, the Mary Livingstone character took on added significance. Ethel Shutta, George Olsen, his band members and the NBC announcers that Benny and Conn had incorporated into the comic dialogue abruptly left the show. Because she was now the most experienced member of the supporting cast, Mary's part expanded, as she stepped up to inherit the comic stooge and straight-man roles that Olsen and Shutta had filled.

As the previous chapter discussed, in addition to the cast changes, the sponsor in mid-November introduced an additional writer, Sid Silvers, to be added to the program. Silvers devised a new narrative focused on Jack as a theatrical impresario with Sid as his assistant, a large part for himself that came at a diminishment of Mary Livingstone's lines and importance to the plot. The episodes do not exist in recorded form, but the scripted dialogue reveals Sid's character to be unappealingly brash and lazy, and he speaks to Mary in a condescending and belittling manner. Jack all of a sudden starts chasing chorus girls, while Mary mopes on the sidelines. In the ruckus of Benny, Conn, and Livingstone demanding that sponsor Canada Dry remove Silvers from the program, *Variety* claimed that it was Mary Livingstone who remonstrated the most, in order to regain her leading role. The protest was successful, and Canada Dry relented.

Mary's increased involvement in Benny's radio show was noticed by critics and audiences, and the couple was often mentioned in articles about the sudden prominence of husband and wife teams in radio. In November 1932, the *Washington Post*'s radio critic noted that Mary was much more than just a "straight man" or appendage, unlike other female assistants.[31] Mary fully took over the roles in parody skits portraying sophisticated, sexually aware women. On the December 29, 1932, program the Benny cast performed the sketch "She Lived, She Loved, and She Learned," in which Mary, as a bored and wealthy wife, pushed her lackluster husband (played by one of the band members) out the door on a business trip. Soon afterwards, the milkman knocked and Mary rejected him as it was the *Canada Dry Program* (thus he was representing a competing product). Jack entered as the lover, who soon had to hide in the closet. On January 15, 1933, they performed a skit based on the scandalous Broadway drama of sexual promiscuity in the South Seas, *Rain*, calling it "Snow." Mary, in the Sadie Thompson role, sang a few bars of

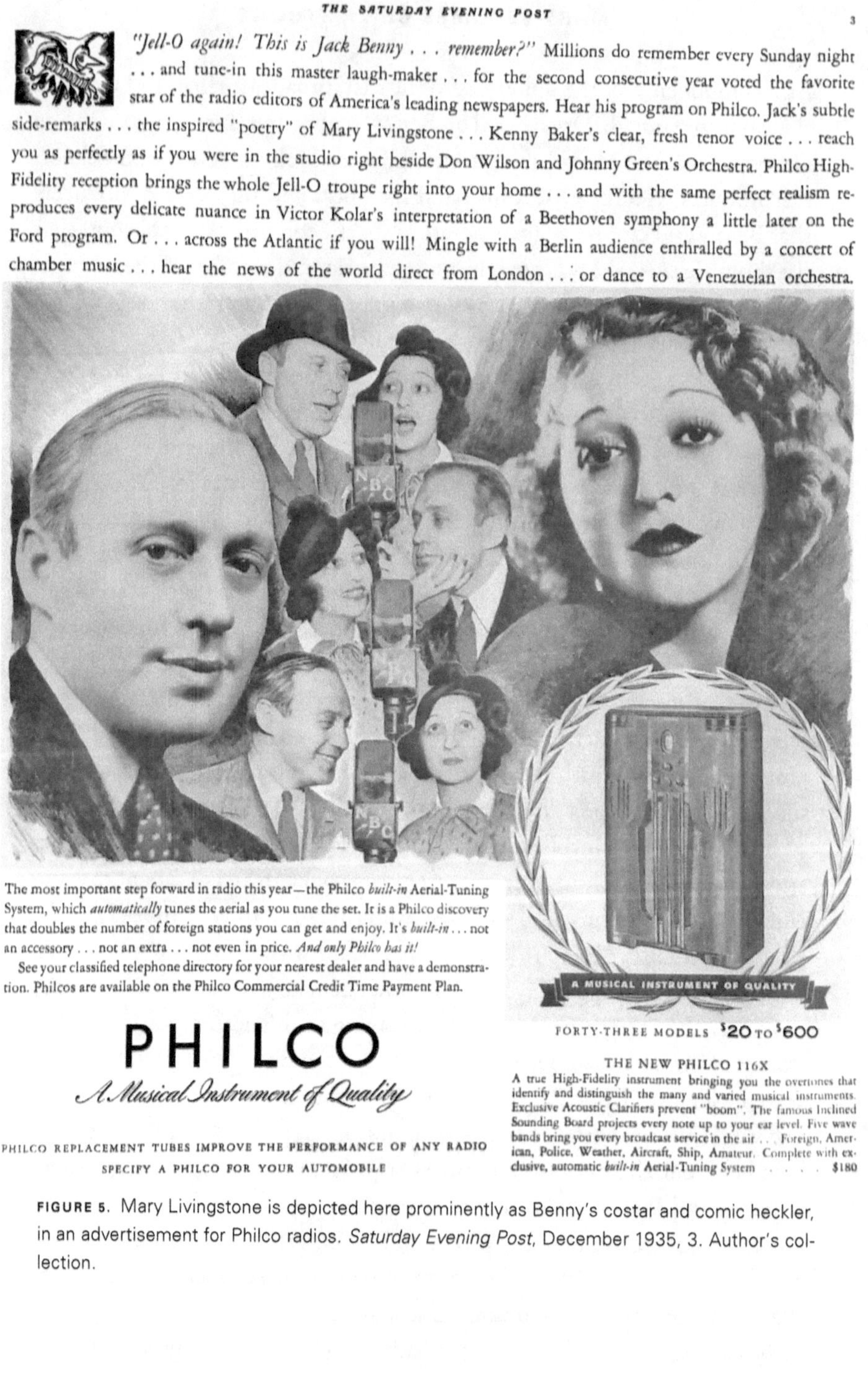

"*Jell-O again! This is Jack Benny . . . remember?*" Millions do remember every Sunday night . . . and tune-in this master laugh-maker . . . for the second consecutive year voted the favorite star of the radio editors of America's leading newspapers. Hear his program on Philco. Jack's subtle side-remarks . . . the inspired "poetry" of Mary Livingstone . . . Kenny Baker's clear, fresh tenor voice . . . reach you as perfectly as if you were in the studio right beside Don Wilson and Johnny Green's Orchestra. Philco High-Fidelity reception brings the whole Jell-O troupe right into your home . . . and with the same perfect realism reproduces every delicate nuance in Victor Kolar's interpretation of a Beethoven symphony a little later on the Ford program. Or . . . across the Atlantic if you will! Mingle with a Berlin audience enthralled by a concert of chamber music . . . hear the news of the world direct from London . . . or dance to a Venezuelan orchestra.

The most important step forward in radio this year—the Philco *built-in* Aerial-Tuning System, which *automatically* tunes the aerial as you tune the set. It is a Philco discovery that doubles the number of foreign stations you can get and enjoy. It's *built-in* . . . not an accessory . . . not an extra . . . not even in price. *And only Philco has it!*

See your classified telephone directory for your nearest dealer and have a demonstration. Philcos are available on the Philco Commercial Credit Time Payment Plan.

PHILCO
A Musical Instrument of Quality

PHILCO REPLACEMENT TUBES IMPROVE THE PERFORMANCE OF ANY RADIO
SPECIFY A PHILCO FOR YOUR AUTOMOBILE

FORTY-THREE MODELS $20 TO $600

THE NEW PHILCO 116X
A true High-Fidelity instrument bringing you the overtones that identify and distinguish the many and varied musical instruments. Exclusive Acoustic Clarifiers prevent "boom". The famous Inclined Sounding Board projects every note up to your ear level. Five wave bands bring you every broadcast service in the air . . . Foreign, American, Police, Weather, Aircraft, Ship, Amateur. Complete with exclusive, automatic *built-in* Aerial-Tuning System $180

FIGURE 5. Mary Livingstone is depicted here prominently as Benny's costar and comic heckler, in an advertisement for Philco radios. *Saturday Evening Post*, December 1935, 3. Author's collection.

"St. Louis Woman" to help paint the appropriate picture for the listening audience.³²

After Benny's group was fired by Canada Dry in early 1933 and hired by Chevrolet (meaning a return to NBC), new decision makers chose male vocalists for the program. Benny's success in negotiating a favorable salary and prominent co-comedian role for Mary Livingstone was noted admiringly in the trade press.³³ Mary Livingstone was now the only woman in the cast (now billed as a comic program with musical interludes). Mary proved popular with radio audiences and critics, who complimented her assertive character. A review of the *Chevrolet Program* in June 1933 remarked:

> Seemingly, every comedian must now own or operate a stooge to be on any major payroll. Mr. Benny's wife, Mary Livingstone, stooges as an impudent secretary but refuses to be submerged in the classic dumb-dame department. She gives as well as takes and the two of them together account for a total of twelve to fifteen minutes of unwatered frivolity [during the half hour program] which you'd do well not to miss.³⁴

On March 31, 1933, the cast performed a sketch parodying Mae West's new hit film *She Done Him Wrong*. In Lady Lou's dressing room, Mary as Mae West hummed one of her signature tunes, "Frankie and Johnny," and purred lines like "Hullo, Dark 'n' Handsome," and "Listen, hon, why don't you come up some time?" Harry Conn had a long-standing Mae West connection, as one of her scriptwriters since the 1920s.³⁵ Now that West was a national sensation, Benny and Conn wondered if Mary could carry off Mae West's distinctive voice as well as Ethel Shutta had the previous fall. Mary Livingstone enthusiastically took up the challenge of transmitting Mae's vocal personality, and she was an unexpected success. *Washington Post* radio reviewer Robert Heinl in April 1933 praised her:

> Mary Livingstone distinguished herself as an imitator of Mae West during a program over the networks recently. Miss Livingstone mastered Miss West's dulcet speech of *She Done Him Wrong* during a single sitting at the performance of the popular talkie. "But I was never so nervous in my life," said Miss Livingstone (Mrs. Jack Benny out of office hours). "I worried a lot about the imitation, for after all, there's no one talks just like Mae West!"³⁶

The reporter noted a month later, "Mary Livingstone's imitation of Mae West... invariably gets a 'rise' out of the studio audience. Mary's inflections bring applause and laughter from the studio visitors."³⁷ Mary's expanding vocal comedic abilities added layers of verve and life to this well-known transgressive character.[38]

Conn and Benny wrote the Mae West character into at least ten of the subsequent skits on the Chevrolet radio show in 1933 and 1934, as Mary was called upon to play sophisticated or sexually aware characters that broadened her "regular" identity as addlepated secretary/companion. In December 1933 the cast performed a parody of *Uncle Tom's Cabin*, in which Mary played Liza with a Mae West accent. In subsequent years, as Mae-mania abated, Benny and his writers incorporated Mary's popular vocal characterization into her portrayals of a succession of tough girls. Over the next fifteen seasons, Mary continued to play a series of sultry-voiced, gun-wielding wives, lovers, and cigarette girls (named Gertie La Strip or Mitzi La Rue) in the Captain O'Benny murder mystery skits. Mary's brazen, confident characters shot their milquetoast husbands, and weren't sorry in the least.[39] The characters anticipated the femme fatales who would lurk in the shadows of film noir detective films of the postwar years. Mary performed these provocative roles in at least nineteen episodes of the Benny radio show between 1935 and 1942, and at least a dozen more between 1942 and 1950.

MARY'S MID-1930S RADIO STARDOM

The expansion of Mary Livingstone's role as Jack Benny's chief stooge brought her a great deal of publicity, although she always remained in Jack's shadow.[40] A *Boston Globe* reporter in 1935 seemed nonplussed at Mary's popularity: "Today Jack Benny and Mary Livingstone constitute an inseparable combination. Jack without Mary is like Amos without Andy. Listeners wait for her poems and wisecracks as eagerly as they do for Jack's 'Hello again' and his gags at the expense of Don Bestor's spats. Mary's 'OK, Toots' has become a national catch-phrase. They even wrote a popular song about it."[41]

Mary's scatterbrained character and recurring specialty bits did start to grate on a few critics' nerves. Larry Wolters of the *Chicago Tribune* complained about the repetitive quality of Mary's poems.[42] On the other hand, Mary's poems were one of the most heralded features of the Benny group's personal appearance tours. In 1934, a newspaper promotion challenged Pittsburgh fans to complete the final two verses to "Oh, Pittsburgh!" to win prizes. In Detroit in 1936, the city's newspapers made Mary the center of publicity around the Benny troupe appearance; they held a cash prize contest for fans to send in their own bits of doggerel imitating Mary's style, which she would purportedly judge.[43] They christened Mary "the punk poetess of the air, who appears with Jack Benny as his interrupting stooge on all this programs."[44]

Some of the public commentary on Mary's achievements referenced the paucity of other successful female entertainers on radio. A *Variety* headline on November 21, 1933, declared "Few Femme Radio Favs," bemoaning the dearth of women's names as lead performer among the twelve most popular radio programs. The article noted that Gracie Allen was the top woman as part of Burns and Allen, and that several women such as Mary Livingstone and Portland Hoffa supported their spouses in comedy. (Hoffa, who portrayed a dim-witted young female companion to husband Fred Allen on his radio program, once described herself as "Wooge" or female stooge. It's a delightful term, but I have not yet found other references to it.[45]) The dreary situation for women in radio in the 1930s differed from the dominance of female stars in Hollywood film, where women were the top-paid actresses (if behind the scenes, there were few directors or major screenwriters still at work after their 1920s heyday).

In the 1930s, Mary's comic persona was most frequently compared to that of radio's most prominent female star, Gracie Allen. Famous for what her partner George Burns called her "illogical logic," addlepated verbal games and linguistic somersaults, Gracie seemed brainless on the surface. However, Gracie was not so much a "Dumb Dora" as a nearly uncontainable female force, who twisted around the heads of everyone she encountered until they were befuddled.[46] Radio historian Susan Douglas remarks that Gracie's unruliness was legendary—"her absolute refusal to obey orders, her defiance of instructions, her willful misunderstanding of the language."[47] Scatterbrained but loveable, Gracie always escaped whatever predicaments she caused, while George stood at her side, critiquing her and her stories in a resigned sort of exasperation. In the imaginative space of radio, George couldn't quite "contain" her as thoroughly as he would be able to later on television within the confines of their suburban home setting. Radio historian Leah Lowe credits Gracie with overcoming the worst social prejudices about gender in which 1930s culture could frame her as a "Dumb Dora" through her portrayal of "an exuberant femininity oblivious to many of the limitations imposed on women by patriarchal authority."[48]

A highlight of Gracie's comedy for radio audiences, Leah Lowe suggests, was having to piece together the crazy reasoning Gracie presented for the

FIGURE 6. Mary Livingstone is given the glamorous cover girl treatment as befits one of radio's most popular stars. *Radio Guide*, October 19, 1935. Author's collection.

bizarre things that she did, for in Gracie's mind, the ending outcome was always logical.[49] As George Burns said of Gracie's illogic, "If you listen to Gracie's prattle on the radio, you may notice that her logic is faultless, though usually completely mistaken... Gracie gets her laughs—we hope—because we often THINK the way Gracie TALKS, but we pride ourselves that WE never talk the way Gracie thinks."[50] Gracie did many things that no other female partner accomplished on primetime network radio programs—she was the focus of the show, the plots always revolved around her antics, and

George was the sidekick stooge who fed her straight lines, sighed in exasperation, and puffed on his cigar. George called Gracie out for her craziness, but she was never really punished for the chaos she caused, unlike the troublesome Baby Snooks, who got spankings from her exasperated father, or Our Miss Brooks, who was thunderously called on the carpet by her principal in every episode. Gracie, like Mary, was also always presented as an attractive, tastefully dressed upper-middle-class woman. While male characters on the Burns and Allen show may have criticized Gracie's seeming lack of intelligence, none ever disparaged her looks. In contrast, Bob Hope regularly insulted the man-chasing "debutantes" Brenda and Cobina, Archie cracked on Miss Duffy on *Duffy's Tavern*, and the Kingfish called his nagging wife Sapphire "The Old Battle Axe" behind her back.[51]

As with Mary Livingstone, Gracie's comic timing in delivering her lines was impeccable and her laughter was a "crucial element of her vocal performance," as Leah Lowe notes. (George Burns used his cigar to help the couple's comic timing, as he could always take a puff if the audience laughter continued.)[52] Lowe states that "much of what is funny [on the radio] arises from the vocal delivery of scripted dialogue rather than scripted dialogue in and of itself."[53] Like Mary, Gracie frequently laughed at seemingly nothing, and when George asked her why, she followed with a non sequitur or said "I don't get it" rather than make a joking, critical comment.[54] Gracie's laughter fell over George's dialogue lines and disrupted the flow of the conversation, whereas everyone on the Benny show paused when Mary laughed, to relish the sound, and to find out what she thought was amusing.

Like Gracie's ridiculous stories about her brothers, Mary's reading of letters from her mother back in Plainfield allowed her to ground some of her comedy in domestic and family situations. The letters from Mary's Mama (which began tentatively in June 1934 and became a regular feature in April 1935), contain humorous stories about misbehaving uncles, brothers, father, and life on the farm.[55] Mama was a strong-headed and forceful woman who often worked masculine-type jobs like driving a milk delivery truck and pummeled her misbehaving, lazy, drunken husband, Papa. Mary's brothers, uncles, and cousins suffered ludicrous accidents, took strange jobs, and did crazy things that were fodder for the wry jokes, bad puns, and working-class-focused humor that enlivened these letters, all read in a lighter tone than Mary might otherwise take when criticizing Jack. Mary's sister Babe, the man-hungry pipefitter or steamroller operator, entered into the Benny show's narrative in the 1940s. Even as the Mary character's tone sharpened in the

1940s, the letters from her mother seemed to soften her character by association. The put-down jokes about Babe were the closest the Benny show comes to putting down Mary herself, although Mary always appeared superior to her hapless sister.

Letters from home were the limit of Mary Livingstone's domesticity, however. Unlike Kate Smith, who was portrayed as a homemaking expert when her program was sponsored by a food company, or Fibber McGee's Molly, (even Gracie, who kept house for George after a fashion), the Mary Livingstone character was never shown to be cooking or cleaning. It is ironically amusing that, during the eight years that the Benny show was sponsored by Jell-O, Mary never entered a kitchen to whip up a batch. Announcer Don Wilson, who emoted so enthusiastically about the product, spoke as if he was well-versed in preparing it. In Jell-O magazine and newspaper advertising, a cook or even Jack himself prepared the Jell-O or Jell-O Ice Cream Powder. In a 1936 full-page color comic pages newspaper advertisement, "Jack Benny Pulls a fast one on Mary Livingstone," Jack in an apron and chef's hat beckoned to Mary and said "Mary—If you'll promise not to write any more poems, I'll make dessert tonight!"[56] Although Mary shared equal billing with Jack on the cover of the Jell-O recipe booklet given away by the radio show's sponsors in 1937, the closest she ever came to the actual product was a spoon to eat it with.

There was always some trumped-up confusion about whether Jack and Mary were actually married, because their stage names were different and they did not play a married couple on the radio. Undoubtedly most of the public knew they were a couple, but fan magazines could exploit the mystery. The *Detroit Free Press* played up this angle in a 1933 interview: "Jack Benny, the merry fellow who entertains you via the air, and Mary Livingstone, his pesky girlfriend, are doing their scrapping in Detroit this week. Only they're registered at the Book-Cadillac Hotel as Mr. and Mrs. Benny, and they point with pride to the fact that they are going to celebrate their seventh wedding anniversary soon." An advertisement for the August 1935 issue of *Radio Stars* raised the question "Why Did they Marry?" "Read—The Love Story of Mary and Jack Benny." "Is it true that Mary Livingstone, the cute girl on Jack Benny's program, is his wife in real life? How did they meet? What is their love story?"[57] But marriage also had its realistic downside, to which female fans could also connect. A 1941 *Pittsburgh Post-Gazette* article, "Wives and Husbands Make the Best Radio Teams," darkly hinted, "Who, for example, knows better the foibles and all too human weaknesses of that perennial radio heel, Jack Benny, than Mary Livingstone?"[58]

In interviews, Mary Livingstone spoke of the stage fright, mike fright, and nervousness in front of audiences that plagued her. She continued to downplay her performing talents and walked away from opportunities that other actresses would have leapt at. A 1939 fan magazine article noted, "Mary Livingstone attracted considerable attention as a vocalist when she sang the title role in the Benny air version of 'Snow White' last season, and two or three times a year she's coaxed to vocalize. Mary's opinion of her own voice, however, isn't as high as her critics' so it's only at the insistence of Jack that she sings."[59] Mary appeared in one motion picture, Paramount's 1937 *This Way Please*, a light romantic comedy about movie theater ushers featuring radio personalities Jim and Marion Jordan, bandleader Buddy Rogers, and rising film starlet Betty Grable. The *Los Angeles Times* film gossip columns noted, "Enter Mrs. Jack Benny as a motion picture star. And just why has that debut been delayed so long—considering how much she contributes to the entertainment on the famous Benny radio program?" While Jack incorporated mentions of Mary's upcoming film appearance into the radio show, and in October 1937 Jack read out on the air a review published in the *Hollywood Reporter* that complimented Mary's performance, Mary didn't like to talk about the film or her experience. Mary went to the trouble of having plastic surgery done on her nose in 1940 to make her appearance less ethnic and more glamorous for possible movie roles, but she did not expand her film career.[60] (The procedure also seemed to make her radio voice sound less nasal.) Even though Paramount kept offering film contracts, Mary never appeared in the movies again, lending only her voice to one scene in 1940's *Buck Benny Rides Again* and the 1959 Warner Bros. cartoon *The Mouse that Jack Built*.[61]

MARY'S LAUGHTER BECOMES MORE INCISIVE

Mary's greatest asset, her show-stopping laugh, was bright and lengthy, and Benny and his writers utilized it to great advantage.[62] Jack would be chattering away with other characters, ridiculous boasts flying, and then Mary would launch her hilarious reaction. After a beat of silence, Jack would respond, "What're you laughing at, Mary?" Then Mary would sharply quip her retort, which at its best was a clever pun that punctured Jack's hubris. During the Benny program broadcast of February 14, 1937, for example, Jack and Phil were exchanging remarks with the guest star, bandleader Ben

Bernie. Each had greeted the other in elaborate fashion as "Maestro." As their discussion continued:

JACK: Say Ben, come 'ere a minute, let me ask you, man to man.... Now he's *supposed* to be funny, but I can't see that fellow Fred Allen, can you?
BEN BERNIE: No I can't.
PHIL HARRIS: I can't see him either!
MARY: Hahahahahahahaha!
JACK: Mary, what're you laughing at?
MARY: Three blind maestros.

In the 1930s, radio advertisers actually gauged the success of the comedy programs they sponsored by counting the number of laughs emanating from the studio audience during a performance, and measuring the duration of audience reactions. Benny's writers and producers informally kept score during the broadcasts, and audience response to Mary's jokes and laughter was consistently the highest for any Benny show cast member.[63] Other than her witty retorts, however, much of Mary's humor during the first five years on the air hinged on her misunderstanding of situations or lack of intelligence. When Kenny Baker was hired as the new tenor in November 1935, following in the footsteps of the somewhat sophisticated, wisecracking singer Frank Parker, Benny and Conn decided to make Baker's character be a young and foolish brat. In her autobiography, Mary recalled her character's early immaturity, and that "when Kenny came on, the writers made him dumb, too. It didn't take Jack long to discover that two dopes weren't as funny as one. That's when I became Jack's smart-aleck girlfriend."[64] When Bill Morrow and Ed Beloin joined the program as writers in Spring 1936, Mary's character especially began to become more intelligent, her laughter more of a comic weapon, and her critical barbs launched at Jack more biting. This sharpening of Mary's character coincided with developments of Jack's own radio persona to become less of the polished master of ceremonies and more the bumbling, egotistical "Fall Guy."

In his 1939 guide, *Handbook of Radio Writing*, Erik Barnouw discussed the problem of how to avoid "vanishing characters" in crafting multicharacter narratives for broadcasting. He argued that Mary's radio lines made an unexpected positive use of the tendency of characters to disappear into the background of radio dialogue.[65] Barnouw stated that if the radio listener didn't hear a character speak for a while, that character became invisible. He counseled prospective writers that, when they needed a radio character to give a long speech, to occasionally insert references to the person he is speaking to into the text, to acknowledge them and, in Barnouw's words "keep them alive." Otherwise, long speeches should be regularly interrupted by others' comments, or those silent characters seemed to "die." Barnouw reasoned that the problem of invisibility was why the dialogue on most programs came in spurts of repartee.[66] However, Barnouw found that Benny comedy program turned this liability into an asset:

> In the world of Jack Benny's comedy... the writer doesn't care a hoot about the prosaic worry of keeping characters alive. Sometimes, in fact, he derives a definite value from letting them die. Mary Livingstone isn't in the picture continuously. Sometimes she has silent intervals during which she drops completely from our consciousness. This, as a matter of fact, is what makes her sudden reincarnations so delightfully abrupt and shattering. This same abruptness couldn't quite be conveyed on the stage. It owes its punch to the very fact that, a moment before, she didn't even exist.

Barnouw provided an example from the *Jell-O Program* in which Jack and Don Wilson had been conversing, alone, for several minutes:

WILSON: Mr. Benny, there's one more question the ladies in particular would be very much interested in. Do you MIND telling us your age?

JACK: What's that?

WILSON: Do you MIND telling us your age?

JACK: I'm just 31.

MARY: He minds.

"A quick stab like this is the more effective," Barnouw concluded, "because, like the door, or the telephone that rings, Mary comes into existence just as that moment."

WOMEN'S HUMOROUS ASSAULT ON MEN IN THE BENNY NARRATIVE UNIVERSE

Jack Benny's radio program, like those of many other comedies, dramas, and soap operas of the 1930s, 1940s, and 1950s, was framed around tensions in the relationships between women and men. However, unlike most other comedies and dramas broadcast in prime time, Benny's show showed marked sympathy for the women's point of view in the battle of the sexes. Mary Livingstone and the other female characters on the Benny radio program wielded considerable social, psychological, and economic authority over the men, and they most often wore the pants in their families. Strong-willed, smart, and confident female characters such as Dennis's mother—the battle-axe-waving, milk-truck-driving Mrs. Lucretia Day; Mary Livingstone's feisty mother (who ran the household, held down jobs, and browbeat her lazy husband and male relatives on the farm in Plainfield); the frosty female movie stars who disdained Jack, the diner waitresses who dished out sarcasm with the food, and Gertrude and Mabel the telephone switchboard operators, all gave trouble by telling the truth to Benny and the other men on the radio program. The female characters were nearly always working women—all held jobs and supported themselves and often their entire families. In the Benny radio world there were no frail ingénues, no cloyingly sweet innocent girls, and no happy housewives, no nurturing aunts or grandmothers—no subservient, dependent, or sentimental women whose goal in life was to serve and to please men.

Benny's radio world was a place where traditional gender relationships were turned upside down. While conservative listeners might laugh derisively at the women on this show for denigrating the sanctity of marriage and the family, other listeners appreciated how the Benny program could "audaciously turn the tables on women's usually subordinated position."[67] Benny and the other men fell short of stereotypical definitions of heterosexual masculinity—weak, timid, immature, old, lazy, unemployed, and often drunk (the only exceptions being film actor guest stars and stern sponsors). As the next chapter will further explore, men on the Benny program desperately hung on to the last shreds of patriarchy by a thread. Mary Livingstone's character led the show's vanguard of females unafraid to make a spectacle of themselves—women who had to work with and live with these men, and laughed at them with abandon, knowing that they were going to have to carry their own weight.[68]

Benny's program complicated the gender norms espoused on other radio comedies. Gerard Jones notes in his history of the genre that "unhappy wives had always been a staple of sitcoms, of course, but their image had always been counterbalanced by that of the happy wife, either the protagonist or a loving spouse."[69] On the Benny program, there were no compliant females to counterpoint Mary's independence and caustic criticisms, and there was no "sentimentalized portrayal" of family life.[70] Meanwhile, the narratives of other popular radio comedy programs hewed to stereotypes about women and their behavior. Bob Hope's women were either objectified as sex objects of Hope's wolfish desire, or scorned as man-hungry harridans like Vera Vague or Brenda and Cobina (doppelgangers of high society debutantes of the day). Hope, Eddie Cantor, and Red Skelton created comic worlds in which the gender divisions between men and women were so calcified that the boundaries could rarely be crossed. Ridiculing women made men feel part of a group united against their opposites. Jokes about women allowed men to deal with their anxiety about the power of matriarchy and their own insecurities about their heterosexual masculinity. Even the Benny program insulted women who behaved unconventionally or didn't meet societal standards of beauty (like Mary's sister Babe, or Jack's meager girlfriend Gladys Zybisco),[71] and Mary Livingstone gleefully made catty comments about them. Nevertheless, male misbehavior was reprimanded on the Benny program more regularly than it was on the other programs.

The humor of Benny's narrative world seems feminist inflected, even as it was produced for twenty years on radio by male scriptwriters. The show's humor reflected a down-to-earth cynicism about duties and pleasures of everyday domestic life, as it acknowledged that husbands did not often resemble Prince Charming, and that families bickered. Yet, with humor somehow we will get through this and everything will be OK. A cynical view of a world of endless amounts of work especially around the house binds the women in the Benny narrative world to the women who make the Jell-O, and gives them tremendous sympathy for Rochester. With the introduction and expansion of the Rochester role, we start to see Benny at home, living in the domestic world, away from work. As the show's narrative played with more issues of Benny taking in laundry, bottling chili sauce, selling Christmas cards, we do flesh out his character as a male person much more fully than a sitcom dad who goes off to mysterious work, or just comes home and reads the paper.

Even though the Benny narrative world was a workplace sitcom, its male and female characters over the years seemed to build the close bonds of family. Despite all the insult humor and Mary's endless jabbing at Jack, there is always a family-familiarity to the show, like squabbling siblings who do indeed care for each other. The insults in Benny's world are the family fights of familiar characters that are bound together. Radio historian Susan Douglas suggests that joking insults assumed a familiarity between characters like battling siblings or spouses, so insult humor on the air made characters feel familiar with each other, and more familiar to the audience.[72] Douglas says of the Cantor program, "Men's conceits about their attractiveness and sexual prowess, about their intelligence and general mastery over life, were pierced into flaccid, deflated balloons. But at the same time masculinity was recuperated, its resilience, toughness and instant ability to respond to a challenge celebrated week in and week out." Conversely, Benny and his radio characters recuperated very little of their masculinity in their exchanges with women.

An example of the sympathy toward women that the Benny program portrayed is a comic Grape Nuts Flakes midprogram commercial (November 8, 1942) about house-husband Mr. Twink (Benny) who dishes up the Grape Nuts Flakes while his wife works a war job at the shipyard, and all the other service people who deliver milk, coal, mail, whatever, are saucy women who flirt with Benny.[73]

DON: The scene is the little cottage of Oglethorpe J. Twink in Glendale, CA. It is breakfast time, and Mr. Twink, played by Jack Benny the eminent politician ["Hooray for Benny!" interjects writer Ed Beloin as a drunken voter] is awaiting the arrival of Mrs. Twink, his wife who is a welder on the nightshift in one of our huge aircraft factories, curtain, music....

JACK: Oh dear, 7 am and Clarabelle isn't home yet. It's payday too. I hope she didn't get into a crap game with some of the girls.[audience laughs]. Oh well she works hard, she's entitled to a little a little fun, I guess.

[knock on door] Now I wonder who that is, come in? Why its the *ICE* girl [audience laughs], hello Gloria.

SARA BERNER: (flirty voice) Any ice today, Twinkie?

JACK: Darn you, Gloria for the third time today, no. I am a married man!

SARA: Aw come on. Don't you want a cake of ice, sweetie?

JACK: No and take your *foot* out of the door. [audience laughs for 4 seconds] If my wife finds you here heavens knows what will happen, now scram!

SARA: OK cutie, I'll see you tomorrow. (door slam)

JACK: That Gloria's fresher than the Fuller brush girl.[audience laughs] Well I might as well start getting breakfast ready for the twins, they love those toasty brown, sweet as a nut Grape Nuts Flakes. (sings) I'm dreaming of a white Christmas [audience laughs] ... Just like the ones I used to know, where the tree tops glisten ... (door opens)

JACK: Clarabelle where have you been, its almost 8 o'clock.

MARY: (in her tough girl voice) Now, now honey stop nagging and give me a kiss.

JACK: Get away from me with those *greasy* hands, I've got a clean apron on[audience laughs] . . . now you tidy up.

MARY: OK, hand me the Dutch Cleanser, I want to wash my face. [audience laughs]

JACK: Here you are. . . . (singing) I'm dreaming . . . just like the ones I used to know. . . . You want some breakfast, dear?

MARY: Yes, but first give me my kiss.

JACK: Now Clarabelle . . .

MARY: Come on, kiss me. (small sounds of a tussle)

JACK: Not so early in the morning! Don't be so rough! Clarabelle, the children will hear. . . . Now you broke the clasp on my slave bracelet!

MARY: Well I'll take it to the plant tonight and weld it for you. By the way, why aren't the kids up?

(Joe and Josephine now appear, played by Phil and Dennis in childlike voices; they express excitement about eating their Grape Nuts Flakes, and Dennis complains that he wants to play the part of Joe)

JACK: Aren't you going to have breakfast, dear?

MARY: Not until you give me that kiss.

JACK: Not in front of the children! Now you let me go!

PHIL AND DENNIS: (sing-songy voices) Momma's kissing daddy, momma's kissing daddy!

JACK: Children behave yourselves. . . . (singing) I'm dreaming of a white Christmas . . . (knock) Oh, oh its Gloria.

SARA: Hey Twinkie honey, did I leave my ice tongs here?

MARY: Oh, so she calls you Twinkie, eh, so you've been playing around with that ice girl!

JACK: No, no I haven't.

MARY: You're going to have a white Christmas. . . . bandages.

JACK: Clarabelle put me down! Ouch! Ouch!

DON: Chin up but with blackened eyes [a soap opera reference], Mr. Twink will serve breakfast.

BALANCING MARY'S BITING LAUGHTER WITH SOFTER ASPECTS OF HER CHARACTER

Writer Milt Josefsberg recalled that Mary "was one of [the show's] most valuable components because she could most frequently and fearlessly puncture his pomposity. Perhaps because she didn't technically work for Jack and the program, and because she was also an attractive gal whom Jack occasionally dated, she could get away with more frequent and sharper insults than anyone else on the show. They were many, and they were funny."[74] Mary's humorous attacks on Jack's foibles became more pointed as his own vanities grew. Mary's occasional "shut up!" jokes became potent laugh-getters. These were so shocking in their day (such sharp words to a man, coming from a woman) that they could be used only infrequently, but when sprinkled into the scripts every so often, Mary's ripostes were the most powerful putdowns Jack's character experienced. When later asked about which were his very favorite jokes across his program's long history, Benny would of course nearly always mention the "Your Money or Your Life" skit. But his second-favorite audience laugh-getters always involved Mary. Many times he marveled that Mary got a huge audience response and long laughter with "just three words." For example, when opera singer Dorothy Kirsten guest-starred on the April 25, 1948, episode, she and Don Wilson exchanged erudite opinions:

DON: Oh, Miss Kirsten, I wanted to tell you that I saw you in *Madame Butterfly* Wednesday afternoon and I thought your performance was simply magnificent.

DOROTHY: Well, that's awfully kind of you, Mr. Wilson, but who could help singing Puccini? It's so expressive—particularly the last act starting with the *allegro vivacissimo*.

DON: Well, that's being very modest, Miss Kirsten, but not every singer has the necessary *bel canto* and flexibility or the range to cope with the high *tessitura* of that first act.

DOROTHY: Well, Mr. Wilson, didn't you think in the aria "Un Bel Di Vedremo" that the strings played the *con molto* exceptionally fine, with great *sostenendo*?

JACK: Well, I thought....

MARY: OH, SHUT UP!

Jack recalled in a 1969 interview, "Mary's simple three worlds, 'Oh, Shut Up!" practically stopped the show. If I had to choose only one bit as being the funniest, that's the one I would have to pick."[75] As other elements of the program's comic world increased in intensity over time (Jack became more and more preposterously cheaper each year so that the newer jokes would "top" the previous ones), Benny's writers used Mary's sharpest rebukes, and most acrid tones, more often. By her final appearances the Benny program's final episodes, Mary did come off as a pretty sour companion.

What may have saved Mary's puncturings of Jack's ego from being too ugly was the underlying context that the radio-listening public understood in the 1930s–1950s. No matter how sharp and mean Mary's retorts to Jack might have been, she was nevertheless a loyal companion. She never left his side; she was always right there to go on crazy adventures in the Maxwell, to have dinner at his house, to go out for sandwiches after the show. Whenever the Jack character was sick or injured or sad, she was the first one there to visit (even if all she contributed as a nursemaid was a mustard plaster fashioned from an omelet made with Vicks Vapo-Rub). It was Mary who always accompanied Jack to public places. Another element ameliorating her harsh words was the obvious affection Jack exhibited toward Mary. Warmth was always in his voice when he spoke of her, such as when she was ill and had missed a program. At the end of a program, he would call her by his nickname for her, "Doll." No matter how much she flayed his ego, the radio-listening public knew very well that Jack and Mary were the long-wed Mr. and Mrs. Benny in real life, and the public seemed to play along well with this double knowledge.

Another facet of Mary Livingstone's character that may have tipped audience sympathy towards her was her continued recitation of silly poems. One of the best was this one, included in the January 1, 1939, broadcast, "Goodbye 1938, Hello 1939":

> Oh Happy New Year, Happy New Year
> Please don't be a sad and blue year
> These last twelve months have been sublime
> So goodbye 38, hello 39
> [Jack: Well, so far, nobody is screaming. Mary: You just wait.]
> I wonder who, this coming *yar*
> Will be our favorite movie star?
> Will it be Garbo, or Sonia Henie (HY-knee)?

So goodbye 38, Hello thirty-*niney*.
[Jack: Niney?]
What has this year in store for us
For thee and thou and thy and thus
Will Don get fat, will Phil be gay?
Will Kenny get knowledge with a capital K?
[Jack: I doubt it.]
I'd like to ask you, if I dare
Will Jack continue to lose his hair?
[Jack: Mary . . .]
And when its gone, will it stay away?
Goodbye 38, hello toupee
[Jack: Mary! Get to the last verse, will you? Mary: It's coming up now.]
Oh Happy New Year, Happy New Year
Please don't be a sad and blue year
We will give you one more chance
So goodbye Broadway, hello France.
[Jack: Well!]

Mary's poems (which ended in the early 1940s) and her playful reading of letters from her Mama in Plainfield revealed Mary's softer side. No matter how sophisticated, tart, or icy Mary might have seemed, the letters from Mama still made her seem like a naïve girl.

An additional softening factor for Mary's personality in the later 1940s and 1950s was the unexpected opportunities that arose when she flubbed her scripted lines. Mary's on-air dialogue-reading gaffes, which occurred more frequently after the war (probably as she became even more anxious with mike-fright), took her down off her high perch. Her hilarious mistakes gave Jack the only reason he ever really found to criticize her, and triggered a lot of laughter among both studio and home audiences who were attuned to listen closely to the dialogue and thus catch the gaffes. Although Benny was not known for his ability to ad lib, when it came to correct timing and reading of lines on the program, Jack was quick as lightning to respond and to reprimand any scofflaws. When Mary flubbed lines, like saying "grass reek" instead of "grease rack" or "chiss sweeze" instead of "swiss cheese," pandemonium broke loose with cast and audience. Benny's writers did a great job of making the most of Mary's inadvertent mistakes by working them into follow-up jokes for weeks afterward.[76]

Meanwhile, Mary's determination to avoid the publicity spotlight meant there was significantly less discussion of her than in the 1930s in the entertainment trade press and fan magazines (other than an occasional interview where her views about Jack were solicited). In the wartime military camp shows, there were jokes about Mary being pursued by pilots and junior officers. The character of a maid was added (first Butterfly, and then Pauline) to give her an added person with whom to exchange bits of dialogue. But Mary the "star" was becoming Mary the supporting character. Behind the scenes, she played an important production role. "Mary Livingstone is the spark of Benny's Show," noted a St. Joseph, Missouri, reporter, covering the Benny troupe's broadcast from there in 1945, "The least obvious person seated at the long table was Mary Livingstone. And yet her presence was a tangible thing, like the unseen string that holds the string of pearls together.... Her actual speaking part on the broadcasts is only a minor factor. For Mary is called upon by the writers, by the rest of the cast, by Jack and even the sound boys when they want a constructive opinion on a gag, a line or a noise."[77] Benny, too, regularly attested to Mary's skill in judging the laugh-getting potential of script lines and comic scenarios. In a 1952 interview, Jack noted that Mary would make an excellent producer for radio or television programs, and CBS had offered her a position if she ever wished to take it. Benny claimed that Mary possessed an innate sense of production values, that she "can usually tell us in advance whether or not a certain routine will play. Her clairvoyant judgment has been a big factor in our radio success."[78]

Instead of continuing on as a major character in front of the microphone on Jack Benny's radio program, or behind the scenes as a producer, however, Mary Livingstone chose a gradual retirement from performances and public life in the 1950s. As CBS began to allow them to prerecord episodes, Benny and his radio producers were able to take advantage of the technology, and Mary began to record her radio dialogue lines from home and have them spliced into the master tape (with substitutes like daughter Joan Benny or assistant Jeanette Eyman reading Mary's lines with the cast at the studio in front of an audience). Benny and his writers made her speaking parts shorter and shorter. The decline of her role as Jack's chief heckler meant that the Rochester character took up a steadier position in show narratives as Jack's companion, both on radio and on TV.[79] Mary joined Jack only on his third television broadcast in May 1951, then largely begged off the television shows until he coaxed her back on to take a smaller role in a score of filmed episodes at mid-decade (for which she would not have to appear before a live audience).

She claimed that it was nervous mike-fright that drove her from public performances:

> In the beginning my appearances on the radio shows were fun. I actually enjoyed working once a week. But ironically, the more shows I did the more nervous I became. I still can't figure it out, but it ended up with every Sunday being the most tortuous day of the week. I explained to Jack how much this was taking out of me and told him I couldn't go on any longer. I was quitting and he would have to hire somebody else.... but Jack persuaded me to go on. Finally I went to Jack and broke down and told him.[80]

Eve Arden, whose tart-tongued cynicism in film roles and in the *Our Miss Brooks* radio and TV programs came the closest of any Hollywood performer to matching Mary's, once related the story that Benny approached her at a party and suggested that she would be a fine candidate to take Mary's place on his television show, but nothing ever came of it.[81] In 1970, President Richard Nixon took credit for getting Mary out of retirement for one more brief appearance on one of Benny's semiannual TV specials. *Variety*'s Jack Hellman reported that, "At their last meeting Nixon said to Benny, 'When are you going to bring Mary back? I liked her laugh.'"[82]

CONCLUSION

Mary Livingstone's unruly, attention-getting laughter; her impertinent, genial nonsense; and her razor-sharp deflations of Jack's egotism were cornerstones of the Jack Benny radio program's humor. Sadye Marks Benny, the reluctant performer, and Mary, her semifictional mouthpiece, accomplished what few other women in radio or film were able to carry off in the 1930s and 1940s—she enacted the persona of an independent, feisty young woman who could speak truth to male vanity and yet not be punished for raising her voice. Mary was joined in the narrative world of the Benny program by other disruptive women—frying-pan-wielding mothers, disdainful Hollywood actresses, sassy and murderous cigarette girls, put-upon waitresses—all of whom had to make their way in the world surrounded by Jack and the other imperfect men in their lives. In Benny's world of gender representations, there were no sweet ingenues, and no self-effacing maternal figures; women may have been feared, but never despised by the men on the program. Unlike on some of the other radio comedy shows broadcast into American homes during this era, given that the basis of much humor was insult laden and putting people into their place, the Benny program stood out. On this show, there was a great deal of respect and affection for women, and feminist sympathies, on a program that was always produced by male writers. Female characters on the Benny show spoke up for themselves and gave their radio audiences a space to laugh at life's absurdities.

The next chapter turns to examine the representation of masculinity on Benny's radio show, and how the project of turning Jack into the Fall Guy in every way possible meant that attacks on patriarchal authority, and stereotypical heterosexual identity, became major sources of the program's humor.

THREE

Masculine Gender Identity in Jack Benny's Humor

Jack Benny's radio comedy played with gender identity, continually blurring the boundaries of what were at the time very narrow definitions of masculinity and femininity and strictly divided models for appropriate gendered behavior in society. Benny's humor complicated and questioned what scholar Carole Vance terms the "implicit cultural ideology of fixed sexual categories."[1] His character explored varieties of masculinity that ranged from demanding patriarchal employer to insufficiently virile heterosexual male, to assimilated Jew, and from a straight man with a predilection for cross-dressing to a person of indeterminate sexual identity who impishly performed with effeminate and homosexual mannerisms.

As Jack Benny's radio character transformed from a self-deprecating but suave master of ceremonies into the "Fall Guy," the unfortunate soul to whom ridiculous and frustrating incidents happened, he became the target of an increasing number of humorous insults lobbed at him by his cast members. The show's narrative world expanded to incorporate Benny's frustrated attempts to rule over his home and his workplace, his painfully awkward dealings with Hollywood celebrities, and his exasperating experiences with shop clerks, waitresses, railroad station ticket sellers, and cab drivers. In the process of devising ever more ways in which Benny's character could be vexed and scoffed at, his writers seized on nearly every possible way to belittle his masculine identity as an employer, a celebrity, and a heterosexual male. At times this escalated in the postwar years. While the move to television, during an era of hardening ideals of appropriate gender roles, brought new scrutiny of visual displays of identity, Jack appeared on TV as a nattily dressed, handsome, upper-middle-class man who looked years younger than his age. Despite losing the imaginative radio wordplay with which his cast could describe his lack of heterosexual physique and mannerisms, Benny and his writers in the visual arena of TV still occasionally engaged boundary-questioning humor, particularly in 1952 and 1954 episodes featuring Jack's uncannily accurate impersonation of comedienne Gracie Allen.

Benny's representations of masculinity have been the focus of academic inquiries (by McFadden, Doty, Balcerzak, and others) who have explored an archeology of possibilities for queer representation embedded in historical mainstream media. They have made insightful analysis of how Benny's character can be read across a variety of audience interpretations.[2] Their studies have detailed Jack's comic involvement in homosocial relationships and his failures of heterosexual prowess. His effeminate characteristics and humorous suggestions of homosexual activities could have been enjoyed by some listeners in the 1930s, 1940s, and 1950s, while they could have been abhorred by others, and understood by many as just another way to demonstrate Jack's failure as a heterosexual patriarch. At the same time, Jack's slyly incorporated outré sexual references possibly sailed right many many listeners' heads, while they were acknowledged and enjoyed by some, and shocked and angered others.

The masculine gender identity of Jack's character contained complexities and contradictions. Sometimes he made jokes that played with expressing gay preferences, other times he stood up for a heterosexual patriarchal authority to which his wealth and fame gave gives him access, and sometimes he titillated the audience with mentions of his enjoyment of feminine ways of behaving.[3] Jack could more often be characterized as lacking in sexual desire or energy, rather than filled with sexual drive, more often asexual than overtly homosexual or heterosexual. Instead of focusing only on one moment, an examination of the complications inherent in gender identity that encompasses the breadth of Benny's radio career over thirty years can help further explain Benny's popularity with audiences across the sexual-political spectrum. It will also gain Benny even greater credit for his fearlessness, self-confidence, and wit.

Representations of female identity in radio and television have garnered the lion's share of feminist analysis, as media scholar Rebecca Feasey notes, because these mediums were consumer oriented and geared to female viewers, or otherwise feminized.[4] However, "masculinity and male heterosexuality continued to be understood as fixed, stable, unalterable and therefore beyond inquiry."[5] As Judith Butler and other scholars have argued, gender is not biologically innate but is performative and culturally created, and there have always been many types, varieties, alternatives, and levels of masculinity that men and women can perform. When Jack Benny created his comedy in mid-twentieth-century U.S. culture, the dominant stereotypes of masculine identity were narrow, and the differences between men and women were considered to be extremely wide.

Feasey suggests that popular culture provided models of gendered identity that formed "a hierarchy of acceptable, unacceptable and marginalized models for the male,"[6] with a hegemonic masculinity as the desired ideal. "The hegemonic male was said to be a strong, successful, capable and authoritative man who derives his reputation from the workplace and his self-esteem from the public sphere," writes Feasey.[7] Even though very few people might reach it, it was a standard measuring stick "to which men are supposed to aspire." Some lived in tension with it (such as minorities and "effeminate men") and thus "command[ed] less power," but most were, as Michael Kimmel says, "still complicit in sustaining this hierarchic model."[8] The Benny show narrative explored how the immutable, fixed categories of proper masculinity could crack to reveal possibilities of multiple forms of masculinity. While in other areas of popular culture, boundaries of gender representation were hardening, on Benny's program, they were continually blurred.[9]

How did Benny's gender-themed humor over the airwaves make up for limitations of listeners not being able to see the visual cues that constructed gender identities? On radio, as scholar Lori Kendall similarly suggests of computer-mediated online discussions, "the bodies of others may remain hidden and inaccessible, but this if anything gives references to such bodies even more social importance."[10] Gender characteristics of disembodied radio voices could be fluid and uncertain; hints were given by the tone and pitch of the performers' voices. From Mary's throaty laugh to Mrs. Day's intimidating growl to Frank Nelson's snideness, performers' voices on the Benny show played with stereotypes. Benny and his radio writers also lavished attention in scripted dialogue on visible gender differences. To fill in the spaces of listeners' imaginations, Benny show dialogue often described what the characters were wearing, especially if it was different from heterosexual, white middle-class norms. After his appearance in the film *Charley's Aunt* (20th Century Fox, 1941), Jack's adventures in cross-dressing costumes were added to the radio show, and the Benny gang joked about what Jack looked like in female clothing, or how he did not fill out the shoulders of his suits. Jack ribbed Phil Harris and Rochester about the loudly colored jackets they wore that aligned them with zoot suit culture. Mary and Jack made merciless fun of the overalls Babe wore to work on her construction jobs. Explorations of gender identity, and humor based on upending listeners' expectations of how male and female characters would look and behave, was central to Jack Benny's comedy.

FRUSTRATED WORKPLACE PATRIARCH

Jack's character was at its most hegemonically masculine in his role as the star and producer of his radio show, and employer of his cast members at work and of Rochester at his home. Jack became depicted over the years as a demanding and churlish boss, traditionally patriarchal, paying his workers little, and trying to squeeze much work from them. He criticized Don's weight, Phil's drunkenness, the band's lack of musical ability and slovenly habits, and Dennis's craziness and stupidity (earlier, it was Kenny Baker's craziness and stupidity). He attempted to fire the Sportsmen Quartet numerous times. His one retort to Mary's insults was to threaten to send her back to work at the May Company department store. "The Mean Old Man," a parody radio soap opera referenced on the show, took Benny as its model of a heartless landlord.

The insults swapped back and forth between Benny and his employees fit the traditions of workplace comedy, especially of the humor made in male-dominated factories and workshops. As Susan Douglas argues, radio comedy's insult humor established a pecking order, and reminded the workers that Benny was the paternalistic boss.[11] But the employees nearly always gave back worse than they got. Benny once explained the sources of comedy on the program from the point of view of an employer: "The humor of Phil Harris is, how can a man that is supposed to be working for me go on getting drunk, chasing women, insulting me, and still I don't fire him? The humor of Rochester is— how can he get away with it? If Rochester and I share a bedroom on a Pullman he rushes in first and grabs the lower, and I have to sleep in the upper berth."[12]

For all his petty power in the radio studio and at home, Jack nevertheless was terrified of his own bosses. Jack quaked in his boots every year when it came time for the sponsor to pick up the show's option. From the earliest episodes in which Jack made outrageous ads for Canada Dry and wondered if his sponsor would fire him, Jack's fear of his sponsor continued throughout his years on the radio. The sponsor was rarely an executive visiting the studio, but more often an unheard voice on the other end of a telephone, whom Jack begged for another chance (helplessly remonstrating against the sponsor's unheard accusations "But ... but ... but ... but!")

While the stereotypical male authority figure was expected to remain in control of rationality and reason, keeping his emotions in check, Jack frequently lost his temper and yelled at annoying underlings—especially the Sportsmen Quartet, who often spun out of control while singing the program's middle commercials. Benny and his writers orchestrated Jack's "slow burn" build ups of infuriated responses ("Wait a minute ... wait a minute! ...WAIT A MINUTE!" and "Now cut that out!") into crescendos of yelling voices, demonstrating that his leadership was always on the verge of collapsing into chaos.

Race as well as gender entered the picture of employer–employee relations in Jack's management of Rochester. Jack as the employer of a household servant was a despot. He not only paid Rochester next to nothing but constantly ordered his servant to perform mountains of labor. Rochester could complain but could not say "no." In the earliest years, Rochester was supposedly lazy and even stole from his employer. As Benny and the writers removed those stereotypes to make the character less offensive to African American critics, Rochester became a bit more feminized, a very diligent and selfless employee, despite his miniscule income. Jack could order Rochester to do anything, such as to spend all night searching for a lost golf ball. Despite how much Jack abused him, Rochester never considered quitting. The frustration of Rochester's impossible work situation would inspire a violently imagined conclusion in Amiri Baraka's short play "JELLO" (1970).[13] To the credit of Anderson, Benny, and the show writers, although Rochester the housekeeper was stuck obeying Jack's imperious demands, Rochester's ability to talk back to Jack and to criticize him through humorous putdowns of the boss's cheapness, vanity, and lack of virility created the sharpest humor on the radio program.

To add another deflating comic twist on Jack's patriarchal authority, Benny's writers began to make Jack parsimonious, unwilling to play his proper role in consumer culture. Accusing someone else of being cheap had a very long history; it was a staple of Italian commedia dell'arte conflicts between the employer and his servants, and vaudeville routines poking endless fun at thrifty Scotsmen. Jack eventually became rich as a prominent radio star, and he had money in every bank in town, plus a massively fortified vault in his basement, but he was increasingly loathe to spend a dime. As Mary commented in a 1950 pre-Christmas episode, whenever Jack went out to purchase something, there was trouble.[14] He was the nation's worst consumer. The clerks always gave him grief, and Jack balked at the price of everything. Frank Nelson confronted him everywhere as a belittling department store floorwalker or obstreperous railroad station ticket seller. Mel Blanc, as a department store clerk, was annually driven to insanity by Jack's impossible demands made while purchasing the cheapest possible Christmas present for Don Wilson.

The blurring of real-life persona and fictional character in Jack Benny's quest for patriarchal authority on his radio program occurred, most fascinatingly, in those fleeting moments live on the air in which Benny the performer let it slip that he indeed was the exacting director of his own show. Although Benny had a very limited ability to ad lib in response to other people's jokes in real life, while in the middle of a radio broadcast, he was lightning fast to complain about a flubbed line of dialogue, or a missed ring of a telephone sound effect. He made sharp, cutting, fabulous ad libs that took the miscreants to task. Cast members hooted with delight the few times they caught the boss himself botching a line. Her microphone-fright increasing after the war, Mary began making more mistakes in reading her dialogue lines. As wide a berth as Jack otherwise took in criticizing her in their dialogue, when Mary flubbed a line, Jack immediately leapt on these mistakes and barked at her, to terrific comic effect. Those moments were the one time he could really "punish" her and put her in her place, to make up for all the insults she tossed at him.

The Jack Benny–Fred Allen radio feud of 1937 drew its spirit from the traditions of insult talk that are a central part of male interaction in workplaces and social situations. From gangs of boys who learn to fight as "play," to Shakespearian insults hurled by gifted actors at one another, exchanges of ritualized insults in many cultures have enabled the players to duel, establish pecking order, show off their skills, and form mutual bonds with the audiences that cheered them on. Scholar Elijah Wald quotes jazz musician Mezz Mezzrow linking the African-American tradition of "the dozens" to an improvised jazz performance:

> The idea right smack in the middle of every cat's mind all the time was this: he had to sharpen his wits every way he could, make himself smarter and keener, better able to handle himself, more "hip." . . . On the Corner the idea of a kind of mutual needling held sway, each guy spurring the other guy on to think faster and be more nimble-witted.[15]

Communal events like a contest of the dozens could hold a variety of meanings, suggests Wald. "One person's bitter insult was another's comic masterpiece, and what one observer interpreted as predatory bullying another might interpret as the fascinating survival" of old traditions.[16] Women could toss the insults, but traditionally this has been a masculine endeavor (which undoubtedly added to the sting of Mary's insults of Jack, as a woman was not supposed to be as adept at this game as men). The insults themselves needed to be wildly exaggerated, their absurdity providing the insurance that it would not be personally hurtful, but also making them humorous. While philosopher Jerome Neu suggests that too-truthful personal insults could result in the opponent swinging punches, if the insultee launched a reciprocal insult back in return, the incident became a game. Neu argues that insult games are ways of claiming superiority. They are all about asserting masculinity and cultural identity, claiming honor and defining the self, in shows of verbal and intellectual skill and dexterity.[17]

After the ten-week Benny-Allen feud climaxed in a hugely promoted meeting in a Manhattan ball room on March 14, 1937, instead of ending, the conflict continued and took on a life of its own. Fan magazine *Radio Mirror* published an adapted script of "The Mighty Benny-Allen Feud" in July 1938, and fans wrote to say that they had reenacted the skit as a party game.[18] GIs on the battlefronts of World War II greeted Benny's USO appearances with signs that said "Welcome, Fred Allen." When Allen appeared as a guest on the erudite radio quiz sho, *Information Please*, host Clifton Fadiman focused mostly on jokes about how much Allen must hate Benny.

After the war, Benny continued the fun in several radio episodes with "Benny's Boulevard," sketches in which he parodied Allen's Alley, with a clothespin affixed to his nose.[19] In others, Benny and Allen swapped tall tales of their earliest encounters backstage on the hinterlands vaudeville circuit. These sketches were opportunities to mix playful boasting, insults, and accusations of plagiarizing each other's acts with delightful reminiscences about acts like Fink's Mules and Japanese flash acrobats (jugglers who tossed wooden barrels with their feet), which gave Fred and Jack the chance to work the word "bunghole" into the script.

Usually acerbic radio critic Harriet Van Horne commended Benny and Allen on the extended feud in 1947:

> By professing to hate each other they have instigated more humorous situations and basked in more free publicity than any other would be haters in show business. By this time you might think that the situation was arid of humor. That neither could find in the other a single attribute to insult. But no. Mr. Benny finds new terms of derision for Allen's program and the bags under his eyes. Fred, on his part, had endless variations on the theme of Jack's stinginess, stupidity, conceit and clumsiness with the violin.[20]

FIGURE 7. Fred Allen and Jack Benny cleverly extended their feud long after its 1937 beginnings. Here in 1943, Fred reacts to the supposed rotten smell of Jack's poor jokes. *Tune In*, May 1943. Author's collection.

A classic feud exchange occurred that year in live performance onstage at a New York City movie theater, as *Variety's* review noted:

> Jack Benny, according to Fred Allen during the historic tete-a-tete during Benny's opening show at the Roxy, killed vaudeville 15 years ago, and now has returned to the scene of his crime ... The Allen intrusion was one of the

historic moments in vaudeville, wherein two top radio personalities on a friendly feuding basis had a chance to exchange insults.... Allen started the business by demanding a refund on his admission. After all, he argued, it was guaranteed that he'd die laughing, and inasmuch as he was still alive, he felt that he had his dough coming back. Benny argued that the Sportsmen should be worth 15 cents. Marjorie Reynolds was worth a quarter, and Rochester should be worth 20 cents. There was some disagreement on Phil Harris' value, and after an initial demand of 10 cents, price was pared down two cents lower. They tossed for the balance, with Benny winning, and Benny shielded a dime for personal expenses.[21]

Critic John Crosby recalled another escapade as the feud's best example of Allen's triumphant, insulting wit. "Once Benny was appearing on the Paramount stage and Allen sat in the front row and fueled one witty insult after another at his old friend. After one quip, Benny, nonplussed, waved a twenty dollar bill at the audience and offered it to anyone who could top Allen's last gag. Instantly Allen was on his feet, topped his own gag with a better one, and walked up and claimed the twenty dollars."[22]

BENNY AND JEWISH MALE IDENTITY

To what extent was Jack Benny identified by audiences and critics as a Jewish male comic? Benny did not want to be pinned down to one stringently defined identity. "The humor of my program is this," Benny explained in a 1948 interview, "I'm a big shot, see? I'm fast talking. I'm a smart guy. I'm boasting about how marvelous I am. I'm a marvelous lover. I'm a marvelous fiddle player. Then, five minutes after I start shooting off my mouth, my cast makes a *shmo* out of me."[23] "Shmo," noted Leo Rosten, in *The Joys of Yiddish*, was a Yiddish term coined in America that meant idiot or cuckold, a lighter form of the more pejorative term "schmuck." A shmo was a dull, stupid, obnoxious, or boring person, a shnook, a schlemiel, a hapless, clumsy, unlucky jerk who was the butt of other people's jokes.[24] Benny internally defined his character in terms of Jewish humor, but put him in an outwardly assimilationist package.

Benny's complex relationship with Jewish identity, as explored by numerous scholars, seemed dependent on his listeners' point of view and how they wished to define the man and his comedy. To mainstream Christian radio listeners, Benny presented himself as a highly assimilated Jew. Unlike some other performers from immigrant backgrounds, he did not speak with an ethnic accent or dress in ethnic costumes, and he used almost no Yiddish phrases in his work. Throughout his radio career, his shows celebrated Christmas and Easter as well as Mother's Day and Halloween, but never touched on Jewish religious holidays.[25] Radio listeners occasionally wrote into fan magazines to ask if Benny was indeed Jewish. To some commentators, however, Benny seemed to hide his ethnic identity to the point where it had disappeared.[26]

Early in his career, Benjamin Kubelsky (like hundreds of other first- and second-generation ethnic performers) changed his birth name to a stage moniker that sounded slicker and more assimilated, first Ben K. Benny, then (when bandleader Ben Bernie objected to the similarity) to Jack Benny. Holly Pearse suggests that Benny's early years, spent in his hometown of Waukegan, Illinois, a small manufacturing city of 10,000–20,000 people an hour north of Chicago, assisted him in the adoption of an assimilated personality. Instead of being raised in the densely populated Lower East Side of New York City, with its extensive Jewish immigrant communities and rich culture (the backgrounds of Eddie Cantor, George Jessel, and George Burns), there were relatively few Jews in Waukegan. Benjamin Kubelsky learned the flat Midwestern accent shared by his schoolmates.[27] As an adult, Benny was apparently not an actively religious person, rarely attending services. His faith was important to him—he married a Jewish woman, he contributed generously to Jewish charities, and he socialized in large part with other Jewish-heritage performers—but it remained a private aspect of his life.

Within the American Jewish community, Jack Benny was acclaimed as a beloved and prominent member of the faith, although certainly not as Jewish-identified to the extent of Eddie Cantor, who made his religious and ethnic identity a central part of his performing identity.[28] Benny garnered only a modicum of coverage in the Jewish press over the years, but he cropped up occasionally, such as when an Atlanta-based publication celebrated him in 1948 with a full-page photograph captioned "America's Greatest Jewish Comedian." Benny figures prominently in most studies of Jewish performers in American entertainment history, as a prime exemplar of a second-generation immigrant who became prominent in mainstream American popular culture.[29] His comic themes and performance style drew on many themes that scholars have typed as Jewish—the self-deprecating humor, the miserliness, the slight stature, the personality of the hapless "schmo," the violin playing, the effeminate mannerisms.[30]

Stephen Whitfield characterizes nineteenth-century American humor as "cocksure patrimony"; "frontier humor exalted those who exhibited mastery, those who triumphed over rivals or enemies, those who demonstrated can-do supremacy." On the other hand, Whitfield notes that Jewish humor centered on "self-deprecation and victimization." "Jews continued to exhibit a proclivity for humor that underscored failure rather than success, marginality rather than influence and puniness rather than power," he writes. Whitfield finds Jewish humor in twentieth-century American culture in the character of the antihero who was "self-mocking" and "exposed his own weakness," and thus he judged Jack Benny to be the comedian to be the most associated with Jewish cultural themes.[31]

Other scholars have argued, however, that self-deprecating humor is common among many ethnic/marginalized groups, and that it's not exclusively a Jewish trait.[32] Benny was very sensitive about anti-Semitic slurs made against him in public that might damage his career (as exemplified by the horrid examples collected by the FBI at the time of his smuggling prosecution in 1939).[33] Racial hatred was also his biggest concern about undertaking of the "I Can't Stand Jack Benny" contest in late 1945, when he was careful to employ readers to remove any entries that spouted prejudiced attitudes. The identity blurring that Jack Benny was able to accomplish was to appear outwardly to look and sound very assimilated into American culture, but to draw on his Jewish cultural framework for his humor.

Despite Benny's assimilationist tendencies for his own comic persona, his radio program did include occasional appearances of Jewish-identified characters. In the early 1930s, Harry Conn created a Jewish comic character who became a semifrequent visitor to the Benny radio program—Shlepperman, played by Sam Hearn. Shlepperman was an urban trickster, popping up when he was least expected, announcing himself with, "Hello, Strangzyer." Shlepperman had a thick Yiddish accent. He was sharp with retorts but otherwise a pleasant fellow. Conn utilized the Shlepperman character as part of his collection of ethnic voices inserted into the end of a skit's dialogue to surprise listeners. After the Benny show permanently relocated to the West Coast, Shlepperman appeared much less frequently. Hearn himself milked his Shlepperman role for years on the East Coast, putting on performances in theaters and clubs where he would portray the wily character, conversing with a recording of Benny, or telling Benny-related anecdotes.

When the new group of writers joined the Benny program in 1943, they experimented with adding new characters, such as Herman Peabody, the timid insurance salesman; bombastic Belly Laugh Barton, the writer; and brash Steve Bradley, the public relations agent. Mr. Kitzel first appeared on January 6, 1946, when Jack and the gang attended the Rose Bowl football game, and they encountered a funny little man with a Yiddish-inflected voice, selling hotdogs up in the stands. Kitzel was played by Artie Auerbach, a radio actor and photographer. Both Kitzel's jingle ("Pickle in the middle and the mustard on top!") and his character were popular with radio listeners. The writers began bringing him back regularly onto the radio show. If Shlepperman had darted in and out of Benny's program with an urbanized vibe, Mr. Kitzel instead was a gentle greenhorn. Kitzel's humor rose from his "cultural incompetence" in Michele Hilmes's term, his confusion and lack of knowledge of American society. Kitzel substituted Jewish names for Anglo-Saxon-named celebrities, events, and objects. His tentative voice and reaction to Jack's comments, a surprised "hoo hoo HOO," marked him as an unassimilated immigrant. Fred Allen's character Pansy Nussbaum made similar types of remarks when she appeared in "Allen's Alley" skits. Cantor had the Greek Parkykarkas and "Mad Russian" characters on his radio program, and Mrs. Nussbaum was joined in Allen's Alley by a Yankee farmer, Southern senator, and a drunken Irish lout. Benny, like the other comics, distanced himself from these ethnic personalities by his smooth, superior use of language. There was debate within the Jewish entertainment community in the late 1940s and 1950s as to whether continuation of these broadly stereotyped Jewish ethnic characters like Kitzel stimulated prejudice against the Jewish American community; performers like Sam Levenson argued for ending them.[34] Benny incorporated Kitzel into nearly 120 of his radio program episodes in the late 1940s and 1950s. Kitzel also made an appearance on Benny's first TV episode, and thereafter the character was still used occasionally, until Auerbach's death in 1957. Kitzel's numerous radio appearances added to many of the continuing themes of Jack's humor meant that reminders of Jewish ethnic identity remained embedded around the edges of Benny's radio program.

BENNY'S FEMALE IMPERSONATIONS

In Benny's mid- to late-1930s radio episodes, Jack occasionally requested that his male cast members take female roles in their movie parodies. Their skits drew on the long tradition of male crossdressing in comic stage performances, which had been popular with mainstream entertainment audiences for hundreds of years.[35] When the Benny group did a takeoff of the film *Girls' Dormitory* (20th Century Fox, 1936), the male cast members made titillating jokes while complaining about having to dress as characters of the opposite sex. Words like "girdles" and "stockings" were worked into the dialogue to add visual humor to the audience's imagining of the scene. On other occasions they performed skits about a football team or the all-male crew of a submarine, and Mary got to grumble about having to wear shoulder pads and threatened to add lace to her uniforms.

The most prominent occasion of group cross-dressing on the Benny radio show in the 1930s occurred when Jack and the cast performed a parody of the film *The Women* (MGM, 1939). The film's publicity had highlighted how unusual it was to have an entirely female cast. Benny and his players performed a wickedly funny sketch, with Jack preening at the opportunity to play Norma Shearer, and Eddie Anderson grouching about having to wear mascara as the maid. Jack, Don, Phil, and Dennis had a high time playing gossipy society women complaining about the faithless men in their lives, while Mary introduced the play's acts with meowing side-comments. The skit was so popular that the cast was asked to reprise it several times at entertainment industry functions in Hollywood.

Historical case studies of the sexual naiveté and resistance of the 1930s American movie-going public, especially in smaller towns, who when encountering older men in relationships with Shirley Temple in Shirley's films either could not conceptualize or angrily rejected the possibility of pedophilic inferences, are small but telling examples demonstrating the power of dominant heterosexual ideology. Heterosexual ideology was so strong at midcentury that many people were incredulous about alternative sexual identities or desires, and many were unable to speak of, imagine, or acknowledge them. Others actively refused to.[36] Media scholar Karin Quimby has suggested that "straight" audiences could use the concept of "disavowal" to downplay any homosexual content in popular media and understand the program's humor as being within a normative heterosexual content. Other audience members might understand the scene to represent both straight and gay connotations. Disavowal, Quimby writes, "allows some audience members both to acknowledge gay male difference . . . and to disavow this difference through the heterosexual fantasy" that sees the characters, like themselves, as straight. Quimby argues that this openness of interpretations in media audiences' reception dynamic allows such programs "to attract and keep audiences who may be somewhat uncomfortable." Quimby argues that the "dynamic of contradiction or disavowal" can be built into the program's narrative, through storylines, the visual look or sound of performers, and their understated acting to make them seem as "acceptable" or noncontroversial to straight audiences as possible.[37] Benny's programs, like those of other radio comics, played with outré, unusual, or forbidden sexual humor in this way. In radio performances, dialogue and descriptive language created imaginative worlds that listeners could configure to their own pleasures. Suggestive euphemisms were easier to slyly bypass unsophisticated audiences, although infamous encounters such as Mae West with Charlie McCarthy on the Bergen and McCarthy radio program in 1937 could draw wide criticism and reaction.[38]

"Male-to-female transvestitism is a complex phenomenon that is often confused with other manifestations of male-to-female cross-dressing, e.g. drag performance," argues feminist scholar Samantha Allen.[39] She notes that although studies have shown that as much as 87 percent of people who wear clothes of another gender identify as heterosexual, it has been widely assumed in American and Western culture that this is a sign of homosexuality. A sharp historical gender divide of clothing and behavior has mandated that "the clothes one wears must match one's felt sex which must be opposite to the sex one desires."[40] Men have had a variety of reasons over the years for wishing to wear female clothing, both erotic and performative. They have taken pleasure in confusing or shocking the gender-identity distinctions of those who view men in dresses, or a pleasure in performing or inhabiting female identity.

Sexual-themed humor was prominent in radio comedy, as it had been in vaudeville and the stage. Matthew Murray, in his study on radio censorship, argues that radio networks were fully cognizant of its popularity and potency as a ratings-getter and selling tool. Like the interplay between movie producers and the film industry's censorship organization, radio network administrators attempted to negotiate the tensions between material that titillated some audiences and offended others, and material that reflected "modern" values as well as the maintenance of conservative values of propriety. In 1934, NBC established a Continuity Acceptance Department, headed by Janet MacRorie, to scrutinize the scripts of material that sponsors intended to broadcast over their airwaves.[41] Comedians, with their penchant to joke about the forbidden, gave these radio censors headaches. Fred Allen earned their frequent ire over the years for his allusions to barnyard bathroom humor (chickens straining to lay eggs, cows with unruly udders). Eddie

Cantor, Bob Hope, Charlie McCarthy/Edgar Bergen, Ed Wynn, Red Skelton, Jack Pearl—all the comics gave the censors trouble at one point or another with questionable humor. Radio authorities did not seek to completely remove instances and themes of transgressive sexuality, but to contain and tame it. They sought to reincorporate taboo topics as much as possible into norms of white middle-class culture and standards of appropriate male and female representation and behavior.[42]

Not only did Benny's radio program play with male cross-dressing, but the show likewise occasionally incorporated situations and jokes that could to some listeners be perceived as having gay, queer, or effeminate connotations. Some listeners chuckled at the outré comedy, while conservative straight audiences could explain away the dangerous ideas in this humor as being nonoffensive, a foolish parody of normative heterosexual ideologies. During the May 29, 1938, episode, which took place at Paramount Studios, Jack ordered Rochester to read Joan Bennett's lines as Jack practiced a love scene for his upcoming film appearance in *Artists and Models Abroad* (Paramount, 1938). Don, Mary, and Phil listened in from outside the dressing room while the two rehearsed. Jack complained that Rochester was not acting with sufficient emotion:

JACK: Rochester, you're not giving me anything. How can I be romantic when you won't put any feeling into your lines? I wish you'd get into the mood of it.

ROCHESTER: Mood? I did everything but kiss you! I started out driving your car, and now I'm your leading lady.... Are we on our honeymoon yet?

The lines were greeted with ready laughter from the studio audience. Radio listeners might have complained to the network or sponsor or their local stations, but there is no evidence in the trade papers or archives that this occurred. Because these sexually outré moments were created by Benny and his writers, and performed by his cast with sly humor, mainstream audiences could understand them as just absurdities, grotesque burlesques of behavior appropriate in other situations like movie love scenes. While historians such as George Chauncey have found evidence that gay male radio listeners in the 1930s understood the Benny show's humor to incorporate homosexual-related humor that they found pleasurable, Benny's program at the same time could be perceived by mainstream heterosexual listeners to be inoffensive to their ideological beliefs.[43]

Public reaction to Benny's comic cross-dressing in radio and film and his flirtations with gay humor changed over time, from the 1930s to the mid-1950s. As Benny's enjoyment of the roles and the humor he created remained the same, the media form he appeared in made a difference in critical reactions, and the culture kept changing around him. While some critics have interpreted these cross-dressing performances to strongly link Jack the character and Benny the person to homosexual identity, I believe that Benny found pleasure in not choosing any particular identity, in keeping listeners, viewers, and critics titillated, confused, and guessing, wondering about how Jack was blurring the sharp distinctions between male and female behavior and heterosexual and homosexual identities through a variety of comically erotic ways of behaving.

From his start on-air in 1932, Jack Benny had been considered one of the network's least problematic performers by the NBC Continuity Acceptance Department and the network executives who worried about complaints from offended listeners and special interest groups. Benny made one mild allusion to outré sexuality in an early program in his first three months on the radio, when he read out testimonials from animals at the zoo proclaiming their fondness for Canada Dry Ginger Ale. It was an excuse for terrible puns. Mr. and Mrs. Leopard claimed that Canada Dry "hit the right spot," and the mountain lion was glad that the soda was sold at all "mountains." Then Jack reported from the Monkey House, "Dear Mr. Benny, your Canada Dry Ginger Ale is very good. I love it with a dash of orchid ice cream. Signed Jim Pansy." Benny slyly commented, "Ahh, they even have them in the zoo!" This association of the forbidden with the product, along with Benny's other outrageous humorous in-program commercials for Canada Dry, led his sponsor to demand that he choose much less controversial paths in which to advertise their ginger ale.

Archival records of NBC's Continuity Acceptance Department are only partial and can't provide definitive answers about which radio programs or performers caused them the most concerns. Several documents mention Benny's program, but network executives usually were quick to note that complaints about his show were rare.[44] Listeners who wished to voice complaints about Benny's show might also have directed their comments to the sponsor or to the advertising agency that produced it. Here too, unfortunately, archival evidence is very scarce, leaving historians with just a few tantalizing clues about censorship problems that the Benny program encountered.

In January 1937, NBC vice president Bertha Brainard complained to West Coast NBC executive John Swallow about her frustration over the network's lack of control over radio performers when their programs originated from Hollywood, far from the New York–based Continuity Acceptance Department's oversight:

> I listened to the Jack Benny program last night and think there are perhaps certain things which you, in your diplomatic fashion, can suggest to Jack. The line "I think you are nuts" I have never felt belonged in Mr. Benny's copy. He has always been above reproach and this phrase we have found to be disapproved by a large percentage of our audience. I felt that there was a definite tendency toward effeminate characterizations, particularly by Frank Parker. I feel strongly about this, especially when a tenor with a high voice has the line. I'd like to see anything of the lavender nature all out. Jack doesn't need this sort of material to get his humor.[45]

It was the popular tenor, Parker, not Benny, who was giving hints of sexual transgression in his performance, and Parker did it through his delivery (as his written dialogue had been approved by NBC authorities). The only other significant objection about possible homosexual inferences in the Benny program in the archived Continuity Acceptance Department files was a complaint about "effeminate men" lodged about the Benny show in 1939.[46] In March 1942 NBC executives had lengthy discussions about their problems with risqué jokes being told on nearly all the comedians' programs—Allen, Benny, Cantor, Gracie Allen, Skelton. The worst offender, they claimed, was Bob Hope. Network executives were receiving little help from sponsors or ad agencies in toning down the raucous humor, which in Hope's case was becoming such an issue that several Midwestern stations threatened to band together and refuse to carry his program. These relatively few complaints about offensive humor in Benny's show were all that appeared to exist in the records in the archival NBC radio collections.[47]

BENNY PLAYS CHARLEY'S AUNT

Following a successful 1940 Broadway revival of Thomas Brandon's 1892 frequently performed slapstick, the cross-dressing farce *Charley's Aunt* (which had featured a young Jose Ferrer in his first starring role), in August 1941 the 20th Century Fox film studio released a film adaptation, starring Benny. Set at Oxford University in the 1890s, the play's slight narrative concerned two male undergraduates who convince a third (Fancourt Babberly, played by Benny) to pose as a wealthy old lady, Charley's Brazilian Aunt Donna Lucia, to chaperone visits of the boys' girlfriends to their rooms. Complications ensued when Babberly, dressed as the aunt (in long Victorian crinolines and a grey wig), attracted the interest of all the old men on campus, from doddering professors and the girls' crusty uncle to his classmate's father. The men were mostly attracted by the aunt's wealth, but the old professors also appeared to romantically desire the old woman. Pratfalls and rump-kicking abounded, and then pretty Kay Francis (the real aunt) arrived. Eventually the truth of the identity of Charley's aunt is revealed, the young couples are united, and Babberly falls in love with the "real" aunt.

Fox's publicity campaign for the film focused on Benny's gender boundary crossing, featuring tag lines such as "She is the funniest thing in skirts! And most important of all—she is a HE!"[48] Broad physical slapstick and cigar chomping were emphasized in photographic and cartooned advertising illustrations to reassure conservatives that nothing about Benny or his performance was actually effeminate. Nearly all newspaper reviews of the film concurred in finding that the film was hilarious simply because Benny wore female clothing. Many delighted in detailing Benny's costume, underclothes, and wigs. The *Chicago Times* noted:

> Benny makes a very pretty picture indeed as he peeks coyly out from behind a black lace fan, as he toys with the white silk fichu around his neck. Flutters his eyelashes and tosses his curls—a poor copy of Whistler's mother. His awkwardness in skirts, his coy simpering and mad efforts to escape from a pair of romantic gentlemen who both yearn to make him a bride, provide the picture with considerable hilarity.[49]

A small number of conservative reviewers claimed to be offended by the film. *Family Circle Magazine's* reviewer wrote: "Everybody at the theater laughed fit to bust. Made me feel like an outsider. But I'm the killjoy at the party who doesn't go into gales when Joe puts on Mabel's hat."[50] The *Albany (New York) Knickerbocker* noted," Now this critic, while no prude, confesses that he has never been able to detect the slighted gleam of humor in such a masquerade of the sexes.... There is something fundamentally vulgar about it. But the dear public eats it up."[51] Other reviewers reassured potential moviegoers that the film was purely heterosexual fun, with no exhibition of alternative sexual connotations. The *Los Angeles Herald Express* reported, "[Benny]

FIGURES 8 AND 9. The humor of Jack Benny's 1941 film adaptation of the old farce *Charley's Aunt* was promoted by local theaters as the surprise of a man dressed in women's clothing. Colonial Theater (location unknown) souvenir, 1941. Author's collection.

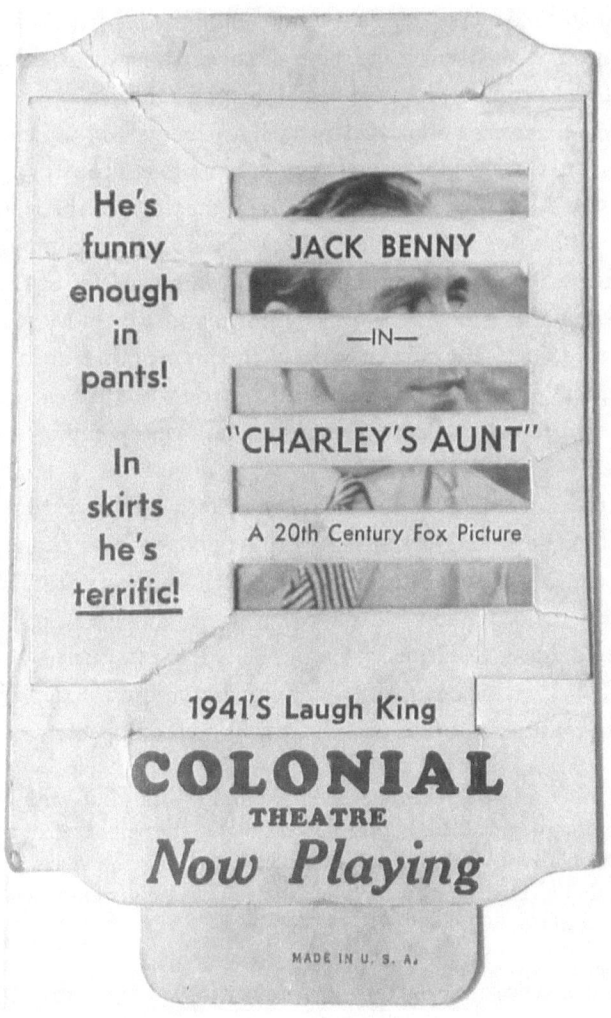

plays the part without swish and in almost his natural voice."⁵² Howard Barnes of *New York Herald Tribune* wrote: "He has the wisdom to play the famous part straight. There is never a question of effeminacy in his portrayal. That, I think, makes the difference between an uproarious redaction of the Thomas farce or a dull museum piece."⁵³ The *Los Angeles Times* calmed readers' qualms by claiming that the Babberley character "loathes the masquerade that he has to put over, but the young men, his associates, have him on the rope."⁵⁴ On the other hand, for the *New York Post* reviewer, Benny's own effeminate tendencies particularly suited him to the part: "As for Jack Benny, his long established screen and radio character, somewhat lacking in the more virile traits, fits snugly into the demands of an aunt role."[55]

A few reviewers, nonplussed by the sharp loudness of audience laughter in response to the film, connected its popularity to rampantly accelerating war fears. The *New York Morning Telegraph* mused over the riotous reaction at the film's premiere at the Roxy: "There's no explaining it, no more than there was any explaining the astonishing success of the José Ferrer stage version that took Broadway by storm last Winter. Maybe it has something to do with the current state of the public mind, bordering close on hysteria anyway, maybe it has something to do with the weather."[56] Another paper termed it "a blitzkrieg of furious fun, wordy humor and deep belly laughs."[57]

At the Academy Awards ceremony, held in Hollywood in March 1942, Bob Hope presented Jack Benny with a faux award, to "honor" Benny for portraying "the best sweater girl on the screen." It was a gold-toned Oscar-like statuette, dressed in long skirt and tiny grey wig, with a cigar in its mouth, and was dubbed "Oscarine."[58] The publicity this joke garnered in newspapers and fan magazines demonstrated the growing cultural anxiety over the instability of traditional gender roles. Benny himself quipped:

> I should have won the Academy Award for my acting in *Charley's Aunt*. But the voters were baffled. In that picture I played the part of a man and the part of a woman. I was exceptional in both parts, but the voters didn't know whether to elect me best actor or best actress. I don't know whether to be jealous of Gary Cooper or Joan Fontaine.[59]

Once or twice a season, during the ensuring wartime years, Benny and his writers incorporated mentions of cross-dressing and sexually outré behavior into Benny's radio routines. In October 1942 Jack and Rochester were in the kitchen putting up Mother Benny's Apple Butter to sell. Both wore aprons, and visiting cast member Dennis Day asked, "Why are you wearing dresses?" On the October 24, 1943, show, Jack joked about sharing a train sleeping berth with Don Wilson and Dennis Day. Train travel during wartime was overcrowded, so most listeners found humor in that context of shared inconvenience. Jack's character was thoroughly defined by his cheapness by this point, so others laughed at the misery caused by Jack refusing to book separate accommodations. Still others might be amused to imagine the corpulent Wilson crammed into the small space with Jack and Dennis. But the suggestion that three men were sleeping together was available to titillate some listeners with a sexual connotation.

On the October 8, 1944, episode, Jack told Mary a story about wearing his Charley's Aunt dress to enter the Palladium dance hall (a place where men had to pay double the admission price of women). Penurious Jack claimed it was accidental that he'd just left the film set of *Charley's Aunt* in costume, and he used it to get in at half price:

JACK: Mary, I'm not dressing up like a girl again. I'll never forget what happened last time.... hmmm. A guy buys you a drink, he thinks he OWNS you.

JACK: (in a girlish voice) What I went through...

MARY: (laughs) Jack, Jack it was bad enough being dressed like a girl to get in, but you didn't have to let a fellow buy you a *drink*.[60]

JACK: well for goodness sake Mary I *danced* with him all evening, I deserved SOMETHING. What a rotten dancer he was ... Say, Mary, I wonder what he'd have thought if he knew who I really was, especially when he tried to put his arm around me?

MARY: He tried to put his *arm* around you? Well gosh Jack, why didn't you tell him?

JACK: I didn't have the heart to, he was a Marine and he was going overseas in the morning.

Network radio programs in the 1940s and 1950s usually depicted the occasional gay character in stereotypical ways, as weaklings with high voices and nervous temperaments. These characters were generally greeted with "horror, laughter, pity or disgust from a mainstream heterosexual audience," as Feasey notes of later 1960s TV episodes. Straight characters were free to make derogatory jokes about homosexuals—it was considered "entertaining" and appropriate to marginalize them. Feasey notes that homosexuality was still presented for comic value fifty years later on the TV series *Friends* (NBC, 1994–2004) when its main characters became upset and felt humiliated at being mistaken for gay or encountering gayness. At mid-twentieth century as well as for the rest of the era, most straight white men expressed a great deal of uneasiness around being associated in any way with issues of homosexuality. Thus, it's all the more remarkable that, on the Benny radio program in the 1940s and early 1950s, while the jokes about cross-dressing, effeminate behavior, and sleeping arrangements were meant to insult and humiliate the characters (mostly Jack), there was no gay bashing or malice shown toward characters who hinted at outré sexual identities. On the program, there was tacit acceptance of "less than" or "different than" heterosexual ideals. Most radio audiences of the day did not outright reject these characters and situations. There were no public boycotts of programs. Mainstream audiences probably assumed that these were the harmless quirks of absurd characters.[61]

On the Benny radio program, although Mary and Phil constantly insulted Jack about his lack of masculinity, they did not do it with disgust. His activities were presented as just a facet of his character of the schlemiel. Jack's body was regularly criticized, and sometimes instead of making pronouncements about his weak, thin, or old appearance, the cast members joked about his womanly physique—especially his shapely legs and feminine walk. Jack joined in this humor, explaining the circumstances, and not embarrassed but accepting of his own body and sartorial choices.[62] Jack was presented most frequently as asexual or neutered and very rarely as expressing sexual desire. It is likely that most audience members of the day considered Jack harmless. Mary once claimed that embracing Jack was like kissing a dead fish.[63]

In the late 1940s, the occasions of outré sexual innuendo occasionally rose on Benny's radio program, even as public attitudes toward appropriate expression of gender identity were hardening. On occasion, however, Benny and his writers took chances and pushed the edge of the acceptability envelope. One of the program's most outlandish radio program skits based around cross-dressing and sexual desire involved someone other than Jack doing the costumed play, as Jack took a familiar role as the "Fall Guy" who was the victim of the practical joke. At the opening of the radio show on November 2, 1947, Don, Jack, and Mary discussed their past weekend activities:

JACK: I had a lot of fun Friday night, too, Don. You know I went to a Halloween party in Beverly Hills, and I met the most *wonderful* girl, and she was so cute, you know she came dressed up as Little Bo Peep.... Kids, I got to tell you about this girl, she wore a little black mask that seemed to ... oh I don't know ... she was just wonderful ... I really went nuts about her.

MARY: *Well*, I've never heard you talk like *this* before.

JACK: I can't help it ...when she came through the door, I looked at her, and she looked at me, and I could just feel something run up and down my spine.

[Dennis enters the conversation, and after his usual distractions, he informs Jack that Phil Harris had also attended the party.]

JACK: Phil was there? Gee that's funny, I didn't see him. What was he dressed as?

DENNIS: Little Bo Peep.

JACK: Little Bo Peep? . . . Phil!!!

PHIL: Kiss me, Pumpkins!

JACK: No, no wonder he wouldn't take off his mask.

MARY: Phil, you mean Jack danced with you all evening?

PHIL: Not only that, Livvy, he asked if he could drive me home.

MARY: No!

PHIL: Yeah. Say Livvy, have you ever seen the lights of the city from Mulholland Drive?

JACK: I can't understand it, how could he shave so close?

MARY: Phil, I think you carried it too far, why didn't you tell Jack who you were?

PHIL: What, and spoil an old man's evening?

JACK: Alright Phil, look, you've had your joke, now let's forget it.

PHIL: Forget it? I want those nylons you promised me, Alice could use them.

JACK: Look, you're *not* getting those nylons and I'm not putting you in pictures either. Now look we've got a show to do.

PHIL: Look Jackson, come here a minute, [takes Jack aside, in low tones] I want to ask you something.

JACK: What is it?

PHIL: (whispers) Come here I want to ask you something. . . . Do my eyes still twinkle like two stars in the summer sky?

JACK: (loudly) Oh boy, do you fall for everything you hear! I really put one over on you, bud! (lower) But I still don't understand how he could shave so close.

In the recording of the live broadcast of this episode, there were an extraordinary thirteen seconds of studio audience laughter and applause caused by Dennis's revealing of Phil as being Bo Peep. The loud laughter seems a little more nervous and edgy than usual. Benny, his writers and cast members were perfectly aware of what they were doing in playing with possibly sexually suggestive, queer humor. Writer Milt Josefsberg recalled the times the scriptwriters would put really outrageous jokes into the script just to draw the wrath of the network censors, to distract them from the more slyly subtle joke that got slipped in elsewhere.

In the postwar era of increasingly conservative public attitudes toward appropriate heterosexual gender roles and rising unease, fear, and policing of homosexuality, some media critics, upholding virile masculine standards, disdained the Benny's shows hints of titillating homosexual humor. John Crosby of the *New York Herald Tribune* commented in February 1948:

> One of the stock characters in radio comedy is what might charitably be described as the male spinster. He is the man who says "Mr. Berle, we are not amused!" He's the postal inspector on the Dennis Day show who said "Mr. Day, I LOVE you!" He's the man who sells Jack Benny the ticket to Cukamonga [sic].... He is waspish, supercilious, sarcastic, vaguely effeminate, and he lives in a state of perpetual irritation. He usually occupies a position of minor authority and uses it tyrannically. Invariably he appears when the comedian wants comedy badly and is in a hurry. He gets a sure-fire laugh from the studio audience not for what he says but for how he says it and, in spite of their affection, I'm damn tired of him and I'm sure a great many others are, too.[64]

Crosby, like the NBC Continuity Acceptance Department administrators thirteen years before, claimed that most inferences of homosexuality came from minor characters on the Jack Benny program, such as Frank Nelson in his "nasty man" roles. Although Crosby's description could have fit Jack to a significant degree, there may possibly have been repercussions in the industry had Crosby gone so far as to label such a big star as homosexual. I have not yet uncovered a significant number of other public criticisms of Benny radio episodes for their aberrant sexual humor. This perhaps implies that the majority of radio listeners assumed that Benny's shows were unproblematic family fare. Either radio audiences did not notice these examples that hinted of alternative sexual identities, or they found these characters simply absurd. Certainly other groups were listening closely, such as the African American listeners and critics who paid very close attention to Rochester's role on the program, but this sexual innuendo did not seem to draw much comment. Given the paucity of complaints in the archives, the increased amount of sexually titillating humor on the Benny radio program in the early 1950s is fascinating to examine. The scandal magazines of the late 1940s and 1950s, like *Confidential*, would have a field day exploiting photos of Benny in his Gracie Allen costume as purported evidence of his outré sexual behavior. As we will see in the chapter addressing Benny's challenges of moving his radio program to television, TV critics and TV audiences would begin to complain about the visuality and intrusion of sexual images broadcast into the home. Wouldn't those concerns and conservative cultural values have created a greater amount of criticism of Benny's occasional blue humor on the radio airwaves than we have been able yet to find? The imaginative aspects of the unseen radio medium must have allowed for greater latitude for audiences not to complain about things that they heard, that would have upset them had they seen them.

BENNY IMPERSONATES GRACIE ALLEN

The pleasure in cross-dressing that Jack Benny took, over the years, found its finest expression in his imitation of Gracie Allen. Jack created the Gracie impersonation for a private, members-only West Coast Friars Club charity fundraising entertainment, probably in 1949, perhaps earlier. The Friars programs (as they had traditionally been done in New York) featured only male performers, while women were invited to be part of the audience. In the 1948 Friar's Frolic program, Danny Kaye impersonated modern dancer Kay Thompson, with Benny, George Burns, Jack Carson, and Van Johnson performing as "her" evening-suited back up dancers, the Williams Boys. In April 1949, the *Los Angeles Times* reported that "the girls numbers" were a big success.[65] The highlight of both 1949 versions of the Friar's Frolic show in Los Angeles was Benny and Burns. Benny did a full-on impersonation of Gracie Allen, not a broad burlesque performance, but one paying careful attention to get the costume and behavior as close to the original as possible. The Benny-Burns skit was reported fairly widely in the American press, accompanied by as many or more slyly titillating comments and details as had greeted Benny's performance as Charley's Aunt eight years previously. Fan magazine *Radio and Television Best* ran a two-page photo spread, "Meet Gracie (Benny)" detailing Jack's transformation with makeup, false eyelashes and lipstick, silk stockings, corset, curly wig, and feathered hat.[66]

JACK BENNY GETS INTO

Meet Gracie (Benny)

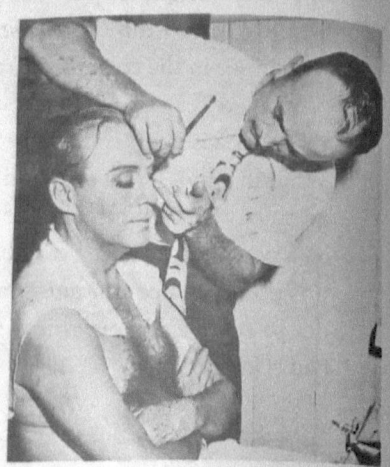

George Burns got a new, but not necessarily better, half at a recent benefit performance in Los Angeles. Donning feminine make-up, figure and clothes, Jack Benny masqueraded as Gracie Allen. These pictures show how the man from Waukegan was transformed into a seductive beauty whose only glaring fault was his lack of feminine charm, something the wardrobe department couldn't supply.

1. Jack gets his first good look at real femininity through his false eyelashes. Overcoming the desire to do something about the hairy chest, a make-up man brushes the lashes.

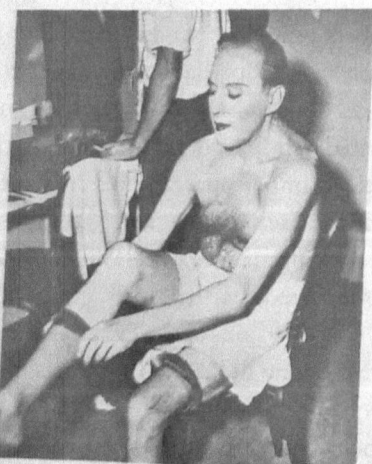

2. His lips curving coquettishly, his eyes alluring behind their silken lashes, the emerging "Gracie" makes sure that the seams are straight as he dons the sheer silk stockings.

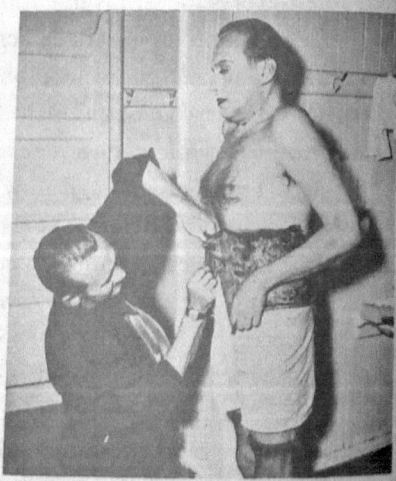

3. Anybody can wear lipstick and silk stockings, but as wardrobe man Lonnie Dorsey forces him to squeeze his hips into a corset, Jack begins to like the figure of the man he was.

FIGURE 10. Even before Benny performed his Gracie Allen routine on television, fan magazines were obsessed with reporting the details with which Benny transformed himself for private stage performance with women's clothing and makeup. *Radio Best*, October 1949, 34–35. Author's collection.

THE ACT WHILE GEORGE *"BURNS"*

4. Jack is rapidly getting into shape for his new role as George Burns drops in to take a look at "Gracie" and pauses to admire the beautiful face and figure.

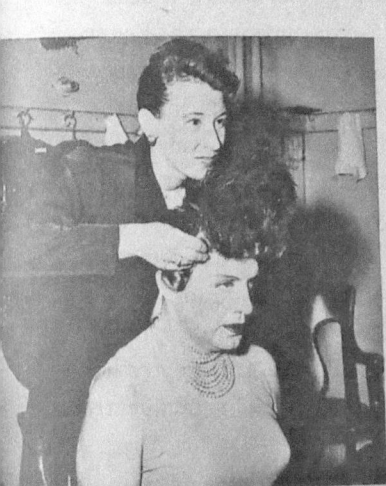

5. "Never thought I'd see the day," says Jack, as Mary Hatch, hairdresser, tops the beautiful red wig with a fetching chapeau, a Parisian creation.

6. The transformation complete, "Gracie" looks demurely from under his long, dark eyelashes at George, who thinks it wasn't such a smart idea.

Benny was of course only one of several noted comics doing female impersonations on American television in the late 1940s and early 1950s. Milton Berle had donned outlandish female costumes (Cleopatra, Carmen Miranda) as part of his slapstick vaudeville-style performances on his program. Eddie Cantor and Ken Murray (whose comedy TV show was sponsored, like Benny's, by the American Tobacco Company) appeared in broad, campy, exaggerated kind of drag performance. Benny, on the other hand, created something that delighted some audience members by being so slyly accurate. As one TV reviewer claimed, "Unlike Berle and Cantor, Benny made a handsome, rather than a grotesque woman. Showed a mighty neat ankle, too."[67]

In 1950 and 1951, Benny and Burns repeated their routine at private parties. In March 1952, Benny and his writers crafted a TV show episode to highlight the Gracie routine, expanding the ten-minute skit with a surrounding story about Gracie's disappearance from the guest-starring role she and George Burns were to play on the Benny TV program. In the first half of the TV episode, Jack was hidden behind a backstage dressing room screen as he parried the insults hurled by George, Rochester, Don, and Frank Nelson, the makeup man. Jack also struggled with his makeup, girdle, and other accoutrements necessary to impersonate Gracie. The middle portion of the Benny TV episode displayed the onstage Burns and "Gracie Benny" performance. It was drawn from old Burns and Allen vaudeville routines from the 1920s, and Benny's sly impression of Gracie's expressions, movements, and tone of voice were spot-on. Benny's entrance onstage was greeted with great deal of audience applause, and the intimacy of the television production's close-up shots emphasized the costume and make-up he wore. In the conclusion, after the stage show, Benny was shown sitting in his dressing room sans wig but still in costume and makeup. The real Gracie Allen burst into the room, mistook Jack for a hussy named Tallulah, and slapped him, then vented her wrath about cheating husbands by slapping every man she subsequently encountered (including Jack's sponsor).

Benny's Gracie Allen impersonation aimed for cross-dressing verisimilitude—his costume was subdued and accurate, not an exaggerated clown or drag outfit. The careful attention to seamed stockings, high heels, gloves, and hat, and Benny's reserved channeling of Gracie's mannerisms and ways of speaking were uncannily close and unnerving to some critics and conservatives in this time of increasingly sharp divisions between appropriate male and female behavior. Reaction to Benny's March 9 TV episode was swift and loud. *Variety*'s Jack Hellman reported that "In all his 42 years in the business, says Jack Benny, no show of his occasioned as much comment as his recent TV'er in which he played Gracie Allen. What surprised most of the lookers was his studied trick of playing it straight without any ludicrous trimmings."[68] A network executive at CBS gathered the next morning's most important reviews and telegraphed them to Benny's manager Irving Fein in Hollywood.[69] One was scathing—Ben Gross of the *New York Daily News* titled his response "Not so Funny":

> Maybe there's something wrong with my sense of humor, but I'm one of those odd guys who just can't see anything screamingly funny in a man masquerading as a woman—except in "Charlie's Aunt," of course—well the highlight of Jack Benny's show on CBS TV at 7:30 last night was Jack pretending to be Gracie Allen, teamed up with George Burns. For the first few moments the act produced a few faint laughs on my part, although it wowed the studio audience. After that, I thought it all to be a deadly bore.[70]

On the other hand, Harriet Van Horne of the *New York World Telegram* announced "Benny Panics 'Em in Sequins and Furs," judging that "Poor Jack" had finally created a visually oriented show that overcame the limitations of his aurally based radio humor:

> [When Gracie went missing,] Jack stepped into the breach, wearing a sequin-trimmed dress, platinum fox furs, a plumed hat and high heeled shoes. His foundation garment, it was made elaborately clear, is borrowed from the rotund announcer, Don Wilson. When Burns and Benny made their entrance there was a roar of laughter. Everything stopped while the audience luxuriated in the delicious lunacy of Jack Benny playing Gracie Allen. It was the most spectacular "entrance" I've ever seen on television.[71]

These critics demonstrated the deeply divided responses to Benny's episode.[72] Jack Gould of the *New York Times*'s enthusiastic praise exposed the nervous tension that surrounded Benny's cross-dressing gamble:

> Jack's success came in a form which nine times out of ten spells disaster for the clowns of Broadway and Hollywood: he did a feminine characterization. But this was an impersonation that avoided the clichés to which Milton Berle in particular is addicted—the smeared lipstick, the padded figure and the affected lisp—and instead was essentially a masterly tidbit of hilarious pantomime.... [W]hat made the show was Mr. Benny's walk. He took mincing little steps that in themselves were almost a satirical ballet on all the grand dames that ever lived. Without saying a word he would shrug a shoulder, pat the back of his coiffure or lift an eyebrow. Each gesture was underplayed and disciplined. Yet cumulatively they provided the idea framework for Jack's mastery of deadpan comedy.[73]

Quite a few TV reviewers' responses were negative. One noted: "I can understand the bit [Benny's Gracie routine] at a gathering of show folk, but on a coast to coast telecast I thought it ill-advised, in questionable taste and to no particular advantage. In other words, a broad, burlesque impersonation is one thing but a slick, near-perfect job of the sort that Benny did last night is quite another and much too close for comfort."[74] Andy Wilson in the *Detroit Times* asked, "Without getting into a long winded discussion with psychiatrists and amateur mind-readers: why do comedians think putting on women's clothing is funny anymore? Probably the main reason is that some one is sure to snicker at the comedian's legs and feet and then you get an epidemic of laughs."[75] Reviewers for the *Washington Star* and *Kansas City Star* claimed that this kind of humor was "beneath" Benny and that they cringed "when men dress up as women for laughs." They declared that it was not appropriate for family viewing.[76] The reviews expressed a theme that "proper middle class family values" were being challenged in these TV shows, visually displaying too much sexual innuendo, working-class burlesque, and "poor taste" invading their living rooms in the new technology.[77]

Emboldened by the attention it garnered when broadcast live to a small national audience in 1952, Jack Benny seized the opportunity to repeat this sketch in a filmed television episode broadcast to a far larger audience on April 11, 1954. *Variety*'s review acknowledged that that it still pulled a massive reaction from studio audiences, with Benny's entrance in costume generating one of the "longest laughs of the season."[78] Nevertheless among the reviews there were still a significant percentage of negative responses, noting the reviewers' discomfort with the drag performance, a Boston reviewer calling it a "lowly device of female impersonation."[79] The *Hollywood Reporter* acknowledged the sketch's popularity but questioned its appropriateness:

> Benny ... was an impressive female worthy of wolf whistles anywhere. The material was good too and Burns and Benny dancing between jokes was high style stuff. They'll be talking about this show in the trade for many a moon. And what they're saying is—"Should Benny get his laughs this way?"[80]

Jack continued to reference cross-dressing humor in 1954, claiming in his next television episode (May 2, 1954) that he was picked up by a sailor while wearing his Gracie Allen costume, and in another sketch in fall 1954 set at Jack's house, after losing a bet at cards to Rochester, Jack wore an apron while cleaning his kitchen, and Don entered the scene and mistook him for a woman.[81] Subsequently, however, Benny and his writers chose to pull back

FIGURE 11. The new celebrity scandal magazines seized on images of Jack Benny in makeup for his Gracie Allen impersonation as headline-worthy outré sexual behavior to exploit. *Uncensored*, November 1955. Author's collection.

from further direct presentations or discussions of female cross-dressing in his television programs. They adhered more often to a situation comedy formula in realistic domestic, neighborhood, and studio settings, with Jack playing nothing more outré than a fastidious fussbudget. Milton Berle and the other vaudeville-influenced comics on television were toning down their burlesque-flavored comedy of crazy drag costumes and over-the-top physical comedy. Cultural taboos on appropriate representations of gender and sexuality were hardening. The new celebrity scandal magazines like *Confidential* and *Uncensored* ran photographs of Benny in Gracie Allen makeup and spun rumors about his sexuality. As the nation's culture grew more skittish in the mid-1950s about portrayals of outré gender identity, and Benny himself aged, the space for Benny to create playful aural and visual humor about gender identity closed down. That doesn't mean it disappeared. Jack was comfortable to keep blurring the lines when he could, such as on talk show appearances in the early 1970s. On occasion he would make self-deprecating jokes about how other comics criticized him for his womanly walk, and then gladly demonstrate it.

· · ·

Humorous comments on American constructions of masculinity gender and sexual identity were central to Jack Benny's humor, throughout his career. These examples, stretching across Benny's radio, film, and early TV performances from 1932 to 1954 have shown the slippery nature of the way that he played with masculine gender identity, and his humor's continuities and changes over two decades. His jokes and comic characterization blurred the boundaries of sharply defined categories that became more strictly enforced in American popular culture over time. The humor of his roles was available to be read in many ways by a variety of audiences in his era and today. Reception of Benny's comedy had a wide range of meanings—it could confirm conservative assumptions about heterosexuality and male dominance, and it could create spaces for alternative conceptions of masculinity and religious and ethnic identity. It could open a place for the recognition and acceptance of queerness. By being so adept at blurring the distinct categories of gendered behavior, Benny's comedy created a liminal space in which men and women, Jews and Gentiles, straights and gays, could safely laugh at their differences and similarities.

The next two chapters examine the career of African American actor Eddie Anderson and the construction of racial identity that Anderson, portraying Jack Benny's radio valet Rochester, brought to Benny's radio narrative. Although the Rochester character only joined the Benny program in 1938, he rapidly became one of the most crucial components of the show's humor, and endured the longest as the most effective counterpoint to Jack's egotism, vanity, and frustrated efforts at patriarchal control. Anderson's career, and Rochester's radio characterization, would be impacted by racism and evolving cultural, political, and industrial limitations, opportunities, and pressures across the tumultuous period from Rochester's introduction to the show to Anderson's rise to public acclaim in both the mainstream white media and the African American press by 1940, to Rochester's inclusion as a flash-point of debate over racial representation in the mass media in the wartime and postwar era.

FOUR

Eddie Anderson, Rochester, and Race in 1930s Radio and Film

African American actor Eddie Anderson achieved enormous popularity through his work on Jack Benny's radio program, from his one-time appearance as a train porter on the radio show in March 1937 to a central role as Jack's valet "Rochester" beginning in late December 1937 that continued on radio, in film, and on television for more than twenty-five years.[1] Soon after his incorporation into the Benny program, the Rochester character became a hit with both white and black audiences, despite—and because of—racial attitudes of the day.[2] Rochester's witty retorts to the boss's supercilious demands and egotistical vanities, croaked out in his distinctive, raspy voice, helped to keep the Benny program high in the ratings, made Anderson the most prominent black performer in broadcasting before 1960, and earned him an income of upwards of $150,000 per year.[3]

Success came at a high price for Eddie Anderson, however, for as an African American performer portraying a fictional character created by whites in the 1930s, 1940s, and 1950s, he faced challenges of racial stereotyping, prejudice, and critique from all sides—from racist, rejecting white audiences in the South; conservative, skittish sponsors in New York; and the racially insensitive media industries in Hollywood to disdain from liberal critics, members of the black intelligentsia, and politically active, equality-seeking members of the younger generation of African Americans. Anderson was the only major black performer on primetime network radio. Everyone knew that *Amos 'n' Andy*, the most famous program featuring black characters, was created and voiced mainly by whites. On other radio shows, the minor roles of African American characters were usually portrayed by white actors performing what historians have characterized as "verbal blackface."[4] The few black performers on network radio programs were usually required to use stereotypically uncultured language and accents. Given the intense, widespread racial prejudice during these decades (not only in the Jim Crow South, but across the nation), how did Anderson survive and succeed?

To avoid the "Uncle Tom" catcalls and harsh criticism that film performances by black actors like Stepin Fetchit and Willie Best provoked, Anderson constantly had to negotiate a path through this minefield of cultural, social, and political issues. Meanwhile, Anderson labored to be a top-flight comedian and entertainer, to please Jack Benny, to serve as a conscientious supporter of Southern California's African American community, and to enjoy the fruits of his celebrity. Eddie Anderson stood in a precarious place, benefitting and being denigrated, being held up and held down, expected by many different constituencies to act "appropriately" when whatever was amenable to one group would anger the others.

In making his way through these ambivalent situations, Anderson merged his public identity into that of fictional character Rochester Van Jones. "Where Rochester leaves off and Eddie Anderson begins is often difficult for Eddie, himself, to tell," the *Baltimore Afro-American* reported in 1945. "There are few radio personalities which so completely absorb the identity of their creator in the eyes of the public as that of the Rochester which he created for the Jack Benny show on NBC."[5] Yet, Anderson also began to face increasing criticism for silently acquiescing to (and complacently accepting, some charged) the demands of racially insensitive, white-controlled mass media industries. Another article from the *Baltimore Afro-American* in 1945 complained:

> Some people are critical of the fact that Eddie Anderson, as Rochester, is a comedian, pure and simple. He commercializes the humor of many situations. He "refuses to propagandize" or use his influence—except for fun. In his own words, "a performer is a performer first and last. He has no business making propaganda. People want to be entertained, not educated." He thinks that the things a colored performer does on the stage or radio have no serious bearing on the nature of race relations. He has no strong notions about "what ought to be done on the racial front." Eddie Anderson, colored, is always Rochester, comedian.[6]

These two chapters explore the difficulties Eddie Anderson encountered, his achievements while enacting Rochester's role, and the subsequent impact of this character on black and white popular culture in the radio era. This first chapter retraces Anderson's early career in the 1920s and 1930s to understand the many challenges that black performers faced in vaudeville, film, and broadcasting. Then it examines Anderson's first years on the Benny program, and how its writers constructed and contained the Rochester character. On the other hand, the Rochester character (through Anderson's performance) broke through the restraints of stereotype to become an important voice of interracial understanding in popular culture. Benny's radio show narrative struggled to juggle competing representations of Rochester as a comic star, an African American actor, a stereotyped servant character, and the most intelligent "stooge" among Jack's underlings. Popular understanding of the Rochester character was impacted by cultural change—widely held racist stereotypes and prejudices were being challenged by agitation for racial equality. If network radio in the 1930s and 1940s held the potential to "transcend the visual," as Michele Hilmes notes, the Benny show, nevertheless, like many others, "obsessively rehearsed" racial (and gender) distinctions to cue listeners to characters' racial identity.[7] She states that radio, "in speaking to us as a nation during a crucial period of time helped to shape our cultural consciousness and to define us as a people in ways that were certainly not unitary but cut deeply across individual, class, racial and ethnic experience."[8] Anderson's radio character, however, also divided listeners into camps of those who enjoyed his jokes and were reassured of the rightness of the social order by Rochester's complacency in his servant role, and those who were angry at the belittling stereotypes his position represented.

The representation of Rochester in his first years on Benny's *Jell-O Program* (1937–1939) contained heavy doses of minstrel stereotypes—stealing, dice playing, being superstitious, an obsession with pork chops—but from the beginning these faults were also undercut by his rapier-sharp wit and collegial relationship with Jack. The show's dialogue alternately showcased and contained Rochester in a dynamic relationship with the boss. The show's early tendency to present him as inferior (thieving, carousing) and continuing focus on making his blackness "visible" on the radio made racial identity essential to Rochester's character. It also isolated Rochester from the rest of the cast by assuming that everyone else was white and superior. On the other hand, when Rochester and Jack interacted, it was nearly always Jack who was wrong, inept, or foolish, and it was Rochester who had more knowledge and tried (even if in vain) to steer Jack toward a better path.

This chapter charts Anderson's rise to intermedia fame through his appearance in several Benny films, and examines how his public persona was shaped in white and black media. It ends with Anderson's greatest pinnacles of public achievement, when he was honored at an all-star film premiere in

Harlem, awarded prestigious race relations awards, hailed as being a harbinger of a "new day" in interracial amity and new possibilities for black artistic, social, and economic achievement. The start of World War II only enhanced the possibilities for Anderson's career. The next chapter, however, will show how the long shadow of Uncle Tom on the one hand, and increasingly obstinate white racism in some parts of American society on the other, increasingly dogged his career in the 1940s and 1950s.

EDDIE ANDERSON'S EARLY ENTERTAINMENT CAREER

Eddie Anderson left few traces of his life in archives, and revealed little in interviews with inquiring newspaper reporters and scholars. His reticence to speak about himself, his experiences, or his opinions on racial representation in American entertainment made it easy for critics to downplay his achievements.[9] Anderson's silence can be seen as a consequence of the ambivalent, difficult position in which he found his public life constructed. He was prominent in the West Coast African American community, but he was also beholden to Jack Benny and the Rochester role for his fame. Like other black actors struggling to make a living from Hollywood films and network radio, Anderson constantly had to maneuver, dodging between racist attitudes and pronouncements from white society on the one hand and Uncle Tom charges from black society on the other. Whenever possible, he remained in a silent, neutral position to avoid any controversy that would anger radio sponsors, film studio, Benny, or black critics and scuttle his career. What can be gleaned from coverage of Anderson in the black and white entertainment press shows him to have been a hard-working, versatile dancer, singer, and comic from humble but not totally impoverished beginnings, who reached a modicum of success across many years in vaudeville, night clubs, and film before a radio role made him a huge star—a story not unlike Jack Benny's.

Edmund Lincoln Anderson Jr. was born in Oakland, California, on September 18, 1905, second-oldest of six children (four boys and two girls) of Edmund "Big Ed" and Ella Mae Anderson.[10] "Big Ed," who'd been born in Michigan in 1869, was a comedian and bass soloist who sang and performed with the Richards and Pringle Georgia Minstrels, Howe's Greater London Circus, and Fordham's medicine shows.[11] Ella Mae (also known as Maude), born in 1881 and raised in Kansas, was one of the few African American circus tightrope walkers in the business, but she had to retire early after a crippling fall.¹² They were part of the small West Coast black community, the family traveling with entertainment troupes before migrating to California sometime around the turn of the century.

Eddie's older brother Cornelius was a dancer who had worked as a child along with his father in the Georgia Minstrels; his younger brothers and sisters were also sometime-performers. Eddie told stories of selling newspapers and peddling cordwood for three dollars a load on the streets of San Francisco as a young child. Most accounts credit his famous gravelly voice as the result of injuries sustained from shouting out the *San Francisco Bulletin*'s headlines.¹³ "We really hawked newspapers when I was a kid. We thought that the loudest voice sold the papers, which wasn't true, of course. I ruptured my vocal cords from straining them."¹⁴ Eddie claimed that his father had hoped he would be a singer, and lamented, "You've done gone an' ruined your voice."¹⁵ At age twelve Eddie was dancing and singing with his younger brother Lloyd in San Francisco hotel lobbies and at the Presidio military base for World War I soldiers.¹⁶ By thirteen, he traveled down to San Diego and back in the cast of movie cowboy Art Accord and Edith Sterling's Wild West show.¹⁷ Anderson attended two years of high school in San Mateo; he worked odd jobs, delivering packages for a tailor and driving teams of horses on the Spreckels sugar plantation near San Francisco. The family relocated south to Los Angeles sometime in the 1920s.¹⁸

At fifteen, Eddie performed with his older brother Cornie in a two-man dancing and singing act, sometimes with the "Strut" Mitchell troupe.¹⁹ In the early 1920s they joined with a partner, Larry "Flying" Ford, to form an act they called the Three Black Aces. The earliest mention of Eddie (at age eighteen) in the *Chicago Defender* comes from a November 1923 review of a "midnight ramble" at the Dunbar Theater, located on Central Avenue, the hub of Los Angeles's black community: "The bill was opened by Eddie Anderson who set the house on fire with his eccentric dancing. Naturally a favorite at this house, he started something that had the rest of the bill trying to see just who would walk away with the honors of the evening."²⁰ "I was mainly a dancer," Eddie later told the *Baltimore Afro-American*, "but I always liked comedy. We used to finish off our dance with some comedy and it stuck."²¹

Eddie's most distinguishing characteristic was his unusual voice, a scratchy, octave-ranging sound that emanated from a compact, stocky body with an expressive face and dancer's litheness. "Mr. Anderson's voice was a challenge to describe," noted his *New York Times* obituary:

It was most often associated with gravel, frequently with sandpaper, and was described variously as rasping, wheezing and scratchy, and in valiant journalist attempt, was likened to "a grinding rasp that sounds like a crosscut saw biting through a knot in a hardwood log." Mr. Anderson, himself, noting that his natural voice was actually deeper than his performing voice, once described how he achieved the effect that became his trademark. "I pitch it up and put more pressure behind it to get that vibration" he said. "To me, I'm talking very high, but on the radio it resonates very deep."[22]

Others described his distinctive voice as "possessing much of the same quality of a klaxon horn," "a cross between a calliope and a buzz saw," and "a cement-mixer."[23]

In 1924 the Three Black Aces performed in Southern California night spots for white and black audiences, and played on the Pantages West Coast vaudeville circuit. In September 1924 they joined a sixty-five-member black stage review, performing at the Philharmonic Theater in Los Angeles. The *Los Angeles Record* reported "The dancing of Eddie Anderson, Cornie Anderson and Lawrence Ford as 'Three Black Aces' had in it the primeval spirit of syncopation, elemental, abandoned and whole hearted."[24] Ford left soon afterward, and the act regrouped as "Cabbage" and "Little Aesop" Anderson, the Two Black Aces.

The pair won a spot in another large, all-black stage review called *Steppin' High*. The *California Eagle* characterized these roles as "chorus boy in an all sepia revue," but it was professional show business and the Anderson brothers were undoubtedly glad to be in a major production, which featured Mamie Smith, one of the earliest female blues singers.[25] Ambitiously embarking on a national tour,[26] the *Steppin' High* company ran into financial trouble in its fifteenth week, and folded that summer in Omaha, Nebraska. This ironically was a lucky break for Eddie and Cornie, as an admiring theatrical manager at Omaha's World Theater got the stranded pair a spot, first on his own stage and then on the Pantages Midwestern vaudeville circuit that included theaters in Minneapolis and Kansas City.[27] Eddie and Cornie remained in the Midwest, performing in and around Chicago for a year or two, including fifteen weeks at the Sunset Café with Cab Calloway,[28] and at the State-Lake, Palace, and McVickers Theaters.[29]

Eventually the Andersons worked their way back to the West Coast, playing the Fanchon and Marco and Keith-Orpheum vaudeville circuits. Eddie performed at black nightspots on Central Avenue in Los Angeles, including the Apex Night Club, where Eddie headed the floor show with Duke

Ellington's band, and for several years at Frank Sebastian's Cotton Club in Culver City (a chic nightspot that the *Defender* noted "caters exclusively to white trade"), dancing, singing, joking, and acting as the review's master of ceremonies, with Louis Armstrong, Lionel Hampton, or Duke Ellington's bands providing the music. He ran into repeated troubles with Sebastian for tardiness, occasionally had his pay docked, and eventually was fired.[30] In April 1933 Eddie appeared in an Earl Dancer production, "Fourteen Gentlemen from Harlem," with Etta Moton as featured singer, at the Warner Theater. In 1936 Eddie performed at the Club Alabam on Central Avenue, dancing with Johnny Taylor, performing what one colleague recalled as "zany comedy routines, including a slow motion, delayed action dance that convulsed audiences. A great sense of timing was theirs. . . . Both performers had tremendous talent. They revised, improvised as they went along. And audiences loved it."[31]

Motion picture appearances were the goal of nearly every performer in Southern California, and when he returned west in 1932, Anderson joined other black performers making the rounds of Central Casting, hoping to get the occasional walk-on or extra part. His early film appearances include nine uncredited roles as a butler, porter, sailor, chauffeur, or bootblack. Eddie received a rare bit part large enough to get a screen credit, as a bum in *Transient Lady* (Universal, 1935). The *Defender* and *Los Angeles Sentinel* always reported with optimism on African American performers' successes in obtaining these tiny roles, trying to create a sense of a film community in which blacks had significant impact.[32] In 1936, Eddie landed a feature film part, as Noah, the third largest role, in the Warner Bros. film version of Marc Connelly's stage success *The Green Pastures*. It garnered good reviews for Anderson, but did not propel him to further film advancement.[33] That year he had uncredited bits in *Show Boat* (Universal, 1936), and in sixteen other films produced at the major studios. In 1937 Eddie had a dozen very small movie roles, working at studios from Warner Bros. to Paramount, Columbia, 20th Century Fox, and Republic.

Similar (on a smaller scale) to Jack Benny's early professional journey of moving between entertainment forms, Eddie Anderson was piecing together a solid and busy, if relatively minor, entertainment career in Los Angeles. He was best known in the West Coast black community as a night club emcee, dancer, singer, and comic, at cabarets that catered to the African American community on Central Avenue and at others that attracted wealthy white pleasure-seekers. He appeared in regional-level vaudeville programs and movie theater stage prologues. He was known, but not prominent, in Chicago and New York entertainment circles. The Hollywood film studios kept his roles at miniscule size.

THE MARGINALITY OF AFRICAN AMERICANS IN RADIO

Ambitious to expand his career, thirty-two-year-old Eddie Anderson joined the casting call for a one-time bit role on Jack Benny's highly rated NBC radio comedy program in March 1937. Primetime radio programs were relocating production to the West Coast from New York City. However, Eddie and the other auditioning black actors did not have reason to think the opportunities in network radio were going to be any better than in films. In fact, the situation for them was significantly worse. There were very few African American performers on network coast to coast shows—appearing only as orchestra musicians, church choir singers, or playing tiny roles as servants or minstrel-type buffoons.

Black actors Juano Hernandez and Frank Silvera occasionally got small parts in nonblack roles because they had built strong reputations as "competent linguists" who could perform other dialects.[34] But a great many other black character roles, from Amos and Andy to servants and minstrel show participants, were performed by white voice actors. Like Gosden and Correll, and Marlin Hurt who would originate the role of Beulah the maid on the *Great Gildersleeve* radio program, voice actors might create up to a dozen different roles of various race, ethnic, and gender identities on a single program. Radio producers considered it a cost-saving measure, but the practice contributed to the marked lack of racial and ethnic diversity in American network broadcasting. Radio program producers too often sought easily identified foreign accents and vocal stereotypes, not the depth of variety of subtle accents, pronunciation, and vocal timbre. The technological limitations of radio vocal reproduction multiplied this use of stereotypical dialects and accents.

African American radio actors bitterly complained that radio producers and casting directors wanted the very few roles for blacks to sound stereotypically identifiable to whites, incorporating much more drawl than professional actors wanted to use.[35] The few black performers who were able to audition for radio roles almost always had to compromise by creating vocal characterizations with accents drawn from minstrel shows and "coon song" performers on the vaudeville circuit. Actor Johnny Lee recalled, "I had to learn to speak Negro dialect when I first began acting. I had to learn to talk as white people believe Negroes talked. Most of the directors take it for granted that if you're a Negro actor, you'll do the part of a Negro automatically."[36]

Radio sponsors, their ad agencies, and the networks maintained for years that their fear of alienating white Southern consumer-listeners kept them from using black performers, similar to the "myth of the Southern box office" that film producers alluded to when they refused to create prominent movie roles for black actors. Radio sponsors claimed to be terrified that prejudiced white listeners would associate a black performer negatively with their products and refuse to buy.[37] As well, although there were some European-ethnic radio stations broadcasting in the North, Jim Crow restrictions kept African American–operated radio stations from opening until after World War II.[38]

The black press protested for years, in vain, about the dearth of African American performers in prominent roles on the airwaves. Black newspapers, the NAACP, and social critics also had to fight hard to reduce and remove blatant racism from the network radio airwaves, as was exemplified by the controversy and threats of boycotts surrounding Will Rogers's on-air repeated use of a racial slur when describing spirituals, comments made in a January 21, 1934, episode of his *Good Gulf Oil* program for which he subsequently was very reluctant to publically apologize.[39]

Nevertheless, optimists hoped that the absence of black performers on network radio could be ameliorated. In April 1937, two weeks after Eddie's one-time appearance on the Benny program, the *Louis Armstrong Orchestra* variety program debuted on the NBC Blue network, Fridays at 9:00 P.M., sponsored by Fleishman's Yeast.[40] Hopes were high in the black community for its continuing success. Yet there were disappointments from the start. The *Pittsburgh Courier* complained that the opening program's dialog (written by Southern white dialect novelist Octavus Roy Cohen) was "typical Uncle Tom Negro" fare and only a burlesque of how actual black people spoke.[41] Armstrong forswore any use of the minstrel-type language, but conservative whites still objected to his jazz-musician-style vocabulary and the intonation of his voice. Despite a promise to relocate the program to Sunday evenings, the sponsor backed out and the Armstrong show was soon cancelled.

Meanwhile, the most famous "black" performers and characters on the radio were Amos and Andy, performed by white actors Freeman Gosden and Charles Correll. Melvin Ely, Michele Hilmes, and other scholars have explored the vast popularity, cultural impact, and many controversies surrounding the *Amos 'n' Andy* show, which began broadcasting in its earliest form from Chicago in 1928 and became a huge hit for NBC as they moved the broadcasting to New York and the show's setting to Harlem. Gosden and Correll played all the characters for a decade, before adding black performers Lillian Randolph and Ernestine Wade to portray the female roles. In the late 1930s, the fifteen-minute program broadcast five evenings per week, while no longer the smash hit that did so much to popularize serialized radio comedy, was still a very solid ratings getter, beloved of white audiences and some black listeners as well. Going into his 1937 radio audition, then, Eddie Anderson probably hardly even dared to hope that this single appearance on the Benny show would amount to much more than a few dollars in his pocket.

ANDERSON'S APPEARANCE ON THE BENNY PROGRAM, MARCH 1937

Jack Benny's radio program in the 1930s frequently contained minor roles that utilized ethnic characters with strong accents—Italians, Russians, Greeks, Scots, Irishmen, Germans, Schlepperman the urban Jewish trickster, Appalachian hillbillies, and tough gangsters. They were portrayed by voice specialist actors Benny Rubin, Patsy Flick, Sam Hearn, and occasionally writer Harry Conn. Conn had maintained that the surprise of an ethnic accent it was one of the surest ways to get a laugh from radio audiences. Nevertheless, among the dialect characters, the Benny show had utilized African American voices only infrequently, as waiters or bellhops at hotels—performing single lines that might have been covered by his ethnic comics. African American actor Clarence Muse had been hired twice in early 1936, to perform brief one-shot roles as a fellow jail inmate and a train porter. But nothing more came of that.[42]

Benny recalled in his autobiography that writers Bill Morrow and Ed Beloin, (who had been on the job one year) drafted an episode to be broadcast March 28, 1937, Easter Sunday, which involved the cast traveling to the West Coast on the Santa Fe Super Chief after the denouement of the Benny-Allen feud. The writers wanted to create a scene with Jack meeting someone on the train trip who, like so many waitresses and store clerks, would annoy him. Instead of the conductor or engineer or a passenger, they chose a Pullman porter who would impertinently frustrate him. Benny assumed they could utilize Benny Rubin for this small role, but Morrow pointed out that Rubin would look so incongruous to the studio audience at the live broadcast, a small white man playing a black character, that the audience would be too distracted to laugh in the correct places.[43] Jack suggested Rubin could wear blackface, and the writers again objected that it would hurt the mood of the scene. Benny described the racial insensitivity that he, his writers, and most of white society held in the era that framed their notions about the character they sought to create: "He was a traditional Negro dialect stereotype. He had a molasses drawl and he 'yassuh-bossed' me all over the place. He was such a drawling, lazy, superstitious stereotype that even the original Uncle Tom would have despised him. However, in those days we were not aware of these racial aspects of comedy."

With just a short time that week to get the part cast and episode rehearsed and broadcast, they auditioned five black actors. Eddie Anderson had not performed the most outstanding acting job of the group in reading the lines. Benny was nevertheless very attracted to the sound of Anderson's voice, recalling that "he had a deep husky growl in his voice and his words came up through his larynx like there was a pile of gravel down there.... During the reading he modulated into a high pitched squeal that was marvelous. It sounded like 'hee hee HEEEE.'"[44] Anderson won the small part and earned $50 or $75 for his few minutes of work on-air.[45]

The scene—Jack and Mary are aboard the Super Chief

JACK: Gee, what a long trip.
MARY: Say Jack, look out the window... (giggles) They sure dress funny here in Hollywood.
JACK: Those are Indians... this is New Mexico.
MARY: Oh.
JACK: Hey porter, porter!
PORTER: Yessir?
JACK: What time do we get to Albuquerque?
PORTER: What?
JACK: Albuquerque!
PORTER: I don't know, do we stop there?
JACK: Certainly we stop there!

PORTER: My, my!

JACK: Hmmm...

PORTER: I'd better go up and tell the Engineer about that.

JACK: Yeah. Yeah, do that!

PORTER: What's the name of that town again?

JACK: Albuquerque.

PORTER: Hee, hee, hee! Albuquerque. What they gonna think up next?

JACK: Albuquerque is a town.

PORTER: You better check on that.

JACK: I know what I'm talking about.... Now how long do we stop there?

PORTER: How long to we stop WHERE?

JACK: In Albuquerque.

PORTER: Hee-hee! There you go again.

"I remember that first Sunday," Eddie later recalled. "I wasn't nervous—I had been a performer for years and if I ever had stage fright, it was so long ago I forgot it."[46] Eddie Anderson's lively portrayal of the sassy porter who gave Benny a hard time by claiming to never have heard of Albuquerque made an impression on listeners and critics, as public reaction was apparently quite positive. Benny later recalled, "Eddie was a riot on that show and I was surprised nobody picked him up. We got so much mail, I decided to make him a regular, which I did after the summer. I made him my butler and chauffer on the show."[47] While Benny's quote made Anderson's incorporation into the show seem smooth and inevitable, in actuality, Benny and the writers did not have a solid idea for a permanent addition. They brought Anderson back on a second show on May 2 as an impertinent waiter (Pierre) in the "Buck Benny" skit, because they liked his voice.[48]

In a half a dozen other appearances on the Benny *Jell-O Program* that spring and the subsequent fall, Anderson played anonymous characters. Meanwhile, Anderson continued his day-labor in films and appearances at nightclubs, and also picked up several small one-time parts on other radio programs. Anderson was finally featured as a major continuing character on Benny's December 26, 1937, episode. The episode revolved around a holiday party Jack was holding at his house, and the fact that he had hired a valet named Rochester Van Jones. The episodes contained some prominent lines for

Anderson. Rochester's wife (unheard) continuously called on the telephone, and Jack and Rochester took turns answering the calls (the wife very soon disappeared from the program's narrative). Rochester sang a verse of a song, and Don Wilson involved him in doing the middle Jell-O commercial.

How the name "Rochester Van Jones" originated was a matter of debate. A 1939 *Defender* article claimed of the scriptwriters' choice, "Rochester, they said, was phonetically perfect. Van has a tony touch and Jones is used as a sort of a great big let-down." In a 1968 interview, Anderson maintained that it was Benny who thought up the name. "Jack modestly said that he can't really remember, but the minute the name Rochester was mentioned, he knew it was the right one.[49] In his autobiography, Benny noted, "Rochester was a good name for a butler because it does sound kind of English and it was incongruous for me to have an English butler. Also the word has a good hard texture. It's a name you can bite in to. If I was mad at him, I could yell 'RAH-chester.' It was an ideal name when I lost my temper."[50]

After Rochester's introduction as a recurring character on the Benny radio program, Anderson appeared on about every third episode in early 1938. After the show writers made a few experimental attempts to include Rochester in the "work" of the radio program, appearing in the parody skits the radio cast undertook, the writers settled instead on a narrative frame in which Rochester was clearly Benny's servant working at his home, not a cast member or employee of the radio station. As Benny explained Rochester's role to a *New York Times* reporter, "Never is he supposed to be an actor or a part of the program. Always the audience thinks of him as my valet. That is why we never mention his name in the cast. The trick is to keep him in character."[51]

The decision to keep Rochester's realm of activity separate from the radio cast ended up expanding the situation comedy elements of the Benny program. The show's writers worked to vary the program narrative, from episodes that completely followed the radio program production, to others that mixed in preparations before or after the show, to those that took place entirely away from the radio studio and had almost nothing to do with the show. To incorporate Rochester into the action, they began to experiment more often with comic scenes taking place between Jack and Rochester at home, or when Rochester phoned his employer at the studio, or when he drove Benny and the cast around town in the Maxwell. Rochester interacted only infrequently with other members of the cast, although as more shows included scenes at Benny's home, Mary Livingstone frequently appeared and the two of them together would critique Jack's vanities. When Jack found himself the owner of a pet polar bear, Carmichael (who had an appetite for gasmen), Rochester assumed another household duty in caring for him.

Because Rochester was separated in the show's narrative from the others as valet and private person, not as a radio show performer, script dialogue referred much less often to Anderson's other real life performances outside the world of the radio program than it did to the other cast members' outside activities. While Phil Harris could brag about his band's appearances at the Wilshire Bowl, and Kenny Baker could publicize his appearance in the film *The Goldwyn Follies,* Rochester did not get to talk about Eddie Anderson's appearances at Los Angeles night clubs or the roles he played in films like *You Can't Take it With You, Jezebel,* or *Gone with the Wind.* This has led some critics to argue that there was a persistent prejudicial downplaying of Anderson's status on the show.[52] The radio program's dialogue sounded uneasy as characters begin to acknowledge Anderson's skyrocketing celebrity as Rochester (especially when the radio-themed films were released).[53] The show's reticence to publicize Anderson's doings also made Rochester the most fictional of the show's self-reflexive characters who so thoroughly blended radio character and real-life identities.

On the flip side, Anderson soon found himself publically subsumed into Rochester's identity, in both black and white popular culture. Everyone began calling Eddie "Rochester," even his wife.[54] As the radio scripts' changing of Sadye Marks Benny's name to "Mary" in indications of her lines meant that the actress had adopted her stage name in real life, it's probable that people connected with the program were calling Anderson "Rochester," as well, for the scripts list him as "Rochester" starting in October 1938. A July 1939 interview in the *Defender* claimed, "Anderson has become so accustomed to being called 'Rochester' that it is hard for him to remember his real name."[55]

REACTIONS TO ANDERSON AND ROCHESTER IN THE BLACK AND WHITE PRESS

Soon after his regular role began on the *Jell-O Program,* both white and black newspapers made especial efforts to inform radio listeners that Anderson was actually a black actor performing a black role.[56] Given the paucity of African American participation in network radio programs, the black press had previously given little regular space to network program guides, oftentimes restricting their listings only to noteworthy appearances of black musicians and singers. In February 1938, the *Atlanta Daily World* and *Chicago Defender* began including the *Jell-O Program* in their radio guide—listed as "Rochester—NBC Red—Sunday 7 pm."[57] The *California Eagle*'s entertainment reporter in April 1938 acknowledged his readers' reluctance to engage with radio when "good programs that give Negros more than two lines to say are few and far between." He urged them now to turn on their receiving sets:

> I immediately call your attention to Jack Benny's Jell-O program, which for several years has been voted the most popular one of the air. The newest addition to Jack Benny's cast is Eddie Anderson, a young Negro comic, whose excellent performance as Rochester, the butler, is bringing new and hearty laughs to the program every Sunday.[58]

The *New York Amsterdam News* interviewed Anderson in April, and reported that "He is treated equally well by all members of the cast, including Mary Livingstone, Phil Harris, Kenny Baker and Andy Devine, and is just as popular as any other individual on the program." It claimed that Benny took a personal interest in him and treated him like a protégé. The article was accompanied by a photo of Jack Benny and Eddie Anderson posing in the studio with *New Amsterdam News* reporter Bill Chase. This was a coup for Chase, as few white entertainers were willing to be so photographed. The article also noted Anderson's role in the recent film *You Can't Take It with You*.[59] Director Frank Capra was receiving kudos for supporting improved race relations, for the equality with which Anderson and Lillian Yarbro, who played servants, depicted as being treated. A 1939 *Baltimore Afro-American* brief profile when Eddie appeared in person at the Earle Theater was careful to portray him with dignity, mentioning that he had his own valet backstage: "That harsh, croaking voice which you hear when he plays Rochester is only a part of the act and is discarded for a pleasing, clear, deep voice when he is offstage. A reserved, ever smiling gentleman in reality, he never clowns or tries to display any of Rochester's' vocal mannerisms."[60] Optimists began to hope that Anderson, through these radio and film roles, was leading to a new era of more sympathetic depiction of blacks in contemporary American society, through comedy.[61]

Meanwhile the first article about Anderson in the *New York Times* painted a stereotype of a minstrel character: "Jack pushed me ahead and I sure does feel mighty thankful to him," it claimed that Eddie said.[62] Even the black press could occasionally depict Anderson in a similar manner. A syndicated article titled "Radio's Famous Rochester" was published in the

Pittsburgh Courier, the *Atlanta Daily World*, and the *California Eagle* in November 1938. It introduced Anderson as "The bewildering Rochester, who exasperates his boss with his laziness and larceny each Sunday night over the NBC-Red network."[63] It was rife with inaccuracies, and exaggerated Anderson's previous connections to Benny, claiming that Benny saw Eddie in *The Green Pastures* and remembered to invite him to audition, supposedly when Benny was looking to cast a valet. It argued that Eddie paid hero-worshipping-levels of attention to Benny and imitated his cigar smoking at rehearsals.

THE SOUNDS OF RACE ON THE RADIO: MAKING ROCHESTER VISIBLE

Michele Hilmes argues that U.S. network radio program creators were obsessed with delineating race on the radio. The ether and its performers were invisible, but inevitably, cultural construction of racial difference played out in this aural arena. Black characters (when they were included at all on the mainstream, white-dominated network programs) needed to be identified and labeled.[64] To listeners today, the dismaying aspect of Rochester's incorporation into the Jack Benny show narrative during his first years was the heavy load of what radio historian Michele Hilmes terms the "cultural incompetence" the character was made to carry, like the worst aspects of minstrel show characters.

Hilmes discusses the character failings demonstrated by *Amos 'n' Andy*, which made them seem inferior to the presumed "superiority" of radio listeners. When like greenhorn immigrants they did not know how to function correctly in modern society, when they exposed how uneducated, or stupid, or naïve they were, when they were taken advantage of by the Kingfish or neighborhood sharpsters, when they got into trouble, they were labeled as losers. Radio listeners could assume these flaws were natural, even shared by other blacks, and could think Amos and Andy "deserved" their less-privileged status in life because of their "incompetence." Hilmes argues that Gosden and Correll marked their characters as black through the narratives, dialogue, and performances. Amos and Andy lived in an all-black world, first on Chicago's South Side and then in Harlem. They were naïve, foolish, and lazy, and constantly misunderstood or rejected the white-bourgeois rules of hard work and thrift needed to rise into middle-class society. They constantly mixed up and mangled words for humorous effect, although on the flip side, their neologisms and malapropisms were also wry, sharp, and often intellectually insightful.[65] Part of the cultural "trouble" that *Amos 'n' Andy* caused was that racist attributes were totally entwined with admirable aspects of the program. Gosden and Correll were superb writers and performers, with gifts for narrative, characterization, and comic timing. In the late 1940s, radio critic John Crosby would sincerely praise the show's writing as the best on network radio.[66] The show, by thoroughly mixing humorous, sympathetic characters with deplorable stereotypes, historian Melvin Ely has argued, could simultaneously appeal to both white racists and to blacks and whites sympathetic and supportive of the black community and race relations progress.[67] Rochester's character would face similar wrenching and contentious issues of character construction and audience reception.

During his first several years as a character on the Benny radio program, Rochester was saddled by the show's writers with many racially stereotyped, minstrel show–like "cultural incompetence" cues: he was lazy; he stole watches, suits, and money from his employer. He was stupid and incompetent on the job (he burnt the clothes he was ironing, broke dishes, etc.). He had no control over his appetites over food and liquor, partying, brawling, and women; he was obsessed with pork chops, chicken, and watermelon. He shot craps and fought with razor blades. He lied, he bragged, he had a superstitious fear of ghosts. Over the months, nearly every widely held racist minstrel-show stereotype came out in the writers' attempts to set Rochester out as "incompetent," different, and inferior to the other cast members, who could be united in opposition, despite their own many idiosyncrasies and flaws, in their superiority and whiteness. These stereotyped differences helped justify why Rochester "deserved" to be ordered about and yelled at, and paid so little by his employer. Here are a few examples:

May 29, 1938, in a parody of "Tom Sawyer," Jack plays the school teacher conducting a recitation:

JACK: Now, Rochester.

ROCHESTER: Yes, boss.

JACK: Can you name the Seven Wonders of the World?

ROCHESTER: Yes sir!

JACK: What are they?

ROCHESTER: The Sphinx, the Pyramids, the Hanging Gardens, and four pork chops!

JACK: Now Rochester, pork chops are not included in the Seven Wonders of the World.

ROCHESTER: I guess you've never been in Harlem Geography.

October 2, 1938, Jack is at home, getting dressed to go to the studio for the season's first radio broadcast:

JACK: You know, it's a funny thing, but every time you press my pants, you burn a hole in them.

ROCHESTER: Yeah, that is funny.

JACK: Well, don't laugh. Oh well, I'll put on an old pair so I won't be late for breakfast. You know Rochester, sometimes I don't know why I pay you.

ROCHESTER: I don't even know WHEN!

JACK: I told you I'd pay you as soon as I went back to work. Right now I'm short of cash.

ROCHESTER: What's that green stuff in your mattress? Grass?

JACK: Yes, it's grass!

ROCHESTER: Well, I mowed some of it last night.

A further aspect of Rochester's early depiction, which was tied to the idea of keeping him separate and distinct from the radio cast members, was the writers' dogged determination to delineate Rochester's physical and visual racial difference. They did this by repeatedly describing his blackness. In an invisible medium where everything was colored (pun intended) by the listeners' imaginations, the show's writers tried to milk humor, and reinforce awareness of racial difference, by regularly having Jack note the blackness of Rochester's body:

November 13, 1938, Jack, Mary, and Rochester have gone to visit a fortune teller's home, and its dark and creepy inside:

ROCHESTER: This place is darker than a telephone booth in Harlem.

JACK: Well, where are you?

ROCHESTER: Here I am!

JACK: Open your eyes so I can see you.

November 5, 1939, the cast is getting ready to perform a radio skit parodying the current MGM film *The Women*, and Jack insists that all the men on the show have to take female roles (Jack himself is taking Norma Shearer's part); Jack calls Rochester in (as they are short of performers) to take a role as his maid:

ROCHESTER: Your maid? Why can't I be your valet?

JACK: Because I don't want a man in my room when I'm dressing. You're going to be my maid.

ROCHESTER: I ain't gonna wear no dress.

JACK: You are, too.... Now, fellas...

ROCHESTER: I ain't gonna wear no mascara.

JACK: You are, too!... Now, fellas...

ROCHESTER: It ain't gonna show!

Yet these denigrating and derogatory characteristics of Rochester were always counterbalanced by the Rochester character's quick wit, and his irreverence for Benny's authority, accentuated by his inimitable voice and the wonderful timing of his pert retorts and disgruntled, disbelieving "Uh huh" and "Come now!"

ROCHESTER: "When we start on our vacation, does that mean I'm off salary for 14 weeks?

JACK: It certainly does. You're just like me, Rochester. When I don't get it, you don't get it.

ROCHESTER: When you GET it, I don't get it![68]

Rochester annoyed Jack, but also critiqued every order and action. With an air of informality, Rochester usually called him "Boss" and not "Mr. Benny." He also had a far more sophisticated vocabulary than Phil Harris or Jack. The Benny show writers gave Rochester all the punchlines in his interactions with Jack; he had the ability to ridicule and criticize his employer, not having to keep his thoughts silent and to himself. This lively bumptiousness raised his character above the much more stereotypical black characters then current in American radio and film. He always remained a

FIGURE 12. A rare appearance of Eddie Anderson as Rochester in a print advertisement for Jack Benny's radio sponsor's product, Jell-O. The Rochester character here is shown voicing more stereotypical-type language than writers were putting into his radio and film dialogue. Advertisement for Cola Jell-O, *Life*, circa Winter 1942, unknown date. Author's collection.

loyal servant and had to follow Jack's orders, so he was palatable to those racists most resistant to social change, and yet, in a small way, Rochester spoke truth to power, and he was portrayed by an actual African American actor, so he gained sympathy and affection among black listeners, too.

The racial tensions inherent in Jack's relationship with Rochester (employer/employee, superior/inferior, master/slave, and yet informally joking colleagues interacting with some sense of equality) literally collided in the February 5, 1939, *Jell-O Program* episode. The feud between Fred Allen and Jack Benny had reheated. Jack ordered Rochester to drive him and Mary out to Andy Devine's farm in the San Fernando Valley in order to cheer Jack on as he trained for a possible boxing match against his rival. In need of a sparring partner, Jack conscripts a reluctant Rochester. Jack and Rochester start sparring, and we hear sound effects of boxing gloves making contact. Andy says, "Hey Jack, with you and Rochester sparring around, it looks like you are shadow-boxing." Jack then pulls a dirty trick. He calls out to Rochester to look behind him, and when Rochester is distracted, smacks him hard in the face. Jack crows, "Bet I gave you a black eye!" Rochester retorts, "You'll have to peel me to find out!" They spar a little more. Then Rochester calls out to Jack, "Look down at your shoe laces!" and punches Jack in the face in retribution for the sucker punch. Jack collapses on the ground, and shouts in a garbled manner—he's lost his bridgework. While Mary and Andy scramble to search for his missing false teeth, Jack yells that Rochester is fired, while Rochester hides up in the rafters of the barn. As Benny recalled the episode in his autobiography,

> There was the sound of an arm swishing through the air. The crack of a gloved fist meeting a glass jaw. The thunk of a body fitting the floor. "Boss, boss," Rochester cried, "git up, git up!" I rose. So did the South. Thousands of indignant persons below the Mason-Dixon Line wrote in to complain that permitting my Afro-American butler to punch me in the face was an attack on the white race and the dignity of the South. Until [the I Can't Stand Jack Benny contest] . . . this incident brought the heaviest mail we ever received on the program. You've got to realize that most of my life I've been a political innocent. It never occurred to me there was anything offensive in this humorous little episode. I was amazed at this revelation of people's strong feelings on the subject of race. To me, I was just doing a comedy show.[69]

Benny's radio show never again ventured into even hints of physical altercations between Jack and Rochester.

Given that the Jack Benny radio show was airing in 1930s, with the Civil War just seventy years past and race relations in America at a nadir of widespread prejudice and Jim Crow laws, and given how sharply Jack ordered a willing Rochester around, demanding so much for so little in return, some critics have likened theirs to a "master and slave" relationship. Theirs was joined by other uneasy, unequal relationships on the program, from Jack's imperious treatment of his show cast, the Sportsmen, and the band musicians, or Jack's terror of his own bosses (sponsors and network radio executives, film directors, and producers) who treated him as dismissively as well. Dennis Day's overbearing mother Lucretia barked out commands for her timid son to obey, and both Dennis's and Mary's mothers batted their lazy, weak husbands around.

The relationship that Jack and Rochester played with was rooted in ancient stock characterizations and comedy plots, found in Greek comedy, Italian commedia dell'arte's Harlequin and Pantalone, French farces, and Shakespearean comedies to Mark Twain satires, drawing room comedy, and vaudeville and silent film's slapstick zaniness. European and American literary and theatrical history has been filled with stories involving trickster slaves, witty servants, and grumpy old, demanding masters. Whether they are deviously helping young lovers unite in spite of parental opposition, tweaking the old master's vanity, or being sly jesters telling the truth to old men, sly servants overrode their subservient positions in every possible way, while just trying to get enough food (and/or love) to survive another day in a harsh world.

In the decades that the Benny program aired, many listeners would have been familiar with another famous model of a sagacious valet/butler much smarter than his employer—Jeeves and Bertie Wooster. British novelist P. G. Wodehouse created Jeeves in 1915 as a "Gentleman's personal gentleman" serving wealthy, stupid, and foppish young British aristocrat Bertie Wooster, in a series of eleven novels and thirty-five short stories that stretched from 1919 to 1974. Jeeves was incredibly smart and well read, wryly humorous and totally in control of "Master" Bertie's life. Jeeves's brilliant plans managed to extract Bertie from whatever sticky social situation in which he ineptly and regularly immersed himself. Jeeves could solve any problem. Attempts were made to translate the stories to film in the mid-1930s with Arthur Treacher playing Jeeves, but they weren't half as inspired as what Benny and Anderson were creating.

Nevertheless, the American cultural context of the relationship of Jack and Rochester, created within the historical legacy of slavery, widespread prejudice, poor race relations, and huge racial divides, made it very possible for radio listeners to understand Jack and Rochester's relationship as plantation based, with Rochester's acceptance of his meager lot taken as the way African Americans "should" acquiesce to white authority, accepting never being anything more than servants, loyally caring far more about the welfare of employers' families than their own. It would comfort conservative whites who might see the relationship through the prism of the appropriateness of Jack ordering Rochester around and the servant having to do the master's bidding under pain of punishment. But for black listeners, the fact that Rochester acquiesced to Jack's demands, that he didn't quit because of lack of wages or poor treatment or for a better opportunity, led some other listeners to categorize Rochester as a stereotypical Uncle Tom, comfortable in his subservient role, no matter how oppressed he might be.

Why didn't Rochester just quit? What kept him tied to Jack, and accepting of the endless indignities of his servant role? The radio show's narrative always struggled with explanations. Rochester would say he could not leave because he loved his boss so much. On the other hand, when Jack grumbled about Rochester's thieving and cast members would ask why Jack didn't fire him, Jack would reply with an excuse like "I can't. He's got some letters I wrote to Garbo, and he won't give 'em back!"[70] To newspaper reporters, Benny explained that Jack's relationship with Rochester as based on affection: "He knows I like him, and no matter what he says or does he knows I won't fire him."[71] Their relationship seemed like a family obligation, a strong bond of love and obedience and desire for approval that seems more like parent and child, or husband and wife. A paid employee should not have to owe such patient allegiance to an employer that treats him so badly. Writers who defended the Jack and Rochester relationship talked about Rochester having a deep-down love and affection for Jack, a determination to put up with the guff and do his duty. On the other hand, liberal critics began to chastise Anderson for acquiescing to the role. *The Defender* would try to head off criticism with denials in 1939: "No Uncle Tom is this man 'Rochester.' He makes it clear that he is valet deluxe to comedian Jack Benny and polar bear Carmichael only on the radio and in the movies. Outside of work, he is plain Eddie Anderson."[72]

ROLES IN BENNY'S PARAMOUNT FILMS MAKE ANDERSON AN INTERMEDIA STAR

In late 1938, the Paramount film studio hired RKO director Mark Sandrich to resuscitate Jack Benny's movie stardom after a string of lackluster musical variety films. As I recount in the Intermedia stardom chapter, Sandrich developed the idea of incorporating Benny's radio identity and the sound, pacing, and energy of the top-rated *Jell-O Program* into the movie *Man About Town*.

After putting Phil Harris into a role, Sandrich decided to incorporate Eddie Anderson into the film, too, playing a valet named Rochester who worked for theatrical producer Bob Templeton (Jack). Anderson had been a regular cast member of the Benny radio show for about a year, and Rochester's popularity had been growing rapidly. During the weeks of film production, however, on the radio show, while Jack and Phil joked about happenings on the Paramount sets, no mention was made of Anderson's involvement in the filming; the narrative was intent on keeping Rochester contained as Jack's private employee. Meanwhile, Sandrich kept expanding Anderson's role as the film was in production, adding to Anderson's comic repartee with Benny and involving him in several musical numbers.

Even the best-intentioned efforts, then as now, in exploring humor that is connected to race can go awry, because no matter what intent a joke maker puts into a jest, it is always open to a variety of interpretations by different audiences. Sandrich saw something he thought was amusing while Anderson was performing a solo dance number in a large courtyard set that was surrounded, for some obscure reason, by a collection of live zoo animals in cages. The *Los Angeles Times* reported the incident as "Dance-Minded Chimp Will Appear in Film":

> Some of the most unusual scenes in motion pictures happen by accident. Scene: the country estate set of an English gentleman, which boasts a private zoo and aviary. Eddie Anderson, erstwhile Rochester and valet to Jack Benny in "Man About Town" at the Paramount studio, is performing a comedy dance routine. Mark Sandrich, director, is suddenly attracted to an offstage scene which is going on while the cameras are recording the dance. A big chimpanzee in a cage is not only jumping up and down, but he is keeping time to the rhythm of the swing band which is playing, in a dance of his own. The director ordered another take and the simian did it again. Yesterday Sandrich shot a scene of the dance-minded chimpanzee doing his stuff. And it should be one of the best laugh scenes in *Man About Town*.[73]

It is difficult to watch this movie scene today and not think that Anderson and the animal are being paired, and that it seems denigrating. Perhaps the scene was understood by others at the time differently—some spectators might have been so enthralled with Anderson's dancing that they hardly noticed the background commotion, and others, whose prejudiced sensibilities might have been rankled by the visible equality of Benny and Anderson in their co-starring scenes together, might have been mollified to see Anderson's stardom undercut by a chimp imitating him.

Man About Town, a lightweight film, was far funnier and fresher than anyone had anticipated. Benny and Anderson had more screen time together than any nearly any other black and white actors had performed in Hollywood film. Their radio relationship seemed even closer when vividly portrayed on the screen with an easy informality. Anderson got a chance to shine, throughout the film, with excellent timing in his comic banter, and a lively, engaging performance as actor, dancer, and singer. The film's press book touted a new star, as if Anderson had never appeared in movies before:

> It has Rochester—who must be given special mention because it the screen debut of Benny's famed radio stooge—and what a debut! Rochester (Eddie Anderson) has delighted millions on the air—and he'll have your patrons flat on their backs in the aisle, both with his straight comedy role and with his hysterically comic dance routines.[74]

Man About Town received an extraordinary level of intermedia promotion at its June 1939 premiere. Paramount Studios, radio sponsor Jell-O, Young & Rubicam, and the NBC network all contributed to a massive premiere and celebration held in Jack Benny's hometown of Waukegan. While the elaborate festivities were all supposed to honor Jack Benny the film and radio star, Eddie Anderson and the Rochester character were celebrated as co-stars. Anderson was given nearly as many special awards, keys to the city, and fireman and policeman's badges as hometown hero Jack Benny. No other African American media star had received a reception like this outside of Bill "Bojangles" Robinson's fetes in Harlem. The promotional week in Waukegan involved parades, speeches, and special awards dinners. Over 100,000 people flooded the streets of the gritty northern Illinois town and a thousand policemen were required to keep order.

Reviews of *Man About Town* in the trade press and newspapers across the country reacted with surprise to the humor and sprightliness of the film, and to the raucous reception it received from audiences. Moviegoers were delighted with Anderson's performance, white and black, Northern and Southern. New York's *Cue* magazine was taken aback:

Brightest star in the picture is, oddly enough, not Benny but the ebony-hued, sand-paper voiced, irrepressibly funny man-stooge, Eddie Anderson. Eddie is the handy man-valet known on the Benny radio program as Rochester. In *Man About Town*, Benny has generously afforded Rochester plenty of footage, lines, dances, songs, close-ups and pricelessly funny gags, giving him the cinematic opportunity of his life—and Rochester responds nobly.[75]

Even one of the deans of the New York film reviewing community, Howard Barnes of the *New York Herald Tribune*, found something nearly utopian in the possibilities for representation of black people, after seeing *Man About Town*.[76] He excoriated Hollywood for "foolishly ignor[ing]" talented black dramatic performers in the past, and saw a glimpse of something new in this film: "Anderson's Rochester was obviously designed as nothing more than a foil for his [Benny's] wise cracks and antics. And yet you are likely to come away from the picture remembering the colored player's laugh-provoking and versatile performance as vividly or more vividly than the star's."

After his prominent role in *Man About Town*, the African American press detailed Anderson's burgeoning fame in mainstream white popular culture. The *Defender, California Eagle, New Amsterdam News, Atlanta Daily World, Baltimore Afro-American*, and others published large spreads of photographs, interviews with Anderson, biographical sketches, and praise for the film.[77] Black movie theaters both across the segregated South and in the North advertised the film featuring Rochester's name as starring over Benny's, and many white theaters listed Benny and Rochester on their marquees as co-stars. Anderson spent the summer of 1939 on a triumphant tour of leading black entertainment venues in Chicago and New York and a lucrative series of headlined engagements at major theaters across the nation before the fall radio season began.

When the Jell-O radio show resumed broadcasting in October 1939, the program's narrative struggled to deal with Rochester's on-air, on-screen, and public fame, given that his radio character was supposed to be a private servant.[78] Paramount meanwhile rushed Benny and the radio cast into a new film to capitalize on their success, titled *Buck Benny Rides Again, (BBRA)* with Mark Sandrich again directing. Anderson, Don Wilson, Phil Harris, Dennis Day, Mary Livingstone, and Fred Allen would all contribute this time. Dialogue on the radio show revolved for weeks around the new film's production. In a December 1939 episode, Jack and Mary discussed the filming going on at Paramount, and Jack mentioned that Phil and Andy Devine would be appearing in the picture. "Did you leave anyone out?" Mary asked, in an opportunity to heckle him:

JACK: "Oh yeah ... Rochester is in the film, I forgot."
MARY: "You'll remember when it comes out."

Paramount mounted an elaborate promotional campaign for *BBRA* in April 1940, focusing nearly equally on Anderson and Benny. Paramount's press book for *BBRA* was awash in photos of Anderson (whom it identified only as Rochester), dancing, singing, wrangling Carmichael the polar bear, and interacting with Benny. The press book offered local theater managers a quarter-page newspaper photo spread of Rochester and Theresa Harris dancing, titled "Doing the Rochester Shuffle-Off." The Paramount publicity department declared, "This strip sequence of Eddie Rochester Anderson doing the 'Rochester Shuffle' should appeal equally to jitterbugs and followers of Fred Astaire. Rochester's' a natural space-stealer as well as a picture stealer. Plant this strip now!"[79]

Newspaper advertisements provided for the film prominently featured illustrations of Anderson along with Benny. In small ads, Rochester's face was paired with Carmichael the bear. The larger ads and theater posters linked Rochester to both Benny and to Fred Allen. Rochester was depicted, cigar dangling from his mouth, clinging to the top of a large cactus, holding a portable radio by its handle. Fred Allen's voice emerged in a text balloon from the radio, quipping, "Imagine that tenderfoot on a horse! If Benny ever gets on a jackass, you won't know who's riding who!" In a dialogue balloon, Rochester said "Mr. Allen sho' do say funny things." Benny, riding in the Maxwell, retorted, "Oh shut up, Rochester."

While this huge publicity buildup of Eddie Anderson was occurring, Hattie McDaniel had a much more contested reception surrounding the December 1939 premiere of *Gone with the Wind*. Jill Watts and Matthew Bernstein have documented the refusal of white Atlanta municipal authorities to allow McDaniel to publically participate in the world premiere of producer David O. Selznick's film in that deeply segregated Southern city.[80] Even though McDaniel was nominated for and won the Academy Award for Best Supporting Actress for her role, Southern whites did not want to celebrate her performance. Southern blacks rejected the film entirely for its depictions of racial attitudes, slavery, and the Confederacy. Even though

Anderson and McDaniel both portrayed servants in these films, popular understanding of their performances (and public reaction to their stardom) was impacted by a myriad of factors, highlighting the differences between historical melodrama and contemporary musical comedy, and the relationships of Jack and Rochester versus those of Mammy and Scarlett. While it is fascinating that Anderson could gain so much more public appreciation of his star performance, his success came at the price of seeming to be submerged in the role of what both racist whites and the black intelligentsia would label as "public clown."

So differently than what MGM had done in Atlanta, in April 1940 Paramount's publicity department mounted twin premieres of *Buck Benny Rides Again*, one at the flagship Paramount Theater in Manhattan (which broke all box office records for the first day's shows), and the night before, a huge celebration at the Loew's Victoria Theater in Harlem, a 2,400-seat picture palace located on 125th Street, adjacent to the Apollo Theater. The Harlem events received live radio coverage and extensive stories in the black and white press. "'Hollywood Goes to Harlem!' is the slogan adopted by Paramount for the first world premiere of a motion picture ever held in Harlem,"[81] the black press gleefully reported.

The *BBRA* premiere week in New York City was the highest point of Eddie Anderson's star career. It started with a ceremonial parade held in Harlem the Thursday before, when Anderson alighted at the 125th Street station to be greeted by area African American dignitaries. More than 3,000 people jammed the sidewalks to see the group parade up several blocks to the famous Theresa Hotel, with Anderson riding a large black stallion.[82] On Sunday evening, the Benny cast performed their radio show from the stage of the Ritz Theater. On Tuesday night, a huge parade brought Anderson, Benny, Sandrich, Benny cast members, Fred Allen, and New York entertainment celebrities to the Loew's Victoria Theater. Coverage was broadcast on radio station WHN. Crowds estimated at 150,000 filled the streets, 20,000 people gathering outside the Loew's Victoria to see the celebrities arrive. Three hundred city police on horseback kept pushing into the crowds, aggressively maintaining order.[83] A *New Amsterdam News* reporter maintained it was a bigger public event than Marcus Garvey's parades or even the welcome home reception for Jesse Owens returning triumphantly from the Olympics in Berlin.[84]

Inside the theater, with the local broadcast continuing, Willie Bryant acted as master of ceremonies on stage, Bill Robinson introduced dignitaries in the audience, Jack Benny and Rochester performed a skit on stage, and then Fred Allen spoke. The principals stayed to open the second screening, then everyone repaired to the Savoy Ballroom, where a huge testimonial reception was held to honor Anderson.[85] Everyone in Harlem society was there—including Ella Fitzgerald, Louis Armstrong, Bill Robinson, Ethel Waters, Jules Bledsoe, city dignitaries, and prominent African Americans in city and state government, the police and fire services, and the military.

Reviews of Anderson's performance in *BBRA* were uniformly laudatory, although some articles in the mainstream white press twisted things around to give most of the credit for Rochester's role to Benny, and a few betrayed deeply held racial attitudes. The *New York Showman's Trade Review* reported that Rochester

> smashes through to the spotlight on several counts. For one, he sings "My My" especially written for him, in a voice as charming and soothing as a cement mixer. He displays an amazingly delicate talent as a dancer and he tops the Benny gags with something funnier at every shot made by the master. It is with a spirit of bland generosity that Benny steps back and lets Rochester have the spot, for while he sacrifices himself as an actor, he proves himself tops as a showman.[86]

The *New York Herald Tribune*'s critic Howard Barnes, who had waxed eloquently about Anderson in *Man About Town*, joined the chorus of appalled serious film critics who excoriated this film for being so radio-focused and uncinematic. On the other hand, he was delighted at the opportunity that black performers had been given: "Once more he [Anderson] and Miss Harris demonstrate that the photoplay is a natural medium for Negro performers and that they should have a bigger hand in its exploits."[87]

The impact of Anderson's and Benny's unusual position as interracial co-stars in a Hollywood film contributed to fascinating little moments of possibility in the black community's popular imagination. In fall 1939, Dr. Benjamin Mays assumed the presidency of Morehouse College, the prestigious all-male undergraduate component of Atlanta University. The college faced dire financial challenges, which Mays addressed by careful fiscal budgeting and much more strictly enforcing payment of tuition bills by the students. By spring of that school year, just as *BBRA* was playing in both Atlanta's segregated black and white movie theaters, Morehouse students started to kiddingly call Dr. Mays "Buck Benny," to honor his frugality. The nickname stuck. For the rest of his career, students, faculty, staff, and alumni affectionately used it. Yet as the years rolled on, this utopian interracial moment faded, and everyone forgot about the movie. Students still called Dr. Mays "Buck Benny," but no one could remember where it came from.

Other African Americans optimistically appreciated what this film and the hoopla surrounding it could possibly mean for a movement toward loosening of racial boundaries and amelioration of inequalities in the entertainment world. A letter to the editor of the *Chicago Defender* noted:

> Dear Editor: I take this means of congratulating Eddie "Rochester" Anderson for his splendid work in *Buck Benny Rides Again*. There has been much favorable comment from the white people of this town. They say it was really Rochester's picture and they seem to have enjoyed it much more than some other pictures. I know it was much better than some I have seen similar to this one. Two of the pictures I may name were *Imitation of Life* and *Gone with the Wind*. Both of these were outstanding pictures, but somehow *Buck Benny Rides Again* seems to bring about the good will between the white and colored races which has been and is being fought for so vigorously by a people who are approaching the shouldering of arms for a flag and country they have not the privilege of serving sincerely. I feel we should not overlook any opportunity to encourage our people. I sincerely hope all colored people who have not seen this picture will do so at their first opportunity.
>
> S. Springfield 503 Fifth Street, Coffeyville, Kansas[88]

During the week after the big celebrations in New York, Anderson flew up to Boston. He'd been invited to be guest of honor and entertainer at a Harvard Freshman "smoker," a big stage show that was also to feature Cab Calloway's band. En route to Boston by airplane, he was intercepted at a layover in Providence by a group of MIT students masquerading as his Harvard hosts. They "kidnapped" Anderson, drove him to Cambridge, and kept him sequestered in their fraternity house for several hours, before finally taking him to his scheduled performance (in a motorcade of twenty-five cars) over at Harvard. After the show, in the early hours of the morning, a full-fledged riot ensued between the rival university students, complete with sixty policemen called in, punches thrown at students, water balloons tossed at the cops, false fire alarms set off, traffic snarled in Harvard Square, and eight Harvard students arrested.[89] Entertainment industry people shook their heads in wonder, marveling that no producer could buy such great publicity that Paramount had just gotten for free. The next evening, Anderson, in connection with the opening of *BBRA* at the Metropolitan Theater, was greeted by a crowd of 10,000 (Boston's black population predominating) who lined a torch-lit parade through the South End to a special reception at a restaurant on

Tremont Street, where Anderson was made an honorary member of the fire department and was feted by the leaders of Boston's black community.[90]

UTOPIAN RACIAL HOPES, AND ANDERSON'S CAREER IN HIGH GEAR

In 1940 and 1941, Eddie Anderson found prominence everywhere at the national level—in radio, film, and stage appearances, and in the press. He garnered film awards from the black community. The Sepia Theatrical Writers Guild, a West Coast newspaper writers group, named him comic male star of the year for *Man About Town*.[91] The NAACP's California branch honored Anderson and Theresa Harris for their work in *BBRA*.[92] In Los Angeles, Anderson won the honorary title of "Mayor of Central Avenue." The role was not merely ceremonial: the "mayor" acted as a private intermediary with the Los Angeles mayor and police departments, trying to stem the brutal treatment that black Angelenos received at the hands of the city's cops.

The success of Eddie Anderson's co-starred films with Jack Benny fueled optimistic hopes in the black press that prejudiced racial attitudes could be softening in the white South. Rochester was hopefully opening a wedge to destroy the old myths that racist Southern whites refused to watch or listen to black performers, the myths to which film and radio producers so stubbornly clung. *Pittsburgh Courier* film editor Earl J. Morris lauded Anderson as a "goodwill ambassador" bringing a message of respectability and equality to whites in Hollywood and across the nation.[93] On screen he was *not* an "insolent, ignorant Negro ... his lines contain witty wisdom" and he was "sagacious":

> Eddie "Rochester" Anderson is Public Valet No.1. He is the patron to the colored domestic workers throughout these United States. "Rochester," diminutive prince of pantomime and comedy king, is the "Little Napoleon" of the vast empire of colored domestic servants. "Rochester" and Jack Benny have improved the lot of maids, cooks, butlers, valets and what have you. They show their appreciation to this stellar comedy team in every way that they can. About three million maids, cooks, butlers, et cetera, serve as many families "the delicious flavors" and make them like it. And the Negro motion picture audience turns out en masse to see the comic antics of this pair on the screen.

FIGURE 13. By the 1940s, Eddie Anderson had become the most prominent African American star in Hollywood, and tourists sent home postcards of his elegant home. Circa 1942. Author's collection.

Anderson and Benny both received nationwide press coverage in spring 1941 for being chosen among a dozen recipients of citations from the New York City–based Schomburg Center for its Honor Roll in Race Relations for 1940. The Schomburg's director, Dr. Lawrence Reddick, saluted a dozen African Americans and six whites "who had done the most for the improvement of race relations 'in terms of a real democracy.'" The center honored "Eddie Anderson, better known as Rochester, for his Harlem premiere of *Buck Benny Rides Again* and for his Sunday evening performances with his fellow-comedian Jack Benny" and "Jack Benny, for recognizing dramatic talent irrespective of color. His fellow comedian Rochester is cast in roles that are neither personally humiliating nor indirectly derogatory to the Negro people."[94]

With war looming closer, and the importance of black workers to the U.S. war effort becoming more widely recognized, a better share of equality for African Americans became a prominent topic in the black community, and also among leaders in Washington. Within the continuing climate of tendentious race relations, some members of the African American community were gaining hope. There was potential for black workers to get better jobs, and anticipation that black performers in film and radio could get more prominent and respectable roles.

Eddie Anderson's stardom positioned him to represent the optimistic hope that perhaps race relations and opportunities for blacks were improving. The terrible and hurtful representations of blacks in the mass media of the past could finally be put aside. The *California Eagle* voiced these hopes in an editorial titled "Rochester, The New Day."[95] It claimed that after twenty-five years of dreadful representation in American mass media,

> two years ago America became conscious of a new thought in Negro comedy. It was really a revolution, for Jack Benny's impudent butler-valet-chauffer, "Rochester Van Jones" said all the things which a fifty year tradition of the stage proclaimed that American audiences will not accept from a black man. Time and again, "Rochester" outwitted his employer, and the nation's radio audiences rocked with mirth. Finally, "Rochester' appeared with "Mistah Benny" in a motion picture—a picture in which he consumed just as much footage as the star. The nation's movie audiences rocked with mirth. So, it may well be that "Rochester" has given colored entertainers a new day and a new dignity on screen and radio.

. . .

In April 1941, editors in the African American press could celebrate the hopeful aspects of not only Eddie Anderson's performances but also his character of Rochester—created by white writers for mainstream network radio programs and Hollywood films. The worst of the minstrel stereotypes with which Rochester had been saddled in his early appearances on Benny's radio show had receded. Through the narrative device of Jack Benny's radio show, in which all the characters he interacted with irritated him, insulted him, disparaged and undercut Jack's patriarchal authority, the Rochester character was able to voice something new in American media—a black man who could talk back to a white man. Rochester's retorts, jibes, and criticisms were very mild, to be sure, and constrained by cultural ideas of the "proper" mode of address and social place across the racial divide. So he was (except for the boxing incident) inoffensive to the most conservative white listeners. But Rochester had a voice—on nationwide, primetime network radio. With his talent, Anderson brought to that voice a distinctiveness and individuality, aided by scriptwriters who gave him wryly humorous lines of dialogue. Anderson became even more visible in American popular culture through several film appearances with Jack Benny in their Paramount musicals. Rochester brought high ratings to Benny's radio program and box office success to his films. Working as a member of Benny's ensemble provided Anderson a way to expand a stereotyped role into a popular individual character that amused both white and black audiences. Optimists anxious to see further racial inclusion hoped that perhaps it was "A New Day."

The next chapter shows how tenuous and fragile were the film industry's attempts to expand and cash in on the popularity of Anderson and this partial-integrationist ideal. Cultural and political battles of the wartime years over civil rights would throw monkey wrenches into the plans of both white media and black performers to continue the positive representations of 1941. With the rising tide of expectations within the African American community for equality, a new generation of cultural critics would claim that Rochester, and Anderson, were no longer symbols of hope but deficient remnants of an old order that must be replaced. How Anderson, and Benny's radio program, dealt with these challenges, follows.

FIVE

Rochester and the Revenge of Uncle Tom in the 1940s and 1950s

By 1941, after four years on the radio with Jack Benny, playing the sly comic servant Rochester, and three films at Paramount in which he and Benny practically co-starred, Eddie Anderson had achieved unprecedented levels of popularity in mainstream American media and broken new ground for interracial acceptance. Hopes in the African American community were high that Anderson's success was the harbinger of a new era of increased opportunities and recognition for black performers. Despite the occasional lapses into stereotypical minstrel show–type behavior with which Benny's radio writers still saddled Rochester, Anderson used his unique voice, wit, intelligence, and great sense of comic timing to transform the role of valet, butler, housekeeper, and chauffeur into a complex, very human character. With the start of World War II and the government's efforts to promote racial tolerance and greater inclusion of African Americans in the labor force and military, Anderson's professional prospects expanded further, as he served as a useful spokesman for those ideals. He was now a big star, with a multifaceted career that spanned movies, radio, musical shows that toured the country, and recordings of novelty songs, with every indication that it would only continue to grow. Anderson was offered a major role in an all-black-cast film at MGM, and minor but prominent roles in other Hollywood films.

Massive cross-over success almost coalesced for Anderson. But then, unanticipated events and complex cultural change conspired to heap as much criticism as praise upon his head. Accusations that Rochester was an "Uncle Tom" rose from black critics on the one hand, and objections to his egalitarian relationships with whites erupted from white racists on the other.[1] To be acceptable to whites, Anderson, like other veteran black performers who tried so hard to carve out careers in movies and radio—such as Hattie

McDaniel, Ethel Waters, Louise Beavers, and Clarence Muse—had to make many compromises with which liberal critics were increasingly dissatisfied. Benny and his writers further moderated Rochester's disreputable habits during the war years, but unfortunately, again and again, the limitations of their ability to permanently change their own racial attitudes when writing scripts set off uproars within the black community.

In his history of African American culture in Los Angeles in the 1940s, R.J. Smith describes the ambivalence that black listeners experienced when they heard Rochester on the radio—"every appearance on the Benny show was likely to simultaneously further and undermine stereotypes."[2] Much of the racialized humor on the program was old and stereotypical, black audiences judged, but there was nevertheless something new in Rochester's relationship with Jack. Rochester called his employer the more informal "Boss" rather than "Sir." Jack was far more often the butt of the jokes than Rochester. Rochester could give voice to criticisms of Jack, mock him, and make numerous complaints about his never-ending duties and lack of pay, yet he was never punished. Rochester, more than the other servant characters in broadcasting and film, was authentically black. Even if this only meant carousing through Los Angeles's Central Avenue and Harlem, Rochester had a life outside of working for "the Boss." "It was this license to speak openly that made Rochester a hero on Central Avenue," Smith concludes.[3]

This chapter chronicles the difficulties Anderson faced in the 1940s, when often-simultaneous eruptions of white racism on the one hand, and black criticism on the other made his career more challenging than ever to negotiate. Even while Anderson prospered in the Rochester role and created superb comic repartee with Benny, cracks in the utopian vision of interracial stardom appeared, and compromises on all sides came hand in hand with success. Anderson was the most prominent and highest paid black performer on primetime network radio, but too often he still had to make jokes about craps shooting, and enact minstrel show behaviors. He landed a role in a prestigious film, 20th Century Fox's *Tales of Manhattan*, but then faced backlash from a new generation of black critics who disdainfully charged him with being an Uncle Tom. Anderson's leading part in the MGM film *Cabin in the Sky* was a hopeful sign of increased media stardom for black performers, but race riots in the summer of 1943 placed a damper on movie theater managers' desires to showcase them. Southern backlash against his appearances in mixed-race films made Hollywood film producers even more skittish of working with him.

In the postwar period, Anderson faced mounting approbation from critics who decried the prevalence of accommodating and buffoonish servant roles in the media and lumped Rochester among them. On Benny's radio show, as the writers placed Jack in domestic situations and adventures outside the radio studio, he was brought into even closer contact with Rochester, and their relationship became, as historian Joseph Boskin noted, "extraordinary in its depth and sensitivity" and something "far beyond the typical employer-employee association."[4] Nevertheless, in 1950, Anderson would face outrage in the black community over the broadcast of a Benny radio episode awash in creaky old examples of Rochester's Harlem debauchery, and frustration in trying to start a radio program of his own.

ANDERSON'S PRECARIOUS PERCH BETWEEN BLACK AND WHITE WORLDS

Articles about Anderson in both the black and white press in the early 1940s dwelt on his economic and social success. They emphasized his lavish spending on cigars, clothes, a large house, cars, a boat, and race horses, one of which, "Burnt Cork," he entered in the Kentucky Derby. The tenor of articles in the black press was prideful in these public displays of wealth. In the white press, stories betrayed more ambivalence that he might be appearing to act "above his station." Reporter Earl Morris argued in a *Pittsburgh Courier* story that it was politically purposeful for Anderson to ostentatiously wear good clothes and drive fine cars; through his efforts, whites might now better tolerate black people's economic success and increased participation in consumer culture. "He has subtly injected racial propaganda, been a sort of good will ambassador for his minority."[5]

The price of fame in mainstream white American culture for an African American actor was enduring the many humiliations imposed on him, intentionally and unintentionally, by insensitive writers. In 1943, Anderson was one of the rare black celebrities to be the subject of a feature article in the *Saturday Evening Post*, one of America's most widely read magazines.[6] Author Florabel Muir patronizingly looked down her nose, sniffing that the suit Eddie wore was rumpled and that his pretentious twelve-room mansion located near Central Avenue was an exact copy of Benny's house in Beverly Hills. A feature article on Anderson in the fan magazine *Radio Mirror* described him as "the eye-rolling eight ball."[7] Both black and white newspapers also downplayed Anderson's talent and instead emphasized the debt that he owed to Benny for his fame. An *Atlanta Daily World* article by Ruby Berkeley Goodwin maintained:

> Rochester, through the generosity of Jack Benny, was lifted from obscurity to stardom. I don't mean that Rochester can't stand on his own feet as a comedian. He can! But not in another fifty years will you find a man like Benny who will act as a stooge for Rochester.... I have nothing but the highest praise for Jack Benny. He doesn't talk Americanism—HE LIVES IT![8]

The black press emphasized the friendly, egalitarian nature of Anderson's relationship with Jack Benny, in radio, films, and in real life, and Rochester's ability to critique his employer's actions with an attitude of equality that no other black character in film or radio was allowed to express.[9] "Jack Benny and Rochester are what, in the old days of vaudeville, would have been called a team," asserted the *New Amsterdam News* in 1943:

> The relationship between Rochester and Benny is both classic (deriving from Carlyle) and democratic, in the American sense. Although Benny is no hero to his valet, neither is he a villain. And if Rochester, the gentleman's gentleman, isn't much of a help, neither is he a very serious hindrance. So, in effect the arrangement is a nice cozy one, in which the distinction between master and servant is practically non-existent.[10]

The article concluded, "The professional relationship between Benny and Rochester is a landmark in the history of the entertainment world, and a tribute to Benny's astuteness."[11]

Benny's radio show even occasionally acknowledged how central Rochester was to the program's popularity, such as on the April 2, 1944, program, when Jack was being interviewed for a story by Hollywood gossip columnist Louella Parsons. The rest of the cast used Rochester's popularity as a way to puncture Jack's overblown sense of his own talent:[12]

LOUELLA: How long have you been in radio?

JACK: Thirteen years.

LOUELLA: And of those thirteen years, how long would you say you've been a star?

JACK: Seven years.

LOUELLA: And how long has Rochester been with you?

FIGURE 14. Eddie Anderson and Jack Benny parlayed their radio popularity into film successes. They were promoted as the first interracial buddies in American movies in the early 1940s, co-starring in Paramount films *Man About Town*, *Buck Benny Rides Again*, and *Love Thy Neighbor*. *Movie Radio Guide*, December 20, 1941. Author's collection.

MARY (BREAKS IN, ARCHLY): Seven years.

JACK: Yes, he's a wonderful butler.

PHIL: He's pretty good on the radio, too.

JACK: Once in a while I let him take a line when I'm short an actor.

Despite utopian hopes in the black community that Jack Benny was a race relations hero, as Benny was honored with awards in 1941 for promoting interracial understanding and expanding opportunities for black performers, it was nevertheless still easy for him and his writers to slip into old attitudes. Puzzling out Rochester's place in white-dominated society in a way that would provoke laughter from studio audiences and mainstream radio listeners, Benny and his writers thoughtlessly incorporated older racialized humor into the program that struck ambivalent notes about the idea of interracial progress. The writers occasionally incorporated blackface jokes into the show. Even in these scripted situations, Rochester was able to resist having to perform blackface routines and to argue that minstrelsy was no longer acceptable to him or the black community. On the February 11, 1940, program, Jack and the radio cast took a long automobile trip in the old Maxwell, traveling from San Francisco to Yosemite for a skiing vacation. While Rochester was driving them along, Jack required him to sing to provide some entertainment because the car lacked a radio. Rochester complained to Mary:

ROCHESTER: At eight o'clock, he wants me to imitate Amos and Andy!
JACK: Well?
ROCHESTER: I can't do that blackface stuff!
JACK: You can try, you don't have to be perfect. . . .

On the March 29, 1942, program, Jack led the cast in putting on an abbreviated version of an "old-fashioned" minstrel show.[13] The cast joked about the burnt cork they would be wearing (and Rochester joked that he spent his make-up allowance on a bottle of gin with a cork in it). Unexplained raucous laughter erupted from the studio audience when Anderson came to the microphone; it could be that either he wore a costume or signaled by a gesture that he thought the performances absurd. Rochester did not have to take part in the ritualized minstrel humor, but was given a stand-alone feature role, singing "Somebody Else, Not Me," a comic ballad made famous by Ziegfeld Follies entertainer Bert Williams.[14] In one of the final references to blackface on the Benny radio show, on the February 27, 1944, program, Jack and the cast talked about seeing Al Jolson down on his knees, participating in a dice game. Jack compared Jolson to Rochester, remarking that they were just alike. Rochester retorted, "But after it rains, I'm still Rochester." Such lapses of racial sensitivity would continue to sporadically erupt on the Benny show in the coming years, bringing increasingly strident complaints from black critics.

THE *TALES OF MANHATTAN* CONTROVERSY

His reputation in Hollywood having risen after his success in the three Paramount films, Anderson was offered several visible (if small) film roles that blurred the boundaries between his radio character and his identity as a media star. He appeared as the chauffeur in *Topper Returns* (Hal Roach Studio, 1941) with Joan Blondell and Roland Young and was pictured in the poster and lobby card advertising. He played a dancer in the Mary Martin–Don Ameche backstage comedy *Kiss the Boys Goodbye* (Paramount, 1941). In the variety show film *Star Spangled Rhythm* (Paramount, 1942), he danced and sang in a "zoot suit" specialty number. Through his popularity on the Benny radio show, Eddie Anderson also received invitations to make guest appearances on other broadcasting comics' programs. Nearly all his roles limited him to the character of Rochester, however. He appeared on Fred Allen's program in 1940, interviewed as Rochester on the "people you are unlikely to meet" segment, and Allen egged him on to tell secrets about Benny's cheapness. He was on the Eddie Cantor program on June 24, 1942, in an episode noted by the *Defender*'s Harold Jovien as among best of the year.[15] His guest appearance on *Duffy's Tavern* in January 1943 was highly anticipated in the black press as a rare occasion for Rochester to trade quips with Eddie Green's character of the black waiter, who was the only sane employee of that crazy establishment.[16]

In early 1942, Anderson landed a plum role, a part playing alongside Paul Robeson and Ethel Waters in a film production that featured a dozen prominent Hollywood actors, 20th Century Fox's *Tales of Manhattan*. The anthology film's plot concerned an actor's tuxedo jacket, supposedly cursed, which fell into the hands of four different owners. In the final sequence, the tattered coat was tossed out of an airplane by gangsters. It landed in a Southern sharecropper's field. Impoverished, naïve, and deeply religious farmers Paul Robeson and Ethel Waters, along with other laborers (played by members of the Hall-Johnson Choir), took the coat to their preacher (Eddie Anderson), and they found its pockets stuffed with $50,000 in cash. They collectively decided use the heaven-sent gift to purchase their farmland. The black characters were very stereotypically drawn, but the film was touted during its production as being quite prestigious, and it premiered to admiring reviews.[17]

When the film began playing a preview engagement in Los Angeles, however, on August 7, 1942, a group of ten young black journalists, led by *Los Angeles Sentinel* publisher Leon H. Washington Jr. and *Los Angeles Tribune* editor Almena Davis, picketed outside Loew's State Theater. They marched with banners that shamed Robeson, Anderson, and the other black actors for appearing in the film, and claimed the closing scene was "fraught with 'Uncle Tommism.'" The *Defender* reported that "members of the picketing committee stated the move against the picture was part of a general movement to discourage the making of pictures which obviously hold the Negro character up to ridicule and burlesque."[18]

A front page essay by young *California Eagle* editor John Kinlock, published the same week as the picketing, railed against the prevalence of Uncle Tom characters in mainstream white media:

> Ofays [slang term for whites] and people like that enjoy to consider Uncle Tom with their eyes slightly misty with crocodile tears and assorted cracks about the inhumanity of mankind during the lamentable period of slavery.... He is the kind of person who is always playing Jack Benny to some peck's Rochester. He probably disseminates more affirmatives in one afternoon than the whole motion picture industry in the course of six months, which is saying a great deal, indeed. Once upon a time, Uncle Tom was an ancient character with little intelligence except an uncanny insight into what the Boss Man wanted him to do-say-or-think at any given time. The type of Joe who might utter "You sho' is one GOOD white man, and kick me some mo' please, suh, and sho' laks you' boot toe."

Kinlock broadly charged all black performers who worked in Hollywood films and Los Angeles night clubs with enacting the new version of "streamlined Uncle Thomas."[19]

The Hollywood black establishment was horrified at this public eruption of intragroup conflict and criticism. Rumors spread around town, to film producers and studio executives, that it was the actors themselves who had done the picketing.[20] Eddie Anderson secretly gathered a group of the top black performers together to draft a statement distancing themselves from the protest.[21] Uncle Tom charges continued to spread in the black press, however. A letter to the editor of the *Defender* from a Chicago reader queried in early September: "Why must Rochester, Sunshine Sammy and a few more of our male Negro actors continue to play right into the white man's hands? Don't these fellows realize that the parts they play are doing serious harm to their race? Their roles are used to depict the Negro's lack of initiative, both mental and physical."[22]

Walter White, national secretary of the NAACP, in February 1942 made a well-publicized trip to Hollywood to meet with studio executives, but not the established black actors, to advocate for more dignified representations of blacks on screen. White recommended the employment of new "serious" actors (like his protégé Lena Horne) who would forge new ground by refusing to play roles as servants and comic clowns.[23] White issued statements from the New York NAACP offices supporting the *Tales* protests. Anderson and other members of the black acting community were frustrated at White's neglect of their input and advice. The veterans claimed that these agitators from outside the acting community—the militant members of the black press and the NAACP leadership—were not supporting them, but trying to undermine their efforts, and replace them with other actors.[24] The veteran actors worried that if they stood up and loudly protested, their careers would be affected, so they were reluctant to say negative things in public about the studio system.

In September 1942, the black performers released a further elaboration of their response to the *Tales* picketing, making public some of their behind-the-scenes efforts over the years to improve conditions for blacks in the film industry. "Colored actors themselves, without the aid of outsiders, have broken down former practices of segregated dressing rooms, studio cafes, washrooms and rest rooms, and accompanying signs that once were common, such as for 'colored men' or for 'colored women.' A large square black screen used by camera crews, formerly called the 'n—r' is now called the 'gobo'."[25] Their statement detailed several of the most painful instances of racial insensitivity in film productions that they had been able to thwart in recent years:

> Clarence Muse objected to the Nat Turner-like leader of a slave rebellion in Paramount's *So Red the Rose*, [1935] humbly repenting and kissing the hem of his mistress's dress. Director King Vidor said "All right Clarence, you rewrite that sequence yourself tonight, and we'll shoot it tomorrow," and it was done, while Margaret Sullavan the star got bawled out for objecting. Take *Imitation of Life* [1934] which catapulted Louise Beavers to fame. Although she was then an unknown, she told the Universal studio officials during a story conference that her people hated the word "n—r" which ran freely all through the screen story. Out it came, and the word "black" was substituted by director John Stahl. And then believe it or not, their eyes having been opened, they cut a whole sequence that depicted a near-lynching when Peola, pretending to be white, accused a young colored man of attempting to flirt with her. Just as they have strung him up, she breaks down with remorse and screams "Don't do it, I'm a 'n—r' too"!

The actors' catalogue of film production horrors climaxed with an incident involving the pair that readers might have been least likely to expect—

Anderson, on the set at 20th Century Fox, where he was shooting the film *The Meanest Man in the World*, with Jack Benny:

> There was a scene where Rochester was to be hidden in a woodpile. Benny was to call, "Rochester, come out of that woodpile." But the famous comedian [Anderson] quietly explained that the inference of the old saying "n—r in the woodpile" would bring a laugh for the whites, but indignation from colored movie fans. "Yes he's right, Eddie's right," said Jack Benny to the director, "better take it out."[26]

The veteran actors claimed that their efforts had been going on long before Walter White began agitating for better representation of blacks in Hollywood films. The group claimed to be glad for his assistance, but more ambivalent about his lack of support for the actors who were already in the business. The black actors who had footholds in Hollywood were upset at being criticized for taking the roles; they claimed they would gladly play parts as bank presidents, but until Hollywood screenwriting and casting changed, or a black consortium could establish an alternative film studio, the actors were going to have to play the roles that existed, or see all black characters disappear from American films. Walter White did finally acknowledge some of the actors' concerns, as he retold Anderson's "woodpile" anecdote in one of his newspaper columns. Nevertheless the NAACP executive would continue to rail against the black community's acquiescence to the status quo in Hollywood.[27]

Meanwhile, Anderson also had to negotiate his role as an entertainment industry spokesman for the U.S. war effort to the African American public. There was widespread dissatisfaction in the black community over the irony of being asked to fight fascism and racial oppression overseas when they were treated as second-class citizens in their own country. To win over a skeptical black population (and smooth tense race relations with whites), the government's Office of War Information used black celebrities to make persuasive pitches to support the war effort. Like other stars, Anderson was regularly asked to volunteer to give radio speeches and make personal appearances at war bond sales rallies. On March 30, 1941, Anderson took part in a special broadcast put on by the National Urban League to encourage racial fairness in hiring practices in defense industry jobs in "The Negro and National Defense," broadcast over the CBS network. His speech, which he presented as if Rochester was giving a "practice run" of it privately to the "Boss," was geared to persuade doubtful whites of their paternalistic responsibility to deal fairly with the black community:

It seems to me that Mr. and Mrs. America have been so busy in this great program of national defense that they sorta overlooked one of their children. One who has always been a great fighter—loyal, conscientious, and willing to do his bit at all times. It seems that this child is having a little trouble convincing the principals and teachers of this great defense program that he should be in there too and that he could come with flying colors if only given a chance to. He knows that he is a Negro and is glad to be. But first of all, he is an American, so let him be an American. . . . They have scientists, inventors, philosophers, machinists, mechanics—and that's something like me at the house, eh Mr. Benny? In fact they have almost every other skill that is known to man. . . . I realize the whole thing is just an oversight and I know that Mr. and Mrs. America have been so busy that they kinda overlooked the one son that they can put up against the wheel and rest assured that nobody can tell him anything else but push. So, Mr. and Mrs. America, give this child of yours a chance to make you just as proud of him today as you've always been in the past.[28]

Anderson's popularity with white audiences made him a nonthreatening spokesman for black rights, historian Barbara Savage notes. By presenting his message in an entertaining way, he might have caught the ears of listeners who might otherwise tune out serious policy discussions. Response to the Anderson program in newspapers across the nation was very positive.

During the war, Anderson remained active in support for soldiers and homefront activities. He appeared with Benny in special comic segments of "Command Performance" recorded by the Armed Forces Radio Service (AFRS) to entertain troops around the globe. He also a frequent guest star on the AFRS program "Jubilee," which featured skits and musical performances by black actors, singers, and orchestras.[29] Anderson joined the steering committee of the Negro Division of the Hollywood Victory Committee, organized and led by Hattie McDaniel, to provide entertainments for black soldiers.[30] In January 1944 he gave a show at Tuskegee Army Airfield.[31] Anderson also invested in a parachute-production factory in Southern California, which would be staffed by forty black workers.[32]

1943 – *CABIN IN THE SKY*, RACE RIOTS, AND BUTTERFLY MCQUEEN

In early 1943, Eddie Anderson signed a lucrative deal to appear in five upcoming films, earning $25,000 for each one. He was offered his largest role yet, in the MGM black-cast musical *Cabin in the Sky*, adapted from the Broadway musical, which two years before had featured Ethel Waters, Dooley Wilson, and Katherine Dunham.[33] Eddie took the lead male role of "Little Joe," while Ethel Waters repeated her role of Petunia and newcomer Lena Horne played temptress "Georgia Brown." Horne's film career was blossoming as she was also appearing in the 20th Century Fox black-cast musical *Stormy Weather* (co-starring Bill Robinson) which would be released two months after the April 1943 release of *Cabin in the Sky*.[34] Louis Armstrong, Rex Ingram, Butterfly McQueen, and other prominent actors also had small roles in the film.

The plot, a retelling of the Faust legend, opens with loose-living "Little Joe" getting shot over unpaid gambling debts. His devout wife Petunia prays for his soul. An angel and devil visit Little Joe and give him one more chance. The sensuous floozy Georgia Brown is sent up to seduce him, but Petunia's fervent entreaties to the Lord ultimately win the day. *Cabin in the Sky* (like *Stormy Weather*) presented mixed messages in attempting to answer critics' calls for better representations of blacks in film—it symbolized an increased black visibility in Hollywood film, but it was also filled with obvious stereotypes. Reviews of *Cabin* connected the film to the wartime government edict to attract more black workers to war production jobs to the unprecedented push to feature black performers in major film roles to serve as models of racial acceptance.[35] MGM placed large advertisements for the film in both the white and black press, predicting wide success for it across the nation. But the film seemed more like a religious-tinged folktale fantasy than a drama with any connections to the realities and challenges of contemporary black life.[36]

Appraisals of *Cabin in the Sky* in the black press were mixed. Some reviews emphasized the benefits to interracial understanding, pride in the visibility of the black actors and praise for their performances. *Los Angeles Tribune* critic Phil Carter approved of *Stormy Weather* but disliked *Cabin*, claiming "its ideology was certainly as bad or worse than the worst examples of Uncle Tommism of 20 years of screendom." *Defender* critic Rob Roy expressed frustration that Lena Horne flaunted the exposure of her undergarments while singing in the film, wishing that black actors could be allowed to act and be costumed in a more dignified fashion. He accused the film studios of playing down to Southern white expectations.[37]

The race riots that erupted in Los Angeles and Detroit in June 1943 and which spread across the nation to Mobile, Alabama; Beaumont, Texas; Harlem, and other places through the hot summer weeks, were due to racial tensions boiling over into violence, and not directly connected to release of these black-cast motion pictures. Tens of thousands of Latinos and African Americans had migrated to booming, overcrowded industrial cities in the North, Midwest, South, and West Coast. In Los Angeles, groups of young draftees, inebriated and bored while on weekend leave, encountered young Latino and black males wearing the extremely nonmilitary fashion of "zoot suits." Soldiers and sailors accosted the young men.[38] Clashes between young whites, blacks, and Latinos expanded into riots in Detroit and other cities as whites resented the blacks and immigrants who'd moved there to take war jobs, and the new migrants were frustrated with the racism and poor working and living conditions they continued to face. In three days of violence in Detroit, 34 people were killed, more than 400 injured, and property valued at $2 million was destroyed.[39]

In the midst of the race riots, from *Variety*'s entertainment-focused point of view, the expensive all-black musicals and interracial films that were being shown in urban centers were inevitably linked to the violence. The riots were occurring downtown in entertainment districts, and the big movie theaters were flash points for violence, or so writers in *Variety* feared. In June and July, *Variety*'s front page contained reports of the downtown damages and widespread closure of theaters, baseball parks, and other entertainment centers, and paired them with reassuring stories that *Cabin in the Sky* was drawing "extraordinary business" in the fifth week of its engagement at the Criterion theater on Broadway.[40] Yet on June 30, *Variety*'s headlines also warned, "Hollywood Holding up Pix Releases in Which Whites, Negroes Mix," fueling the fears of skittish film exhibitors and movie producers that these films were too controversial to play. "Many pictures with colored performers are being withdrawn from current release due to the race riots in various parts of the country," *Variety* noted. "Those films in which Negroes are shown mixing with whites are being pulled especially in Southern territories. Scenes showing whites and blacks on the dance floor in *Stage Door Canteen* are to be deleted through the South and other spots where feeling is running high. Likely also the Ethel Waters footage in that picture may be severely trimmed for Dixie screenings."[41]

Two weeks later, *Variety* reported that the film exhibition situation for these films had turned even grimmer, with local censors across the South "hacking scenes indiscriminately." Newsreel footage of black troops in battle, Cab Calloway's performance in *Sensations of 1945*, and Lena Horne's scenes in *Broadway Rhythm* were being excised in Memphis and other Southern cities.

The *Chicago Defender* substantiated some of the distressing stories about how the fallout from race riots and conservative Southern resistance was impacting the box office success of these films. "Think Race Riots Hurt Negro Films," proclaimed one worried observer:

> Loss of millions of hours in manpower in Detroit during the recent race riot will be nothing compared to the loss suffered by the motion picture industry, is the startling information that has come from reliable sources.... MGM's "Cabin in the Sky" was hailed as a sure money maker for theatres waiting their turn to play it, and encouraged by "Cabin's" success, 20th Century Fox's "Stormy Weather" was being eagerly awaited. But this feeling has changed, and there is fear that it will affect others on the market as well as several in production.[42]

In early August, a front page story in the *Defender* told of "an angry mob of white townspeople" in the small central Tennessee town of Mt. Pleasant who forced a theater manager to halt the showing of *Cabin* in a segregated theater that had been filled with white and blacks patrons, even though the exhibitor had checked with the police department before booking the film. Local interracial labor strife was cited by the theater manager as a contributing factor to the disturbance.[43] Reaction from prejudiced white Southerners had also been more severe than the film companies had anticipated. The skittish Hollywood studios began to pull back on their commitments to showcase black performers. The "Myth of the Southern Box Office" was alive and well, operating through fears and rumors. The studios were allergic to political controversies that would keep audiences away from the box office, and local theater managers were always anxious to compromise on the side of Jim Crow to keep racist elements of their audiences at bay.

Jack Benny returned to the air in September 1943 after his summer hiatus from broadcasting (during which time he traveled across North Africa, performing for soldiers with a small USO troupe). He faced difficult challenges with his radio program. His two writers for the previous seven years, Bill Morrow and Ed Beloin, had left the program. The show's narrative and ratings continued to drift downward into mediocrity. In order to inject some new energy into the program, Benny's new writers tapped into Anderson's tremendous success on the Benny radio program and in film to attempt to further expand African American roles on the program. Their ideas, however, did not blossom into a character with nearly as much comic potential or human interest as Rochester possessed. Thirty-two-year-old stage and film actress Butterfly McQueen was introduced on October 31, the fourth program of the fall season, playing a new character, Butterfly, who was introduced as Rochester's niece. On this first appearance Rochester brought her to the broadcast of the Benny radio program to sit in the audience with him and laugh loudly at Benny's lame jokes. McQueen used the high-pitched voice she had made famous in her role as Prissy in *Gone with the Wind*. On the Benny program, the writers made her character similar to Prissy—young, naïve, and not very smart. Butterfly asked stupid questions and prattled on about her boyfriend Jerome in the army, who kept misbehaving and running afoul of the military police. She did not reappear on the Benny program until late November, when Mary solicited Rochester's advice on who she could hire to be her maid, and he suggested that he could get Butterfly to work for her.

Butterfly McQueen appeared on the Benny show in the role as Mary's personal servant in every episode during December 1943. She was on three times in January, performing her duties ineptly and telling more tales about Jerome's exploits, then her spots tapered off to every other week in February and March. Having made fourteen appearances, McQueen quit the Benny program in late May, two weeks before the end of the season. McQueen's exit apparently was a surprise to Benny, who had rarely had an actor willingly walk away from the gravy train of association with his prominent program. In a legal document ending her contract, Benny maintained that the role had significantly boosted her career. He enjoined her from taking any similar part: "You are unwilling to continue to portray the role of a domestic servant of my radio program, although I have been and am desirous that you continue in that role . . . you will refrain from portraying a domestic servant on the radio for one year."[44] McQueen was diplomatic in talking of her time on the Benny show, once saying only that she "didn't care for it . . . They seem to like only very broad comedy."[45] "I don't mind playing maid parts occasionally," she told a reporter from *Ebony Magazine* in 1946, "but I feel that I would be disgracing my race by always accepting parts as a menial to be not only laughed at but looked down upon."[46]

McQueen perhaps had the last laugh, for she was able to land several other radio acting jobs that were better than "handkerchief roles," as she referred to those servant parts. She briefly appeared on the Dinah Shore program, and then she portrayed Thelma, the addlepated president of Danny Kaye's fan club, on Kaye's comedy-variety radio show. McQueen's part on this program was fulsomely praised by both *Variety* (which gave Kaye's program a special award for racial amity) and the black press, because the narrative never delineated whether the character was black or white.[47] In a 1976 *Washington Post* interview, McQueen claimed that she left Benny's show because she had been promised that her character would be Rochester's girlfriend, and therefore she was disappointed to end up merely as Mary Livingstone's maid.[48]

1945: ANDERSON'S ROLES CRITICIZED FROM ALL SIDES

During the war, Benny and his writers continued to struggle with the problem of how to create radio shows that would appeal to the military servicemen attending their live shows, while the NBC network broadcast the shows to home audiences who might not appreciate the jokes that resonated with soldiers, sailors, and airmen. When it came to crafting dialogue for Rochester away from the domestic setting of Jack's house, it too often seemed easiest for the writers to send Rochester on a spree. From Rochester's earliest days on the Benny program, the cast's trips to New York had presented radio script writers with the opportunity to have Rochester drink, carouse, womanize, and gamble with abandon in his favorite Harlem gin joints. Rochester's excesses were also ripe fodder for humor at camp shows. Benny and his radio writers also assumed that the excitement-starved men at military bases where they performed would want to hear randy stories of Rochester's louche behavior. But what Benny and his staff did not anticipate were the changing sensibilities of media and social critics in the black community, who demanded more than ever to have black characters in radio and films act like admirable citizens with positive racial representations. Comic material that was relatively acceptable on Benny's program in 1938 was increasingly deemed offensive in 1945.

After four shows broadcast from in and around New York City (where Rochester raucously partied in Harlem), the Benny cast was back on the road. Their February 11 broadcast was made from the naval air station in Glenview, Illinois. Halfway through the episode, Rochester called Benny on the telephone from St. Joseph, Missouri, where he'd journeyed ahead of the rest of the cast to prepare for the next week's program.

"Hello Mr. Benny, this is Rochester," Anderson said, to typically enthusiastic applause from the military audience. Rochester complained that he had encountered financial trouble on the train because Benny had cut his travel funds a little too close for the trip. Rochester explained the he had stopped to purchase a pack of gum at the train station, and weighed himself, and when he went to purchase his ticket, he was exactly six cents short.

JACK: Well, it's your own fault for spending money like that. What did you do then?

ROCHESTER: Well I got on the train anyway, and if it hadn't been for the extreme kindness of some sailors, I wouldn't have had enough money for my fare.

JACK: Why, did they lend it to you?

ROCHESTER: No, they faded me!

JACK: Rochester! Rochester! Do you mean that you started a craps game with some sailors?

ROCHESTER: Oh no, Boss! No! I didn't start it. You see, there were seven sailors standing around in a circle discussing Einstein's theory of relativity...

JACK: Uh huh...

ROCHESTER: Then someone dropped a pair of dice, and Einstein went A.W.O.L.

JACK: But Rochester, you didn't have to get in the game.

ROCHESTER: I know, but one of the boys said "Shoot," and even I couldn't refuse that call to battle stations.

The audience, primed to hear Benny and his cast make jokes geared to the male-dominated crowd of sailors and airmen, laughed heartily at this humor. And most white listeners at home across the nation may have thought it was relatively typical behavior for Rochester, nevertheless it was a type he had exhibited less frequently of late. Black listeners and critics, however, were very upset by the references to gambling and carousing, and more than ever before, they protested it publically. A year before, a *Chicago Defender* commentator had complained, "It's too bad that 'Rochester' comedian on Jack Benny's program has had to resort to Uncle Tom tactics to stay on that program... this columnist could not in the least appreciate his crap shooting skit on Sunday's program."[49] Now, however, that same critic sharply criticized the Benny program and Anderson in particular for his willingness to participate in humor that the critic found degrading:

> We are sick and tired of Eddie (Rochester) Anderson making a fool out of Negroes by portraying the part of a craps shooter on his weekly radio program with Jack Benny. It seems Rochester would have common sense enough to tell his script writers that Crap Shooting and similar buffoonery are not

typical of the better class of Negro citizens who are more concerned with winning the war than listening to clown tactics which he uses just to please white audiences.... If you disapprove of his crap shooting skits, write to Carl Stanton, 247 Park Ave NYC who handles the advertisements for Lucky Strike cigarettes.⁵⁰

Prominent radio writer Norman Corwin encouraged black listeners to collectively raise their voices against such stereotypical representations. "Negro entertainers should be educated. Pressure should be brought to bear against Rochester.... Phone the studio, write letters, publish editorials! Make your protests known. It avails nothing to resent quietly. Go after everything that is caricature, bad taste, incorrect even at the risk of being excessive in criticism." Corwin argued that most radio and film directors and writers created such offensive scenes as the ones on Benny's program out of "unthinking ... inherited ignorance," and not virulent racism, and so they could be educated.⁵¹ Corwin's critique, like others, blurred the lines between disgust with the way the Rochester character was written, and disdain for how Anderson portrayed him, which must have been painful for Anderson to read. The *Pittsburgh Courier* concurred with the critiques, and headlined an article "Negroes Object to Rochester's Crap Shooting on the Jack Benny Show":

> The continuous week after week involvement of Eddie "Rochester" Anderson, ace comedian on the Jack Benny radio show, in a crap shooting episode has stirred up a storm of protest amongst Negro listeners of the program on the West Coast. The matter has become the foremost topic of conversation by persons in all walks of life from the man on the street to milady in the drawing room. General opinion is that Anderson is too funny an actor and comedian to have to read such outmoded and stereotyped lines to draw laughs.⁵²

Anderson was not without his supporters in the black community. They claimed he was being unfairly saddled with blame for reading comic dialogue he did not write, about stereotypical faults that had been attributed to other groups. His old stage revue director Earl Dancer remarked in the *California Eagle*, "I'm inclined to disagree with those critics who label Rochester an 'Uncle Tom.' Other than his expression of 'Boss.' I think his brand of comedy is on a par with Abbott and Costello, Bob Hope or any other dispenser of good clean fun. Some way, somehow, Rochester always comes out on top in all verbal bouts with Jack Benny."⁵³ A Chicago-area reader wrote in to the *Defender*:

> I, for one, don't feel that Rochester is making a fool out of Negroes when I know there are as many white people who shoot craps as Negroes. There are certain neighborhoods where white fellows shoot craps out on the sidewalk. You read articles in the daily papers and hear jokes on the radio concerning white people shooting craps. I heard a white soldier being interviewed on the radio one evening. When he was asked how he spent his spare time. He answered, "Shootin' craps!"

The reader judged Amos and Andy to be far more problematic characters than Rochester because all profits from that show went to whites, whereas Eddie Anderson at least earned a big paycheck for his comic efforts, no matter how questionable.[54]

Anderson himself had rarely spoken publically about the challenges he faced portraying a black servant on a white situation comedy radio program. During this East Coast trip, however (perhaps responding to the critical outcry about the Benny episodes, or approached because of the controversy), Anderson granted an interview to Phil Carter of the *Baltimore Afro-American* in February 1945. Carter pressed the actor for his opinions on what a black performer's responsibilities should be in crafting positive racial representations. Anderson's answers remained as noncommittal as possible. Carter wrote that he "stressed the point that an entertainer should 'keep out of politics and must always appeal to all the people.'" The comic explained the narrow path he threaded between the expectations of different sections of his audience, and how loathe he was to step out of line or address contentious issues:

> People take our broadcasts seriously. Sometimes they complain that Jack Benny doesn't pay his singers enough or that he shouldn't make some of his performers mow the Benny lawn. Some think I'm really his valet. Some of them write that he shouldn't let me take such a bantering attitude. Others are surprised when I don't hold his coat or dust him off when we are out together.

Carter noted that "as Jack Benny's valet in the Rochester character, he has an off-handed, independent bantering attitude toward his boss." "I asked him," continued Carter, "what would happen if a real valet acted like that?" "It might not be so funny," Anderson answered, but still the actor maintained that "I don't portray an insolent character, just funny."[55] Carter questioned Anderson's commitment to improving representations of blacks in entertainment. He argued that the comedy routines that Anderson performed live on stage during his summer tours, especially in black theaters in

Harlem, Chicago, and across the South, contained an even heavier dose of jokes about razors, wild trips to Harlem, dice, and other stereotypes than were heard on Rochester's radio sprees. "On the radio it appears that this is toned down by Benny," Carter wrote. In concluding the interview, Anderson reiterated to the reporter that his audiences should not expect him to be a "race man first" and a comedian second. "I am in this business because I'm a comedian." Reporters in the *Pittsburgh Courier* archly responded to Anderson's refusal to be more proactively involved in cultural change:

> The droll comedian was credited with having stated in an interview which appeared in an Eastern publication recently, that he was first, last and always a comedian given to humor and not solving the race problem. Interested observers here, however, point out that consciously or unconsciously, Negro actors and actresses of radio, stage and screen are ambassadors of either good or bad will for the entire race. This because of the dictates of American life, which thus far are still given to judging the entire race by the actions of the few.

After criticism from the black community, Benny and his writers in a subsequent show would usually provide some way to showcase Eddie Anderson, play up Rochester's importance to the program, or bring on prominent African American performers whose close personal relationship to Rochester would be highlighted.[56] Thus it might not be merely a coincidence that, soon after the Benny cast returned to Los Angeles after the long trip, the March 11, 1945, program's theme revolved around Jack relating the tale of how he had supposedly met Rochester and brought him into the radio program "family." In the story, Jack was driving his old Maxwell car in 1936 in New York City when he crashed into a taxicab that was driven by Rochester, who was employed by Amos and Andy's Fresh Air Taxi Company. Rochester discussed Benny's offer to settle the matter with his employers and the Kingfish, then they all trouped over to Benny's hotel to try and wrangle a large damage payment. When Benny balked at even a $50 charge, Amos and Andy settled for turning over Rochester to Jack's employment. Although audiences at the time may well have enjoyed the rare appearance of Amos and Andy (Gosden and Correll) on Benny's show, listening to it today, the characters interact uncomfortably, the dialogue has not aged well and the dickering for Rochester's services seems belittling.

Some observers in the black community saw this episode featuring Rochester to be Benny's attempt to make amends with critics. The *Chicago Defender*'s columnist "Old Nosey" extended an olive branch over the crap shooting complaints of five weeks earlier. The reporter complimented Anderson and Benny on now offering a much more congenial depiction of Rochester:

> We tip our topper to Rochester [and] this week place ... [our] stamp of approval on the recent broadcasts of the Jack Benny show, starring Rochester and others. Last Sunday's program was one of the best in Jack Benny's long list of stellar entertainment and Rochester didn't have to shoot craps and ridicule his race in order to get a laugh. Instead, bolstered by the fine humor and showmanship of Amos and Andy, the broadcast was such rip-roaring fun, the studio had to space in much greater time than usual for the applause and laugher of the studio audience. Keep up the good work, Rochester and Jack Benny, and you'll both retain your reputations as Ace Comedians of the Air.[57]

FILM BAN ON THE ONE HAND, UNCLE TOM CHARGES ON THE OTHER

No sooner had Anderson gotten past the furor in the black community over Rochester's radio misbehavior, when another publicity disaster struck, coming from the opposite direction. In Anderson's latest film, a remake of the forty-year-old comedy *Brewster's Millions* (United Artists, 1945), he had a featured role as "Jackson," a servant and handyman employed at the home of young military veteran Monty Brewster's (Dennis O'Keefe's) mother. Anderson received fourth billing, with his photo featured in all the advertising. He was the only minority actor in the film, and was shown in collegial relationships with the white characters. Anderson wore a suit, spoke with an educated vocabulary, and worked alongside the hero to help spend the money to meet the terms of Brewster's inheritance. The film received average-to-good reviews in the major newspapers; the *Los Angeles Times* reviewer rated it "rich in laughs and well played by its cast of performers who seem to have caught the comedy tempo."[58]

However, in Memphis, Tennessee, reactionary white leaders objected to the film. Instead of cutting out a few offending scenes, as they had been doing to musical performances by Lena Horne and others in films during the war, now they escalated to a complete rejection—*Brewster's Millions* was banned by the City Board of Motion Picture Censors. Lloyd T. Binford, the chairman, stated that he and his board "considered it inimical to the friendly relations now existing here. We believe it presents too much familiarity between the races. It has Rochester (Eddie Anderson) in an important role. He has much too familiar a way about him and the picture presents too much social equality and racial mixture."[59]

The *Chicago Defender* expressed outrage at the Jim Crow politics on its front page, excoriating the actions of Memphis mayor "Boss" Crump and Binford, and leapt to Anderson's defense as a hardworking actor who had volunteered his time for the war effort.[60] On the front page of *Variety*, Lillian Smith, author of the bestselling novel *Strange Fruit*, lashed out at the timidity of the Hollywood for not standing up more firmly to racism. "She declared the industry's lack of courage, shown by its catering so easily to southern prejudice, is feeding racial bias."[61]

Another Jim Crow limitation Eddie Anderson faced was his inability to be able to accompany Jack Benny on Benny's prominent USO tours to perform for soldiers in North Africa, the Middle East, and Italy in Summer 1943, and the South Pacific in 1944. In May 1945, Anderson volunteered to do USO shows for the summer but insisted that he wanted to take along two white musicians from Phil Harris's band. His request was denied.[62] In August, actor Orson Welles, who had become increasingly active in working to improve racial tolerance and civil rights for black performers, took a stand against segregationist military regulations. Welles had recently been the emcee of an awards ceremony for a group called the Interracial Film and Radio Guild, which had honored Bette Davis, Eddie Anderson, Lena Horne, and the Warner Bros. studio for their efforts to promote interracial harmony. Welles chose Jack Benny as the focus of his campaign, publishing an "open letter" to Benny asking him to fight to have Anderson included in his USO tours. Welles boldly took Benny to task for creating the damaging racial representations that he and Anderson had propounded over seven years on the radio program and urged both Benny and Anderson to become much more involved in political action for civil rights:

> Without meaning it at all, you and Eddie have been doing the Negro people a grave wrong. The gags about gin-drinking and crap-shooting are unusually good gags, and Eddie makes them sound hilarious, but through the years they've helped perpetuate a dangerous myth. You and I and Eddie know very well that Negroes aren't chronically irresponsible stooges born to shine shoes and steal neckties. But Rochester is one of your most valuable comic properties and it's Eddie's livelihood. I'm not asking either of you to give up Rochester. I'm suggesting that you put him to work in a good case. You can undo all the harm you've done innocently at home by very deliberately taking

him overseas. Sure it's easy for me to sit here by my typewriter and ask you and Eddie to endure all the strain. It's easy, but you and Eddie are the kind of men it's easy to ask a lot of because you give a lot without taking any bows. Here's a chance to give more.

African American servicemen in the field also were beginning to protest against the representations that they encountered in films and radio programs. "Our GI's in South Pacific Fiercely Resent 'Uncle Tom' Roles," wrote a correspondent for the *New Amsterdam News*, who poignantly described the silent exodus of black soldiers from camp theaters when they encountered servants in Hollywood films enacting stereotyped behavior. Eddie Anderson was one of their main targets as the most prominent black performer on the air, along with actress Hattie McDaniel, whose servant roles in films were being severely criticized by soldiers and sailors.[63] Militant young members of the black press now published pointed accusations that earlier journalists had dared not make so boldly—"Rochester heads list of theatre, radio players we can do without," wrote a columnist for the *Baltimore Afro-American*. Unlike Anderson, who apparently made no public response to any of these charges, Hattie McDaniel personally answered these negative letters from black GIs and published letters to the editor of various publications defending the humanity and compassion she tried to bring to these very limited film roles.[64]

Even Dr. Reddick, director of the Schomburg Center, who in 1941 had honored Anderson and Benny as leaders in promoting interracial understanding, now four years later publically proclaimed that Rochester was a detrimental character and buffoonish comic servant: "'A stereotype conception,' complete with 'razor toting and gin drinking'; is the manner in which radio treats the Negro."[65]

In 1946, media critics also voiced increasing complaints about the use of broadly stereotyped Jewish and other ethnic figures in radio comedy, along with continued reliance on minstrel-show depictions of blacks. A group called "The Writers Board," in promoting racial tolerance, judged Benny's show harshly: "Jack Benny gets a dud for his use of the dialect hot dog salesman in his program [Mr. Kitzel, played by Artie Aurbach].... This character tends to hold up a nationality to ridicule, just as the Rochester stereotype makes fun of Negroes." Jack Benny's loyal supporters, such as *Variety*'s Jack Hellman, were very defensive about the charges:

> What's wrong with a clean characterization that makes millions laugh? If you were to ask Eddie Anderson (Rochester) or Amos n Andy what the reaction

of Negroes to their delineation has been they'd show you stacks of fan mail from colored people praising their antics and even making heroes of them. . . . . It's all fun—good, clean fun—and never have we heard exception taken.[66]

The postwar era was a mixed bag of personal success and continued frustration on many fronts for Eddie Anderson and other black performers who tried to carve out careers in broadcasting. The veterans of the Hollywood black acting community were finding even fewer film roles. In radio, Hattie McDaniel played the role of "Beulah" the housekeeper. Gosden and Correll used a somewhat larger number of black actors to play supporting roles on *Amos 'n' Andy*. In July 1948, NBC attempted to create the first all-black cast primetime network radio program, a musical variety show to serve as a summer replacement for Dennis Day's situation comedy. Originally titling the program *The National Minstrel Show*, NBC programmers filled it with stereotypical comedy routines (performed by Lucky Millender and Moms Mably). Pressure from the NAACP and critics in the black press convinced NBC to delay the broadcast, and change the show's name first to *Modern Minstrels*, then to *Swingtime at the Savoy*. Although by August the program finally had some promise, with an appearance by rising star Ella Fitzgerald, the show never found a sponsor, and was cancelled after five weeks.[67]

Anderson remained the most prominent black performer on the radio. After critical outbursts about Rochester's stereotypically minstrel-like behavior during the war years, furor over the character died down, at least public complaints in African American publications. Benny and his writers steered their scripts further away from racialized humor for Rochester, even as they increasingly involved the Rochester character into the situation comedy.

The new 1946 magazine *Ebony* published a feature essay in its third issue on black representation in network broadcasting, "Radio and Race."[68] "Radio is growing up in race relations. . . . Uncle Tom is doing a fadeout," it optimistically asserted. While taking Anderson to task for his unwillingness to publically support civil rights measures, the article still noted that his radio character was becoming less offensive to critics. "Biggest name is radio today among Negro performers is Rochester, whose routines with Jack Benny are heard by 25 million Americans every Sunday night. Never notable for his racial consciousness, even Rochester has been mending his mike manners and steers away from razor and dice clichés of late." Other black newspapers kept their focus on the new generation of younger performers (Dorothy Dandridge, Lena Horne, Nat King Cole) and largely left Anderson out of the spotlight.

A ONE-TWO PUNCH OF TROUBLE FOR ANDERSON IN SPRING 1950

As 1950 began, longtime members of Benny's radio cast, including Eddie Anderson, were optimistic that they could achieve wider broadcasting success. Several years before, Dennis Day and Phil Harris had fruitfully expanded their careers through popular spin-off radio comedy programs (*A Day in the Life of Dennis Day* and *The Phil Harris/Alice Faye Show*) that brought them additional income and professional prominence, and they and their talent agents were investigating what they might do in TV. Mel Blanc, who appeared regularly on the Benny show as well as in small roles on fifteen other radio programs, had been given his own situation comedy program, *The Mel Blanc Show*, which ran on CBS network radio for a season.[69] An advertising agency was considering the creation of a radio situation comedy featuring Mr. Kitzel. Rochester's popularity had many wondering when Anderson would have his own spin-off program.

Finally, in early February 1950, advertising executive Adrian Samish of the Dancer, Fitzgerald, and Sample ad agency worked up ideas for a radio program to feature Anderson.[70] It was an unsettled time in network radio, however, as financial support of the largest sponsors was shifting to television. Daytime radio was still quite healthy, however, and its lower costs meant that smaller sponsors could be courted to invest in programs. New programs, however, had an uphill battle to fight for support, as sponsors tended to gravitate to programs with proven track records. Success of the daytime comedy *The Beulah Show* emboldened the Dancer, Fitzgerald, and Sample agency to advance its plans.

Samish faced problems getting the American Tobacco Company to allow use of the Rochester character in a spin-off. Their delays apparently scuttled a fascinating program idea that Samish pitched to the new potential sponsor (Franco-American canned spaghetti, a subsidiary of Campbell's Soup)—a parody of currently popular detective mystery shows, to be tentatively titled "The Five O'clock Shadow." With the Lucky Strike makers' hesitations and limitations, Samish ended up proposing to Franco-American a fifteen-minute daily situation comedy, to be called "The Adventures of Rochester."[71]

The program's narrative focused on Rochester, living in a small apartment near Central Avenue in Los Angeles's black district, interacting with his landlady and neighborhood characters. Given the wit, ingenuity, and intelligence of the Rochester character that brought such verve to the Jack Benny program, these sample episodes Samish produced are quite disappointing. The show was a pale imitation of *Amos 'n' Andy*, with Rochester reduced to the role of gullible, naïve, stupid Amos. All the other characters took advantage of his trusting good nature, bamboozling and humiliating him as if he was the greenest rube just off the farm. Eddie Anderson found that he had very little control over the character he had worked so hard to create over thirteen years. Negotiations stalled, and plans for Anderson's program dissolved.[72]

In late January 1950, while this deal was percolating, Anderson hurried by train with the rest of the Benny radio show cast to broadcast two episodes of their radio program from New York City. Writer Milt Josefsberg recalled a combination of problems upsetting their scripting routine—the train trip cross-country was rough, Benny and Mary Livingstone both caught colds, and the writers were ill as well. While Benny's radio show episodes in early 1950 had been some of the sharpest and wittiest that the writers ever concocted, this week left them harried and out of ideas. On Thursday the troupe was still scriptless with Sunday looming ever closer. Josefsberg said that, amid the turmoil and lack of creative inspiration, "Jack's personal secretary, Bert Scott, remembered a script that Jack had done in New York almost exactly ten years ago. A copy of this script was dug up, updated, and shoved in as an emergency measure."[73] The script Scott had excavated was originally broadcast on December 15, 1940.

The episode began with the standard routine of Don introducing Jack, who talked about his New York adventures and the cheapness of his room at the Acme Plaza Hotel. Soon afterwards, Jack complained to Mary, Don, and Phil about Rochester's absence and the fact that his brown suit was missing. Jack threatened to fire his valet when he found him. In the second half, Jack found a telephone number to call in Harlem to attempt to locate Rochester. A man answered, announcing the Harlem Social, Benevolent, and Spare Ribs Every Thursday Club. He told Benny that Rochester had entered the club on one knee, and pulled everyone into a craps game. The fellow provided Jack with a second number to call.

JACK: Hello?
MAMIE: Hello, Mamie Brown, the sweetest gal in town talking.
JACK: Miss Brown, this is Jack Benny.
MAMIE: Oh oh . . .

JACK: I'm trying to get in touch with Rochester, Is he there?

MAMIE: He *was* here.

JACK: Oh, well, do you think he'll come back?

MAMIE: In all modesty, I can *guarantee* that.

JACK: Well, when he returns will you please tell him to call my hotel . . . and you can also tell him I'm stopping his salary.

MAMIE: Oh, that ain't gonna bother him. He now *owns* the building that houses the Harlem Social, Benevolent, and Spare Ribs Every Thursday Club.

JACK: Oh yes, I heard about that,. He wins from everybody, doesn't he?

MAMIE: Yeah, when I opened the door and he came in on one knee, I thought it was a proposal.

Mamie Brown provided Jack with a third number where Rochester could be reached and, when Jack inquired if that was another woman's residence, she claimed if so, she would cut Jack's brown suit to ribbons. Finally Rochester himself telephoned Jack, and Jack demanded that Rochester not lie about the whereabouts of the suit, while Rochester prevaricated. Rochester also claimed he started on his spree after being frightened by a black cat outside Jack's hotel. Jack sighed in frustration, "This happens every time I bring him to Harlem."

"We had hardly signed off the air when the network's switchboard lit up a like a computer gone berserk," recalled Josefsberg. The writer claimed that "Jack, a gentle soul, was amazed at the unfavorable reaction. He remembered that when the material had been done ten years previously it had caused hardly a ripple."[74] While no mention of this contretemps was made in any of the major newspapers or in the entertainment trade press, the *Chicago Defender*'s front page headline blared, "Jack Benny Show Stirs Harlem's Ire." The *Defender* reported that "A storm of protest broke Sunday night over the Jack Benny show on the Columbia Broadcasting System for the American Tobacco Company. As listeners blasted a stereotype 'Rochester in Harlem' sequence, the NAACP, through acting secretary Roy Wilkins, wired a strong protest to CBS, and spokesmen for the network told the *Chicago Defender* that it was receiving many telephone protests shortly after the program Sunday night."[75] Wilkins's telegram asserted that:

> NAACP protests script material for Rochester on Jack Benny program February 5. All the old inaccurate and derogatory stereotypes were pulled out

of the hat by writers who used knifing, woman-chasing, drinking, dice games and stealing of wearing apparel in skit. Most writers for radio long ago learned these situations are not typical of Negro life and are not likely to make friends and influence people among them for products sold by such means. CBS, Benny, Rochester and script writers are old enough in this knowledge to know better and do better.[76]

Benny, his writers, and the CBS network, in a probable attempt to make amends with angry black critics, and to stem the tide of this protest that caught them so unexpectedly off-guard, quickly invited the prominent black musical group the Inkspots to make a guest appearance on Benny's next program (February 12, 1950). They showed up to Benny's cheap Manhattan hotel room to sing a parody of their hit song "If I Didn't Care," rejiggered to serve as the middle Lucky Strike commercial. In this episode, Rochester was a busy professional valet, taking care of Benny's personal business, and commenting wryly on Benny's cheapness. He exhibited no more roistering around Harlem.

Nevertheless, angry responses from the black community kept coming. Furious *Defender* columnist Lillian Scott fumed that neither Benny, Anderson, sponsor, nor network would take responsibility for the offensive episode:

> So round, so fully packed—so stereotyped and stupid; best describes the celebrated Jack Benny show last Sunday over the Columbia Broadcasting System for the American Tobacco Company. Mr. Benny—they call him a comedian! Didn't miss a single one of the old gables about Negroes. Aided and abetted by Eddie "Rochester" Anderson who should have been named for Buda-pest or Grand "Coolie" instead of that nice Upper New York State town.... There was much buck or should it be Benny passing after the show. The Lucky Strike people said Benny was sole arbiter of the entertainment portion of the show, and CBS allowed as how Monday morning they hadn't had enough protests to issue any formal statement. Personally we'd like to know just how listeners felt all over the nation. Drop us a penny post card or letter, *Chicago Defender*, 101 Park Avenue, NYC 17, willya? CBS didn't say anything because it took for granted that not enough of us would care enough to bother telling them.

Scott claimed the sponsor's slogan now meant "Lucky Strike Means Foul Treatment" and suggested that black listeners boycott the brand.[77]

Anderson planted a face-saving story with a friendly *Defender* columnist, who wrote in the same February 18 issue, "Maybe you'd like to know that Eddie 'Rochester' Anderson, whose lines on the Jack Benny program were

FIGURE 15. The pairing of Jack Benny and Eddie Anderson on the cover of *Look* magazine in May 1950 was touted in the African American community as one of the first nationally prominent representations of black celebrity and interracial equality. *Look*, May 1950. Author's collection.

criticized last week, objected to the script when he first read it but time would not allow its being changed."⁷⁸ Benny, too, tried to mollify the protestors, after his return to Hollywood on February 25, releasing a statement published on the front page of the *Pittsburgh Courier*, expressing "regrets... that his program had caused 'ill feeling.'" Benny's publicity manager Irving Fein denied that the show creators had intended any harm, and argued instead that racial minority groups were "inclined to be too sensitive" about comic representations of ethnic characters. "Rochester, who is usually portrayed as a hardworking valet, is entitled to shoot some dice and take a drink once every ten years," Fein claimed, and acknowledged that "it was ten years prior to the 1950 incident that Rochester had portrayed similar characteristics on a New York-originated broadcast." "Most Negroes liked the portrayal," said Fein, maintaining that they protested not "against the portrayal but against the general practice carried on in the radio industry of presenting the Negro in same type of roles without offering any other regular presentations what would give balance to or counteract the regular stereotype portrayals."[79]

The same day, the *Defender* responded to the Benny's mild excuses and the still-roiling controversy with an editorial, "When Racial Jokes Aren't Funny:"

> Many Negroes protested the recent Jack Benny radio show which had a Harlem sequence that featured some crapshooting, low brow characters who have been traditionally identified as typical Negroes.... To some whites, such protests seem unjustified and they insist that Negroes are too sensitive, too thin-skinned about this race and colored business. They point out that jokes are made about the Irish, Scotch and other national and racial groups and no offense is taken. These whites do not know what a Negro experiences when he tried so get a job or get a promotion in his position. If they did, they would understand why those racial jokes and clownish characterizations are not funny.... There is nothing funny about being a second-class citizen and being denied opportunities for economic and cultural advancement. We believe that there is plenty of material for humor that does not involve perpetuating stereotypes that impair our chances for getting out of the much created by bigotry.[80]

"Jack Benny certainly laid an egg, to use theatre parlance, with his recent broadcast about Rochester's adventures in Harlem," claimed the *Los Angeles Sentinel*.

> Newspaper reports have it that Benny, his sponsors and CBS are all puzzled by the outbreak of criticism and each of them is protesting that no harm was meant. That's probably true, just as it is true that the man who kills his friend with an 'unloaded' gun is sorry for the result. The trouble is that the victim is still dead in the shooting instance and that Negroes have been cast in a bad and unwarranted light by the Benny show.[81]

After being denied a radio program of his own, and being lambasted by black media critics for the "throwback" New York radio episode, Anderson received one small bit of positive publicity, his photograph in color on the cover of *LOOK* magazine's May 9, 1950, issue. Benny and Anderson were paired looking quizzically in opposite directions of each other. (The cover accompanied Leo Rosen's article "Jack Benny: the Ultimate Fall Guy.") The

Atlanta Daily World and *Los Angeles Sentinel* lauded it as a sign of positive interracial public relations, the *World* noting, "Rochester, radio aide to Jack Benny, graces the cover of the current issue of *LOOK* magazine which appeared on the newsstands here this week. This marks the first time from the information obtainable that a Negro has appeared on the cover a multi-million circulation magazine."[82] This accolade was overblown, as Anderson had been depicted on the cover of *Liberty* magazine in 1942 (with a hatchet, trying to dispatch a large Thanksgiving turkey), and Jackie Robinson had appeared on the cover of *Time* in 1947, and would be pictured on the cover of *Life* (albeit in black and white) the very same week as Anderson's cover.[83]

ROCHESTER ON TELEVISION, AND HIS LEGACY

Eddie Anderson would continue to play a key role in Benny's situation comedy narrative on radio and television for the better part of the next fifteen years. Rochester was the first major cast member introduced on the inaugural 1950 TV program, showcased in a sketch that featured him singing and dancing while cleaning Benny's home and bantering with Polly the parrot. As Mary Livingstone and Phil Harris appeared on the show less frequently, Rochester became an even more central character in both the radio and TV show's narratives. Jack and Rochester interacted at Jack's home more frequently like household partners, and more than ever, Rochester had the dialogue lines that punctured the Boss's outsized ego. Media historian Donald Bogle has characterized them as television's original interracial Odd Couple.[84]

Anderson appeared with Benny on nearly all the 250 Benny radio episodes between January 1949 when the program moved to CBS, through its last episodes in May 1955. Television was a different matter. Anderson appeared in only half of Benny's TV programs between fall 1950 and spring 1955. Even the *Defender* noticed that Rochester was being used significantly less on TV than he had been on radio.[85] In the next four years of the show's sponsorship by Lucky Strike, however (1955–1959), Anderson was on much more often—about 80 percent of the shows. In the following three years (fall 1959 to spring 1962) Anderson's nagging health problems were probably a reason why he was reduced to appearing on only half of these shows, and only in a quarter of the TV programs between fall 1962 and spring 1965.

Criticism surrounding black representation on early 1950s television centered on *Amos 'n' Andy* and *Beulah*. At the time, black media and social critics were also concerned about the inappropriateness and detrimental qualities that the Rochester character posed for beneficial representations of black manhood to U.S. media audiences. But for a number of reasons, Rochester and Eddie Anderson were not as targeted as often for protests and calls for the cancellation of Benny's show. One factor must have been Jack Benny's power as a leading entertainer. It would ultimately be his decision (with the sponsor having a big say, too) if Rochester would stay or go. A second reason would be the importance and value of the Rochester character to the Benny show. On television, Rochester emerged as the most prominent character who talked back to Jack, criticized his poor decisions and cheapness with smart jokes and witty retorts, and who interacted with him most regularly. The longevity of Rochester's relationship with Jack, and the fact they were played by the same actors for all those years, also contributed to make them a taken-for-granted part of the media landscape. Anderson's performance as Rochester—the amazing voice, sense of timing, skeptical wit, and charm that Anderson brought to the role—undercut many of the dialogue lines he was given that resembled Uncle Tom stereotyping. The fact that he was just one part of an ensemble cast, and not the title character, also perhaps kept him from being a lightning rod for criticism.

. . .

Largely, the Rochester character successfully negotiated the cultural and political tensions of 1950s broadcasting and popular culture. Benny's scriptwriters could nevertheless still unthinkingly manage to create awkward situations on the program, such as when Rochester's friend Roy appeared on radio episodes (one or two a year between 1949 and 1954). There was one in particular where Roy had been assisting Rochester in cleaning up the dishes at Benny's home after a party (January 18, 1953), and Benny jokingly bantered about how little he intended to pay Roy. When Benny behaved this way, to a worker who had not been rude to him like the store clerks or waitresses he encountered, then suddenly it was not the old, joking penurious relationship that Rochester complained about, but something meaner.

When UCLA sociology graduate student Estelle Edmerson conducted interviews in 1953 for her thesis research, examining the difficulties faced by African American actors in network broadcasting, and the many limitations placed on representation of black characters on radio shows, criticisms of Eddie Anderson and the Rochester character remained a significant issue.[86]

In an era of reduced activity for black performers, Anderson was still the most prominent and best paid black star in broadcasting with the longest tenure on the airwaves. Yet Edmerson found Anderson to be as frustrating to interview, and as evasive in his answers, as had any previous investigator had experienced:

> Eddie "Rochester" Anderson, actor on the Jack Benny show, answering the question relative to his problems as a Negro in radio, said that he had had "none." "Rochester" commented on the Negroes' criticism of the Negro actors' radio presentations, he, evidently, did not feel that the criticisms had been a problem for him, even though his role as Rochester had been severely criticized by many Negro groups and newspaper columnists. . . .
>
> "I haven't seen anything objectionable. I don't see why certain characters are called stereotypes. There's no one originating any new characters. The Negro characters being presented are not labeling the Negro Race any more than 'Luigi' is labeling the Italian people as a whole. The same goes for 'Beulah' who is not playing the part of thousands of Negroes, but only the part of one person, 'Beulah.' They're not saying here is the portrait of the Negro, but here is Beulah. There were no objections when the part was played by a white person."[87]

Asked about blacks' opportunities in radio, Anderson said, "I believe those who have shown that they had something to offer have been given an equal opportunity."[88] However, black actor Frank Silvera commented, "In some instances, it may be said that due to the few opportunities, Negro performers tend to become protective, they seek to gain for themselves and let the rest go hang. They shrink from protestation, and find justification for all of this in proclaiming the industry a 'rat race' or 'dog eat dog' business."[89] Edmerson concluded:

> Generally, a great number of critics have contended that the "overbalance" of stereotyped portrayals had been their main object of complaint. Also, most of the Negro artists, themselves, including those who participated in and were favorable toward the stereotyped portrayals, accused the radio industry of presenting a one-sided picture of the Negro. . . . The criticism of Miss McDaniel, Rochester, etc. usually stems from the fact that they are domestics in the home, subject to the orders, whims and wishes of white people.[90]

In the racial tumult of the 1960s, some sources claimed that there had never been any anger within the black community about Benny and Rochester team A 1968 *Chicago Tribune* article claimed,

Not only was Jack the only one to have a Negro on his program for years, but the relationship established between Jack and Rochester was unique in that it never stirred up criticism when Negroes began their campaign to have Hollywood eradicate the servant stereotypes so prevalent in movies. Undoubtedly this was because with Jack and Rochester there was more of a partnership than an employer-employee relationship. Rochester, in fact, frequently outsmarted Jack in situations—much to the delight of audiences everywhere.[91]

On the other hand, playwright Amiri Baraka would espouse a very different solution to the dilemma in his 1965 play *JELLO* that turned longing for equality into seething, murderous rage, when his Rochester character kills the other radio program cast members.[92]

At the conclusion of his November 16, 1968, television special, the hiply titled "Jack Benny's Bag," Benny engaged Eddie Anderson in a brief exchange commenting on the changes occurring in depictions of racial interaction, to suggest that the old master and servant relationship was now a thing of the past:

JACK: Rochester, the reason I brought you out, I want to tell you about a great idea for a series we can do together next year.

ROCHESTER: Good, good, what is it?

JACK: We can be two tennis players who are really spies working for the CIA.

ROCHESTER: Hold it, hold it—that was done last season.

JACK: Oh. Well, then we can play two bounty hunters in the post–Civil War period.

ROCHESTER: Hold it—that's being done this season.

JACK: Oh. Well, I have another idea—how about you coming back to work for me as my valet?

ROCHESTER: Blue eyes, we don't do that anymore.

JACK: Oh, that's right. Come on, let's go get a hamburger.[93]

SIX

The Commercial Imperative

JACK BENNY, ADVERTISING, AND RADIO SPONSORS

"Jack's success as a salesman in moving goods, first for General Foods and then American Tobacco, was absolutely incredible,"[1] recalled legendary broadcasting executive Sylvester "Pat" Weaver in 1963. Weaver knew what he was talking about, having worked with Jack Benny in radio over twenty years through an advertising agency, a sponsor, and a network.[2] Benny collected accolades from industry observers, critics, and the public throughout his radio career for his ability to merge entertainment and consumer product advertising. As soon as he started in radio, Benny learned that commercial broadcasting had a wider variety of masters to please than he had experienced in vaudeville or in film. Each group he worked with in radio promoted different agendas. Harried network vice presidents attempting to keep sponsors satisfied tried to shape Benny's program. Persnickety sponsors interested in promoting their product and pleasing their own cultural tastes tried to dictate what Benny did on air. Advertising agencies sought to bend Benny's radio show to their own marketing interests. To navigate this minefield, Benny became what the television industry today would term a "show runner"—not only a performer, but also an involved, hands-on co-creator and manager of his own entertainment product. Getting the support and resources he desired, and creating comedy in these circumstances was not easy. After all, Benny ran through four sponsors in his first two and a half years on the air.

Consumer advocate groups and radio critics bemoaned the commercial imperatives of radio in the 1930s and 1940s, despairing at the professional, aesthetic, and ethical compromises that program creators had to make for the sake of selling things.[3] As no one was more successful than Benny at working within the context of advertising, he could easily be dismissed as a "sell out."

Given the industrial factors in the contemporary entertainment world pushing advertisers back into production of media content, however, there are lessons to be learned in analyzing how Benny negotiated, over nearly twenty-five years in radio, the complex relationships and restrictions of the sponsor system.

By involving himself in the creation of commercial advertising messages, Benny could enhance his radio program in several ways. He could have more control over the content of the twenty-seven minutes of his show that fell between the bookends of opening and closing commercials. This helped Benny shape the "flow" and continuity of his program. Especially as Benny and writer Harry Conn began developing characters and story lines (as opposed to presenting a collection of one-line jokes), the comedy benefitted from lack of the jarring interruptions of ad verbiage so common on other shows. Benny turned his radio announcer from the pompous, dour person who droned dull messages into a joke-making member of the radio family. Benny scripter Milt Josefberg recalled, "Jack's kidding of the commercials became a high plateau of humor on his programs, and the public looked for it as eagerly as the rest of the show."[4]

Crafting the middle commercial themselves also allowed Benny and his writers to do some ideological work on the sly, whether it was the mischievously subversive Canada Dry and Lucky Strike ads, or the more generally ironic attitude toward consumer culture woven into the ads for Chevrolet, General Tire, and Jell-O. Benny's humorous commercials helped further break down the barriers between the production orientation of traditional American culture toward one that was more focused on consumption. Even if Benny's character was unwilling to spend a dime, the commercials in his programs acknowledged that his radio audiences lived in a world of products that fulfilled needs and provided pleasures. The brands that Jack and his cast members mentioned so often on the air became familiar characters in listeners' imaginations.

While previous accounts of Benny's career have generally depicted Benny's business dealings as congenial, in fact, Benny had to struggle repeatedly against sponsors', advertising agencies', and networks' contrary wishes, irrational demands, and attempts to control his program; they tried to alter scripts and program themes, choose their own writers and performers, and constrained Benny's efforts to pursue other entertainment endeavors. The dearth of surviving archival sources probably obscures many other disagreements that must have occurred between Benny and his bosses. This chapter charts Benny's innovative advertising practices, and examines how Benny parried the interfering efforts of his bosses. It focuses on three case studies—the "wild frontier" of humorous Canada Dry advertising in 1932, the synergy of selling Jell-O using humorous "soft sell" tactics from 1934 to 1943, and Benny's creative solutions to the challenge of working for the creator of the most obnoxious, irritant-inducing, hard sell advertising in all of radio—American Tobacco's George Washington Hill.

THE UNCERTAIN ROLE OF HUMOR IN ADVERTISING

"Humor in advertising is greatly admired by creative advertising people, widely noticed and talked about by the public, and seldom used," pronounced advertising executive Draper Daniels (a model for the TV series *Mad Men*'s Don Draper) in a 1959 guide for advertising copywriters. "Frustrated humorists in the advertising business frequently attempt to explain this seemingly contradictory set of circumstances by claiming that it seemingly proves that most advertising people on both the agency and client side of the fence are stuffed shirts." Daniels continued,

> When humor is used in advertising, it is too frequently dragged in in a manner that diverts attention from the product that is the advertisement's sole excuse for being. The problem is to keep the sound of the customer's laughter from drowning out the persuasive words of the sales talk.... Many people look upon the expenditure of money, particularly in large amounts, as something other than an occasion for laughter.[5]

Draper Daniels's distrustful view of the use of humor in commercials had been widely shared by advertising executives across the first half of the twentieth century. Advertising historians Cynthia Meyers, Roland Marchand, and Stephen Fox have analyzed how the professionalization of the advertising business led earlier industry leaders Albert Lasker and Claude Hopkins in the 1910s to develop "scientific advertising" and an approach to ad copy called the "hard sell." Hard sell advertising was serious; it provided as many factual "reasons why" an advertised product fulfilled a consumer's needs as it would take to wear down the customer's objections and leave them no choice but to buy.[6] Hard sell advertising in print was direct, wordy, and obnoxiously insistent. In the early 1930s, agencies' translation of hard sell advertising copy directly into scripts read out by radio announcers made those commercial announcements on the air sound even harsher to listeners' ears.

Despite advertising leaders' insistence that they knew the best way to sell the goods, other innovators considered the potential of humor and light-heartedness in print and radio ads. During the Depression, advertising agencies like Young and Rubicam (Y&R, Jack Benny's agency in the Jell-O years) focused not on selling a product to a rational but uninformed customer, but instead on building long-term emotional relationships between products and customers, and creating brand identity and brand loyalty, in examples like the flippant tone of Postum ads, the comic strip characters it developed to sell Sanka Coffee, and the loveable Borden product symbol Elsie the Cow. "Soft sell" proponents crafted ad campaigns that tapped into psychological ties that bound consumers to products, and presented products as helpful friends that solved their problems, increased their self-confidence, brought them untold pleasures, and guaranteed their success in life. Humor was an emotion that could reduce audience resistance to the commercial messages. Even for soft sell advocates, however, comedy's ability to help sell the goods was warily approached.[7]

"Humor in advertising is a dangerous weapon," Daniels warned. "It is difficult to sell to your boss, difficult to sell to a client, and with reason. Nothing falls quite so flat as an attempt to be funny that fails." The rewards of successful use of comedy in ads were tantalizing enough, however, Daniels reluctantly concluded, that talented and fearless copywriters could give it a try.[8] Daniels praised the ten-year legacy of advertising accomplishments of Jack Benny and announcer Don Wilson for Y&R's Jell-O program "with their integrated personality commercials and deceptively casual, good humored hard sell." Daniels felt that, underneath the surface of soft sell comedy ads, their direct sales pitches worked as pointedly as "reason-why" ad copy of old.[9] Daniels acknowledged the persuasive skills of talented announcers like Don Wilson and "the tremendous contrast with which his breezy, uninhibited approach stood out against the polished, bombastic advertisingese mouthed by the average radio announcer."[10]

Pat Weaver (who had been one of those innovators at Y&R in the 1930s) argued that different products required different sales approaches. Some sponsors' products benefitted tremendously from the development of relationships between an entertainer or mascot and the product, what Weaver called "program association values." If the sponsor controlled the entertainers' entire program (as was the general rule in radio and early TV) and a specific program star was associated with the sponsor's product, it could foster audience affection for the performer. When the advertised product was also one that could be linked in audiences' minds to pleasure, then it could be matched to a like-minded, lighthearted comedy show and happy audience associations would result. Jack Benny and Jell-O could become cemented together in consumers' minds, and listeners would purchase Jell-O to applaud Benny. When the plan succeeded, Weaver called it an "explosive kind of selling."[11]

On the other hand, the 1959 copywriters' guide that quoted Daniels reminded its readers that not every sponsor or advertiser approved of the soft sell approach of intertwining ads and entertainment. George Washington Hill practiced the exact opposite approach with Lucky Strikes, relying on "the shock value of a commercial that contrasted violently with the entertainment."[12] Advertisers like Hill worried that a comedy commercial would too easily be forgotten. Jack Benny's genius would be to merge soft and hard sell techniques completely in his comedy, hammering home brands names in a hilarious, absurd, and sometimes shocking manner, which worked effectively for sponsors as disparate as manufacturers of soda pop, automobiles, tires, desserts, and cigarettes.

THE EFFERVESCENT RADIO COMEDIAN'S AUDACIOUS COMMERCIALS

The advertisements that ginger ale bottler Canada Dry placed in newspapers, magazines, and on the radio in the late 1920s and early 1930s (created by the N. W. Ayer and Sons agency) emphasized dignity, social class, and good taste. Canada Dry's ad managers had modified the hard sell by developing soft(er) sell themes that stressed the atmosphere of refinement surrounding the product, calling it the "champagne of ginger ales" and describing the beverage's popularity among the country club set.[13] Canada Dry radio advertising was presented by a stately announcer with a cultured, well-modulated voice. Nevertheless, soft drinks were a pleasurable, frivolous treat, not a life necessity or something available only to the rich. The product was inexpensive, and commercials educated consumers to order it at soda fountains and to purchase take-home bottles from their grocers—not exactly the daily habits of the Rockefellers.

In April 1932, Canada Dry, which had been sponsoring radio programs for several years, was dissatisfied with its action drama set in the snowy Canadian Northwest Territories, broadcast on NBC. They'd gotten a few too many complaints from listeners about the show's violence, and objections from potential customers always put sponsors in a panic. So NBC executives Bertha Brainard and John Royal searched for a replacement to present to the sponsor and its advertising agency. Canada Dry dithered between sticking with dramatic narratives that made listeners think of Canada, or switching to a light, pleasant musical and "personality act" like the shows currently on the air featuring bandleaders Ben Bernie and Fred Waring. Canada Dry warily agreed to try a program pairing bandleader George Olsen and his orchestra with Jack Benny. In his contract, ad agency N. W. Ayer and Sons stipulated that Benny would "handle the commercial credits" at midprogram himself.[14]

Jack Benny took it as a challenge to use the commercials to explore the satirical side of living in an urban world increasingly filled with sales pitches. On the first program, May 2, 1932, Benny launched into humorous commercials with a vengeance. Describing his meager girlfriend in Newark, Jack claimed:

> She comes from a very fine family, although her father very often partakes of the forbidden beverage. It's all right for me to mention that, as they have no radio. In fact, her father drank everything in the United States, and then went up north to drink Canada Dry. (whistles) Gee, I'm glad I thought of that joke—you know—the one about Canada Dry, I'm really supposed to mention it occasionally. After all, I owe it to my sponsors, and they might be listening in. Seriously though, do you realize, folks, that if you want a drink of Canada Dry—we'll say just a glass—you don't have to buy it by the bottle. You can walk into any drug store or soda fountain that has that big sign, "Canada Dry made to order," ask for a glass, and get it. I know you always have it in your home in bottles, but isn't it nice to know that you don't have to wait until you get home to drink it? Gee, I thought I did that pretty well for a new salesman. I suppose nobody will drink it now.

Benny violated what most advertising executives considered a cardinal rule. As Draper Daniels would mandate, "Humor may be directed at the salesman of the product, the user or nonuser of the product, or at the foibles of human nature and society. It must never be directed at the product.... Irony, satire and subtlety are likely to miss with a mass audience."[15] Benny proceeded to push the envelope edges of vaudeville-like slapstick verbal humor with his Canada Dry commercial messages over the next few weeks of the broadcast.

On the May 23 episode, with Harry Conn on board, Benny's target was the patent medicine commercials that littered the radio landscape with their ridiculous claims of cures, their gruesome details of indigestion, acne, and constipation and the suffering of victims that could only be relieved by purchasing the miracle product:

> Jack—Let me say this, ladies and gentlemen, I do not claim that Canada Dry will cure falling arches, dandruff or baggy knees. But I will say this—I KNOW it is a refreshing drink because last night—believe it or not—I tried a glass of it at the fountain. And it wasn't bad ... it was NOT bad ... in fact, it was good ... I liked it.... Gee, I thought it was swell ... Ladies and Gentlemen, it was EXCELLENT! ... Are you paying attention, Sponsors, hmmmm?

The sponsor was appalled, as these ads shattered the atmosphere of dignity and refinement surrounding the product that they were paying their agency so much money to maintain.[16] Years later, Benny recalled the turmoil:

> The first few weeks that we did it in a satirical way on the Canada Dry show, the sponsor didn't like it and want us to stop it.... We did a lot of satires on the commercials [like "nickel back on the bottle"]. The sponsor wanted us to go back to the straight commercials but the agency liked it and the agency said "they haven't had time to prove whether this is a good way to do it." So they allowed us another two or three weeks. And in the next two or three weeks the mail kept coming in so much to the sponsor that they liked this kind of advertising that they finally let us alone and let us do it.[17]

Benny's Canada Dry commercials cynically ribbed the product with far sharper barbs than other radio shows were doing. The Albert Lasker/eventual Draper Daniels school of advertising would have been shocked to see such levity as the Depression's economic woes were growing ever worse. They fully captured the spirit, however, of the over-the-top parody advertisements then appearing in the satirical humor magazine *Ballyhoo*, edited by former *Judge* magazine cartoonist Norman Anthony, which had debuted in Manhattan in August 1931 and had quickly grown in circulation to sell nearly two million copies per issue. Historians Margaret McFadden and Roland Marchand have analyzed how the magazine's comic strategies sharply critiqued capitalism's failed promises and the ridiculousness of Prohibition, burlesqued the humbug of advertising practices, and provided a devastatingly pointed and bitter humor that mocked big business and the social class inequities that favored the wealthy. *Ballyhoo* was read gleefully by a public battered by economic devastation.[18] *Ballyhoo* printed a fake ad for a souped-up international radio console that offered to provide "All the crap in the world at your fingertips!": "Now you can hear foreign announcers gargle hot potatoes ... it will do everything in the world but give you good programs and Gawd knows no set will do that." The magazine's success spawned a book, a board game, and an off-Broadway revue, *Ballyhoo of 1932*, featuring a young Bob Hope, which was playing that summer when Conn and Benny devised their own satirical ads.

Benny and Conn's commercials deprecated the product, the sponsor, and the practice of visiting soda fountains. Benny claimed that Canada Dry was conducting scientific taste tests, blindfolding factory workers, or tying them up, or approaching desperate, parched tourists who had been stranded in the desert, forcing these poor souls to sample the beverage and reporting that they claimed their sip of Canada Dry was not objectionable. They created a product spokesman, a talking glass of ginger ale with a high-pitched cartoon voice. Benny associated Canada Dry with Mary telling a risqué story about a peeping tom in a train's sleeping compartment, and jokes about homosexual zoo animals, lazy soda jerks, drunks, and stories of torture and cannibalism. If Benny and Conn were pushing the boundaries of acceptable humor, at least they were gaining critical and popular acclaim from their small but growing listening audience. Benny became associated with the advertising catchphrases they coined; Jack became known as "Nickel Back on the Bottle Benny."[19]

The Canada Dry program was joined by several other radio programs experimenting with integrating humor into their commercials, such as the Texaco, Pabst, and Chase and Sanborn shows. *Variety*'s Ben Bodec commented, "With the improvement of entertainment and production levels has come a change of policy in the handling of the plug. Devious ways are being introduced for feeding it to the listener insinuatingly.... The Ed Wynn, Ben Bernie and Jack Benny sessions show that the product's plug can be kidded and at the same time put over effectively."[20] Other programs that attempted a comedic advertising vein were excoriated by industry critics. *Variety*'s reviewer criticized the Gem Razor program with Bert Lahr, for its "bludgeon type of merchandizing." The show's performers were guilty of "doing an awful lot of nudging of ribs to remind listeners that Gem is twice as thick, much sharper, smoother, cheaper, and smarter. It deprives the program of its charm and tends to leave behind a hostile impression."[21]

In his fourth month of broadcasting for Canada Dry, Benny lost the role of chief commercial-kidder—no more squeaky-voiced talking bottles or write-in contests, or crazy commercial monologues. Perhaps the sponsor and agency had finally had their fill. The integrated commercial bits now focused on the program's announcer, an obnoxious boor (played by the erudite George Hicks, who read the opening and closing ads in a dignified manner) who burst unexpectedly into skits and interrupted conversations with shouted-out hard sell plugs for product.

Despite positive critical reaction to the advertising and entertainment, Canada Dry remained dissatisfied with Benny's handling of the program (as we saw in chapter 1) and cancelled its sponsorship on January 24, 1933. Benny next learned that there were pitfalls in being too closely associated with a particular product. He found that few sponsors would consider him, concerned that he had become so closely associated with Canada Dry Ginger Ale that radio audiences would reject his commercials for other products. Old Gold cigarettes passed on working with him. Benny only acknowledged his frustration and humiliation twenty years later on his radio show, through a joking comment made by Mary Livingstone, that she pulled Jack out of his car, trying to kill himself with carbon monoxide poisoning, when his first sponsor fired him.[22]

In late February 1933, after several other radio entertainers changed sponsors without the sky falling, NBC finally convinced the Chevrolet automobile company to pick up Benny's option.[23] Chevrolet was dealing with daunting challenges of its own. The winter of 1933 was the nadir point of the Depression, with lame-duck President Hoover powerless to stem the tide of bank failures, unemployment, and despair flooding over the broken U.S. economy. Who could even think of purchasing a new car? Chevrolet was teetering on the edge of bankruptcy. Radio was the one bright spot in American advertising, so program sponsors counted on it to provide miracles like *Amos 'n' Andy* continued to do for Pepsodent toothpaste sales. Chevrolet had been sponsoring a radio musical program starring Al Jolson, but the temperamental singer suddenly quit his contract. Benny agreed to pick up the final six programs of the season, with Frank Black leading an NBC house orchestra.

The new Chevrolet program debuted on one of the least auspicious dates possible, March 3, 1933, the night before Franklin D. Roosevelt's inauguration. Maybe the Benny gang's cut-ups helped momentarily assuage the "fear" that FDR would focus on in his next day's speech. Even Chevrolet's opening commercial acknowledged that economic worries were paramount on listeners' minds–"Ladies and Gentlemen: if you have some money to invest and are wondering where to put it—here's a suggestion, Take that money of yours and use it to buy a new Chevrolet Six. There's no safer, sounder investment than the purchase of an automobile."[24]

Howard Claney became the program's sixth announcer. Like George Hicks before him, Claney interrupted the characters' dialogue with self-important announcements about new Chevrolet cars. The comic advertisements now were significantly less biting in tone than what Canada Dry had allowed.[25] In October 1933, after an anxious three months off the air when GM withdrew from advertising, Benny's program was shifted yet again, this time to Sunday evenings at 10:00 P.M.[26] Benny was able to carry over bandleader Frank Black, but he had to take on yet another new announcer, Alois Havrilla, and new tenor Frank Parker. Both, however, soon became accomplished comic performers under Benny's tutelage. The Chevrolet show gained steadily increasing audiences, higher ratings, and critical approval. All seemed to be going well for the program, *Variety* praising it for

> the well-conceived kidding manner of the sales delivery, striking a new high in humorous exploitation and likewise a new evolution of that style of plugging. Announcer Alois Havrilla brings in a comedy ad plug that commands good humored respect for its general ingenuity. Along with that, Benny's series of travesties on current plays or pictures permits for a world of latitude ... and a sock of plugs for Chevrolet.[27]

Suddenly Benny's sponsor again threw a monkey wrench into his operations. Marvin Coyle was elevated to the position of Chevrolet's general manager in October 1933.[28] Coyle preferred classical music to the current popular band tunes and comedy featured on Benny's program. Coyle instructed the Ewell Campbell ad agency to reduce Benny's humorous patter to only five minutes and have the musicians fill the half hour with "romantic melodies."[29] Furious, Benny told the sponsor the he flatly refused to either truncate the comedy or change the music, as he felt that light comedy needed light music. He threatened to quit the program immediately if Coyle's changes were made. While this ultimatum temporarily worked for Benny, Coyle cancelled the program on April 1, 1934, and instead picked up a musical program featuring Victor Young's orchestra.[30] Chevrolet car dealers in Nebraska and elsewhere expressed their frustration with the show's cancellation, as they had considered Benny's program a helpful marketing tool: "Benny's programs rate high in this section and seems to have been a good warming point for the salesmen to start off their song and dance with when a customer comes in. . . . April finds the heavy selling just getting under way and with the good listener [program] out, it's unfortunate."

Chevrolet's top executive dictating the content of its sponsored radio shows entered ad agency lore as one of the most boneheaded moves of all time. A 1951 article in *Sponsor* instructed corporate executives to heed Chevrolet's mistake:

The sponsor must be on guard against his own private prejudices. Classic is the incident of the Chevrolet tycoon who passed by Jack Benny just at the start of Benny's first nationwide wave of popularity because he, the tycoon, personally preferred classical music to jokes. Big man though he was, this sponsor was wrist-slapped by the General Motors high command for allowing purely personal preferences to determine corporate decision.[31]

The very public firing mortified Benny. In subsequent years, even when he could joke about being released by Canada Dry, Benny never spoke publically about the Chevrolet episode, maintaining that his show moved directly from Canada Dry to his next sponsor, General Tire.[32]

BENNY GAINS GREATER PROGRAM CONTROL

In April 1934, as NBC executives beat the bushes to locate a new sponsor for Benny's very expensive program at midseason (and not lose him again to CBS), Bertha Brainard alerted president Niles Trammel to Benny's growing list of demands. Having now done battle twice with sponsors who wanted to alter his show, Benny would have no more of it. His program's steady rise in the ratings gave him significant bargaining power, despite the two cancellations, to secure greater creative control.

Benny first sought to be able to make more of the casting and hiring decisions. Benny wished to provide more of a complete "package" program to present to a potential sponsor. Benny could count on Mary Livingstone's services, of course, and he had paid writer Harry Conn out of his own earnings since 1932. Now he sought to employ his own announcer. It was an indication of how important keeping that comedic element of commercials integrated into the program was to Benny that he chose to hire the announcer, rather than a singer or band leader (they would still be under contract to the sponsor, ad agency, or network).

Second, Benny wanted more control over where he broadcast from, and what he did in between weekly episodes. In 1934, Benny increasingly began traveling back and forth to Hollywood to make movies, and MGM pressured him to make a full slate of films. NBC and most East-Coast-based sponsors were very unhappy, however, with the idea of Benny broadcasting from California. They tried to prevent it, or put major restrictions on where Benny could broadcast the radio show. Benny sought to be able to take his cast west, even though it might mean having to pick up a different orchestra, bandleader, and singer in Los Angeles, as bands based on either coast sought to play steady engagements during the week to supplement their radio incomes. Making personal appearance tours at major theaters across the United States was a significant boost to Benny's own income between radio broadcasts, and Benny sought more ability to take the radio cast on the road to maximize their public exposure and income opportunities.

Bertha Brainard reported to Niles Trammel that "Benny insists clause be in contract permitting him to make pictures in Hollywood at any time he can. He to pay wire charges. Also clause in contract definitely stating program formula and his style must be accepted as is and at no time will he permit direction from agency or client on style of program."[33] She also warned Trammel, "Again wish to emphasize Benny on General Tire follows Ed Wynn and we believe it would be bad programming and are not in accord with idea." Benny was frustrated about his lack of input into decisions about where his program fell in the network's evening schedule. In the same way that vaudeville bills had been organized not to place the comics one right after another, Benny did not want his quiet humor to follow a raucous comedy program. NBC offered little help in this regard, as radio program scheduling in the 1930s was far more organized around sponsors "owning" of specific schedule times as opposed to the network building a strong lineup of programs that would help each other build audiences.

Brainard finally located a possible sponsor. General Tire had been sponsoring a dramatic show called *Lives at Stake*, but some listeners thought it too violent.[34] However, the company had relatively few advertising funds available—the tire industry had been devastated by the Depression, and close to 80 percent of workers in the chief rubber production center of Akron, Ohio, were then unemployed. General Tire was only able to afford a six-month sponsorship. To get Benny back on the air in midseason, the radio program's broadcast time shifted again, to Friday evenings at 10:30 P.M., and the show had to pick up yet another new orchestra leader (Don Bestor), but was able to retain popular tenor Frank Parker.

Benny hired Don Wilson to be the eighth announcer on the program in two years. Instead of just having Wilson shout advertising slogans, Benny and Conn slowly returned the comic integrated commercials back to more of the silly things they had done with Canada Dry. Wilson soon blossomed as a fine comic stooge and became a full member of the cast; in skits parodying romantic melodramas, Don's character climbed ladders to help Mary's character elope; Jack began joking about Don's girth. Jack and Don played a hilarious sketch in which Don invited Jack out to the Wilson home for the weekend to meet his parents, with disastrous results. Fans responded enthusiastically. Marya Davis of El Paso, Texas, won a $10 prize from fan magazine *Radio Mirror* for a letter on how that "necessary evil," of commercials might be converted into a program asset. "Advertising can be both funny and effective—if made part of the program itself. Consider the riotous way Jack Benny sandwiches in references to General Tire. We don't resent such advertising because it is presented humorously."[35]

Come October 1934, it was time to switch to the alternate sponsor, which would mean upheavals in broadcast time and agency management. General Tire tried to make the best of the awkward change-over. Don Wilson read a telegram on air sent by Bill O'Neill, president of General Tire, to Jack:

> Except for your interference on these programs, Don Wilson could have told our audience much more about our new corkscrew tire. You insist the show's the thing, and on that score I want to compliment you and the cast on 26 weeks of fine entertainment. Until we resume these programs next March, you will be broadcasting for General Foods. The only connection between General Foods and General Tires is that we eat their products and they wear ours. You have to eat to live, but you have to live to be able to eat—so the more people we put on General Tires, the more customers we keep for General Foods.[36]

The 7:00 P.M. Sunday slot in which General Food's Jell-O division scheduled the Benny show was a no-man's land for radio entertainers and sponsors alike. While Eddie Cantor had been able to pull in massive audiences with an 8:00 P.M. Sunday program, others (especially anything earlier) fared poorly, making Sunday overall the lowest rated night of the week.[37] Early Sunday evening presented Benny with audience taste challenges. Conservative Christian families attended church services on Sunday evenings and might not be available, or would decline to listen. Many families were eating Sunday dinner—would they be too preoccupied to listen? Other families travelled to visit relatives or took Sunday drives out into the countryside, and while a growing number of automobiles now featured radios, would passengers tune in Benny's radio program while on the road? For two years, Benny's program had been broadcast late in the evening, usually after 10:00 P.M., and critics thought his humor was sophisticated and adult focused (if rarely blue). Now he was going on the air three hours earlier. Would Benny's humor be considered appropriate for all members of the family audience? Furthermore, a program at this early edge of the prime time evening schedule had no lead-in shows preceding it to build a ready-made audience. Broadcasting a comedy program on early Sunday evening was a gamble only a desperate sponsor might make.

JELL-O—A PRODUCT IN DIRE STRAITS

A forty-year-old gelatin dessert product, Jell-O was a lead weight in the General Foods brand portfolio. Sales had fallen by two-thirds since the company had been incorporated into the General Foods conglomerate of packaged food lines in 1924. Jell-O's problems were threefold. First was the product itself—it didn't taste as good as the competition and took a long time to prepare. Packaged gelatin was one of the most processed food products imaginable, fabricated from ground-up cow and pig hides and hooves, with artificial colors and flavors added to the sugar that filled 60 percent of the box. In 1933, General Foods' chemists improved the fruit oils used in creating Jell-O, expanded the flavor range to six flavors, and reduced by half the time it took housewives to fix it. A second problem was Jell-O's outmoded marketing focus. For the previous forty years, most of Jell-O's advertising had been addressed to children; magazine advertisements featured the pretty blond "Jell-O Girl," cartoon zoo animals, and illustrations of children preparing the product (to demonstrate how easy it was to make, and how fun it was to eat). Competing products, however, were appealing to sophisticated young homemakers.

A third problem was even more deadly. *Fortune Magazine* reported that General Foods' operating principle was to "take an unnecessary but established product, dress it up with all the art of the industrial designer, spend plenty of money in advertising it, sell it with every variety of high pressure that the art of the sales promotion manager can devise, and try to collect a long profit." However, as in the case of Jell-O, these actions "attract[ed] competitive swarms of smaller concerns which are willing to work at a shorter profit and which more than once have cut ground out from under General Foods products." Increased competition in the gelatin field was destroying Jell-O's market share. Royal Gelatin, produced by rival packaged food manufacturer Standard Brands, was considered better tasting. The A&P grocery store chain started marketing its own private label gelatin, Sparkle, and both these products as well as other small label competitors sold for significantly less than Jell-O. Jell-O cost 10–12 cents per package in 1929, while competing brands sold for only 6 cents. Especially as the Depression's hard times diminished consumers' incomes, they purchased less expensive foodstuffs. Perhaps only a marketing miracle could rescue this dying product.[38]

Executives from Y&R pitched to General Foods vice president Ralph Starr Butler a plan to save Jell-O by cutting prices, boosting sales, and redirecting the marketing focus. The ad agency had brought massive marketing success to other General Food brands such as Post Cereals, Postum, and Maxwell House coffee. Y&R, as Cynthia Meyers discusses in her history of radio advertising, was especially devoted to the soft sell approach, and its work with Postum and other General Foods brands in print and on radio demonstrated that advertising could be tremendously successful in creating consumer awareness and emotional loyalty to both the sponsors' programs and products.[39] Now Y&R advocated changing Jell-O's advertising strategy to focus on homemakers, reduce the product price, and spend much more on radio and print promotions. Despite the Depression, packaged foods represented a growing segment of the American consumer market. Food expenses represented a massive 37 percent of American family budgets during the 1930s. Convenient, inexpensive packaged foods were poised to take a more prominent place in busy families' market baskets.[40]

Y&R advised Jell-O's product managers to drop their current radio advertising sponsorship of a *Wizard of Oz*–themed children's program, and instead join one of the most popular trends in radio programming—the comedy/variety program. Most of the top comedians, however, such as Will Rogers and Eddie Cantor, were already locked into long-term contracts. Y&R suggested Jack Benny for the role, but General Foods had concerns that Benny's was one of the most expensive programs on network radio, and Jell-O's annual sponsorship costs would triple. Y&R executive Lou Brockway later recalled that "We were very frank with our client in presenting Benny. We said he was not our first or second or third choice but he was available and he had a good, if not outstanding, record."[41] Jell-O's management cautiously agreed to pick up the program, but warned that product sales must rapidly increase in order for the show to remain on the air.

Under orders to produce impressive results in advertising as well as sparkling comedy, the first Sunday night Jell-O broadcast (October 14, 1934) enthusiastically integrated commercial messages into the entertainment. A chorus introduced the new musical signature, cheerfully singing out the letters "J-E-L-L-O," a bit that orchestra leader Frank Black had composed on the fly. After the opening commercial (a newsboy shouting Jell-O headlines), Jack opened the program with a new twist on his regular greeting, turning "Hello again" into "Jell-O again everybody!" Jack joked with Don Wilson about the many ways they could be incorporating the sponsor's product into the show's dialogue. Don claimed he had purchased neckties in six colors to represent the six delicious flavors, while Jack quipped that Don has already gotten a strawberry flavor stain on an orange tie. Jack cautioned Don not to be too obvious when he worked mentions of Jell-O into the show, for example, not to say "Los An-Jell-O." Mary soon entered, spouting jokes about blown-out tire tubes, and the cast laughed that she was a week too late. In the second show, Don broke into the middle of the dialogue in Benny's parody of the film *The Barretts of Wimpole Street*. When Mary as Elizabeth cried out that she felt she was lost in the desert, Wilson leapt in to announce, "Speaking of DESERT, you will find that Jell-O is the grandest DESSERT your family has ever tasted, and you can get it in six delicious flavors, strawberry, raspberry cherry, orange, lemon, and lime!" The studio audience laughed heartily at the pun.[42]

The revamped Benny program was an immediate ratings success, but sales of Jell-O did not budge. Mary recalled General Foods' anxiety that improvement was not occurring quickly enough for the company to be able to justify the expense of sponsoring the pricey program. On the verge of cancelling the program, General Foods executives mandated that the entire cast take pay cuts. Mary and Jack told the sponsors that they would rather carry the burden themselves, and the two of them worked without salary for weeks to keep the rest of the cast on a living wage. Finally, after three months, Jell-O boxes started flying off grocers' shelves. Don Wilson in a closing commercial in December 1934 went to great lengths to praise the radio audience for purchasing Jell-O in such large quantities.[43] Relieved executives from General Foods and Y&R hosted a cast party at the Benny's New York apartment, and the sponsor made a show of presenting Jack and Mary with a check representing all of their back pay. Mary recalled her chagrin at being overheard chiding a maid who had appeared with a huge platter of Jell-O (sent by the sponsor) to "put that crap wherever."

A radio critic in 1951 attested to the powerful synergy that Don Wilson's vocal talents and friendly personality brought to Benny's commercials: "There's much in a voice. It can be strong, vibrant, confident; warm, persuasive, infectious. The voice of [Don] Wilson, currently heard on the Jack Benny Show . . . has these qualities. It has been termed: 'America's finest selling voice'."[44] Wilson had first entered into radio in the 1920s in California as a singer and announcer, where his color commentary at Rose Bowl football

FIGURE 16. Unlike previous sponsors' unease with Jack Benny's thorough mixture of impertinent mentions of the product into his comedy, Jell-O was pleased to promote his ratings and product sales success. Plymouth Theater program, Boston, November 26, 1934. Author's collection.

games and other sporting events brought him attention and an invitation to move to New York in 1932. Jack Benny hired Wilson for the *General Tire Program* in spring 1934, after hearing him read just a few lines, recalling, "He had a warm voice, he could read a commercial with laughter in his throat, and he proved a great foil to play against." Descriptions of Wilson emphasized his "beaming good-naturalness" and his "infectious laugh"; he was "the jocular, rotund radio announcer who joked and winced at Jack Benny's wisecracks" about his extreme girth (in reality Wilson stood over six feet tall and weighed 240 pounds). Wilson soon began placing high in annual polls of best announcers, and earning awards from the *Radio Guide*, *New York World Telegram*, and *Motion Picture Daily*.

Wilson advised aspiring radio advertising copywriters that "The warmth and acceptability of the announcer . . . who is sincere and whose voice is recognized by the listener as that of a friend in the house. . . . will then make all the difference in the world to the quality of the message itself."[45] Wilson's personality-imbued vocal performance, matched with expressive, emotional language provided by Y&R copywriters, such as this March 1936 example, turned even the "straight" opening and closing commercials for the Jell-O program into synesthetic sensory experiences for listeners to taste, see, and smell:

> One of the strongest influences in our lives, I think, is color; black and white is fine for an etching, but we all need bright colors to keep our spirits up. When it comes to colors, that is where Jell-O shines, it's the liveliest, gayest dessert you can find. Sunshiny orange, shimmering green, the deep rich tones of rose and crimson, six different colors from which to choose, every one lovely, clear and glowing. . . . And when it comes to taste, AHHH, that is where Jell-O shines again, for its packed cram full of delicious real fruit flavor, flavor as truly luscious as the fresh ripe fruit itself.[46]

Radio writer Charles Wolfe claimed that the "personalized salesmanship" that the best announcers brought to their performance played the most important role in making radio a potent sales tool. "Radio's employment of the human voice adds living vitality, immediacy, warmth, sincerity, individuality and persuasiveness which give radio a unique distinction among advertising media and which are largely responsible for its selling power."[47] In this April 16, 1939, closing commercial for the Jell-O program, Wilson explained the synergy between announcer, evocative ad copy, and the audiences' receptive mood that created such a marketing juggernaut:

A friend of mine paid me a REAL compliment the other day. She said, "You know, Don, when you describe those Jell-O desserts over the radio, you just make me HUNGRY for them." Well naturally I was pleased, and tonight I have another new Jell-O dessert I know will make a hit with everybody. A combination of raspberry Jell-O and cottage cheese, and I'm TELLING you, Ha, it's swell and easy to make, too. Dissolve one package of raspberry Jell-O in one pint of hot water and turn into a ring mold and chill until firm. Then unmold it and fill the center with cottage cheese. Serve it with toasted crackers, and THERE is a TRIUMPH of desserts. Clear, shimmering raspberry hello with its EXTRA rich flavor and creamy cottage cheese, SMOOTH and tempting. So try it. Ask your grocer tomorrow for raspberry Jell-O.[48]

As the purported comment attested, a key aspect of the Jell-O ads' effectiveness was Don Wilson's ability, through a combination of his vocal performance and the commercial texts, to make multifaceted appeals to the listeners' senses and emotions, and make as many positive associations with the product as possible.[49]

Most of Don Wilson's integrated mentions of Jell-O do not read humorously in scripted form. The wry comedy came from his tone of voice, quick quips, and butting into dialogue with the catch phrases "big red letters on the box," "genuine Jell-O," and six delicious flavors. The name "Jell-O" was sprinkled liberally throughout the scripts, from characters on a ship called the "Jell-O-a" or a family's children being named Orange, Lemon, and Lime, to skit titles such as "The Count of Monte Jell-O" and "Romeo and Jell-O-ette." A reviewer claimed to have heard the product name mentioned thirty times in a single show. When *Radio Mirror* published several Jack Benny program scripts in 1937 to give listeners a way to re-create the pleasure of listening to the show during the late-summer months the cast was off the air, even the scripts included integrated commercials.[50] Jack boasted about being a musician and having played the violin in concert halls "long before I knew anything about strawberry, cherry, orange, lemon, and lime." Don interjected, "You left out raspberry," and Mary retorted, "I'll bet the audience didn't."

JACK BENNY AND JELL-O MERGE IDENTITIES

By 1935, Jack Benny had become the embodiment of Jell-O, indelibly associating the product with his light, zany, character-gang-driven comedy. Cartoon images of Benny and Mary Livingstone were found in brightly

FIGURE 17. Jack Benny and Mary Livingstone are transformed into cartoon characters happily consuming the playful product in this popular Jell-O giveaway recipe booklet. Millions of copies were given away by mail in 1937. Jell-O booklet, 1937. Author's collection.

colored Jell-O ads placed in all the major women's and family magazines. In 1937, General Foods published *Jack and Mary's Jell-O Book*, featuring the stars, photos of their faces superimposed on stick-figure bodies, telling ridiculous Jell-O-related puns and offering elaborate recipes. The booklet was available for a few cents plus some proofs of purchases mailed to General Foods. The company received 67 million Jell-O box tops in response. Confused housewives were said to ask for "Red or Green Benny" at the grocery store. A New York City luncheonette's bill of fare listed strawberry Jell-O as "Jack Benny in the Red," and hotel banquet menus offered "Dessert a la Benny." A 1939 poll of consumers found that 92.5 percent of Jack Benny's radio audience automatically identified him with his sponsor's product.[51]

Benny's connection to Jell-O was also cemented by his film studios. In an elaborate two-page cartoon-caricature ad MGM placed in *Variety* in November 1935 to promote *A Night at the Opera*, a cartoon in which Benny took a prominent place among a dozen comics gathered in theater seats to praise the Marx Brother's "comeback" film. Benny quipped, "*A Night at the*

Opera is great entertainment with its six delicious flavors—strawberry, raspberry, cherry, Groucho, Chico, and Harpo."[52] When Benny and his radio cast appeared onstage at the Paramount Theater in New York in 1939, promoting their new Paramount film *Man about Town*, *Variety*'s reviewer marveled, "When Benny mentioned his sponsor, Jell-O, it evoked a burst of applause, probably some sort of record—a dessert being applauded in a Broadway deluxer."[53]

The downside of this close identification of Benny with Jell-O, for the sponsor, was if Benny garnered negative publicity. That is what happened in 1939 when Benny and George Burns were indicted in federal court on jewelry smuggling and tax evasion charges. Newspaper headlines across the country blared sordid details of the case. Benny was terrified that his program would be canceled and his career would be ruined. His sponsor was nervous about public backlash. NBC executives forbade network comics to joke about the case on the air.[54] The advertising trade press declared it risky to have too much dependence on individual celebrities to sell their products.[55] Fortunately for Benny and Burns, the judge slapped them with a sizable fine rather than jail time, and with help from Y&R, they were able to overcome the incident.

Jack Benny's success in the 1930s mingling entertainment and product marketing took place in a climate of growing public outrage against radio's domination by commercial advertising. Between Dr. Brinkley's goat gland shilling, and the never-ending stream of loud, obnoxious ads for products to combat bodily malfunctions, consumer groups, critics, and the public were increasingly raising objections. An April 1936 *Billboard* review of a new Lever Brothers comedy program featuring Ken Murray claimed that the unfunny ads intruded vulgarly and aggressively into the body of the program, and held up the Jell-O program as an unmatched model.

> It was Jack Benny, who, we believe, started the vogue of referring via gag material to his sponsor's product. But there is only one Jack Benny. And everybody who knows the degree of Benny's wit and personality register compared with any other comedian on the air will admit that only Benny can talk about Jell-O and its flavors without working up a feeling of revulsion in the listening audience.[56]

Despite, or perhaps because of, the widespread criticism, accolades for the Jell-O commercials accumulated.[57] In 1938, Benny's commercials won an award from the 10 million members of the Women's National Radio Committee for "first place for good taste in advertising."[58] In February 1940 the trade journal *Advertising and Selling* presented Y&R with a "Medal Award" for the "appetizing" tenor of its Jell-O commercials:

> Attracting and holding attention, explains Y&R, building conviction and stimulating sales have all been done in an APPETIZING manner. By deftly blending salesmanship with entertainment—keeping it always a part of the program, this series has demonstrated to listeners and broadcasters alike what effective selling by air can mean. Don Wilson's jovially reiterated sales points, like "six delicious flavors" and "look for the big red letters on the box," have become national catch phrases. Further evidence of this continuity skill is found every Sunday night, when commercials woven into the body of the show draw delighted, spontaneous applause from the studio audience. When consumers can be subjected to advertising—and LIKE it—the advertiser can be sure the job is being well done.[59]

Ad agencies played essential behind-the-scenes functions in the 1930s and 1940s in the creation of top radio programs (developing concepts, casting, scripting, and packaging). Assessing Y&R's role in the success of the Jell-O program, agency vice president Everhard Meade recalled,

> Y&R didn't build the Benny show—Benny built it. But in building it, he had agency guidance, counsel and help [with] production at every turn. As in other historical cases, an agency played the crucial role. Enough enthusiastic, skilled people had faith at the right time to go to bat for Jack in the now forgotten days when it was touch and go whether the great man would get his first Jell-O renewal.

Meade claimed that Y&R's most important service to radio sponsors included "the act of going out on a limb and saying to a client: 'Because we think so, because research backs us up, because we have a damn good hunch, buy this show—it costs a million bucks.'"[60]

Y&R was staffed with young creative minds who believed in the promise of radio promotion for inexpensive packaged food, drug, and toiletry products. Benny worked with talented people at this agency with whom he would work frequently during the rest of his career, including Pat Weaver, Tom Harrington, Ted Lewis, Don Stauffer, and Bob Ballin. Y&R's radio department was hugely successful in the 1930s in handling their radio programs, sensing when to leave them alone and when to tweak them. Y&R staffers knew how to work with performers, too. Weaver especially endeared himself to Fred Allen and Jack Benny, running interference for Fred Allen to spare the prickly star unnecessary interactions with broadcasting bureaucracy. Weaver recalled that "Allen hated agencies, clients and networks indiscriminately." According to Allen, Weaver's efforts "at least made life bearable."[61]

Despite their vital importance to Benny's work, records documenting advertising agency interactions are largely missing both from Benny's archives and their own. Benny and his writers created an omnipotent "Sponsor" character for the radio program, who could reduce employee Jack to a quivering heap with a phone call or telegram. The Benny program's workplace situation comedy narrative of the 1930s and 1940s, however, did not include characters from advertising agencies. Agencies remained invisible in Benny's narrative world until the early 1950s, when American Tobacco switched its account to Batton, Barton, Durstine, and Osborne (BBDO). Benny and his writers then occasionally incorporated jokes into the program about the name BBDO sounding like boxes falling down some stairs, and Jack briefly dated a flirtatious secretary who worked for "Lil' Old Mr. Osborne."

With so little documentary evidence of Jack Benny's relationships with his ad agencies, I will relate only one story from December 1936, when Y&R executives brainstormed a publicity idea. Jack Benny and Fred Allen had been acquaintances (if not close friends) for years in vaudeville and radio. In fact, Benny mentioned Fred Allen on his early radio programs more often than any other comic. It was nothing more than an offhand jest on December 30, 1936, however, when in the talent show portion of the *Town Hall Tonight* program, Fred Allen complimented the violin performance of young Stuart Canin, by saying Benny would be envious of the boy's prowess. By chance, in the earlier, scripted half of the episode, Allen and his partner Portland Hoffa had mentioned Benny. Ditzy Portland claimed that Jack's latest film release was "Benny's from Heaven" (having confused it with Bing Crosby's movie *Pennies from Heaven*). Fred took the opportunity to disparage both Jack and his hometown of Waukegan. Perhaps Benny was on Allen's mind as a target that evening.[62]

There is little firm evidence of what happened next. Only years afterward, industry insiders admitted that it was a Y&R executive who suggested to Allen and Benny that they cook up a fake dispute; not coincidentally, Y&R handled both programs. The agency publically denied any responsibility, so that Benny and Allen could maintain that the feud sprang up organically. It would make much better publicity fodder that way.

FIGURE 18. Young and Rubicam, the advertising agency for the Jell-O program, maintained that their "soft sell" approach which completely integrated advertising and comedy in their top show, not only made the Benny program highest in the ratings but brought awards for commercial writing, and sold the product at extraordinary rates. Young and Rubicam ad, *Fortune*, February 1937, 121. Author's collection.

Pittsburgh Post-Gazette radio columnist S. I. Steinhauser was one of the few journalists to spill the beans on the manufactured Hatfield and McCoy gimmick: "All of this 'shooting' is the smart idea of one Don Stauffer, a former Scottsdale, Pa. boy, who directs programs for one of radio's biggest advertising agencies."[63] Apparently, fast-thinking Don Stauffer suggested to Benny and Allen in mid-December that they turn the incident into a continuing media event. Fred Allen's program scripts from these broadcasts contained a separate section added to the show with up-to-the-minute Benny insults that played off barbs that Benny had thrown just three nights before.[64]

Allen's portion of the feud was launched on his January 13, 1937, program. Benny retorted the next week with injured reactions and returned threats. Allen's program followed Benny's Sunday program on Wednesday nights, and for nine weeks the entire nation eagerly anticipated the exchange of insults. Before its denouement on March 14, 1937, the Benny-Allen feud garnered hundreds of stories in the press and fan magazines, a publicity and ratings bonanza for their shows. Y&R executives patted themselves on the back for a superb stunt. Steinhauser noted at the feud's conclusion how it had benefitted the performers as well as the ad agency, sponsor and network:

> Fred Allen is dumb like a fox. Since he started his "feud" with Jack Benny, his program has moved up 5.1 percent in coast to coast popularity, according to the latest accepted survey. Jack has moved up only one-tenth of one per cent, according to the same survey. Which proves that Fred has the upper hand in the "argument" if surveys mean anything. But Jack is still Number One comedian, according to the survey and has been for years.... Our personal choice in a "feud" is Fred Allen because he is faster on the trigger, writes his own quips, ad libs many of them—a thing Jack Benny simply can't do—and can move his jibes at Jack in and out of the full hour program without spoiling the show. Jack, on the other hand, plans an attack on Fred, shoots the works, and then returns to his program routine.[65]

The comedians got the last laughs, however. The idea of the feud provided priceless material for the two performers for years to come, long after they had acquired new sponsors and ad agencies. The public loved playing along that Benny and Allen were bitter enemies, and delighted in their inspired verbal sparring over the years when the two met to insult each other, to vie for sponsors, to recall who had the superior vaudeville act, or to satirize the other's radio narrative formulas.

LEAVING JELL-O, AND GETTING LUCKY?

Despite the award-winning commercials, enormous product sales, and synergistic fame that the relationship brought both Jell-O and Jack Benny throughout the 1930s, fissures in the Benny–General Foods collaboration nevertheless grew. Benny tussled with Y&R over the control of cast member contracts. The agency had insisted on managing Kenny Baker, the young tenor Benny had developed into a rising star. Y&R did little to hold Baker, however, and he left the program, and Benny in the lurch, in spring 1939. (Benny was, however, able to put Baker's replacement Dennis Day under personal contract.) Benny refused to renew his own Jell-O contract in spring 1940 unless he was given absolute control over the cast, orchestra, sound effects, writers, and producer in the future,[66] and thus negotiated the strongest management held by any performer in the radio industry.

By late 1940, General Foods found that they were reaching the upper limits of Jell-O sales. The corporation had already added two extensions to the product line, Jell-O Puddings and Jell-O Ice Cream Mix, to ride on the coattails of Benny-generated sales success. The company spent $790,000 for 39 weeks of the Benny program, a cost that represented a little more than 2 cents for each dollar of Jell-O sales (at 6 cents retail per package). Jell-O sales accounted for 25 percent of all General Foods income, but the corporate accountants could not advise continuing this enormous marketing expense.[67]

General Foods needed their expensive but successful salesman to remain in their fold and advertise other products, but Benny balked. He didn't want to lose such a rich and colorful source of humor, and the sponsor's plan to switch him to the Grape Nuts account was unappealing. Benny flirted with Old Gold cigarettes and Campbell soups. General Foods, Y&R, and NBC executives scrambled to placate the comedian. Campbell's was nearly successful in stealing the comic, and industry gossip said that only heroic efforts by Y&R's Tom Harrington and NBC's Bertha Brainard kept Benny and General Foods together.[68] Y&R made tremendous hoopla over a celebration of Benny's tenth anniversary of broadcasting, with awards, dinners, and commemorative sections published in the trade papers. NBC came up with the last-ditch idea of "gifting" Benny with the Sunday 7:00 P.M. time slot, which would be forever his, no matter what sponsor he was with, an entitlement that had never previously been granted to a performer.[69] These compliments (and a raise) closed the deal in April 1941, and Benny remained with Jell-O.[70]

Just twelve months later, however, sudden wartime sugar rationing in spring 1942 curtailed Jell-O production, and the gelatin division could no longer afford Benny. General Foods announced that it was switching Benny's program to Grape Nuts and swapping in the significantly less expensive to produce Kate Smith program. Cereal supplies were not limited, General Foods optimistically reminded Benny.[71] Unfortunately, no matter how Benny's writers tried, Grape Nuts and Grape Nuts Flakes were just not as ripe for silly commercials as Jell-O had been, with a few exceptions like the Twink Family skits in 1942 (discussed in the Mary Livingstone chapter).

By early 1944, Benny had grown weary of General Foods. Despite the outward happiness of their relationship, Benny was frustrated that his ratings were steadily declining, and the sponsor was not supporting his program with sufficient investment in advertising and public relations to help him regain ground.[72] Benny put his show up for bid. He had complete control over NBC's Sunday 7:00–7:30 P.M. time slot, which he had done much to build into what was now the preeminent broadcasting segment in all of network radio. General Foods thought differently—*they* had financed the Jell-O broadcasts and thought the time slot should remain theirs, and fought hard to keep Benny. "There were five different companies that went after whatever deal we wanted," Benny later recalled. "The two of them we were trying to decide on were Campbell Soup and American Tobacco and I finally picked Lucky Strike because of a man in the agency [Don Stauffer] that I happened to know who represented Lucky Strikes at that time." Despite the dreadful reputation that American Tobacco had earned for its outrageous ads, Stauffer convinced Benny that he could run interference with one of the most fearsome sponsors of them all.[73]

In February 1944, *Variety* headlines proclaimed that the American Tobacco Company had snared Benny for Pall Mall cigarettes.[74] Benny's requirements included nearly complete control of the program's writing, casting, and payroll, time off in the summer, and flexible scheduling to allow him to make personal appearance tours, radio guest appearances, and to work in motion pictures. His new sponsor not only upped Benny's salary package by 10 percent but also promised Benny a three-year contract, and a $250,000 "slush fund" budget for public relations expenses. *Variety* said that George Washington Hill was "so desirous of obtaining Benny that he is willing to offer all kinds of concessions."[75]

Benny, the master of soft sell advertising, was taking on a huge new challenge in working with Hill, creator of the most irritating and obnoxious ads on radio. Model for the rapacious, impossible sponsor Evan Llewellyn Evans in Frederick Wakeman's 1946 tell-all novel *The Hucksters*,[76] Hill was an advertising evil genius and lived for selling Lucky Strikes and his other cigarette brands by any means.[77] Hill had been an early adopter of radio advertising, sponsoring the *Lucky Strike Dance Band* beginning in September 1928, underwriting programs of popular hits and dance music for three decades. Hill was infamous for forcing NBC president Aylesworth to dance to the broadcast tunes with Bertha Brainard while Hill looked on, to make sure the tunes appropriately fit his standards of dance music.[78]

Lucky Strike's radio advertisements were notorious for obnoxious slogans, shouting commercials, and vulgar brashness. Earlier print ads had touted "Reach for a Lucky instead of a Sweet," and "Its Toasted." Shouting announcers in 1940s radio ads proclaimed "Lucky Strike green has gone to war!" Such huckstering didn't seem to correlate with Benny's smooth style of advertising humor at all. January 1944 (several months before Benny negotiated with Hill) had seen and heard the debut of Lucky's "LS/MFT" (Lucky Strike Means Fine Tobacco) campaign.[79] The sloganned letters, endlessly repeated with lines of "triphammer" copy, combined with tobacco auctioneer Speedy Rigg's cacophonous chants drove radio listeners crazy.[80]

In 1943, radio producer Dan Golenpaul, whose urbane quiz-show-cum-panel discussion program *Information Please* was rather incongruously sponsored by Lucky Strike, actually sued American Tobacco to try to stop the outrageous advertising campaign Hill demanded be run during the program. Lucky's announcer had been barking "The best tunes of all move to Carnegie Hall!" as many as nine times during the half hour. *Variety* reported that Hill adamantly "held to his philosophy that it doesn't matter how much you irritate the listener, so long as he remembers the slogan and the name of the product." Golenpaul was unsuccessful in court, but Hill did agree to let *Information Please* out of its contract and find another sponsor.

American Tobacco gambled when they assumed the huge expense of sponsoring Jack Benny's radio program in fall 1944. They were switching from purchasing spot advertising across many stations, times, and programs, to longer-term sponsorship of a major program, and concentrating about $3.9 million (or 80 percent) of their $5 million radio advertising budget into one program.[81] At the same time, there was a cigarette shortage, which reduced company income.[82] "We haven't anything to sell, so why spend millions in advertising?" Hill complained.[83] The shortage of Pall Mall cigarettes drove Hill to suddenly switch Benny's sponsorship over to Lucky Strikes in August 1944, before the new fall radio schedule started.[84]

Frankly, American Tobacco needed Jack Benny's radio program for its advertising strategies—a top rated and very respected show, light and humorous and Benny's reputation for making advertising more congenial and would help soften complaints in the 1940s about Lucky's advertising excesses. Cigarette manufacturers, trying to expand their sales and fight off the growing bad public relations of mounting evidence of links between cancer and smoking, paid for advanced research studies that analyzed smokers' psychological motivations and satisfactions. Historian Richard Pollay reports that one study concluded that "Advertising makes cigarettes respectable, and is thus reassuring." How could someone as wholesome as Benny be connected to something unhealthy? *Variety* reports suggested that Benny's popularity with young people was a draw for American Tobacco, but they warned that use of Benny might set off criticism of having a pied piper advertise cigarettes to children.[85]

Reviewing Benny's first broadcast for Lucky Strike in October 1944, *Variety* speculated on how Benny, his writers, and his cast might apply the Jell-O advertising "magic" to this differing sales situation, wondering "just how Don Wilson, who built up those Jell-O and Grape Nuts commercials into an integral part of the Benny comedy package, will tie in with the Lucky Strike format, in view of the standard auctioneering plugs?" Wilson's role was indeed usurped by long opening and closing commercials in which Basil Rysdale hammered home repeated sales points and Speedy Riggs chanted. Wilson now introduced Jack and made various quips about the brand.

The plot of Benny's opening Lucky Strike episode, of Benny vying with Fred Allen to impress a terrifying new sponsor (creating a fictional G. W. Hill character) was one of the strongest episodes that Benny's writers had created in several years. "Benny has again firmly entrenched himself," *Variety* marveled. "It's a safe bet his followers aren't going to desert him. And if the first show did something else. It unquestionably identified him with his new boss."[86] Critics who hated Hill's advertising tactics speculated on Benny's ability to stem or compromise the flow of irritating ads, and what manner of compromises the cacophony would make to the program's comedy. A reviewer in *Woman's Day* noted:

> Such jokes as "With men who know comedians best, its Benny two to one" have helped to take the curse off the auctioneers, LS/MFT, chartering telegraph keys and the rest of the Lucky Strike nonsense. I'm afraid, however, that it was a question of give and take between Mr. Benny and the sponsor. Certainly, to open the show with a couple of minutes of commercial junk

before Benny comes on is exceptionally bad programming. And I'll bet Benny's toupee is several shades whiter for it. Jack probably gave way on this point, though, to gain the end that he could, later on in the show, poke fun at the sacred advertising cows.[87]

Just two weeks later, however, Benny and his radio crew brought down Hill's wrath upon themselves. The entertainment portion of the program ran over time and they missed broadcasting the closing commercial.[88] *Variety*'s radio columnist Jack Hellman gossiped that

> GW Hill was said to have hit the ceiling and an agency account exec lost his job over it. Whether Don Stauffer, radio head of Ruthraff & Ryan, made that quickie out here from New York to impress on Benny the importance of LS/MFT is conjectural.... We're not insinuating that Mr. Hill scared Benny with his ceiling-hitting but what we do know is that the next week the program was short so there was plenty of time for the final LS/MFT and a bumper crop of theme [music].[89]

Stauffer returned to Hill's office in New York with Benny's deepest apologies. Hill wrote to Benny:

> Mr. Stauffer said you wanted me to know what you were going to do, to wit: Sell LUCKY STRIKE cigarettes.... I am even salesman enough myself to know that it's the year's record that counts, not the individual black day from which we courageously attack our problem the day after. But I don't have to wait this time for the year's record, three shows are enough to convince me that you are going to sell the goods.

THE SPORTSMEN QUARTET'S MANIC MUSICAL COMMERCIALS

And thus it went for two years. The next chapter details the general malaise that affected Benny's show during the latter half of the war, as he lost writers and cast members to the draft, and the scripts became dull. The obnoxious Lucky Strike ads did not help. During the first two years of the Benny show's Lucky Strike sponsorship, Don Wilson no longer provided the opening and closing commercials. His role was reduced to introducing Jack and then making some light-hearted references to Lucky Strikes and its ad slogans during the program. For the start of the fall 1946 season, however, in a renewed spirit of program innovation, Benny planned an experiment to bring a novel softer sell approach to the middle advertisements. G. W. Hill died of a sudden heart attack in September 1946, but to his credit, he must have approved Benny's invention—or Benny, his writers, and musical arranger worked with lightning speed after the funeral.

The September 29, 1946, program had Don Wilson introduce Jack to a group of four male singers, the Sportsmen Quartet, who hummed but never spoke a word of dialogue. Their job would be to sing adaptations of popular songs that incorporated Lucky Strike advertising slogans into the lyrics. Like so many characters in the Benny world, the Sportsmen proceeded to drive Jack nuts by quickly spiraling out of control, spinning their tunes faster and faster, dissolving into a cacophony of LSMFT and Indian war whoops that caused Jack to scream to get them to stop. Although Benny later reminisced that he intended the group to only be on the program a few times, the huge positive critical and popular reaction to the Sportsmen moved Benny and his writers to build the group into regular characters.

The Sportsmen Quartet and their antic, hilarious middle commercials were the hit of a new prime time radio season that otherwise was mired in stagnation and sameness. Now Don Wilson "managed" the Sportsmen Quartet. Benny's manager Irving Fein praised Don's contributions to the comic byplay:

> Don was a great foil for Jack. He was the hearty announcer who tried to get the commercial on the air and Jack would try to thwart him. Sometimes Don would have the Sportsmen Quartet sneak in the commercial. Don would tell Jack the Sportsmen were going to do a song. Then they would sing a chorus of a song. Don would then tell Jack they had one more chorus—and they would sing the commercial.[90]

Variety's Jack Hellman called the humming, singing, wildly antic Sportsmen "the most novel innovation of the new season. It has caught on so well that radio editors around the country are playing it up." Hellman snarkily gossiped that American Tobacco's in-house advertising department was a little miffed at the attention Benny's marketing efforts were getting.[91] The ads also upended NBC bureaucrats, as Hellman noted that the cheeky song parodies were "the bane of network vigilantes" who had difficulty ascertaining where the entertainment ended and the advertising began.[92] *Sponsor* chortled that the Sportsmen not only softened criticism of Lucky's obnoxious advertising, but helped the bottom line—"Even the number one exponent of irritant advertising copy, the American Tobacco Company, has recently discovered that the amusing nonirritant middle commercial on the Jack Benny program was doing a much better selling job than the straight rubs-the-wrong-way approach."[93]

The Sportsmen's singing commercials became as subversive and amusingly outrageous as Benny's earliest Canada Dry ads. When the Sportsmen sang the words of American Tobacco's advertising jargon, Lucky Strike's endlessly repeated ad slogans "LSMFT," "so round and firm and fully packed, so free and easy on the draw," "never a rough puff," "quality of product is essential to continuing success," or "Lucky Strike means fine tobacco" seemed to lose any kind of meaning and became totally absurd gibberish. All the silliness, and the Sportsmen's manic performances, could have worked, for some listeners at least, to make the brand, the company and the whole idea of smoking ridiculous, and to cast a cynical suggestion that all of consumer culture could be absurd.

When Jack was sick at home in bed with a cold, the Sportsmen telephoned to cheer him with a version of "Button Up your Overcoat":

> Button up your overcoat
> When the wind is free
> Take good care of yourself
> Careful, Mr. B.
>
> Eat an apple every day
> Go to bed by three
> Take good care of yourself
> Passing NBC.
>
> Be careful in the breeze (ooh ooh)
> Watch it please (ooh ooh)
> Or you'll sneeze (ooh ooh)
> You'll get a cold and ruin your program
>
> If you're really feeling bad
> Call a doctor, too
> Take good care of yourself
> 'Cause we all love you.
>
> When you're buying cigarettes
> Buy the brand you like
> Take good care of yourself
> Smoke a Lucky Strike
>
> When you're driving in a car
> Or you're on a hike

> Take good care of yourself
> Smoke a Lucky Strike
>
> If I may have my say (Please do)
> Don't delay (what's new)
> Start today (ooh ooh)
> Light up a Lucky and you'll enjoy it
>
> Men who know tobacco best
> Smoke the best you see
> Round, firm, fully packed
> L S M F T[94]

The Sportsmen performed their version of "Deep in the Heart of Texas"[95] at Jack's house, where he was getting a rub down from his masseur Mr. Nelson (Frank Nelson, who always played devilishly annoying characters). The hearty handclapping that accompanied the song was merged with Nelson slapping Benny's behind in time to the music, and Jack yelping:

> The smoke they like, is Lucky Strike (clap clap clap clap)
> Deep in the heart of Texas
> Throughout the state, they say they're great (clap clap clap clap)
>   (Benny—ouch!)
> Its Lucky Strike in Texas
> They like the pack, of fine Toback (clap clap clap clap)
>   (Benny—Mr. Nelson! Not so hard!)
> Now you'll be smoking Luckies
> In cattle land, the favorite brand (clap clap clap clap)
>   (Benny—you're hurting me!)
> Is better tasting Luckies

Not only did the Sportsmen sing arrangements of popular standards, but they tackled operatic music, bringing in a famous soprano with the Metropolitan Opera, Dorothy Kirsten, to sing the Quartet from *Rigoletto* with the fellows. And Benny joined them on his whining violin for particularly manic versions of such classics as the "Anvil Chorus" from *Il Trovatore*, Mendelssohn's "Spring Song," the *Poet and Peasant Overture*, and the "Saber Dance."[96] The Sportsmen's song parodies were written by Benny's music arranger Mahlon Merrick, and the lines had to successfully gain the approval of the network, advertising agency, and the sponsor. American Tobacco may have determined that these humorous assaults might deflect some of the growing public concerns over tobacco and health issues. The product was a declining brand in the 1950s, as younger smokers preferred the new filtered tip cigarettes. Lucky Strike's manufacturer still needed to spend money on advertising to keep its older customers loyal to the brand, nevertheless, so they continued to sponsor Jack Benny's television program through June 1959.

• • •

In ways that he never had to consider when performing as a single act on the vaudeville stage or as a hired actor in a Hollywood motion picture, Jack Benny had to create his comedy within a set of challenging guidelines in commercial network radio. The sponsorship system gave extraordinary levels of creative control to the advertisers who provided the funds to finance the program and the advertising agencies who assumed the work of program production. Benny had to learn to manage and manipulate that system (and two firings demonstrate the difficulties of asserting the creative input Benny sought in the face of the sponsors' demands).

The commercial imperative mandated by the sponsors to make selling goods central to the entertainment shaped Jack Benny's comic persona and the structure of the narrative that he and Harry Conn created. Boldly making fun of the sponsor's product instantly established Benny as a fresh and different comic, one who was sophisticated enough to slyly send up the false promises of advertising, but also one who was an ally of an audience who also knew better than to take commercials at face value. His sponsor's outrage at Benny's cheeky middle commercials was the performer's first introduction to the power that sponsors wielded over the creation of the comedy program. Later, it was deliciously ironic that Jack's "Fall Guy" frustrated patriarch would be so cheap and so reluctant to take an active role in consumer culture, and also be so knee-knockingly frightened of his sponsors.

Jack Benny could have remained a hired performer, reading the lines scripted by others and following the direction of the ad agency producers. It's to his credit that Benny leapt at the challenge to gain as much creative control over his program as he could, to become so centrally involved in the production of his program. This impulse led him not only to hire his own writer and shape his own cast but also to assertively shape the advertising content of his entertainment program. Benny was admired throughout the broadcast industry for his extraordinarily ability to meld humor and sales messages. He spawned a host of imitators, but none were able to be as successful. Especially in his association with Jell-O, Benny and his writers created a synergy of humorous product and performer co-identification. His experiences also turned Benny into a hugely successful, creative, and exacting show producer or "showrunner," as we might call that position in the contemporary media industries.

If the commercial imperative was one major factor that shaped Jack Benny's radio humor and his program, another was an industrial imperative. Throughout his career, Benny sought to intertwine aspects of two rival media industries—radio and film. The next chapter will explore how Benny, through his character, his comedy program, his star image, and his business dealings, presented himself as working in both industries, as being an intermedia figure. By talking of California and movie stars, by performing parodies of popular film, Benny brought cultural references about the movies into the center of radio comedy. By working with director Mark Sandrich at Paramount, Benny was able to bring the spirit of his highly popular radio character to Hollywood film, flummoxing respected motion picture critics and earning the studio a welcome fortune at the box office.

SEVEN

Jack Benny's Intermedia Juggling of Radio and Film

After spending three months in the American film capital, interviewing 500 visitors from all walks of life, in January 1937, British journalist Austin J. Putnam completed research for his (apparently never published) book, *Hollywood Tourist*. Based on his survey, as he told a *Variety* reporter, Putnam compiled a list of "The Seven Wonders of Hollywood." Most choices embodied popular fascination with the personalities and playgrounds of the West Coast film colony—Clark Gable and Shirley Temple, the Brown Derby restaurant, Charlie Chaplin's film studio, Grauman's Chinese Theater, and the Hollywood Bowl. Putnam's number one, single greatest Wonder of Hollywood, however, was Jack Benny and the live productions of his radio programs. "More tourists asked me how they could get tickets to Jack Benny's radio broadcasts than any other event. It is positively amazing the hold this droll comedian has on the United States public," marveled the Englishman. "He is the most popular celebrity in Hollywood.... I enjoyed his show at the NBC studio more than any stage play I've ever seen in London or New York."[1]

Indeed, was Jack Benny a movie star who appeared on the radio, or a radio star who made movies? A 1937 *Los Angeles Times* article pondered the question, noting that half of his income came from each medium, and that his intermedia stardom was shared by a growing number of multitasking celebrities, from Bing Crosby and Eddie Cantor, to "Arkansas Traveler" humorist Bob Burns.[2] When asked which was the easier profession, acting in radio or film, Benny gave a purposefully ambiguous reply. The manner in which each medium structured his performance was the issue. Benny declared that "picture making is tougher," noting that, unlike in radio, the actor couldn't carry the script into the film scene to do dialog. Mistakes performers made while broadcasting live on the radio could be considered funny, but mistakes ruined a film scene. Films demanded perfection. On the other hand, however, radio brought with it the time pressures of creating weekly programs.

> [I]n movies you only memorize a few lines at a time and stand under the hot lights for a few minutes. In radio a comic must work fast and keep up with the rewrites. You have to physically express emotion with body more than just voice in the movies; you have to do physical stunts rather than the sound effects man. On radio you can look like anything and dress casually, in the movies you must be handsome and have a good appearance.

Benny concluded, "I think for the time being I'll continue to take a helping of both—and maybe a few personal appearances on the side."[3]

Benny thoroughly embedded his radio career, and his radio program's narrative, in the milieu of motion pictures. This intertwining of rival media forms brought both positive and negative reactions from the radio and film industries. In 1934, a time when most network radio programs were broadcast from New York City, Jack Benny's top-rated radio program regularly emanated from Los Angeles, three years prior to primetime radio's "Swing to California."[4] Like a funhouse reflection of the popular dramatic radio program *Lux Radio Theater* that brought a carefully constructed version of Hollywood glamor to radio listeners, Benny's show drew on, magnified, and critiqued listeners' fascination with the movies and Southern California.[5] The feature films in which Benny starred in the late 1930s also just as thoroughly mixed radio and cinema. His movie stardom owed much more to his radio popularity than to his acting skills or the aesthetic quality of his film productions (with Ernst Lubitsch's 1942 *To Be or Not to Be* the exception). Benny himself roundly disparaged his own film performances. Although they are not remembered as critical triumphs, several of his films were box office hits and boosted Benny (albeit temporarily) into the pantheon of top ticket-selling movie stars. Examination of Benny's intermingling of radio and film in the 1930s expands and complicates our understanding of the many formal and informal ties between two commercial media forms, which were said to be bitter opponents in that era.

Contemporary media studies have tended to assume that media convergence—the synergizing of television, film, the Internet, advertising, gaming, and publishing into multimedia conglomerations that share narrative threads, producers, performers and audience interaction, and that create multidimensional experiences—is a recent phenomenon of industrial production practices and marketing imperatives.[6] Jack Benny's career in the 1930s provides a historical case study of the struggles and success of a convergence media star in an age when radio, film, newspapers, and advertising were (for the most part) separately operated, rival industries. Michele Hilmes and other media historians have examined how, behind all this anxious bluster, beneath the surface commonalities and under-the-table negotiations worked to keep these separate entertainment media cooperating, "sharing talent, technology, aesthetics and business practices for decades," finding commonalities and purchasing stakes in each other's fields across the twentieth century.[7]

As Hilmes writes, Hollywood in the 1930s functioned "as broadcasting's alter ego, its main rival and contributor, the only other force unified and powerful enough to present a viable alternative definition to the uses made of the medium by established broadcast interests, yet a necessary contributor to broadcasting's growth and success."[8] The "interrelationship" and "intra-industry conflict" she examines between the film and radio industries looks somewhat different from the perspective of performers and audiences. What film audiences, radio listeners, record buyers, and readers of newspapers and magazines experienced in their everyday media consumption was not necessarily entirely separate media worlds, but more often an entangled flowing-together of entertainment, led by the performances of multimedia stars across all these production forms. Benny often acknowledged his media industry boundary crossings and thus fueled even higher levels of cross-media identification with his fans.

For listeners across America, Jack Benny's radio program was an embodiment of Hollywood film culture that deepened audiences' familiarity with the movies and encouraged Southern California tourism. From the very earliest Benny radio appearances in 1932, his scripts were filled with punning references to current film releases and stars. Benny's radio programs in the 1930s featured at least fifty skits parodying recent box office hits, from *Grand Hotel* to *The Women*. As the decade progressed, Benny's radio program added jokes about the directors, producers, and studio moguls whom Jack worked with in pictures.[9] Story lines regularly featured backstage activities at the Paramount film studio, where radio listeners heard him whine about the small dressing room he'd been given and undertake disastrous attempts at film acting. His humor deglamorized the movie business, while still maintaining that everyone in Hollywood felt superior to the mere radio performer. Jokes about Jack's vanity and stinginess often involved motion pictures, too, as he insisted on seeing his films again and again, fretted about matinee ticket prices and free theater passes, and dodged insults from Mary about attending screenings of his own films at movie theater Dish Night giveaways to get a free plate in the bargain.[10] Benny's broadcasts helped further cement film's place, as well as radio's, in a nationwide "imagined community" of shared everyday cultural experiences.[11]

Despite the potential benefits of cross-promotion, other factors inhibited Benny's ability to mingle references to radio and film and to move between these competing mediums in the 1930s. The jealous rivalries of the separately owned media, each afraid of losing their audiences to the other, the interference of program sponsors who feared giving publicity to competing products, the contentious relationships between film producers and local film exhibitors, and between network radio and local radio stations, and between radio and local newspapers, all threw up challenges to Jack Benny's intermedia promotions.[12]

HOLLYWOOD CELEBRITY—THE CORE OF BENNY'S VAUDEVILLE AND RADIO ROUTINES

Like other major stage, vaudeville, and musical performers of the early 1930s (such as Eddie Cantor, Al Jolson, Ed Wynn, Fred Allen, Will Rogers, Bing Crosby, and Fred Astaire), Jack Benny explored options for his career in a variety of entertainment media during a time of technological change and economic upheaval. Benny appeared in narrative feature films, variety-show-style revue films, comedy film shorts, Broadway shows that mixed scantily clad showgirls with comedy routines, vaudeville turns, and guest appearances on various radio programs. Separate entertainment media forms were converging and mixing, some suddenly blossoming while others were declining, and a savvy group of performers dipped toes into many mediums, trying to ascertain which streams were drying up and which might flow toward continued success.[13]

After his well-received appearance as master of ceremonies in MGM's first talkie *The Hollywood Revue of 1929*, Jack Benny increasingly interpolated references to Hollywood personalities, current films, and his own exploits in the movie industry into his vaudeville humor. Al Boasberg, who had scripted the dialog for the film, wrote Benny a routine concerning his experiences in Hollywood working at MGM. It connected to core aspects of the classic Benny character and style—it was a mixture of urbanity and sly, self-denigrating humor that enabled him to belittle his manhood and poke fun at his unsuccessful attempts to become a leading romantic actor. It shattered any pretentions he might present that he was a debonair movie star who would appropriately be co-starred with Greta Garbo. It assumed that audiences were familiar with his work in films, and for much of its topical humor it drew upon vaudeville audiences' broad interest in the movies.[14]

Benny's earliest appearances on radio also linked him to the film world. In October 1929 he was on a program broadcast from a California station in connection with MGM's promotion of the *Hollywood Revue*. Benny also guest starred on an episode of NBC's *RKO Theater of the Air* in September 1931. Jack Benny was supported in these endeavors by the Hollywood film studios, which Michele Hilmes notes made major programming, publicity, and ownership forays into radio broadcasting as "talkies" connected film much closer to other recording, music, and Broadway theatrical industries.[15] When Benny had a brief guest shot March 29, 1932, on Ed Sullivan's New York City–based radio program,[16] (an appearance he referred to in subsequent years as his first big break in radio), Benny opened with a self-deprecating greeting that played up the intimacy of his entering American homes: "Ladies and Gentlemen, this is Jack Benny talking. There will be a slight pause while you say, 'Who cares?'" The rest of Jack's three-minute talk was drawn directly from the Garbo vaudeville monologue:

> I am here tonight as a scenario writer. There is quite a lot of money in writing scenarios for the pictures. Well—there would be, if I could sell one. I'm going back to pictures in about ten weeks. I'm going to be in a new film with Greta Garbo. They sent me the story last week. When the picture opens, I'm found dead in the bathroom. It's a sort of mystery picture. I'm found in the bathtub on a Wednesday night. I should have been in Miss Garbo's last picture but they gave the part to Robert Montgomery. You know—studio politics! The funny part of it is that I'm really much younger than Montgomery. That is, I'm younger than Montgomery and Ward. You'd really like Garbo. She and I were great friends in Hollywood. She used to let me drive her car all around town. Of course, she paid me for it.[17]

Benny reused this favorite Garbo bit several times on his early radio shows, particularly when he changed sponsors and was introducing himself to audiences in a new time slot.

Deprecating his own film career as an entrée to making humorous comments about Hollywood remained a staple of the comic routines Benny and his script writer Harry Conn crafted when Benny began his radio broadcasts for Canada Dry, although NBC was touchy about allowing him to mention that his film studio was MGM, because that would be advertising without payment. Benny and Conn liberally sprinkled the Canada Dry show scripts not so much with radio-themed humor but rather with movie-related jokes (such as claiming he worked as assistant lover to Ramon Novarro, and that he had dated Peach Pitts, sister of scatterbrained film comedienne Zasu Pitts).[18] As he had in his earlier vaudeville performances, Benny incorporated discussion of his real moviemaking activities into the radio dialogue, to add a sense of personal connection to his audiences. Working discussions of his other media activities (film shoots and live stage appearances on tour with his radio cast) into his radio dialogue also helped promote all these various endeavors.

A recurring skit in the Benny radio program's early years featured Jack reporting as the "Earth Galloper," a gossip columnist who loosely parodied the broadcasts of Walter Winchell, whose career had blossomed in 1932. Benny's "Earth Galloper" continually made joking references to the sizes of Garbo's feet and Clark Gable's ears, and the onscreen romantic prowess of Mae West and Maurice Chevalier. Celebrity quirks seen in the newsreels were also fodder for Benny's topical humor, such as George Bernard Shaw's long beard and Mahatma Gandhi's loincloth. The Benny show's humor revolved around demystifying fame and humorously acknowledging radio listeners' interest in Hollywood gossip.[19]

Benny's fully formed radio persona began to emerge in skits in 1934 that concerned Jack's unsuccessful struggles with his film director to make his part larger or to avoid having his love scenes cut out. Jack's filming of *Transatlantic Merry Go Round* (RKO, 1934) was the inspiration for the funny and effective radio skit broadcast about his film screen test, in which Jack spectacularly flopped as a romantic actor.[20] Even greater discussion of Jack's movie career in his scripted radio exploits came after Benny's move to Paramount studios in 1936. Sometimes the radio program's narratives involved the show cast visiting Jack at the studio and discussing the deficiencies of his dressing room (which was often merely the men's lavatory or a broom closet). Jack rehearsed an upcoming love scene (which would not actually appear in the film) with either his filmic leading lady (Joan Bennett), or with Rochester taking Joan's role. Jack was depicted as a terrible movie actor who continually muffed his lines. At other times, Jack (with Mary tagging along to witness his embarrassment) waited in vain in the outer offices of a real-life film director or studio executive who would not even deign to meet him. In 1937, when Benny was filming *Artists and Models* at Paramount, he and his writers (Morrow and Beloin) began to incorporate an even more direct references and connections to his movie-making activities into the radio show's narrative. This demonstrated strengthening cooperative intermedia ties between Paramount, NBC, ad agency Young & Rubicam, and sponsor General Foods.

Another effective way that Jack Benny and Harry Conn incorporated references to Hollywood and film culture into their radio show came from lampoons of recently released movies. Benny and Conn asserted that they were the first to create film parodies on radio, but others were experimenting as well—Ed Wynn was lampooning the librettos of popular operas and many of Eddie Cantor's comic sketches were film related. The parodies began in the early months of the Canada Dry program in 1932, when the cast performed several ten-minute take-offs on MGM's 1932 all-star melodrama *Grand Hotel* (dubbed "Grind Hotel"). The sketches were so popular that they were reprised several times on the program over the next two years. As the dashing Baron (a character played on film by John Barrymore and on radio by Jack) and tragic, reclusive ballerina Grusinskaya (Garbo's film role, played by singer Ethel Shutta in the radio skit) pursued a surreptitious romantic rendezvous in her hotel room, the dying accountant Kringelein (bandleader George Olsen taking Lionel Barrymore's scenery-chewing role) ran about shrieking that he only had five minutes to live. Nearly dead Kringelein became something of a recurring character, adding extra absurdity to the Benny radio troupe's antics in the subsequent months.

In the next years, the Benny radio cast performed at least fifty hilarious take-offs on films such as *I Am a Fugitive from a Chain Gang, She Done Him Wrong, Little Women, Dinner at Eight, The Barretts of Wimpole Street, Charlie Chan at Radio City, Snow White and the Seven Dwarfs, The Count of Monte Cristo, The House of Rothschild, Mutiny on the Bounty,* and *The Women.* Sharp writing and bountiful comedic skills were required to make the parodies funny, and their success rested on a substantial audience familiarity with the film, titles, characters, and stars. The skits also benefitted the radio show, providing useful alternatives to the increasingly stale vaudeville jokes that other comedians clung to. In a 1934 interview in the *San Francisco Call*, Benny commented: "Our humor is getting more subtle. The change came, I suppose, with the introduction of true satire on the air, with which I had something to do. We began kidding current pictures and plays, giving the comedy a crazy impromptu style. In radio work you can't stand still."[21]

In the mid-1930s, several new radio programs debuted that featured dramatic adaptations of recent Broadway plays and films for radio, adding more intermedia connections for radio listeners and more spark for Benny to contrast the humor and absurdity of his skits with the seriousness of these other productions. Louella Parsons's radio program *Hollywood Hotel*, on the CBS network, incorporated twenty-minute preview vignettes of new movie releases into the program's production, often featuring the film's famous performers. The *Lux Radio Theatre* program, which became the most prestigious dramatic series on network radio by presenting well-crafted adaptations of Hollywood films and featuring movie star performances, began broadcasting on the NBC Blue network in 1934. The program, originally based in New York, featured adaptations of Broadway dramas, before switching two years later to programs based on film dramas, in a show produced in Hollywood on the CBS network and hosted by famous movie director Cecil B. DeMille. The popular program most often focused on melodramas, offering only a few adaptations of comic film fare.[22]

Benny's parodies of recent movies also served as useful promotional publicity for the targeted films and stars. Benny assumed that the film studios would welcome these efforts, but such was often not the case. Benny, his writers, advertising agency handlers, and network bureaucrats had to obtain written permission from the movie studios to use the titles, characters, and any dialogue or plot elements from a film. Original authors and the film studios yelled when too many spoilers were revealed, or when the humor was subpar. Eugene O'Neill withheld permission from radio programs after a few lousy takeoffs on his plays, but allowed the Benny cast to attempt *Ah, Wilderness*. Movie theater owners across the nation continually begged the film studios not to allow radio adaptations of current films to give away too much of the plot, the climax, or conclusion, for fear it would keep too many of their local clients home from the theaters.[23] Film studios grouched about Benny dragging out parodies of *Anthony Adverse* and *Tom Sawyer* over multiple episodes.[24]

To avoid giving away too many details, the Benny movie parodies had only the most tenuous connection to the actual film they caricatured. The skits would focus on the star personae in lead roles (often substituting the star name for the character's name). After establishing the leading stars and/or characters and setting, soon these parodies shifted away from any connection to the film toward vaudeville-style jokes about illicit extramarital affairs or verbal slapstick absurdity. This tactic generally mollified the film studios, but Benny would face trouble in the early years of television when he performed his takeoff on *Gaslight*, which he had first done on radio October 14, 1945, with original star Ingrid Bergman. Benny reprised the sketch on live TV

January 27, 1952, with Barbara Stanwyck, but when he and his production staff sought to do it a third time, capturing it on film in June 1953 (again with Stanwyck) for TV in a skit titled "Autolight," MGM had clamped down and would only give permission for current releases to be skewered. Benny performed the episode anyway. MGM sued and blocked the show from being aired. MGM, Benny, and CBS sparred in a multiyear law suit over the creative limits of parody, CBS appealing the case all the way to the Supreme Court. The court found that Benny's parody was too similar to the original film.[25] Finally, Benny paid to license an adaptation of the film and aired his sketch in 1959.

For all the movie talk, however, in the 1930s, Benny's radio program rarely included guest star appearances. Only Andy Devine, the jocular, rusty-voiced movie cowboy, appeared regularly between 1936 and 1938, participating in "Buck Benny" Western parody sketches. Robert Taylor appeared once in 1936, and Joan Bennett (Benny's co-star in *Artists and Models Abroad*) made two appearances. The stars would only start shining more frequently on Benny's program at the end of World War II, when Ronald and Benita Colman led the way. Benny's radio and TV programs would then be known as shows that were protective and kind to stars—Humphrey Bogart, Jimmy Stewart, Claudette Colbert, and Marilyn Monroe would make rare broadcast appearances with Benny.

BENNY'S CONTRIBUTIONS TO HOLLYWOOD TOURISM

Not only did Jack Benny and his radio cast talk incessantly about the movies—the geography of Hollywood and Southern California also suffused the program's narrative. Early band leader Don Bestor plugged his orchestra's performances at the Brown Derby restaurant, and Phil Harris was shameless in promoting his band's shows at the Wilshire Bowl. Joking mentions of Pasadena, Glendale, the Rose Bowl, the May Company department store (where Mary had sold hosiery before she met Jack), Jack's house in Beverly Hills, the NBC studios, orange groves, trips to Palm Springs, and (in the later 1940s radio shows) trains leaving Union Station for Anaheim, Azusa, and Cucamonga filled radio listeners' imaginations with images and stories of both the real and an imagined Los Angeles.

California held alluring fascination for a great many Americans during the Great Depression. Tourist publications, WPA guidebooks, and annual winter articles in Eastern and Midwestern newspapers all encouraged vacationing in Southern California, touting sunny skies, warm weather, a variety of outdoor sports, festivals and parades, beaches, breathtaking scenery, and of course Hollywood.[26] Tourism to the Los Angeles area grew rapidly in the 1930s, expanding from 200,000 to 1.6 million visitors between winter and summer, making it the region's largest industry second only to petroleum production, and far ahead of motion pictures and the orange crop.[27] Michele Hilmes notes radio's ability to create a sense of nationality, Americanism, a leveling of social class, and gathering of immigrant cultures together to become a nationwide audience having a universal experience.[28] The Benny show's emphasis on Los Angeles played a role in creating an "imagined community" in Benedict Anderson's phrase, to which all Americans could belong. In a 1940 *New York Times* interview, Benny explained how he used Los Angeles references strove to keep his radio program "typically American, not Broadway-ish":

> That is why I wouldn't want to go on the air from New York for a whole season. We couldn't be as rural or homey as we are in California. Out there we all feel that we are in a small town and can go places and do things as the people all do. It's all right to come to New York for two or three weeks. But in the East we find ourselves acting like tourists. I'd never get a feeling for my Maxwell car or going to the country in New York.[29]

While visiting Hollywood ranked high among tourists' goals, their expectations were nearly always crushed when they reached the intersection of Hollywood Boulevard and Vine Street, (then, as now, a pretty lackluster stretch of real estate), for there was little of the movie business that could actually be seen by the public. "The bitter truth, as most tourists learn, is that it is next to impossible to get inside a motion picture studio without knowing some on in the industry," confessed one *New York Times* article. "Still it is possible to find plenty of Hollywood glamour outside the studios. The visitor may see his favorite screen star driving along Hollywood Boulevard, lunching at famous movie restaurants, playing polo or golf, or attending one of Southern California' colorful motion picture previews." The film studios were surrounded by high walls, big gates, and security guards. They didn't hold tours, and it was nearly impossible to get in without a solid industry "connection." "No industry receives more requests for permission to tour its factories and no industry, on the surface anyway, is more loath to accede," warned another article.[30] The movie stars were busy at work, and it was difficult to even get a glimpse of them at the Brown Derby, Ciro's, or the Cocoanut Grove. Tourists had to be well informed and lucky to discover in which suburban theater a "sneak preview" of a new film was being held. The disappointed fan was stuck with studying a map of the movie star's homes, or staring at the cemented celebrity footprints in the courtyard of Grauman's Chinese Theater.

Into that celebrity-gawking vacuum came radio broadcasting. NBC and CBS opened studios in Hollywood in 1938. Sixteen of the highest-rated primetime network programs originated in Hollywood by 1939.[31] While a greater percentage of a day's overall programming was still produced in the East, the West ruled the night.[32] The big radio shows were always anxious to attract audiences of tourists to provide laughter and applause. The studio auditoriums were not large (the one Benny used held only about 350 people), but tickets could be obtained at the studios, hotels, and the Chamber of Commerce ahead of time for free.[33]

The availability of radio performers to be seen by the public, in a town notorious for desire of its famous residents to avoid the masses, further boosted the association of Jack Benny with Hollywood. It was a newspaper-worthy event in the small upstate New York village of Ft. Plain in 1941, when an area man, John Galvin, who unexpectedly found himself mentioned on the *Jell-O Program* (Benny had stumped the visiting junior intellectuals, the Quiz Kids, with the question of who was the manager of the Penn Theater in Wilkes Barre, Pennsylvania). Galvin played Hollywood tourist himself and sent back a postcard, which his hometown newspaper editor gleefully published—"The former Fort Plainer sends a card—a picture of the Beverly Hills home of Jack Benny and Mary Livingstone, with the following note: 'Dear Hugh, with Mary doing the dishes and Jack at the wheel of his favorite Maxwell. Rochester and myself did some FBI work hunting the gas man [whom Carmichael, Jack's polar bear, was suspected of having eaten].'"[34]

Benny's occasional broadcasts from the desert resort town of Palm Springs also added to the cachet of Southern California as a playground for the rich and leisured. Not only were the locals agog, but as the Benny show featured the town in the narrative of the program, it created valuable publicity to bring more Eastern tourists to see the sights Benny named. In 1941, the *Palm Springs Desert Sun* reported that "This village has never witnessed anything like the Benny broadcasts. Accustomed to celebrities of every kind and supposedly blasé, it went into a dither about Benny."[35] The newspaper estimated there were 3,000 requests for tickets for the two shows to be held at the local

FIGURE 19. Fan magazines were anxious to give their readers the inside scoop on what a live broadcast of a popular radio show like Benny's looked like, so they could imagine joining in with the studio audience. *Radioland*, March 1935, 8. Author's collection.

750-seat theater, and a sales representative from General Foods had to rush in to help restore order. "[W]hile stores, newspapers, Chamber of Commerce, hotels and others are fully appreciative of the wonderful publicity and entertainment he is giving the town, they will breathe a collective sigh of relief when it's all over."

THE CHALLENGES THAT RADIO'S SWING TO CALIFORNIA BROUGHT TO THE MOVIES

By the time the broadcasting networks' shows moved to Hollywood, in order to capitalize on film industry glamour, attract more movie stars to guest shots on their programs than they'd been able to do in New York, and to accommodate the intermedia activities of top stars, Jack Benny was already firmly situated in Southern California.[36] Having the radio and film industries in the same city brought benefits and challenges. A concern for both broadcasters and film company executives dealing with the increased number of movie stars in guest appearances on radio shows was that some savvy stars and their talent agents were making these radio deals outside their contractual obligations to the movie studios. Film studio moguls were upset that movie stars were trading on their studio-created fame to benefit themselves. Stars might overexpose themselves, or (the studios claimed) injure their reputations by appearing on unsuitable programs. Movie companies sought to rein in their stars' activities in this rival medium, while the movie actors and their agents fought for career autonomy and the welcome extra paychecks.[37] Young and Rubicam executive Tom Harrington (Benny's program manager) warned advertising agency radio departments in October 1936 that

> radio has gone Hollywood, but it has gone Hollywood in a way that threatens its very future. We can't help but feel that unless some action is taken we will find ourselves in the position of having crated a Frankenstein that will eventually be our undoing. Competition among the advertising agencies has become so strong with all the variety shows being broadcast from the coast as guest stars are at a premium and the scramble becomes a riot.

Rival advertising agencies searching for movie star power for their radio programs were bidding salaries for top stars up to unheard of heights of $5,000 per radio appearance.[38] Radio industry people feared that radio would be reduced to just being a promotional outlet for motion pictures. *New York*

Times radio reporter Orrin Dunlap warned that the film studios saw radio entirely as a promotional medium, not one of artistic creation, and that radio executives should worry that overdoing the publicity would make "radio suffer as an entertainment medium and the public will forsake such programs because of the ballyhoo."[39]

This cross-pollination of media stardom caused consternation for both film studios and the nation's movie theater owners, who had mixed reactions to what they termed "the radio question." "Some exhibitors say an airing [of movie stars on radio shows] hurts show business, others that it helps. Some studios are fighting to restrain that broadcast impulse, or at least to secure compensation for star loan-outs, while others encourage it or at any rate look the other way when it boils over."

Because radio could be listened to for free, film exhibitors and studio executives worried that having their movie stars exposed too abundantly on radio robbed them of potential revenue at the box office. Others saw promotional benefits from putting film stars on the airwaves, as the Paramount studio insisted that its contracted film performers give one free radio broadcast in connection with each film they made. Featuring radio stars in the movies might generate useful publicity for the film industry and draw otherwise reluctant ticket buyers to local theater box offices, but it might also represent a dangerous intrusion of the rival media form that would steal away paying customers from the movies.

Lurking beneath Hollywood filmdom's façade of glamour in 1937 and 1938 laid a crisis that undoubtedly fueled the film studios' jealousy of radio broadcasting's invasion of its turf—the movies were in a severe economic slump, and studio moguls feared the industry might never recover.[40] Catherine Jurca details the unhappy news faced by Hollywood film executives that too many new movies were lousy and that audiences were voting with their feet to stay away from theaters.[41] Meanwhile, radio listenership continued to climb. Jurca points out that movie executives, on the offensive, began to search for what film audiences wanted, and if the answer was less glamour, more "natural" heroes and heroines, and more believable plot lines, then they developed and promoted "believable" stars like Myrna Loy and produced "family films" like the Andy Hardy series.

In February 1937, movie industry leader Will Hays held nearly seven hours of closed-door meetings with NBC West Coast executive Don Gilman and CBS executive Dick Thornburgh about "the motion picture artist situation," to discuss the tensions between radio and film. Hays claimed that local film exhibitors across the nation were the ones angry about movie stars appearing on the rival medium (hitting them hardest at the box office). Gilman countered that NBC's hands were tied—it was not in the networks' control what programs the advertising agencies and movie stars' managers put together; he claimed that "we can't very well refuse programs which have been created outside of our control and which are acceptable as to the artists, material and product." Gilman claimed that Hays understood that any actual loss of audience from theaters for free radio "is so minor that to be wholly unimportant," but Hays reiterated that it didn't matter what he thought, that it was local exhibitors who were upset. Hays diplomatically hoped that radio and film could work smoothly together as "cooperation ... may cause them both to realize that broadcasting is a friend of the picture house."[42]

Local radio broadcasters could be just as testy as local theater owners about film industry propaganda trying to persuade listeners *not* to stay at home. In October 1938, an angry radio station manager in Buffalo, New York, castigated NBC:

> At the end of the "Good News" show from Hollywood last Thursday night October 20, the NBC announcer said " ... and remember, *Movies are your best entertainment*." I wonder if this is sound policy for radio to be used to plug movies in this manner? ... NBC policy prohibits boosting a BLUE [network] show on the RED, and vice versa, on the theory that it is unfair to one client on the RED to have his potential audience INVITED, and URGED, to tune in on a BLUE show running contemporarily on a competitive network.... Would it not be better for us to say *"RADIO is your best and cheapest entertainment, and movies are your SECOND BEST"?*[43]

NBC's Royal sent this complaint to the Continuity Acceptance Department and asked its head, Janet MacRorie, to draft a response. Her internal memo, "Radio's Contributions to the Motion Picture Industry," was sent back up the line to executives up through NBC president Lenox Lohr.

> Radio provides a ready-made audience for the motion picture theatre.... Many personalities, built up through radio, have become popular screen actors and big box office attractions for the motion picture producers. [She lists nineteen performers, starting with Jack Benny] ... Review the expansion necessary in NBC properties alone at Hollywood and it will readily be seen that radio has to follow its own talent to Hollywood when radio personalities are found to be good box office for the movies.... If the motion picture industry contemplates any move to undermine the radio industry, it must indeed be blind to the benefits that is has accrued from this same source.[44]

"LET'S DON'T SNEER AT BENNY MUSICALS": BENNY'S RADIO-FLAVORED 1930S FILMS, AND THEIR INTERMEDIA MARKETING

Jack Benny's MGM film *Broadway Melody of 1936* (1935) boosted dancer Eleanor Powell's film career, if not Benny's, and his subsequent feature, *It's in the Air* (1935), was a mediocre film that, despite its title, concerned daredevil airplane pilots, not broadcasting. Frustrated at not being placed in better parts at MGM, Benny switched to Paramount, but found, however, that his roles did not appreciably improve. In *Big Broadcast of 1937* (1936) and *College Holiday* (1936), Benny's part continued to be that of a producer struggling to mount a talent showcase for college kids, crooners, or scantily clad chorus girls. Benny cracked some jokes, not very well timed, and exhibited lackluster chemistry with whichever leading lady or stooge he was paired with. His subsequent films for Paramount, *Artists and Models* (1937) and *Artists and Models Abroad* (1938), were again hamstrung by particularly weak narratives. These medium-budgeted, barely-better-than-B-level films drew little more than sniffs of disdain from film critics. The purpose of these movies, however, was to reach out to American movie audiences in the suburbs and hinterlands and offer them familiar and relatable characters. Pollster George Gallup's surveys showed these audiences were bored with Hollywood's overwrought dramas and brittle glamour-pusses. Benny's mediocre films weren't as weak at the box office, however, as some of the other dramatic and comedic bombs, which were contributing to the nationwide movie slump.[45]

As part of the film industry's effort to reattract disaffected moviegoers in 1938 came a renewed effort by Hollywood studios to tap into radio performers' popularity—radio singers such as Alice Faye, Dorothy Lamour, Kenny Baker [famous due to his role on the Benny program], Lanny Ross, Martha Raye, and Frances Langford were tapped for movie roles. Paramount hired popular radio storyteller "Arkansas Traveler" Bob Burns to appear in features (he made twelve by 1940). Rising young comic Bob Hope was chosen to appear in Paramount's *Big Broadcast of 1938*, and Edgar Bergen and Charlie McCarthy, breakout stars on the radio in 1938, were given lead roles in two films at Universal, *Letter of Introduction* (1938) and *Charlie McCarthy, Detective* (1939).

Paramount lured away rising young director Mark Sandwich from rival RKO to help improve the quality of Benny's films. The thirty-seven-year-old director had worked his way up from two-reel comedy gagman to innovator of the Fred Astaire and Ginger Rogers musicals that interpolated music so ingratiatingly with the film plots. Sandrich's first musical comedy breakthrough, a profile noted, had actually been "*So This Is Harris* [RKO 1933], a novel three-reel musical, starring a noted bandleader that startled the picture world with his unusual treatment of music. He made music MOVE—on the screen. He also incorporated the simple, but hitherto unused method of filming a musical in which the story ... plot and situations ... predominated."[46] Perhaps Sandrich's fruitful experience with Phil Harris made him amenable to working with the bandleader's radio boss.

Sandrich's solution to the Benny problem was to focus on how to make Benny seem more comfortable on screen; the director oversaw the scripting, incorporating more of Benny's radio-flavored dialog into standard filmic practices and utilizing other members of Benny's radio cast. Sandrich and screenwriter Morrie Ryskind adapted a story Ryskind had co-written about an American show producer and his troupe stuck in London into a screenplay reminiscent of Benny's radio comedy milieu. While Sandrich retained the story's fictional narrative structure that gave Benny the film role of "Bob Temple," Sandrich added radio cast members Phil Harris and Eddie Anderson, who in 1938 was quickly becoming popular as new cast member "Rochester" on the *Jell-O Program*. Sandrich structured the film like Benny's radio program, incorporating established radio characters' personalities and their typical bantering dialogue.[47] But Sandrich also expanded the world of the radio show by significantly increasing Eddie Anderson's part in the film, having him sing two big production numbers, and having him interact onscreen prominently with Benny. Sandrich's efforts made *Man About Town* a surprise hit for Paramount, and incidentally, one of Hollywood's earliest interracial buddy movies.

Benny's broadcasting bosses General Foods, Young and Rubicam, and NBC brought an unprecedented intermedia marketing synergy to the world premiere of *Man About Town*, in late June 1939, investing time and a substantial amount of promotional funding to make it one of the splashiest publicity events of the year in either film or radio. Radio, advertising, and motion picture production corporations cooperated to mount a huge cross-media celebration of Jack, his radio show, and the new film in Benny's hometown of Waukegan, Illinois. The gritty working-class town north of Chicago was inundated with an extraordinary five-day circus of media publicity events, with 300 journalists on hand to cover multiple parades, 150,000 spectators, several episodes of Benny's Jell-O radio broadcast, dinners with town officials, downtown rallies with the stars, and simultaneous film premieres at the town's three movie theaters. More than 2,300 extra policemen, national guardsmen, and boy scouts were brought in to Waukegan to help maintain order.

Paramount's lavish promotional junket to Waukegan was part of a two-year film industry plan to increase business and brand awareness across the hinterlands by staging exploitation events in places far from Hollywood. Paramount had just held the world premiere of *Union Pacific* in Omaha. Warners (in Dodge City, Kansas, with Errol Flynn's *Dodge City*), Fox (in San Francisco with *Alexander Graham Bell* and Joplin, Missouri, with Tyrone Power's *Jesse James*), and MGM (in Atlanta with *Gone with the Wind*) participated in the outreach effort as well.[48]

Plans for the cross-media premiere-night spectacular, linking events onstage, on screen, and on the airwaves from Waukegan ran into a nearly disastrous last-minute snag, however, courtesy of the U.S. government. *Variety* reported, "When [the] Federal Communications Commission got wind of the airing in a theater where admission will be charged, it set down a heavy foot." Radio producers were never allowed to require audiences to pay to attend a national radio broadcast. "Just about the time the Paramounters decided to split up the ceremonial; [General Foods] stepped in to announce it would buy out the house that night."[49] Jell-O pitched in to give away the combined movie-radio show tickets for free. Promoters estimated the premiere's $125,000 price tag was shared between General Foods, Paramount, NBC, and Young and Rubicam.[50]

Paramount promised welcome relief to beleaguered local film exhibitors in their publicity releases for this film, crowing "It's Your Year to Rake in the Jack" and "There's Plenty of Jack in Paramount's *Man about Town*."[51] *Man About Town* made a strong showing at the box office, earning 20 percent more than the average film during the summer slow season, when moviegoers usually stayed away from unairconditioned theaters and studios traditionally dumped mediocre films and light fare. Benny's films were also released in the summer so as not to compete with his October-through-June radio show, and to capitalize on radio fans' missing Benny while he was off the air.

Most reviews praised Sandrich's efforts to blur the lines between radio and film entertainment, lauding Anderson's performance as Rochester and noting how much more relaxed and natural Benny's performance seemed compared to previous films.[52] *Variety* complimented the screenplay, which they judged was "precisely tailored for Benny's radio and screen personality."[53] *Picture Reports* claimed, "At last the screen captures the full flavor of

Jack Benny's distinctive radio character. Heretofore, the Benny pictures have missed the spark that has made the comedian the top ranking star of the airlines, season after season, but the man in *Man About Town* is the same boastful, blustering, likeable fall-guy millions tune in and laugh at every Sunday evening."[54] The *Motion Picture Herald* applauded Sandrich's keen understanding of what made Benny radio shows work: "It has Benny in a jam and Benny the butt of the jokes and gags."[55] *Box Office* agreed, remarking, "It is the most advantageous screen vehicle yet concocted to parade the comedy talents of Waukegan's gift to radio and films and, with its blend of mirthful story, situations, deftly timed gags and lavishly staged production numbers, should be reckoned a strong stimulant to ailing summer box offices."[56]

On the other hand, *Man About Town* received only dismissive acknowledgements from the major New York or Los Angeles film critics, who disdained most of the radio-themed movies released by the film studios. "Let's don't sneer at Benny musicals," reviewer Archer Winsten pleaded in the *New York Post*, praising the "good lines and comical situations" in the film that pleased audiences looking for simple pleasure.[57]

BUCK BENNY RIDES AGAIN — MERELY A FILMED RADIO PROGRAM?

Signed to a long-term contract by a grateful Paramount studio, and promoted to producer/director, Sandrich proceeded to push the integration of radio and film even further in his second Jack Benny picture, *Buck Benny Rides Again* (1940). Sandrich hired Benny's radio writers Ed Beloin and Bill Morrow to craft the dialog script, based very loosely on an expansion of the series of "Buck Benny" Western skits that had been performed on the radio show in 1936 and 1937. Sandrich incorporated even more members of Benny's radio cast into the film, this time not only Harris and Anderson, but also announcer Don Wilson, tenor Dennis Day, and film actor Andy Devine who had played a continuing role on the radio program during the Buck Benny skits. Unlike in the previous film, the major performers in the film used their stage names and performed in their radio personas—Phil was overly attracted to the ladies, and Jack was penurious, vain, cowardly, and awkward around women.

Sandrich incorporated novel radio touches into the standard film context—Don Wilson read out the film's title credits instead of them just being presented as text. Mary Livingstone and Fred Allen appeared, too, but

FIGURE 20. Jack Benny created invaluable intermedia marketing synergy by playing up the radio cast's experiences on the set at Paramount producing their film *Buck Benny Rides Again*. It spelled both high broadcasting ratings and strong box office for this radio-themed film, set at a Western dude ranch. Movie Radio Guide, February 1940. Author's collection.

only as voices emanating from onscreen radio sets (both performers were very reluctant to appear on film). Sandrich also made special efforts to make key imaginary aspects of the show visible on film. Carmichael the Bear and the Maxwell jalopy appear in the movie, to the delight of many film reviewers. Still there were limits to how much Sandrich was able to completely integrate these rival media forms—he had to cut out several lines Morrow and Beloin had written in which Jack and Mary (via radio) discuss the fact that the season of radio programs had concluded. Some intermedia lines were not crossed—there was no mention of Jell-O or radio commercialism in the film.

The Benny program's characters were integrated into a narrative that incorporated Benny's typical radio-style insult-swapping into a standard Hollywood romantic comedy. Ellen Drew played Jack's love interest as part of a sister singing trio seeking to break into radio. Their efforts to get Jack to help them kept misfiring, and Jack's crush on Ellen was not reciprocated. The film cast traveled west to a dude ranch where comic mix-ups with cattle rustlers occurred, and pretty chorus girls danced and sang. Sandrich added a twist to the film plot that drew on a unique aspect of the Benny radio show, something not occurring elsewhere in mainstream Hollywood films, in that Eddie Anderson as the Rochester character again played a very substantial, co-starring role in the film as Jack's sidekick. Anderson even got a romantic interest of his own, actress Teresa Harris, playing servant to the three singers.

Promotion of the film involved an impressive attempt at integration of separate entertainment media forms. On the radio, the Jell-O radio program's fictional characters discussed their activities participating in the actual filming all during the movie's production in December, and then throughout the spring building up to its premiere in April 1940. The radio characters' dialogue dwelled on how much more popular Rochester had been on-screen than Jack in the previous summer's *Man About Town*; it provided yet another new way to puncture Jack's pretentions of being a successful movie star. Leading up to the premiere of *Buck Benny Rides Again*, the entire Jell-O radio cast journeyed across country to New York City for three weeks of broadcasts, plus guest appearances on other Young and Rubicam–managed radio programs. In an unusual and innovative intermedia promotional push, Paramount went to the extraordinary effort to stage not one but *two* world premieres of the film, one at the Paramount Theater in Manhattan, the other in Harlem at the Loew's Victoria Theater.[58] The gala interracial and intermedia event is discussed in the first Rochester chapter. Paramount's *Buck Benny* press book presented ambitious language (if not followed through with more concrete promotional assistance from the studio for local theater owners) to demonstrate that a full intermedia publicity campaign could be possible for *Buck Benny Rides Again*—that radio, films and commercial sponsors could create synergies that would benefit local exhibitors:

> Jell-O backs your showing with big co-op campaign! The distributors of the nation's leading dessert—the sponsors of the nation's number one air show, put their full power behind the cooperative selling of *BBRA*—launching a campaign to top their previous selling smashes on Jack Benny hits. Get out

and get behind this enormous General Foods tie up, that links Jell-O merchandising and the drawing power of Jack Benny's Sunday night air show, with your own box office on the new Benny show.

Paramount claimed that every episode of Benny's radio program on the air, and every box of Jell-O on display at local groceries and chain stores, represented advertisements for this film. Meanwhile, the movie studio itself at least provided some brief phonograph recordings of music and dialogue and sample advertising scripts from which theater managers could craft local radio commercials. Paramount also arranged for cooperative advertisements in magazines and window card posters for product tie-ins with manufacturers of hosiery, overcoats, and typewriters, to help film exhibitors publicize their local screening of the film at cooperating neighborhood stores.[59]

Public opinion pollster George Gallup concluded in a 1940 survey of American moviegoers and moviegoing habits that *Buck Benny Rides Again* was the most effectively presold picture of the year (along with Paramount's Crosby and Hope film, *Road to Singapore*), due to the "direct result of steady plugging on Jack Benny, Bob Hope and Bing Crosby [radio] programs."[60] *Box Office Digest* reported that *Buck Benny Rides Again* was a major hit, doing an impressive 34 percent better-than-average business in movie theaters in cities across the nation.[61]

Reviews of *Buck Benny Rides Again* in the film industry trade press and in newspapers around the nation debated the merits of the film's radio influence.[62] The *Los Angeles Herald Express* called Benny a "comic sensation," claiming that "For the first time in Jack Benny's amazing career in vaudeville, on the Broadway stage, on the air as American's number one attraction and before Hollywood's caustic cameras he has bounced forth with the identical charm, the ready wit and the belittling-of-self attitude that made him great in very other form of entertainment but the movies."[63] *Box Office Digest* said the film was "nearest to giving the comfortable 'at home' feeling to the spectator of spending a corking evening with a succession of Jack Benny air programs that has yet been achieved for an ether personality."[64] *New York Mirror* critic Kenneth McCaleb weighed the benefits and drawbacks of this intermingling of radio and film:

> Radio audiences and motion picture audiences are, in theory, identical; each is supposedly made up of the great bulk of Americans who must watch the nickels closely and who seek escape and low-priced entertainment in these two media for the masses. The chief trouble with this theory is that it has not

seemed to work out so well in practice. Cinematic moguls are still debating whether broadcasting by their stars, as part of radio's standard soap and breakfast food operas, helps or hurts their film box-office standings. Personalities created or largely built up by radio have been borrowed in many cases by the movie makers, with uncertain results.[65]

McCaleb argued that *Buck Benny Rides Again* "is the first which completely transforms to film the radio character which he [Benny] has made for himself." He thus predicted it would be the rare Hollywood movie to truly please radio fans.

On the other hand, the movie was savaged by the established film critics of the New York papers. The *Herald Tribune*'s Howard Barnes "deplored the sorry state of screen fare ... which merely emphasizes the poor judgment which the screen is now displaying in forgetting fundamentals and playing to what used to be called the gallery." B. R. Crisler, reviewing the film for the *New York Times*, waded through the crowds that snaked for blocks around the Paramount theater five abreast outside the box office and incredulously wondered what all the excitement was about. He found it a better than average Jack Benny comedy, but that

> it is still more of a broadcast than a motion picture. There are some worthy people who are wedded to their radio, who like their entertainment handed to them in great gobs of dialogue interspersed with swelling crescendos of background music. And on the other hand, there are equally reputable persons who consider, fairly or not, that the screen is wasted on that type of picture.... Don't blame us if Jack Benny in a cowboy suit hardly seems worth the trip.[66]

Declaring that, "If you can't Abuse 'em, Use 'em, Hollywood makes Pix about Radio," *Variety* discussed film studios' efforts to dive more thoroughly than ever before into radio-themed movies:

> The motion picture industry has ceased to abuse radio and is using it as a background for a score of films, and more to come. Practically every major studio is producing or preparing features dealing wholly or in part with broadcasting. Some of them are built entirely around the microphone, and there is no answering kickback from the exhibitors, who used to protest against the inroads of the ether programs on the film business. Paramount leads the studios in the use of radio backgrounds for the screen, with six features of that nature completed, in production or in preparation.... Throughout the celluloid industry the broadcasting background is a growing rival of the canyons and prairies.[67]

A year-end round up in *Variety* described the added urgency studios felt to discover what the American moviegoing public would pay for, now that the foreign markets, which had brought in about 40 percent of revenues, were seriously curtailed by wartime disruptions.

Gallup's research reports on the habits of American film audiences confirmed that an increasing number of Americans spent more time listening to the radio than attending a movie show. "While 11,500,000 cinemaddicts sit in their favorite cinemansions of an average Sunday, 34,000,000 radio fans listen to Jack Benny on the air. On an average Monday 5,428,000 go to the movies; 26,000,000 stay at home to hear the Lux Radio Theatre program," Gallup noted.[68] Radio was competition that needed to be co-opted, if Hollywood was going to hang on to any audiences in these unsettled, perilous times.

Jack Benny became one of Paramount's top three male movie stars at the box office in 1939 and 1940, and among the top twelve stars industry-wide through 1942.[69] If the public would only come out to theaters to see highly promoted but mediocre films starring radio performers, then Paramount would produce them. Nevertheless, using radio celebrities who broadcast only in the United States made these films questionable for the overseas movie theaters they could still reach. The *Times of London* would consider Sandrich's subsequent Benny effort *Love Thy Neighbor* a poor and forgettable a film, noting that London movie audiences had never heard of Fred Allen, and "the frequent allusions to the Benny-Allen feud will doubtless remain a sealed book to Britishers."[70]

LOVE THY NEIGHBOR AND THE LIMITS OF INTERMEDIA FILM MARKETING

Mark Sandrich attempted to translate the Benny-Allen feud to the screen into a buddy-rivalry film to match the smash box office success of Paramount's other radio-star-flavored success released in spring 1940, Bing Crosby and Bob Hope in *The Road to Singapore*.[71] *Love Thy Neighbor*, however, was a weak and weary film. Sandrich had to beg Fred Allen to participate, as Allen despised both films and being in Hollywood, and it seems obvious from his unenthusiastic performance that Allen's heart was not in the film. Eddie Anderson, the runaway star of both *Man about Town* and *Buck Benny Rides Again*, found his role as Rochester significantly reduced in this film, as he was relegated to third wheel status.

The comic potential of the film was frittered away. Paramount tried to add extra spice to the movie by featuring young Broadway actress Mary Martin, who had made a huge hit in New York performing a scandalous strip tease while singing Cole Porter's comic song "My Heart Belongs to Daddy" in the 1938 musical *Leave it to Me!* The Hays Office made sure to sanitize the song's lyrics and any suggestive dancing before Martin could perform the number on film, however. Further, Martin had no more chemistry in a romantic subplot with Jack Benny than any of his other leading ladies had ever aroused. The movie's jokes weren't particularly funny and the slapstick scenes seemed forced.

Love Thy Neighbor was released in late December 1940, a prime time for Hollywood's family films and box office hits. Although the premiere at the Paramount Theatre in New York was smaller in scale than Benny's previous films, his and Allen's radio programs were at the top of the ratings, and the film earned the largest gross of any film during the holiday week, doing 144 percent of standard business. It was Paramount's second biggest release of the year, surpassed only by Cecil B. DeMille's *Northwest Mounted Police*.[72]

Despite success at the box office, Paramount's promotion of this film gives the impression that the studio was rapidly losing interest in Benny. Radio sponsor General Foods and ad agency Young and Rubicam's efforts similarly also seemed lackluster, in comparison with their previous exertions. Jack Benny undoubtedly noticed this too, for in the aftermath of the film's release, he signed an unusual contract to simultaneously make films at two other studios, Warner Bros. and 20th Century Fox. He also contemplated shopping his radio show to other sponsors. While the press book for Paramount's advertising campaign for *Love Thy Neighbor* claimed "What is far and away the greatest radio campaign ever put behind a motion picture is going on right now," all the studio offered was the appearances of the film's stars on their regular radio programs, and several guest appearances made by the performers on each other's shows to promote the film. Paramount grandly suggested that local film exhibitors could corral all the grocers and Texaco gas station managers in their neighborhood together to support a city-wide celebration of Jack Benny and Fred Allen. Or to display a pile of Jell-O boxes in their theater lobbies. Perhaps most heretical to the minds of local movie theater owners jealous of having their audiences stolen by home radio sets, the press book suggested that exhibitors "rig up a radio in your lobby and have it go on when any of these programs [featuring the film's stars] is on. You can rest assured that there will be something in each of the programs which will help you sell *Love Thy Neighbor*. Do this now!"[73]

Variety characterized *Love Thy Neighbor* as "hardly a picture for the critics,"[74] but New York's top-ranked film reviewers utterly despised the film, panning its surfeit of dialogue and paucity of plot. *New York Times* reviewer Bosley Crowther grumbled that its meager narrative, interrupted by crescendos of music and slapstick, was merely "the tired jibes of a four year old, fake feud."[75] Crowther bemoaned the scourge of radio-themed films in an essay that was supposed to have been an end-of-year discussion of Hollywood's best productions.[76] "From the way some people talk in the motion picture industry you'd think that the radio was a great big measles sign hung on the industry's door, keeping patrons away from movie theatre in alarming wholesale numbers." The rivals had nevertheless been exchanging performers, plots, and formats for nearly ten years, he fretted. He railed at recent films that abandoned "cinematic potentialities" and created merely "as close a reproduction of the air thing as is technically practical." The critic warned that film producers' cynical efforts to make money at the box office were "most deplorable and dangerous, for it fails to regard above all the essential nature of the film medium. It presumes that a picture is merely a show window in which to display a radio attraction, not an artistic entity with definite demands for perfection." Crowther condemned *Love Thy Neighbor* for failing to engage the artistic potential of film:

> Once or twice there are glimmers of some real cinematic inventiveness, such as a speedboat chase sequence in which the boats, making turns, are accompanied by the sound of screeching brakes and sliding tires, and a bit in which Rochester converses with his reflected conscience. But insistently the picture snaps back to the old routine of Mr. Benny and Mr. Allen flaying one another with words.... If the industry seriously suspects the radio of alienating its public, then this seems like a very queer way of meeting the competition—unless, of course, it is really intended as a subtle form of sabotage.[77]

The aesthetic deficiencies that Crowther and the other disapproving critics point to in *Love Thy Neighbor* and Benny's other radio films would parallel complaints about lack of visual interest and physical action that television critics would toss at the radio programs and performers that attempted to transition from the ether to the visual medium in the late 1940s and early 1950s.

. . .

While *Love Thy Neighbor* earned handsome profits for Paramount in early 1940, the studio did not produce the subsequent films for which they had contracted Benny and Anderson. Mark Sandrich turned to serious dramas, and Paramount instead turned to Bob Hope and Bing Crosby to create future radio-inflected comedies. Benny and Anderson appeared separately in successful films for other studios in the early wartime years; they were also paired again in a 20th Century Fox studio adaptation of a George M. Cohan stage comedy, *The Meanest Man in the World* (1943). Major scripting problems resulted in a very mediocre film. By 1946, both Benny and Anderson had appeared in their final major Hollywood movie roles.

The intermedia blending of broadcasting and film in Jack Benny's radio program was extraordinarily successful. Despite the numerous constraints put in place by the rival media companies, sponsors, and local film exhibitors, Benny and his writers had managed to negotiate a path that enabled them to playfully incorporate jokes about both entertainment forms. Benny used his self-deprecating comments about his own Hollywood career to pull back the curtains of movie star glamour. And yet the disdainful cinema stars who showed nothing but contempt for Jack reinforced the mystery of their superiority. The Benny program's innovative parodies of current Hollywood hits helped to dispel the pretensions of sophisticated melodramas like *Grand Hotel* or *The Barretts of Wimpole Street* or *The Women*, while also spreading the fame of those films further into popular culture.

Hollywood stars and movie references became more incorporated than ever into Jack Benny's radio program during its "golden era" of renewed popularity and humorous achievement from 1946 to the early 1950s. The arch disdain of movie star Ronald Colman for his next door neighbor was a superb addition to the radio show's comedy, and created a rich vein of humor that highlighted the difference between Hollywood social class and Benny's Fall Guy failings. The program's reputation among Hollywood celebrities of treating guest stars with kid gloves, making them sound intelligent and funny, won for Benny the appearances of many top actors and actresses (such as Claudette Colbert and Humphrey Bogart) who would not design to be on other comics' programs. But the Hollywood industries, film and radio, would face disruptive competition from New York City–based television, beginning in 1948. The last two chapters of this story about Jack Benny's radio career will examine how he faced the two greatest challenges of his radio career—addressing the wartime creative slump into which his program fell and how he and his production team innovated comedic elements to create that "golden era" of the radio show, 1946–1952. And then how, once back on top of the radio ratings, Benny nervously approached the transition to television.

EIGHT

Benny at War with the Radio Critics

Jack Benny's radio program, riding high in the ratings in 1940, suffered a prolonged slump during World War II.[1] Benny lost his two writers, and key cast members left for military service. He felt obligated to broadcast programs from stateside military camps, which seriously cramped the show's style. His sponsor and ad agency neglected to adequately promote the program. The narrative of the show floundered and the comedy was often listless. The ratings declined precipitously. The bright spots in his wartime recession were his summer overseas tours to perform live USO shows to military camps in African, European, and Pacific battlegrounds. In 1945 the radio program started to improve, as Benny and a new team of writers experimented with adding new characters and comedy routines to the show. Although the innovations took some time to jell together, the Benny show gradually climbed out of its doldrums and recaptured its radio audience; by late 1946 Benny regained his previous high ratings. The re-energized show also reached new levels of popular acclaim; the period between 1946 and the early 1950s became known as the program's "golden era."

Benny's radio wartime fall and postwar revival occurred during a time of aesthetic malaise in network broadcasting. Radio was at its height in terms of revenues, listenership, and influence, but was simultaneously drowning in critics' disapproval. A new breed of radio critics, fresh voices emanating from top newspapers and magazines, thrust aside the curtains cloaking commercial network radio's operation and exposed all of its shortcomings, mistakes, and sins.[2] Jack Benny unexpectedly found himself in the middle of this maelstrom of discontent. As one of the most successful and longest-running of the radio comics, Benny served as a lightning rod for critics' disparaging blasts— Benny's time-worn narrative formulas were dull; his jokes were corrosively nasty, derivative, and repetitive; and fossilized performers like Benny were propped up unnecessarily by sponsors, who would not permit new talent to blossom.

The newspaper critics were led by brash young journalist John Crosby, whose "Radio in Review" column debuted in the back pages of the *New York Herald Tribune* in May 1946. Crosby was joined by other reviewers (Gilbert Seldes, Jack Gould, Ben Gross, and Harriet Van Horne), who energetically attacked the stagnation, overcommercialization, and tastelessness of current radio offerings.[3] They hammered away at Benny, not only as symbol of the strangling control of sponsors over program choices, but also for the legion of imitators who broadcast pale copies of his show. They called for innovative program formats, and higher levels of artistic aspiration. The new radio critics carved out a unique place for themselves in arts criticism, as Amanda Lotz has noted; commenters on the fields of music, dance, the theatre, and even film did not have to negotiate so constantly between the imperatives of a medium that was "at once an artistic and commercial form."[4] The new critics brought a much-needed outsiders' perspective to radio that was not beholden to networks, commercial interests, or the entertainment trade press, and they played invaluable roles in the production of popular culture of the postwar era.

Benny and his writers ameliorated his show's problems with innovations like the "I Can't Stand Jack Benny Because" contest, and the introductions of the Ronald and Benita Colman characters, Professor LeBlanc, the Sportsmen Quartet, and the subterranean vault—and *still* the show was held up by the critics as an example of everything that was wrong with radio. Benny was defensive, hurt by the charges. Nevertheless, Benny and his writers occasionally turned to engage the critics head-on—on the air in comic performance in the case of Gilbert Seldes, and through published replies to criticism and tentative negotiations with John Crosby.

The downside of the sponsor-controlled system, as the radio critics sternly pointed out, was that radio audiences and innovative performers, writers, and producers were terribly shortchanged. The near-sightedness of ratings-seeking sponsors and advertising agencies kept them overreliant on the same top performers and programs for decades, stifling chances for artistic innovation. There was an ironic benefit to this system, however—certain performers, producers, and writers were allowed time to develop finely crafted comedy or dramas over a period of many years. The fragmentation of broadcasting and mass audiences since the 1990s has put tremendous pressure on television programmers to maximize ratings and create immediate viewer support.

Executives have become so fearful of failure that they cancel a struggling new show after just a few episodes, rather than giving it time to develop an engaging narrative and find a devoted audience. Jack Benny often expressed gratitude for having been able to cultivate characters and situations over time in the early 1930s, to work out problems in the mid-1940s, and restructure to his radio program for the needs of television in the 1950s, rather than to have decision makers, frightened by the show's declining ratings at any of these critical junctures, end his program. Benny pointed to Benita Colman's joke about how even the mention of Phil Harris and his band could spoil her appetite. The comedy contained in the dialog's hugely successful punch line was a gag whose pay off laugh could only have been so potent with a twelve-year build up.[5]

BENNY'S WARTIME SLUMP

1940 found Jack Benny a major ratings and box office force across radio, film, and live performance. The success of his Paramount radio films released in 1939 and 1940 (*Man About Town*, *Buck Benny Rides Again*, *Love Thy Neighbor*) would bring Warner Bros. and 20th Century Fox studios knocking on Benny's door, as they asked him to lend them his box office magic. Benny worked constantly, simultaneously making films during the broadcast year and crafting his weekly radio show. Each summer Benny took his radio cast on the road for lucrative personal appearances at urban movie palaces. Disappointed by the increasingly tepid efforts of his sponsor General Foods and ad agency Young & Rubicam (Y&R) to support him with extensive promotional efforts (unlike what Bob Hope and Edgar Bergen were getting), an enormously frustrated Benny saw his rivals surpassing him in the ratings in 1941.

Benny's comedy show faced challenges as soon as the United States entered World War II. The heartbreak of war quickly came home to Benny in January 1942, when his friend and *To Be or Not to Be* co-star Carole Lombard was killed in an airplane crash as she returned to Hollywood from a war bond selling trip. She had been scheduled to appear on Benny's radio program to promote their new film that Sunday. Lombard's death was a psychological and emotional blow to Benny; he cancelled his comedy episode for that week and instead asked his orchestra to provide a somber musical program. The loss soured him on creating the type of highly effective on-air marketing campaign for the film *To Be or Not to Be* like those that had boosted Benny's previous mediocre Paramount films to box office gold.

Pressure to contribute to patriotic homefront efforts also caused problems. Soon after the war started, Benny and his cast began making field trips to broadcast their regular radio program from military bases. Other comics were taking their shows to the camps, and the pressure to do likewise must have been immense. Benny produced eight episodes of his program at camps between January and May 1942, but he was so dissatisfied with the subpar results that he vowed to stop. Camp programs cramped the *Jell-O Program*'s narrative style by gearing the program's jokes towards the boisterous servicemen audiences in front of them and away from its home listeners and Benny's carefully rehearsed control. The writers especially had trouble incorporating Rochester into the narratives. He was the camp audience's favorite character, but Rochester (Jack's valet at his home in Beverly Hills) had almost never been included in skits where the cast was at the studio creating the fictional radio show. The writers resorted to clunky routines having Rochester telephone Benny from a gas station outside the base. *Time* magazine pointedly noted that other comics like the "uninhibited" Bob Hope, "who adores his soldier audience," didn't have such problems doing their patriotic duty:

> Although willing to do special camp shows, fretful Jack Benny, after several attempts, has concluded that he couldn't entertain soldiers and the home folks from the same script. His advertising agency agreed, but its announcement of the disassociation raised a few eyebrows. . . . Benny has found that incalculable whoops and whistles upset his expertly worried lines. No ad-libber, he has to stick to his painfully prepared script, [and] feels that a lot of mugging thrown in for a visual audience is a sin against his radio listeners.[6]

While Bob Hope gained approbation from troops and the public for his camp show performances around the world, not as many people were aware that Jack Benny also made major commitments to entertain troops during the war. His gratis appearances on *Command Performance* and other Armed Forces Radio Service (AFROS) programs were usually not heard stateside.[7] Benny also led a small, intrepid USO troupe to military outposts on the front lines in North Africa, the Middle East, and Sicily in Summer 1943, the South Pacific in 1944, and France and Germany in 1945. Benny blamed lax publicity efforts by General Foods and Y&R for the relative obscurity in which he labored.[8]

If new demands on Benny's time weren't challenging enough, he received knock-out punches to his program from the military draft. First Benny lost the services of Phil Harris and his band to the Merchant Marine in December 1942; Benny used stand-in musicians until Phil returned in March 1943.

Then Benny lost his two writers, Ed Beloin and Bill Morrow, in May 1943. Morrow was drafted; Beloin decided to move on to screenwriting. *Variety* reported that Benny's show writing staff was the hardest hit among the major radio programs, and that the comic was at the end of his rope:[9]

> Jack Benny is threatening to quit radio this fall. He is said to have told friends that on his trip East he will ask General Foods for a release from his contract. Comedian said he wouldn't be averse to doing a few occasional guest shots but that the regular Sunday grind would be too hard on him, what with his writers of the past eight years, Bill Morrow and Ed Beloin, engaged elsewhere.[10]

Y&R executive Tom Harrington and producer Pat Weaver rushed out from the East Coast to Benny's vacation home in Palm Springs to quash the rumors, calm Benny down, and help him rebuild his scriptwriting team.[11]

In the summer of 1943, Benny hired new writers to start working on his program in the fall. Probably nervous about how overly dependent he had been on Harry Conn as his sole scriptwriter in the first half of the 1930s, and then relying on only two scripters, he sought to spread the risk out further and hire four. John Tackaberry, Milt Josefsburg, and George Balzer were originally joined by veteran gag writer Cy Howard, but he was replaced after half a season by Sam Perrin, who like the others remained with Benny for many years.[12]

At mid-war, Benny and the cast regularly traveled across the nation to broadcast episodes at military camps and hospitals. Playing at military bases still didn't mesh comfortably with the program's sense of timing and established situation comedy narratives. Although his role in these shows remained ill-crafted, Eddie Anderson was always greeted with the loudest cheers from the military crowds. Mel Blanc began appearing on these camp programs in November 1943 in bit roles as a common soldier. Blanc also provided the sound effects of fighter planes zipping overhead. The writers also played up the fact that a good-looking woman was on stage in these all-male environments. Benny shows had very rarely discussed Mary's relationships with men since she flirted with band members in 1933, but now in the camp episodes she was being pursued by pilots, officers, sailors, and soldiers who wanted to kiss her.

The war continued to deplete Benny's staff as his long-time personal secretary, Harry Baldwin, was drafted into the Navy in fall 1943. Baldwin had performed many vital functions on the show since 1932, including the role of the man knocking on the radio studio's door (once referred to as "Mr. Bald Dome") who inserted nonsensical asides into the program's proceedings.[13] Then Benny lost tenor Dennis Day to the Navy in April 1944, another major blow to the quality of the show's comic narrative. Benny hired a replacement singer for the duration, eighteen-year-old war veteran Larry Stevens. Unlike the versatile Day (who had blossomed into a talented comedian under Benny's tutelage), young Stevens was rarely used in skits, and there were rumors that he would be replaced.[14] The Benny show lost a vital gaiety and craziness from not having Dennis's juvenile antics, deftly innocent readings of lines, and amusing impersonations incorporated into the program.

Secondary characters in the Benny show's narrative world, such as Jack's crazy boarder Mr. Billingsley (1941–1943) or timid insurance salesman Herman Peabody (1944), did not substantially contribute to the humor of the listless show. Talented radio character actress Minerva Pious journeyed west to the Benny program in Fall 1943 when Fred Allen's program suddenly ceased due to his ill health. The Benny writers did not devise a continuing character for her, however, and Pious left the show in early 1944 to rejoin Allen's program when he recovered. She would go on to play Mrs. Nussbaum of Allen's Alley.

The new writers also did not make thoughtful use of the comedic talents of actress Butterfly McQueen, who portrayed Mary's maid and Rochester's niece "Butterfly" from October 1943 to May 1944. McQueen's cardboard character was a naïve, unintelligent young woman who mostly talked about her boyfriend in the military; she did not spout sharp, witty retorts like Rochester. McQueen quit the show before the end of the season. On the other hand, the Rochester character developed more dimensions than any other persona during the war years. Rochester got more dialogue lines in the scripts, more dignity, and less association with minstrel show stereotypes. The writers created for Rochester an easy informality and equality in his interactions with Benny. These "gains" for interracial understanding were fragile, however, and as discussed in the Eddie Anderson chapters, the unthinking way in which Benny and his writers could reintegrate old stereotypes into the program would bring increasing criticism from the African American community.

"It's not telling tales out of school to say that many in Radio Row felt Jack had slipped badly the past couple of seasons," *New York Times* reporter Jack Gould noted in fall 1944.[15] By spring 1945, the Jack Benny show had fallen out of the top fifteen shows in the Hooper ratings.[16] *Newsweek* noted: "His program abruptly skidded. The comedy became dusty and labored. Listeners demoted him from his customary post among radio's top four or five shows.... The smart alecks whispered that he was finished."[17]

THE BENNY SHOW INNOVATES

With rumors of decline swirling in radio industry circles, Benny worked intensively with his still-struggling young writers to improve the show's quality.[18] They began experimenting with new catch phrases and characters to add to the familiar situations that Harry Conn and then Morrow and Beloin had crafted over the previous twelve years.

In March and April 1944 the writers developed several new routines that emphasized Jack's temper fraying as other people annoyed him. Jack would try to reinstate order or at least stop the madness when a group of characters began yelling or singing at the top of their voices, tossing out egregious insults, the dialogue descending into gibberish. As noisy chaos filled the air, Jack would lose his temper and shout "Now cut that out!!!!" or "Wait a minute, wait a minute, WAIT A MINUTE!!!" Jack and the cast also began deprecating his starring role in the Warner Bros. film *The Horn Blows at Midnight*; insults about the movie began flying in December 1944 when the film was not even released until April 1945.

The increased involvement of versatile voice artist Mel Blanc was a tremendous addition to the show. In January 1945, the writers created an unhinged railroad station train announcer who befuddled Jack by repeatedly calling out "Train leaving on track five for Anaheim, Azusa, and Cucamonga." Angelenos in the studio audience laughed not only at the funny-sounding town names but also because they knew that no train could run between those disparate stops. Terming the thirty-seven-year-old Blanc a "one-man crowd," *Time* magazine informed readers that his chameleon-like talents voiced fifty-seven other characters, including Bugs Bunny and Porky Pig in Warner Bros. cartoons, the unhappy mailman on Burns and Allen's radio show, and characters for Judy Canova, Bob Hope, and Abbot and Costello's broadcasts.[19]

Benny's writers developed numerous comic characters for Blanc. The first was Professor LeBlanc, who was introduced as Benny's long-suffering violin teacher in April 1945. No other character expressed such sheer frustration with Benny as poor benighted Professor LeBlanc, and his lessons, with his witty, insulting rhymed instructions intoned over Jack's scratchy practice stanzas, were priceless comic additions to the program. Mel Blanc also vocalized the sound of Jack's Maxwell. Back in the 1930s the Benny show had used a sound effects person to create the raucous sounds of the Maxwell's motor wheezing to life. Jack donated the Maxwell to a patriotic scrap drive in October 1942. Within a few months Rochester was again chauffeuring Jack around in a rattletrap old car, which went unnamed, but by 1947 Benny and the writers once again called it the Maxwell. Studio audiences especially laughed at Mel Blanc's personification of the Maxwell because Blanc contorted his face so comically in creating noises representing the car's ancient, tubercular engine.[20] The writers further expanded Blanc's repertoire with the introduction of Polly the Parrot as Benny's household pet in October 1945. Unlike previous resident Carmichael the polar bear who only growled (when he wasn't causing the gas man to disappear), Polly the Parrot participated in the show's dialogue. Benny and the writers determined, however, that Polly must create her jokes only by repeating phrases that she had overheard from humans.

In January 1945 Benny and his writers inaugurated the idea of incorporating an underground money vault into the basement of Jack's home, guarded by Ed the vault-keeper, who was played in a deadpan voice by Joe Kearns. Benny's trips downstairs past an array of burglar-thwarting obstacles to meet with Ed, who had been down there so long that he wasn't aware that the Revolutionary War had ended, created a delightful source of humor on Benny's radio shows. As with the Maxwell, the elaborate series of loud and clangy deterrents securing the vault was more satisfyingly imagined in radio listeners' minds than it would be when viewed as a constructed set on a TV sound stage.

Several other new characters joined the program in fall 1945 including sassy telephone operators Gertrude Gearshift and Mabel Flapsaddle, played by veteran radio actresses Bea Bernaderet and Sara Berner. They traded tales of woe about the miserable dates Jack took them on. The Benny radio show also increasingly incorporated Jack's nemesis, Frank Nelson, into the radio program. Nelson had played occasional roles on the show as early as 1934. Beginning in 1945 he appeared regularly in a variety of roles—the rude department store floorwalker, railroad station ticket seller, doctor, waiter, or any number of other annoying people who did their best to thwart and enrage the hapless Jack when he ventured into town.

Benny himself claimed to have come up with the serendipitous idea of having distinguished British film actor Ronald Colman and his wife Benita Colman appear on the show, in December 1945, as Jack's exasperated next door neighbors in Beverly Hills. Benny had referred to them on the program for several years as being among the large group of Hollywood celebrities who disdained him, but they had remained among the celebrities that Jack had never actually met. Benny thought the Colmans would provide a delightful contrast between their upper-class English reserve and Jack's obnoxious lack of manners. "Frankly," Ronald Colman admitted in an interview, "when I read that first script I thought it was pretty corny, but when we started rehearsing it and everyone got laughing, I got into the spirit of the thing." Cleveland Amory wrote that "Benny himself rates their first appearance, on December 9, 1945 as the best single program he has ever had, and claims that the cocktail glass breaking scene . . . was a situation so real that the script girl it the control room actually had tears in her eyes."[21] The Colmans were such a hit on Benny's program that they returned fourteen times over the next three years. Despite Ronald Colman's reservations that he might be made to appear ridiculous, these radio guest shots secured for him and Benita (who blossomed into a delightful comedian with Benny's encouragement, which peeved the jealous Ronnie), starring roles in a delightful situation comedy, *The Halls of Ivy*, which was known as one of the most humorously erudite radio programs of the 1950s.

THE "I CAN'T STAND JACK BENNY BECAUSE" CONTEST

While Benny and his creative team were bandying about ideas in late fall 1945 to draw attention to the program, Benny came up with the idea of "spoofing" the write-in contests that were again so endemic on the radio. Instead of giving reasons why they "liked" some product in twenty-five words or less, or submitting an ad slogan or jingle praising a product, Benny hit on the idea of listeners sending in reasons why they *disliked* his comic "Fall Guy" character. Benny's sponsors had not indulged in efforts to get audiences to write into the program since the mid-1930s when Jell-O had offered listeners autographed pictures of Jack or recipe booklets if they mailed in a couple of box tops, so the novelty of this stunt captured attention in the trade press, as did the chutzpah of the contest's theme. It was one of the most controversial stunts the Benny show ever attempted. *Variety*'s Jack Hellman praised Benny for the idea: "It takes uts-gay to put himself on the spot like that."[22]

Steve Bradley, a new character on Jack's program who was a boorish publicity agent, cooked up the contest in December 1945. Listeners would send in statements of fifty words or less explaining why they "couldn't stand" Jack Benny, and the winners would split $10,000 in war bonds. Jack was robbed of that sum from his vault at gunpoint, and Jack handed the cash over without even considering the choice of "his money or his life." (That Jack acquiesced is an amusing demonstration of how, over the years, Benny's writers would have to find ways to continually increase the absurdity of Benny's faults and frailties in order to keep the audience laughing.)

The *New York Times* noted that "In some quarters it was questioned whether it was a smart decision to invite criticism deliberately, even as a gag."[23] Benny feared an outpouring of anti-Semitism. The war had recently ended, and prejudice against Jews remained a volatile issue. Civic groups called for racial and religious tolerance in public service announcements on the radio, the horrors of the Holocaust were becoming more widely known, and calls for the creation of a Jewish state filled the news columns. As I discussed earlier in the chapter on Benny's masculine identity, like some others in the entertainment business Benny rarely called attention to his Jewish identity, but all of the on-air celebrations of Christmas and Easter on his program would not satisfy the haters. As interviewer Cleveland Amory noted for *Saturday Evening Post* readers, "Since he is Jewish, Benny asked his cordon of 12 contest secretaries to hold out all definitely anti-Semitic letters. Out of 270,000 received, he had only three."[24]

Variety's Jack Hellman took the contest rather too literally. Although he praised its "atomic wallop" to enhance publicity for Benny's program, he assumed the event would point out to Benny what actually ailed his show:

> Neatest trick of the week was Jack Benny's unique contest, which will mount more lineage and lip service than all the orthodox soap giveaways combined.... Letters received in the contest, and they'll run in the thousands, will be smartly indexed and for such a meagre sum as $10,000 he'll find out what's wrong with his show. Among the tradesmen the reaction is mixed. Some say it's a smart move while others feel that he's letting himself in for some unkindly criticism. Many found fault with the inclusion of Fred Allen as judge. That put it strictly in the gag class and may militate against constructive criticisms, which must be one of the main reasons for the $10,000 giveaway.[25]

The stunt generated voluminous numbers of entries. "Half of the letters in the 'Can't Stand Jack Benny' contest are in verse," Hellman noted. "Mail averages around 30,000 entries daily and according to Mr. B. all contestants have one thing in common—they try to imitate Fred Allen. Incidentally, Allen gets mentioned in half the mail." Benny became the butt du jour of other radio comics' jokes (including Milton Berle and Eddie Cantor), garnered quips from public figures (baseball's Hank Greenberg joked that a running gag on Benny's show had left him stuck on third base the entire previous year, so he was going to send in an entry), and of course bon mots from Fred Allen, who was disqualified from the contest by being named chief judge. More than 300,000 entries poured in during the month-long event.[26]

The winning submission was contributed by Carroll P. Craig Sr., a lawyer from Pacific Palisades, California. His name was announced by Fred Allen at the close of the January 27, 1946, program. The next week, Ronald Colman read the winning entry, a poem, on air:

> I can't stand Jack Benny because...
>
> He fills the air
> With boasts and brags
> And obsolete
> Obnoxious gags
> The way he plays
> His violin
> Is music's most
> Obnoxious sin
> His cowardice
> Alone, indeed,
> Is matched by his
> Obnoxious greed
> And all the things
> That he portrays
> Show up MY OWN
> Obnoxious ways[27]

For all the excellent publicity the contest generated for Benny in the entertainment industry and popular press, it did not necessarily fix his problems, and it generated other controversies. Terming it a "neat stroke of showmanship," *Variety*'s Jack Hellman commented that "no contest in radio history whipped up as much dialer interest and trade talk as the 'can't stand Jack Benny' letter-writing derby for the 10G in Victory bonds. It also contributed many laugh lines to a few weeks of scripting and to all intents and purposes it looked like a good deal all around."[28] Yet the contest did not immediately boost Jack's Hooper and Crossley listenership ratings, which remained frustratingly low.

After receiving those hundreds of thousands of entries, Benny did not publicize them. At first, his decision disappointed me as a researcher (and fan) because as I initially began exploring Benny's archives, I had hoped to discover a trove of similarly brilliant, humorous paeans to Jack's faults. But there were none in his papers, or in Fred Allen's, either. I eventually realized that a corporate-initiated publicity stunt was just a publicity stunt, and the other entries probably contained merely some combination of inanity and meanness and did not deserve being saved. As Jack Hellman had commented:

> Contests are tricky things that rarely accomplish any good aside from a mail pull. They have an ungrateful way of biting back and more often than not leave a trail of bad will.... Benny admittedly let himself in for a nationwide round of criticism when he and Judge Allen decided against reading the prize-winning "hate" letters on yesterday's broadcast. They knew full well the logic of their reasoning and also the unpleasant aftermath, but allowed it was an easier escape from public wrath than to have a few thousand women mutter, "mine was better than that." Taking it philosophically, Benny sighed, "so they'll be mad at me for a few weeks." Another annoyance to the comedian was that the capital prize winner was a suburban Angeleno when he had hoped it would be someone from Oklahoma or Vermont.[29]

The dialogue during the episode on which the winners' identities were to be announced ran too long, and Fred Allen was unable to read out more than a few of the finalists' names and addresses. Benny's concern to get middle America involved in his contest at least would have been mollified if the other nine prize winners had been publicized—they hailed from Cleveland; Detroit; Phoenix; Topeka; Greenwich, Connecticut; Portland, Oregon; Fullerton, California; Arlington, Virginia; Burgenville, New Jersey; Bartlesville, Oklahoma; and Jamestown, Texas.[30] *Variety*'s George Rosen reported that the reading of Mr. Craig's winning entry on-air was itself unusual:

> The reading last Sunday of the "Can't Stand" Benny jackpot contribution [brought] ... a division of opinion as to whether it was the smart thing to do. It's reported that Fred Allen, who was the final judge in the contest, did a burn over the decision to air the letter, with others siding with the camp that contends it will invite wholesale beefs from other contestants. On the other hand, many argue that the letter itself was in such good taste and of such superior caliber that it will automatically erase any stigma of cheapness that might be associated with the Benny contest idea.[31]

Meanwhile, Benny and his writers continued innovating to further enliven the show. On January 6, 1946, Artie Auerbach was introduced as an (initially unnamed) hot dog vendor at the Rose Bowl football game, the immigrant Jewish greenhorn, Mr. Kitzel. Dennis Day returned from service in the Navy on the March 17, 1946, episode, and immediately returned his zany, juvenile antics to the program.[32] Benny's ratings started climbing back up the charts.[33] Jack had been vain about his age from the beginning of his radio program in 1932 and for years would not reveal it (while Mary and other cast members delighted in exposing the truth). Jokes about Jack claiming a youthful age increasingly began to crop up in the show during the war years. In 1945 he announced that he was 37 years old (when his actual age was 51.) He claimed to have turned 38 in 1946. He claimed to be 38 years old until his birthday in February 1948, at which time he turned 39, and there Jack remained for the rest of his career.

Benny also began to capitalize more intently on the flubbed lines that performers (especially Mary Livingstone) inadvertently blurted out during the broadcasts. Mary, for instance, mistakenly said "chiss sweez sandwich" in a scene set at a diner. Other comics had teased Benny throughout his career about his inability to ad lib. However, Benny's lightning-fast, critical reactions to his cast members' mistakes showed that he was a superb extemporaneous joker when the situation mattered to him. Benny always insisted on the perfect reading of his scripts with the jokes' timings carefully crafted, and these mistakes exposed how thoroughly invested he was in trying to maintain complete control over his program. Lucky for Benny, his quick shows of temper were deliciously funny for studio audiences to witness and for listeners to hear. His calling cast members out for missing a cue or mangling a line added more spontaneity and liveliness to the radio program. They also added moments of self-reflexive humor in which Benny and the actors momentarily slipped out of their regular characters' roles to comment on the script and their performances. Behind the scenes, the fact that most of the mistakes were made by Mary Livingstone indicated how serious her "mike fright" was becoming. The explosions of laughter from the studio audience that these unexpected moments produced caused Benny's legion of comic imitators to rush to incorporate flubbed lines and jokes about them into their own radio programs.

In 1946, Jack Benny was back to riding atop the radio ratings, and he remained there through the rest of the decade. His rejuvenated radio program, however, now collided with a greatly increased critical discourse about network primetime radio's shortcomings.[34]

"WANTED: RADIO CRITICS"

In a 1940 editorial, *Variety*'s chief radio reporter Robert Landry called for establishment of a professional critical voice to hold radio responsible for its shortcomings and encourage better programming.[35] At a time when the Axis powers' propaganda was strongest, Landry suggested that responsible published criticism would ensure that American radio remained open to democratic discussion and input, and keep pressure groups' influence at bay. He charged sponsors, ad agencies, and networks with being too afraid of angering pressure groups and rushing to censor anything that might offend even one person. They confused cranky complaints with reasoned criticism, and feared both. Newspapers imperiously turned up their noses at a "low-class medium," Landry said, and for twenty years had been reluctant to hire radio critics in jealous fear of radio's popularity. He disparaged the timidity of most radio reporters and their reliance on popularity surveys, which were "a substitute for judgment."[36] He hoped that professional radio critics would elevate radio's standards "by spotlighting the shoddy, the careless, the incompetent, and praising the opposites.... It is easy to dissect the mediocre, difficult to capture the essence of merit."[37]

Radio's vital importance to American culture during World War II, as a source of information, propaganda, solace, and entertainment,[38] sidelined Landry's immediate calls for broadcasting critics. In early 1946, however, there were still few serious appraisals of radio programming being published. What mitigated against the establishment of regular radio critiques? The sheer amount of programming to cover was daunting, with as many as 65,000 fifteen-minute segments of programming broadcast every day for a radio critic to account for.[39] The continued reluctance of newspapers to deal with radio was a second factor. Even though 33 percent of all American radio stations were owned by newspapers, broadcast programming's beholdedness to their own advertisers caused friction.[40] Newspaper publishers feared that advertisers might boycott them if they printed anything too realistic about the companies' sponsored radio shows.[41] Some newspapers refused to list radio schedules, and other papers (angered that they did not receive remuneration for an advertising plug) removed sponsor's product names from the schedules, so that the *Jell-O Program* would be listed as *The Jack Benny Program*. Lack of information about upcoming broadcasts was a problem for radio reviewers, who rarely received scripts to peruse ahead of time to help them prepare detailed analyses. As the programs were aired live and not repeated, reviews seemed superfluous to those who had not heard the broadcast.

As Ben Gross, radio critic of the *New York Daily News*, complained, "regular criticism seldom covered a show after its premiere and there were not enough new openings to keep him busy."[42] The same top programs reappeared year after year, and as one *Variety* reviewer noted wearily, "What can be said about Burns & Allen's act that hasn't been said a hundred times in the last 16 years?"[43] Here was the daunting challenge for the establishment of radio criticism—there was an overwhelming amount of potential programming to cover, most of it was broadcast live, and a reviewer could get little information ahead of time. Every program he or she heard vanished into the ether and would not be repeated.

Variety identified only between forty-five and fifty journalists (across 900 U.S. newspapers) worthy of even being termed radio reporters.[44] Creditable radio editors worked at Cleveland, Milwaukee, and Pittsburgh newspapers, but the major papers in Los Angeles and San Francisco banned all radio coverage. In New York, the corporate center of radio and home of the literary, theater, and film reviewing establishment, Jack Gould of the *New York Times* was the only critic of note, and his weekly reports focused largely on industry issues. His predecessors John Hutchens at the *Times* and Alton Cook at the *World-Telegram* had quit the radio beat in disgust in 1944 and turned to theater and film reviewing. "Except for a very small handful, radio writers have no influence whatsoever," *Variety*'s report concluded:

> They've rapped soap opera for years. Soap opera goes on. They wham excessive commercials, the middle plug, hitchhikes and cowcatchers [extra advertising snuck in between programs]. No one pays any attention to them. Three or four legit theatre critics could close a show (except in very rare instances) with adverse reviews. The radio writers can howl their heads off and, if other factors are present in the show, the Hoopers keep clicking right along.[45]

Indignation over the sins of network radio was heating to the boiling point.[46] In February 1946 the Federal Communications Commission released its blistering report on the status of radio, known as "The Blue Book," which contained scathing findings about broadcasters' lack of responsibility to the public. *Variety*'s editors nodded in agreement. Network radio was in serious trouble:[47]

> Slowly but surely, over the past few years, over-commercialization has won out. Good taste, development of original radio technique and cognizance of public service programming have gone by the boards.... [A] factor that

would have helped tremendously in making the public cognizant of what it had a right to expect would have been a critical press; one that would have constructively played the part of a guide. Even with regulation, radio needs able criticism by men who respect it as a mature medium and accept it on a full par with other arts.[48]

Variety was willing to be a voice of conscience for radio, but it was beholden to the industry's commercial structure controlled by sponsors. Its reporters and columnists could only rap knuckles. It was usually quite gentle in chiding major stars like Jack Benny. *Variety* pleaded for real radio critics. Once the critics arrived, however, the trade journal's editors may have rued what they asked for.

GILBERT SELDES'S CRITIQUE OF INSULT HUMOR

Benny's radio program based much of its humor on cast members insulting the vainglorious, penurious boss, and him dishing it back, creating swirling crescendos of invective. In fan magazine articles such as 1945's "Gags Have Grown Up,"[49] Benny reassuringly claimed that no one was really injured by the cartoonish insults. "We try to follow one simple rule: 'if it hurts, it isn't funny.'"

However famous the Benny show was for its insult humor, Benny was sensitive to anyone seriously criticizing him for it. In the March 1946 issue of *Esquire* magazine, New York–based theater and film critic Gilbert Seldes opened his column of wide-ranging media commentary with a paragraph subtitled "The Young Sadists":

> Next Sunday night, will you please listen to all your favorite comedians and note the percentage of cruel jokes. They may be self-directed, a bit of light masochism, or straight jabs to someone else's jaw. The saucy dummy in Bergen's hands turns out to be relatively mild compared to the snarling and smearing that goes on between comedians and stooges and band leaders and announcers. Fred Allen's trademark is the bags under his eyes; Benny gets it (and takes it) right and left from Rochester and Mary Livingstone; . . . Maybe a philosopher will discover some deep meaning in this mania for cruelty. All I say of it is that it begins to bore me. It's a translation into popular terms of the smart wisecrack, the insults that pass for wit in the comedies of Noel Coward; there's a speak-easy-age staleness over it and I feel that other sources of humor must exist, beyond the physical deficiencies and imputed meannesses of the comedians.[50]

One little paragraph. But someone had dared to pass judgment on Benny for the cruelty of his on-air humor, and his continued reliance on it, which had spread to all the copy-cat radio comedy programs to become the de rigueur form of humor on nearly all radio shows.[51]

Other radio critics disagreed with Seldes, asserting that insult humor's centrality to radio comedy was natural. John Crosby would claim that there was something all-American about masculine-type joking (battles between sharp wits, a comedian deflating his own vanity with self-deprecating humor, and subordinates' barbs lobbed directly at the boss). Crosby traced its history in vaudeville routines, the local saloon, and street corner jousts.[52] "[T]he most astonishing characteristic of American insult, is its amiability," noted Crosby." Americans enjoy insulting one another and, providing it's among friends, even take delight in being insulted."[53] Jack Gould asserted that insult humor allowed "listeners to share in mankind's most ennobling experience—to tell somebody off."[54]

Gilbert Seldes nevertheless stood firm in his disapproval. Benny's writers read the article while the production crew was in Palm Springs and invited Seldes, visiting the area, to attend the February 24, 1946, broadcast. Seldes recalled being curious about what Benny would do. "The question was, how could he turn criticism of his fundamental style and material into a good radio program?"

> [T]he first half of the program was all in the usual vein: Benny was jealous of Mary Livingstone because she got all the requests for autographs; she accused him of falling asleep while dancing with her; the announcer was called "obese"; the orchestra looked like dogs, and so on. Then Benny put me on the witness stand, announced my ideas, and offered to play a sweet show, "sort of a *Ma Perkins* with a band." This part of the program, therefore, consisted of honeyed compliments, excessive gushing, and attempted interruptions on my part, put down severely by Benny.... At the end, Rochester phoned to complain that something had gone wrong with his radio—"Don Wilson's got thin, you got hair...." etc. And Benny asked me which way I thought the program was best, allowing me to reply: "I think it's better when they insult you."
>
> What Benny had done was, of course, the opposite of what he said he was going to do. He had really played his comedy of insult right through, using a different technique and making me the fall guy instead of himself.[55]

After the Seldes incident, Benny and his writers occasionally incorporated comic twists on radio critics' reviews of the program into the Benny show broadcasts, fabricating terrible notices that included deprecating words (like "exacerbate") that neither Jack nor Phil were able to understand. As Milt Josefsberg recalled, Benny and his writers reasoned, "nice is nice, but nasty is funny."[56]

JOHN CROSBY'S "RADIO IN REVIEW"

On May 6, 1946, the *New York Herald Tribune*, one of the nation's premiere newspapers that had disdainfully ignored broadcasting for twenty-five years, started a department of radio criticism to add to its greatly respected theater, book, film, dance, and art reviews. The new column was helmed by someone without broadcasting industry experience, thirty-four-year-old Ivy Leaguer and war veteran John Crosby, frustrated playwright and sometimes theater critic, who claimed he'd never previously listened to the radio. His five-day-a-week column, "Radio in Review," was inauspiciously placed, not in the middle with the other cultural criticism, but buried at the back of the paper between the stock market quotes and the want ads.

From the start, Crosby's essays exhibited a sense of intelligence, withering scorn for shoddy work, and a willingness to take radio seriously. His first column compared a promising young comic, Alan Young, to the tradition of Harold Lloyd's bumbling, quirky, and kind American young man of silent film comedy. Crosby baldly announced his dislike of the program's other comedian, George Jessel, who "somehow got mixed up in the festivities and dampened them considerably." Crosby expressed a fervent hope that risqué jokes about Jane Russell—and Jessel—would both disappear from Young's show.[57] In the next days Crosby took the radio networks to task for the violence in children's programming, suggesting that kids would be better off reading books instead of being exposed to so much screaming and so many murders.[58]

At the end of his second week, Crosby showered effusive praise on Fred Allen. In "Breakfast with Freddie and Tallulah," Crosby judged that "radio's greatest wit" had created a sharp satire of the blatantly overcommercialized morning programs like *Mr. and Mrs. at Home* that exposed the shows' inanities with "explosive violence." Crosby devoted most of the column to quoting the script of Allen's wickedly funny skit.[59] Thin-skinned hosts Ed and Pegeen Fitzgerald immediately took out a full-page ad in *Variety* protesting their rude handling by Allen and Crosby (even reprinting Crosby's column) and arguing that their show's popularity negated any disparagement.[60]

Crosby next addressed the popular situation comedy *Fibber McGee and Molly*, praising the show's insight into small town politics and culture. Its creator Don Quinn understood that small towns were not simply "not a collection of homespun jokes,[but ...], in fact, an intricate web of old feuds, lifelong friendships, local custom and high complicated family relationships." Crosby admiringly concluded that Jim and Marion Jordan as the titular characters "handle this all with genuineness, an air of innocence and good nature about them."[61]

In his third week, Crosby turned to Jack Benny, but instead of the mash notes he sent to Allen and the Jordans, he lambasted Benny for his tired, formulaic humor:

> In the fourteen years he has been on the air, Mr. Benny has joked tirelessly Sunday after Sunday about his age (37), his stinginess, his thinning hair, his jealousy of other radio comedians, his violin playing and Waukegan. Gradually through the years, the jokes on these themes have been foreshortened to the point where they would be unintelligible to anyone who had never heard the Benny program, if there is any one like that. Last Sunday, Mr. Benny and his announcer held the following colloquy: "I'm giving everyone a bonus check. That'll help you get back to California," said Mr. Benny. "Get back to California—with THIS check?" "Turn it over—there's a road map on the other side."
>
> Unless you know Benny pretty well, that gag would mean very little. But, the veteran radio comedian has invented and perfected a sort of radio family joke. Benny's idiosyncrasies excite both laughter and sympathy the same way father does when he leaves his umbrella on the streetcar again. It's not funny to anyone outside the family....
>
> During the last year there have been dark whisperings that Jack Benny was seriously slipping; that his material was old; his scripts poorly written. There's some truth to these charges. The Benny show is no longer put together with the loving care he once lavished on it. Some of his shows were shapeless and floundering, which you could never say about a Benny program in the old days. But I keep listening anyway. I have been listening to Jack Benny for so many years my critical sense is paralyzed. He is like an old friend of whose faults you are fully aware, but are willing to forgive.[62]

To intimate that Benny had retired in place while Allen was at the top of his game must have stung. Benny's supporters tried to spin the "my critical sense is paralyzed" quip positively, but it is difficult not to take the essay as an indictment of Benny's lapses in creative comedy writing.

Crosby brought knowledgeable and demanding criteria to radio's popular programs—he excoriated weak scripts, and identified obnoxious personalities

FIGURE 21. The Sportsmen Quartet, who could only hum in response to Jack Benny's questions, sang parodies of popular songs that turned into delightfully nonsensical Lucky Strike cigarette commercials, winning the Benny show kudos for making the harshest advertising on the radio seem enjoyable. *Radio Best* March 1948, 10. Author's collection.

and poor performers; he published passages of poor dialogue to expose its stupidity. Although he did not discuss his intellectual underpinnings, Crosby's focus on the intellectual values of programs aligned him with late nineteenth-century cultural critics like Matthew Arnold, and the reviewer's contemporaries of Frankfurt School cultural critics, in their belief in the superior value of high culture. However much he would have rather heard symphonies and poetry readings on the radio, however, Crosby was populist enough to unabashedly adore Fred Allen; Edgar Bergen; Kukla, Fran, and Ollie; and even *Amos 'n' Andy*.

As well as hewing to traditional techniques of the arts critic, John Crosby used the tools of a passionate fan, publishing insistent criticism and fault-finding in order to spur performers and the medium to do better. Crosby was especially critical of Jack Benny because he admired him and thought that Benny and his writers were capable of creating much more incisive comedy. Few readers of Crosby's widely syndicated columns rushed to write in to disagree with him about Benny, or the reviewer's denunciations of the excesses and inanities of radio. Only Crosby's diatribes against Liberace (in 1954) created a sizeable public backlash in newspapers across the nation.

The broadcasting industry nervously kept tabs on Crosby's skyrocketing fame and influence.[63] "[I]n general its agreed that he's brought a refreshing note in to the journalistic picture that may prove to spur to additional radio activity on the part of newspapers not only in New York but elsewhere throughout the country," reported *Variety*.[64] *Newsweek* magazine dubbed Crosby "Reporter with a Hammer" and claimed that the critic, whose column was already syndicated in eight other newspapers, "expressed what a great portion of the public had been feeling about certain radio shows." By *Newsweek*'s account, 60 percent of his reviews thus far had been negative.[65] *Billboard* noted the rise in public interest in radio reviews:

> Critical emphasis, less straight reporting, seen as new tack for air editors.... Interesting angle on the whole situation is the emergence in New York of John Crosby's *Herald Tribune* column as a prestige pillar on a plane comparable to Jack Gould's critical writings in *The New York Times*. Level of both the *Times* and *Tribune* critiques is causing much consternation, admiration and wonderment, not only locally, but in areas far removed. It's believed and hoped this is only the beginning.[66]

Radio comedians topped Crosby's list of worst offenders in fall 1946, with Benny directly in the cross-hairs of his criticism.

> Jack Benny returned to the air for his fifteenth year.... Within the first few moments of his opening program Rochester pulled a gag about stinginess. Within the next ten minutes came, in order, a joke about Petrillo, one about those pens that write under water, and another concerning the size of Don Wilson's stomach.... Writing a Benny script must be as precise and standardized an operation as the chant of Speed Riggs, of Goldsboro, North Carolina.[67]

Tongue planted firmly in cheek, Crosby maintained that he was actually being polite to Benny and the other thirty-year veterans of show business who dominated radio's primetime. "When they came to radio they were fresh personalities and highly skilled entertainers. If the bloom has worn off, it's because they have been imprisoned by their own popularity in the same routine.... They have not failed radio. Radio has failed them."[68]

Crosby swung down hard on the top radio comedians in a series of articles on their "growing obsolescence."[69] Crosby blamed the structure of network radio, "a strange and unyielding mixture of oil and water, or show business and advertising." He argued that success in radio had first come to be measured by the volume of studio audience laughter and applause, not by critical appraisal of the quality of the program. "But while this debatable innovation might measure the entertainer's talent, the sponsors had to have some better way to measure the listening audience. Previously show business had but two ways to judge success—the pounding of palm on palm, and the jingle of gold in the box office. The listening public could neither applaud nor buy tickets, so the Crossley rating came into being." Now ratings points, a suspiciously vague reduction of popularity to exact numbers, ruled programming choices. Quality was nowhere to be found as a factor, as the same ratings-getting programs returned year after year without strong competition from programs on networks or other stations opposite their shows. In response, Jack Hellman of *Variety* defended Benny's tried and true formula:

> Most popular format in the comedy line seems to be the one used for so many years by Benny. It combines the best features of joke shows, variety and a segment of continuity. It's really a hybrid, but it has been paying off for years, so what's wrong with that? His is one of the few comedy entries that hasn't reached for something different in trembling fear that the order must change if the parade isn't to scoot past them.[70]

By the end of 1946, John Crosby's tally of critical jabs at the comedians was long. He admitted that he just plain hated Red Skelton and George Jessel (for unfunny routines) and that he nurtured an ever-growing dislike of Milton Berle's radio work (for stealing jokes and formats from other comics, lame puns, and blue double entendres). Crosby announced that he was very weary of the lackluster performances of Jack Haley, Frank Morgan, Jack Carson, Henry Aldrich, and Abbott and Costello (whose finely honed vaudeville routines he admired but whose sloppy radio writing appalled him). Eddie Cantor's humor was sometimes ancient and his songs were too, but Crosby appreciated him shouting out the old tunes. Burns and Allen's formula was really worn, but a bit of Gracie when she'd been off the air all summer pleased him. He was fond of the old but neighborly nonsense of Fibber McGee and Molly and the Great Gildersleeve; he praised Bob Burns for storytelling with a dark bitter edge to his endless supply of family stories, and Lum and Abner's old but amusing corniness. Crosby admired Fred Allen, Henry Morgan, and Bergen's Charlie McCarthy for their original wit, Ed Gardner of *Duffy's Tavern* for his use of language, and *Amos 'n' Andy* for their nonsensical silliness with language, their use character comedy, and for remaining "masters of timing and inflection" even, as Crosby explained, their humor dealt in blackface stereotyped fantasy that had no relations to anyone's real lives. Jimmy Durante he liked for his kindness and wordplay. Crosby had a grudging respect for Bob Hope's hard work but despaired over the comic's reliance on double entendres and formulaic jokes about current topics like Sinatra, nylons, *The Lost Weekend*, Petrillo the czar of the musicians' union, Jane Russell, the housing shortage, and three-way stretch girdles.

While in 1946 Crosby particularly criticized Benny's comedy for being stuck in a well-worn rut,[71] he also heaped scorn on soap operas, giveaway programs, and violent kids' adventure shows. He praised the occasional broadcasting of "good music" and news documentaries about the Normandy invasion anniversary and atomic bomb testing. As he later noted,

> It's extremely difficult to write enthusiasm with distinction. The best critics, or at any rate, the best known critics, have been caustic critics, and their most quoted works have been, in my experience, the most excoriating.. The late great Percy Hammond tore apart a bad play with surpassing skill but approached a good play with the inarticulate enthusiasm of a small boy who has been given a nickel.[72]

Crosby's column had become so famous that on December 30, 1946, the *New York Herald Tribune* editors moved it up from the back pages to reside among the theatrical and music reviews.[73] Editors added a small photo of the handsome author. Ninety newspapers across the nation now syndicated his daily pronouncements.[74]

"THE JACK BENNY MYSTERY," OR "BENNY MAY BE A HOWL, BUT YOU CAN'T PROVE IT BY THE SCRIPT"

Recounting his appearance on Benny's radio program, Gilbert Seldes had noted the unremarkable nature of Benny's printed scripts and how much of the program's humor came from the cast's performance of the written lines: "You add all the cracks tougher and, on paper, it seems that Benny isn't a funny man. You add the show together and you feel that it is insanely funny."[75] However, John Crosby, who admired eruditely written scripts, didn't quite understand that. In January 1947 Crosby drew on the strategy he'd used as highest praise for radio comedy scripts he considered outstanding, of printing portions of them and letting the writing's excellence speak for itself. He tried to use this method to praise Benny, but ended up instead pummeling Benny further for perceived mediocrity.

The incident began on December 29, 1946, when Crosby listened to the Benny Sunday night program and thought it was so outstanding that he quickly wrote a letter of praise to Benny and his writers in California and asked to obtain a copy of the episode's script. Writer Milt Josefsburg, terming the whole affair "possibly the strangest thing that ever happened in the history of the Benny show, and perhaps any show in the history of broadcasting," remembered that the writing staff was extremely proud to have gained Crosby's notice (an indication how much political and cultural power the columnist had gained in just eight months).[76] Just a few days later they were abashed to read Crosby's January 6, 1947, column, "The Jack Benny Mystery."

> One of the most mysterious things in the world, at least to me, is the strange quality of genius that separates a good comedy script from a bad one. A couple of Sundays ago Jack Benny offered his fans a program which to my mind was as hilarious as radio can ever get. Out of curiosity I sent to the west coast for the script to determine, if I could, just what curious essence Mr. Benny had blown into this script to make it that funny. After reading the Benny script I'm as much at sea as ever. Even allowing for Benny's great gift for pacing, inflection and timing, I still don't see why the darn thing should have made me laugh like that. In order that you may, if you like, share my bewilderment, I append below an abbreviated version of the Benny script. You'll just have to take my word for it that the broadcast version was very, very comic.[77]

Here is the dialogue Crosby quoted:

ROCHESTER: Ol' man River, Dat Old Man River

> He must know sumpin but don't say nuthin
> He just keeps rollin, he keeps on rollin'
> Along
> Ol' man Benny, dat ol' man Benny
> He won't waste nuthin,' and don't spend nuthin'
> He just keeps rolling, he keeps on rolling along
> You should have seen him sweat and strain
> When he spends a nickel, he's wracked with pain . . .

BENNY (OFF): Rochester!

ROCHESTER: Tote dat barge, lift dat bale. . . .

BENNY: Rochester!

ROCHESTER: Git a little drunk an' you land in jail. . . .

BENNY: Rochester, I've been calling you.

ROCHESTER: Sorry, Boss, I was carried away with my own voice.

BENNY: Oh fine.

ROCHESTER: Well, I'm becoming quite a popular singer. You know they call Bing Crosby the Groaner?

BENNY: Uh huh.

ROCHESTER: And they call Andy Russell the Swooner?

BENNY: I know. And what do they call you?

ROCHESTER: The Razor's Edge.

BENNY: You sound more like the Yearling. Now Rochester, my cast should be here soon for rehearsal. This is the holiday season and I'd like to serve them the eggnog I told you to make this morning. You did make it, didn't you?

ROCHESTER: Yes sir.

BENNY: Is it good?

ROCHESTER: Wanna smell my breath?

BENNY: No thanks. I'm on the wagon. But you know, Rochester, that's a strange drink. I wonder why anyone would ever think of mixing eggs and bourbon.

ROCHESTER: It's psychological, Boss.

BENNY: Psychological?

ROCHESTER: Yeah. The eggs make you think you're getting something very healthful.

BENNY: Uh huh.

ROCHESTER: And the bourbon makes that fact unimportant.

BENNY: Well that's logical. By the way, Rochester, how much eggnog did you make?

ROCHESTER: About two hundred and fifty gallons.

BENNY: Two hundred and fifty gallons? For goodness sake, Rochester, I want to drink it, not bathe in it.

ROCHESTER: Well, to each his own.

BENNY: All right, all right. Make some sandwiches, too.

(DOOR OPENS)

LIVINGSTONE: Hello, Jack.

BENNY: Hello Mary, Come in. You're the first one here.

LIVINGSTONE: Jack, how come you called rehearsal so early?

BENNY: Well Mary, to tell you the truth, I have a date tonight.

LIVINGSTONE: With whom?

BENNY: Gladys Zybisco.

LIVINGSTONE: Gladys Zybisco? Oh Jack, surely you can do better than that.

BENNY: Look, Mary. Gladys is very nice. She may not be the most beautiful girl in the world but she has a nice figure.

LIVINGSTONE: I know, but does she have to walk that way?

BENNY: Mary, that's not her fault. She's near sighted and she anticipates the curb in the middle of the block. By the way, Mary, would you like a glass of eggnog?

LIVINGSTONE: Sure, Jack. I'd love to. Wait a minute. Who made the eggnog?

BENNY: Rochester

LIVINGSTONE: Uh uh.

BENNY: Why, what's the matter?

LIVINGSTONE: Well, last Christmas I tasted some of Rochester's eggnog and the next thing I know I was at the Rose Bowl game.

BENNY: Oh—you saw the game?

LIVINGSTONE: Saw it, nothing. I was playing left tackle for Alabama.[78]

Crosby's column concluded, "That's just a sample of the Benny dialogue. Just how he manages to wrest so many laughs out of such harmless stuff is his own deep secret."

Josefsburg recalled the bewilderment, shock, and anger the writers felt, to have some of their best work labeled (in Josefsberg's words) "flat, turgid, belabored, and contrived." Crosby had completely discounted the impact of superb acting, vocal inflection, comic timing, live ensemble performance, the structuring of the gags to build upon each other, and the contribution of the audience's reactions in the creation of successful radio humor. Benny did not publically complain about Crosby (unlike Skelton and Hope, who took to the pages of *Variety* to hurl invective at the critic). Benny, however, had Jack Hellman of *Variety* make snide comments about grouchy reviewers.

Benny and his writers sought a truce with John Crosby, who visited with them in Palm Springs while on a junket trip to the West Coast radio production studios in February 1947. The critic published several columns detailing his discussions with Benny's writing staff. He learned more about the weekly pressures and challenges of creating a show; Crosby explained that they put the whole program together from bits like a Ford car, and competed with each other to laugh loudest at their own jokes so that they remain in the overlong script and somebody else's humor is cut.[79] Crosby reported on his conversations with Benny's writers about the challenges they faced of short deadlines and restrictions placed on them by networks and sponsors. Crosby dealt with them sympathetically, if not praising their skills to level that he did with Fred Allen.

CHARGES AND COUNTERCHARGES

In fall 1947, Fred Allen addressed the controversy of radio critics' continued charges—by completely agreeing with them. In his usual satiric mode, Allen used his first radio show of the season to poke fun at the failings of the radio comedians. The episode opened thoroughly disguised as an episode of the crime drama *Mr. District Attorney* (even using that show's theme music and regular announcer), with its lead actor (Jay Jostyn) and his faithful assistant Harrington (Len Doyle) investigating what an amused *Variety* reviewer called

> the NBC Crime—the case against comics (with Allen cited as the chief offender) who return to the air season after season with the old formulas still intact. "That," says the DA, "is a crime against the people." At the show's windup, Allen is in neck deep, with a first degree rap against him, [Allen's] program being labeled "murder."[80]

A few months later, Crosby published his fullest indictment yet of the broken system of American network programming, in an *Atlantic Monthly* essay.[81] "Stalled—Resistance to New Ideas, Fear of Experiment, Reliance on Ancient Formulas, Have Brought American Radio Almost to a Standstill" announced its provocative subtitle. Crosby charged that while the highest paid radio comedians brought in the most listeners, "during the last ten years, the criterion of pure popularity has resulted in a freezing of broadcast standards, a highly developed resistance to new ideas, a distaste amounting almost to revulsion against any form of experimentation, and a widespread and depressing imitativeness." Crosby charged that all of the radio comedians (with the exceptions of Fred Allen and Edgar Bergen) "rely heavily on a [never-changing] formula invented almost fifteen years ago by Jack Benny... at whom all the jokes are directed—jokes about his tightfisted attitudes toward money, his waistline, his hairline, his violin playing, his age. Mr. Benny bellows with pain at each gag and the audience roars."[82] "The Benny formula just happened to work," Crosby argued,

> and consequently has been perpetuated and will continue to be perpetuated. Years ago, comedians new at radio cut records of Benny's broadcasts and played them over and over again to find out what made him tick. They imitated his inflections, his minor characters, his pacing and even his jokes. Today where Benny has Rochester, Jack Carson till recently had Arthur Treacher, Bob Hope has Jerry Colona, and Ed (Archie) Gardner has Eddie Green, each playing Sancho Panza to his master's Don Quixote.

Paul Lazarsfeld's study *The People Look at Radio* had inquired sorrowfully if such unrelentingly derisive comedy was "a general function of humor or is it especially characteristic of the contemporaneous scene?" Crosby angrily responded, "The answer is NO to both questions."

Despite his frustration at the limitations and failings of all the meager replications, Crosby was willing to explore what made Benny's formula the "gold standard" that every other show was trying so desperately to ape. He acknowledged that copying Benny was "not as easy as it sounds":

> Benny, a veteran of years of vaudeville, is a master of timing and inflection, possibly the greatest on the air. The characters who surround him have been selected and developed very shrewdly to exploit the Benny personality. Somehow Benny has contrived to teach each of them his own mastery of timing. In addition, Benny has whittled away at the classic formula of the joke until it has assumed an entirely new shape. A simple "hmmm' takes the place of the punch line, which the home audience can fill in for itself. James Barrie once remarked that the most dramatic parts of his plays occurred when nothing at all was happening on the stage; similarly, the funniest parts of the Benny program occur when nobody is saying anything. The silence at these points is so pregnant with meaning that nothing needs to be said.

Failing to implicate the sponsors or advertising agencies who designed their programs specifically to closely copy Benny's show, and then brought in headliners to star in them, Crosby blamed the radio comedians themselves for this sad state of affairs. He judged that the lesser comics lacked the cultural taste to demand scripts of a more literate, sophisticated level. "While all comedians have writers, they are their own judges of the material the writers give them, and the level of humor in the program is an almost automatic reflection of the level of the critical judgment of the comedian. In the case of Benny, Allen and Bergen it's high. In the case of Bob Hope, Red Skelton, Eddie Cantor and Abbott and Costello, its low—sometimes painfully so."[83]

By November 1948, *New York Times* radio critic Jack Gould, who had previously showered Jack Benny with praise (in 1946 arguing that Benny's program had so improved that he should have won the Peabody Award instead of Bergen),[84] now took up John Crosby's cause and cudgel. In a *Sunday Times Magazine* essay "How Comic Is Radio Comedy," Gould charged that programs were "suffering from ... monotony, undernourishment and repeats." Gould took no prisoners, claiming that Allen's Alley was boring and old with the same familiar characters, "and when will either Jack Benny or Charlie McCarthy let a week pass without a reference to the twin who waved her hair at home?" Gould claimed that the major problem was that radio characters remained the same every week, instead of changing with every production like film or stage roles. He also charged that the influence of sponsors, agencies, and networks placed undue pressures to censor out the kind of edgy, adult themes prevalent in nightclub comedy, and the limitations of maintaining high Hooper ratings were strangling. Like Crosby, Gould charged that these restrictions had reduced radio comedy "to follow a rigid formula" and rely too heavily on topical humor, repetitive running gags, and insult humor.[85]

Jack Benny responded to Crosby and Gould in an essay, "Gentlemen of Depress," published in *Variety* in early January 1949.[86] Crosby actually claimed Benny made good points, and republished a portion of Benny's essay in his own "Radio in Review" newspaper column, titling it "Down with the Critics." While Benny tried to be comic in defending himself against the critics' charges, he did not contemplate altering anything about the way he constructed his program. His claimed that the critics were high-culture killjoys, and that if the public applauded and gave him high ratings, why should he change anything? Benny argued that longevity and the comedians' time-tested, finely honed comic personas were actually the key markers of comedy

FIGURE 22. The studio audience's view of Jack Benny's live radio broadcast, featuring, left to right, Eddie Anderson, the Sportsmen Quartet (Bill Days, Mack Smith, Marty Zperzel, Gurhey Bell), Don Wilson, Phil Harris, producer Hilliard Marks, Jack Benny, Mary LIvingstone, musical arranger Mahlon Merrick (seated behind Mary), and Dennis Day. Mel Blanc is at far right. *Radio Mirror*, November 1948, 34. Author's collection.

success in radio. In his telling, the entire configuration of primetime programming would collapse if any old dog tried to learn a new trick.[87]

. . .

At the end of the 1940s, both Jack Benny and John Crosby were at the top of their respective industries in radio comedy and radio criticism. Benny's biggest concern, fixing the problems with his program, appeared solved. The show had resurged in the ratings and was praised in many places (if not necessarily by the top critics) for its finely tuned scripts and cast. Acknowledgement of his influence and achievements would come in the bitter struggle the CBS and NBC networks waged over his services in late 1948 and his anointment as one of the highest paid and highest honored radio performers. Benny could not singlehandedly fix the broken system around him, where so many other programs aped everything his program did. What might have addressed this problem—perhaps the radio industry listening to the critics? Perhaps only a force such as the network assuming much greater responsibility for improving and diversifying programming could have made a greater change in the dullness of radio programing, rather than having the decisions made by competing ad agencies and sponsors.

Indeed, not only critics' concerns about radio's problems, but also radio's leaders' smug satisfaction at their success would very soon become moot. Television broadcasting was beginning, and that forestalled any concerted effort to make radio better as primetime programming would soon be just about abandoned in a move forward to TV. Even NBC Radio president Niles Trammell had admitted to Crosby in January 1948, "My future is entirely wrapped up in sound broadcasting, but I'm the first to admit that when television comes in, sound broadcasting is finished."[88] Much of the critical buzz of reviews and commentary in radio industry trade press and newspapers by the end of 1948 was starting to be all about television. Even though there were only 25,000 TV sets in all of New York (vs. 60 million radio sets), the new medium's tail was going to wag the broadcasting industry dog. What was Jack Benny going to do about television and the widely predicted death of radio when TV took hold nationwide? Critics, wielding a great deal of influence, would also soon shift their focus to TV. They would speculate about how old-hat radio performers and genres were going to adapt to the new medium (or not). The final chapter explores how Benny, his writers, and his cast attempted to adapt radio humor to the visual medium of TV, and how critics, sponsors, ad agencies, and the public would shape the program through their critical reactions.

NINE

Jack Benny's Turn Towards Television

In 1948, Jack Benny nervously faced the prospect of adapting his iconic radio program to the new medium of television. During more than fifteen years on the airwaves, Benny and his writers, actors, and production staff had crafted a superb comedic soundscape, perfecting a successful brand of aural situation comedy that blended the interactions of quirky characters into a richly developed narrative world colored by radio listeners' imaginations. Audiences in 30 million American homes reveled in the cacophony of Benny's ancient Maxwell automobile engine sputtering to life and the mysterious clangs and roars of the contraptions and beasts that guarded his subterranean vault. Listeners grew to love the familiar patois of the show's characters—from cement mixer–laden rejoinders of Benny's bumptious valet Rochester, to the absurdities of the demented train announcer Mel Blanc, the pained embarrassment of his cultured neighbors Ronald and Benita Colman, the addlepated young tenor Dennis Day's non sequiturs, the jolly announcer Don Wilson's laugh, and acid-tongued Mary Livingstone's put-downs of Jack's egotism. Benny was the leading actor in this multilayered narrative world, who pulled the show together with his mild, Midwestern twang–tinged reactions to the chaos and insults that beset him on all sides. From his longtime informal greeting, "Jell-O again, folks," to the "Well . . . " that introduced his vainglorious lies and the "Hmm" in response to being caught—or the "But . . . but . . . but . . ." of despair as his sponsor berated him and the frustrated bleating of "Now cut that out!" and "Wait a minute, wait a minute!"—Benny had crafted his comic character and the award-winning show by orchestrating a symphony of aural humor with a deft sense of timing.

World War II had stalled TV's implementation, but its arrival was always presented as being imminent. Video stole the trade paper headlines even as radio hit its peak in listenership and advertising revenues from 1945 to 1948, and Benny's show climbed back to the top of the ratings. Now, competing demands from Jack Benny's sponsor, network, broadcast critics, and audiences buffeted him as he sought to transition his radio program to television. As a show producer and a performer, Benny wrestled with obstacles thrown up by the technical, industrial, and aesthetic demands of the new medium.

The burgeoning TV industry was based a continent away from Jack Benny and the radio production center of Hollywood. The dictates of programming practices, combined with the technological limitations of coaxial cable, which had to be strung from city to city to transmit network broadcasts, mandated that nearly all early primetime TV shows would be presented live from the networks' Manhattan studios. The number of TV sets in use was also extremely small. In 1947, the coaxial cable spread north to Boston and south to Philadelphia and Washington, DC, and television stations broadcast three hours of programming per evening. Milton Berle on NBC's *Texaco Star Theater* became the first breakout TV star in October 1948, when only about 350,000 TV sets could tune him in.[1] Influential radio critic John Crosby first incorporated discussion of television into his column in November 1948, describing the television "feast" emanating from New York on Sunday nights (stealing away audiences from Benny's radio show) which included *The Theater Guild*, *Philco Television Playhouse*, Ed Sullivan's *Toast of the Town*, *The Ford Theater*, *Studio One*, and *Actors' Studio*.[2] Sid Caesar and Imogene Coca appeared in the *Admiral Broadway Review* on NBC beginning in January 1949. Ed Wynn starred in a CBS comedy program originating from Los Angeles in October 1949 that was kinescoped for East Coast viewers. Benny's continuing career depended on making a successful leap to TV.

Benny was one of the last senior figures in radio entertainment to start the transition to television while continuing the full-time job of creating and starring in his radio program. Benny made an initial TV appearance on a local program celebrating the opening of the Los Angeles CBS affiliate on March 1949, and then, nineteen months later, he starred in his first network primetime show produced in New York, on October 28, 1950.[3] Critics were already beginning to label some of the first stars of TV "has-beens" before Benny ever made his first tentative steps into video.

He struggled to craft a television program mode and performance style in the face of contentious critical reception of his early efforts. Similar to complaints of the sophisticated film critics of 1940 that Benny's Paramount films were not "cinematic" enough, as discussed in chapter 7, debates raged among the new TV reviewers and industry insiders about how far TV comedy should distance itself from radio's aesthetics—should visual aspects dominate, dialogue be minimized, slapstick action and spectacle be sought, and sophisticated, quieter wordplay in dialogue-based humor be eliminated? Television critics' vehemently negative reactions to Jack Benny's initial television productions in 1950 and 1951 were humiliating to the veteran performer. Reviewers scornfully attacked Benny's aurally focused radio performance style as inadequate for the new medium's demands for visual spectacle and action. The *New York World Telegram*'s acerbic radio/television critic Harriet Van Horne pointed directly to the public reaction that Benny most feared:

> Benny on video is in no sense as funny or as likeable as Benny on radio. When we hear the radio Benny our imagination comes nimbly to our assistance (and to his). Imagination supplies the missing picture. So it has that each of us has created a Jack Benny. We know the "character" so well that we can laugh at his smallest jests ... In television we see something approximating the "real life" Jack Benny. A tired looking man in a well-cut suit who is neither mobile of feature nor flexible of body. He speaks with the slow, deliberate timing that proved a million dollar asset in radio. In television this same timing gives the script a curiously halting gait. The lines may be every bit as funny (and last night there were some excellent lines). But the laughter isn't as joyous or explosive. We realize, a little sadly, how generous have been our imaginations.[4]

Benny, his writers, and the production crew labored to balance critics' desires for substantial changes in the comic performance of his program with the competing expectations of the program's commercial sponsors and longtime fans that the show remain faithful to the characters and aural narrative landscape that Benny had perfected in radio. Benny's powerful sponsor, the American Tobacco Company, and CBS, his broadcasting network after 1948, handed Benny a predicament—they not only demanded that their popular star continue to produce his weekly radio program (based in Hollywood) to service the still-large radio audiences, but also impatiently insisted that he launch full time into television production in New York City. Benny was caught in the middle of these industrial forces, uncertain of how to translate his radio success to television, confused about how his character and comedy world could be adapted to the new medium, and piqued by the critical drubbing he was getting from TV reviewers. Ultimately, Benny modified his own comic performance style in a way that was true to his character but that utilized acting skills somewhat different from those he had previously developed for the vaudeville stage, film, and radio.

Benny's experience provides new insight into TV's upending of the status quo of network radio and the comics who had dominated it.[5] *Variety* cheekily termed the senior comics gingerly entering TV "the nine old men," as if they were aged Supreme Court judges a frustrated president wished would retire.[6] The increased production workload and the draining cross-country commute to New York that Benny faced, while he simultaneously continued to write, produce, and perform a weekly radio program, stretched him thin. His wife Mary headed toward retirement and counseled Jack to do the same.[7]

Why was Jack Benny so reluctant to plunge into television? We have seen how Benny developed his radio format and characters over the first years of the program, but since 1937 it had remained essentially the same, with some polishing and additions of new characters and situations in the postwar years. What aesthetic changes would need to occur to adapt his radio formula to TV? These were central concerns for media critics (and the audiences they spoke for), who demanded to see Benny and his writers meet the new media head on with more visually based humor. How were Benny's carefully crafted radio jokes, based on aural cues, word play, and fantasy, and the rapid repartee of characters standing around a microphone, going to work on TV? What new sources and forms of humor could be developed? Television's difficulties colored the slow and cautious strategies through which Benny approached the new medium.

Meanwhile, his comedy colleagues chose a variety of different paths. Edgar Bergen and Jim and Marian Jordan (*Fibber McGee and Molly*) remained on radio until 1956 and then essentially retired, making a few TV guest appearances. Ed Wynn, who had retired from radio by 1937, had a successful run on TV from 1949 to 1952.[8] Eddie Cantor left radio in 1950 and appeared as one of the rotating hosts of the *Colgate Comedy Hour* from 1950 to 1954 (alternating with Abbott and Costello, and Martin and Lewis). George Burns and Gracie Allen quit radio and moved to New York to co-star in their video situation comedy, initially aired biweekly from New York in 1950, then from 1951 to 1958 from California.[9] Fred Allen's radio program ended in 1949 (chased off the air by competition from a prize-giveaway quiz show). It was said Allen never found a comfortable TV format; in the 1950s he appeared mostly in guest-star or quiz panelist roles before his death in 1956.[10] Health problems also shortened the TV careers of Eddie Cantor and Gracie Allen. Younger radio comics Bob Hope, Red Skelton, and Danny Kaye, who had active film careers that kept them tied to Hollywood, delayed their entries into TV until 1950, 1951, and 1952.

POSTWAR CONCERNS ABOUT TELEVISION, AND THE BATTLE FOR BENNY

In 1947, when *Variety* addressed the issue of how television might impact the very profitable network radio business, amid the utopian hopes for the future were tremendous anxieties about costs, technological hurdles, how prime-time programs and stars might (or might not) transition to the new video medium, and what would be left of radio once TV was launched. An initial concern voiced by the advertising agencies that produced prime-time radio programs was how expensive television was going to be to mount—almost prohibitively costly, given the vast expenditures and the small number of receiving sets yet in operation. Prognosticators in *Variety* speculated that sponsors would not be able to afford to move the top radio shows with their huge talent budgets to TV, not soon or not ever—"Possibility of a weekly tele show featuring stars like Jack Benny, Fred Allen, Bob Hope . . . is consequently extremely remote."[11] Critics suggested focusing instead on lower paid talent in less expensive formats and genres, and not to be so totally reliant on the star-driven comedy and variety programs. They added up the budget items that radio shows had not needed—sets, costumes, lighting, cameras, rehearsal time, plus the stars' high salaries, divided the sum by cost per thousand TV viewers, and judged that the price was ruinously high, fretting that "even then the possibility of any producer using a top star to whom he'll have to pay a top salary is something far in the future."[12]

Queried about his own television plans in summer 1947, Jack Benny was taciturn. *New York Daily News* radio columnist Ben Gross asked radio's top-rated comic, "Do you think your radio show would be equally successful in television?" Benny responded, "'I don't think so. I'd be afraid to try it. We'd have to alter our format radically. In my opinion, the comedy of television will be the comedy of the legitimate stage and of vaudeville."[13] Another article's scare headline proclaimed, "Benny Fears Advent of Television."[14]

Variety's George Rosen saw "alarm and bewilderment" spreading across the radio industry in 1948, as radio broadcasters looked to the future in what was actually their most successful and profitable year. He predicted that TV would not fully take over as a coast-to-coast medium until 1953, but wondered what would happen in the interim. He guessed that the major comics such as Benny, Fred Allen, and Eddie Cantor would become much less important to sponsors, and he thought that Benny had the most to lose

FIGURE 23. The American Tobacco Company marketers achieved a brand promotional trifecta in this print advertisement, combining grinning caricatures of their stable of radio and TV stars, awkward product placement and brash ad slogans into an over-the-top holiday sales pitch. *LIFE* Magazine, December 1950, 77. Author's collection.

because he was so dependent on an "imaginative appeal that visual presentation would destroy."[15]

The senior radio comics might have been skittish about the advent of television, but soon the industry deduced that their ability to draw high ratings would give the networks an advantage in TV. With the guidance of increasingly assertive talent agents, in 1948 Jack Benny and the other radio comedy stars began to plunge into the hustings of deal making.[16] Star systems had dominated the American film and radio industries, and TV executives began to accept that established stars would be needed in the new medium after all. Networks, performers, advertising agencies, sponsors, and talent agencies all began jockeying for position. "Television Raids Scare Radio," *Variety* reported in April 1948, "Air Names Now Want TV Wedge": "Looking ahead into the television future, the major networks, the advertising agencies and the sponsors who plunk down $1,000,000 apiece and more a year for air time and talent are frankly disturbed over the prospects of losing their top stars to rival webs and sponsors.... *Amos 'n' Andy* is being peddled around by MCA, with a tag on it for $30,000 a week for coupled radio and television services."[17]

If Benny the creative performer feared what television might do to disrupt his patented radio formula, businessman Benny, working with MCA agent Lew Wasserman, jockeyed to find the most monetarily and creatively advantageous position in which to approach the new medium.[18] William Paley and CBS entered the fray to wrest top talent from the staid arrangements that NBC held with sponsors and advertising agencies. In late 1948, radio experienced a free-for-all battle, with headlines about the networks' back-and-forth struggle to secure the services of Jack Benny (and other top air comics like *Amos 'n' Andy's* Gosden and Correll, Edgar Bergen, and Phil Harris) filling the industry trade papers.[19] *Variety's* Jack Hellman called it "the most fantastic story in big time radio's spectacular career."[20]

Paley's talent raids of 1948 have been discussed in detail elsewhere, as has Jack Benny's subsequent wrangling with the IRS over whether the sale of his company, Amusement Enterprises, to CBS was legal or just an income tax dodge. In the short term, CBS wanted to increase its primetime radio offerings. It had been considered the second-tier network for many years. Both NBC and CBS were having difficulties developing new programming; ad agencies and sponsors were reluctant to gamble with unproven performers or program formats.[21] In the longer term, the battle for talent was for control of established, proven, name brand entertainers to prepare for the coming of television. For Benny and the other "raided" radio stars, much of the allure of the deal was receiving additional income.[22] During World War II, individual income tax rates had risen to 90 percent, and they remained prohibitively high after the war (still as much as 87 percent in 1950). Stars working for salaries faced huge tax consequences significantly limiting their earnings. Forming corporations that could be sold to a network meant that they would receive payment to their companies taxed at the much lower capital gains rate of 25 percent.[23]

Equally important to Benny, the deal was also about promotion for his program. Benny continually fretted that NBC had not been willing to publicize his show. NBC left promotion nearly entirely up to individual sponsors who provided the programs, and the sponsors and their ad agencies cared far more about their product sales than about the cementing the popularity of performers. Paley and CBS promised to provide much more help for Benny and his show, and indeed the network mounted a full-on promotional push in January 1949 when he joined CBS's radio network, spending $100,000 or more, taking out ads in scores of newspapers and magazines, running hundreds of spot announcements on other CBS radio shows detailing the change, and having Benny make guest appearances on other CBS primetime radio programs.[24] These efforts boosted Benny's CBS radio ratings to the top of the Hooper and Nielsen ratings in early 1949.[25] Benny's *Variety* advocate Jack Hellman crowed:

> Jack Benny's high hop in the Hooper hoopla that caught the experts far off base proved many things. It punctured myth—knocked the pins from under infallibles and revised the thinking of our master minds. It had been dinned in these ears for seasons on end that no one ever improved his rating by moving from NBC down the street to CBS. It would have been heresy to even mutter that anyone could cut into Radio's City's impregnable Sunday bloc. Well, it happened and with a comfortable margin to spare. Two of the so-called "inviolables" came crashing down on the heads of the believers and placed a large doubt in their minds. Dialing habit, they pounded, was so strong that it would take a lot of doing to change the status quo. Secondly, NBC's powerhouse lineups were so strongly entrenched that no amount of battering would budge them. But you know what happened....[26]

As soon as the Benny-CBS radio deal was inked, trade press articles maintained that now Benny was definitely pointed in the direction of television.[27] *Variety* reported:

> Only minor revisions will be required to convert Benny's ether layout to sight and sound.... Fantasy won't be as rampant in video as it is in radio, but tele viewers will see Rochester and Benny riding in the old Maxwell down Main Street. They'll also see the guardian of the squeaky hinged vault in the cellar, the violin teacher, the spare toupees, bashful Dennis Day and his mother, visual proof of Don Wilson's oft-mentioned obesity, and the special Phil Harris brand of braggadocio as he bosses his sidemen around.[28]

The physical reality and visuality required of television concerned Benny far more than this article let on, for he worried that the carefully crafted "picture jokes" and fantasy objects and places he had created over the years on radio were not going to work on TV at all. The *Variety* reporter did reassuringly note that the Benny radio performers had long assumed characteristics that matched their physical looks, so that they would look "right" to television audiences. (This would not be the case with short, rotund radio actor William Conrad, unable to plausibly portray his famous character of Marshall Matt Dillon on *Gunsmoke*, or Gosden and Correll trying to embody their Amos and Andy characters on the video screen.)

CBS and sponsor American Tobacco wanted their star to venture into TV as soon as possible, and on the West Coast the first opportunity that sprang up was an hour-long gala celebrating the opening of Los Angeles CBS TV station KTTV, which occurred March 8, 1949. Benny and Eddie Anderson headed the live program's cast, which also featured singers Margaret Whiting, Bob Crosby, the Andrews Sisters, violinist Isaac Stern, and comics Lum and Abner.[29] Benny found the experience stressful. He recounted in an interview, "One problem . . . encountered in the rehearsals of the show was in keeping the director from switching the camera from one player to another and from changing from long shots to close-up and then back to long shots. In many cases . . . the camera let on that it knew the joke and much of the humor was lost." Although Benny convinced the director to restrain the overactive camerawork, it only added to the anxiety of having to prove himself in a new medium where everyone involved behind the cameras was also new, and there were technical elements he could not control.

Despite high anticipation on the West Coast for the program, many reviews of Benny's first appearance were negative. Even *Variety*'s steadfast Benny supporter Jack Hellman grouched:

> Jack Benny was not flattered by either camera or makeup . . . Rochester (with Benny) will be only as good as his material, and fiddlers such as Isaac Stern have too limited an appeal to stay on too long. It's more than fair to qualify these remarks with the extenuation that the performers were being lensed for the first time in a medium new to them and therefore nervous and ill at ease. . . . But, as any housewife knows, you won't buy the product if you don't like the sample.[30]

On Benny's radio show of March 13, 1949, the cast talked about the KTTV show, cracking jokes that having Jack appear on television was great for the rival theatrical industry, and that Dennis's mother had seventy-two stitches in her hand from punching through her TV screen. One month after the ill-received West Coast TV broadcast, Benny trekked to New York to discuss future TV plans with CBS executives and his sponsor, who had optimistically scheduled Benny to make four TV programs in 1949. While he evinced a confident demeanor and enthusiastic opinion of television to a *New York Times* interviewer in his spacious hotel suite, there were hints of Benny's uncertainty. The reporter described a television set, placed in the room by CBS in order for Benny to better acquaint himself with current New York programming, looming in the background like a one-eyed intruder.[31]

Benny now anticipated that he would have to make major changes to his program format to move from radio to TV. He would revert to the stage-mindedness of his earlier 1920s work as an emcee in vaudeville, in which he introduced the acts, did monologues, and interacted briefly with the various performers. "This is going to give me the chance of picking up where I left off twenty years ago at the Palace Theatre," Benny told the *Times*.[32] Although Benny was loath to jettison the informality, camaraderie, and competitive insult throwing that the radio cast experienced gathered closely together around microphones, he wondered, what did TV audiences want to see? He was flummoxed.

By May 1949, Benny was leaning even further away from his radio routine for his video plans as concerns about the costs involved in trying to visualize radio fantasies mounted. *Chicago Tribune* columnist Larry Wolters reported:

> The Benny video show will not be the same as his radio show. Benny plans to use the variety show format, similar to that employed by Milton Berle and Arthur Godfrey on their TV shows. Benny has dropped earlier plans for bringing his old Maxwell car, squeaking vault hinges and other gimmicks that are merely sound effects in radio to television. If he were to use these, much advance filming would have to do be done. This would prove too costly.[33]

In the panicky rush to figure out what television comedy ought to be, performers hardly knew which way to turn, as critics downplayed and dismissed many of the aural touches that had made radio distinctive and pleasurable for its creators and fans.

"Benny's principal concern over television at the moment is whether he will be able to put on his shows from the West Coast," the interview concluded. Ed Wynn was currently performing his TV show in Los Angeles, with kinescope recordings of it aired several weeks later across the rest of the country. By July 1949, the technical limitations of West Coast kinescopes were becoming more evident. Film and radio actor Jack Carson had worked with an ad agency to create a pilot for a kinescoped TV series to be sponsored by General Foods; the finished product looked and sounded so poor when broadcast, however, that the sponsor ate the entire $6,000 production cost and shelved the program. Other critics complained that Ed Wynn broadcast his show from the stage of a theater so vast that a tiny Wynn seemed lost in a cavernous auditorium.[34] Given the guff Benny had already gotten about the KTTV special, doing a kinescoped program presented many technical and aesthetic drawbacks. Such concerns gave Benny cold feet, and he pulled out of any plans to broadcast television shows from the West Coast or anywhere else in the near future. This could not have pleased his sponsor or the CBS TV executives. *Variety* reported, "Jack Benny will do no kinescope recordings here for American Tobacco unless the quality is considerably improved.... He is favorable to live telecast but believes the strain would be too much, flying back and forth [to New York] each week.... Another reason for bypassing scheduled TV is that he wants to concentrate on his radio show."[35] Now Benny's only "plans" were eventually to "ease into television via occasional guest shots."[36]

Network, sponsor, advertising agency, and talent representatives struggled with Benny throughout the next sixteen months to decide when and where Benny would finally appear on television, since it would have to take place on the East Coast on a live broadcast. They all urged Benny to go on as soon as possible, but for one impeding reason or another, the months dragged on. A July 1949 memo in advertising agency BBDO's files finds CBS executive Frank Stanton pestering BBDO to secure a definite day and time for Benny to premiere a fall 1949 TV series. The memo revealed that "there is still some doubt in some people's minds that Jack Benny will do television this fall. Both Frank Stanton and Ted Scheiver of MCA, when he was in town last week, said they feel certain that Benny will do at least two shows in the Fall and perhaps will stay on an alternate week basis thereafter."[37]

Fred Allen voiced the concerns of many radio veterans skeptical of the new visual medium. In a July 1949 *Life* magazine interview, the comic pessimistically detailed TV's technological limitations, the loss of the intimacy that radio created between listener and performer, and concerns that imaginative input of radio listeners would be lost:

> [T]he [small] screen is a problem. How can you show a glint in somebody's eye? The eye itself is as big as a fly speck. The beautiful girl in television has as much sex appeal as a clothespin. The only way you can register mild

disapproval on that screen is to hit somebody over the head with a broom. And there's something about the television screen that prevents the close, personal contact between the actor and the audience that you had in radio.[38]

In an October 1949 *Radio-Television Life* interview, "Year of Decision; Jack Benny Knows That Television Is Breathing Heavily Down His Neck," Jack Benny seemed to agree with his radio feud rival, expressing doubt that the new visual media could allow for performers to create the intimacy and fantasy of a medium in which he he'd grown so comfortable. Benny admitted, "Truthfully, at this moment I have no television plans.... I don't think bad TV can compete with good radio. It is physically impossible to do both television and radio shows and have them both good. If a performer has been lucky enough through the years to have built up a good show (for radio) his audience will expect him to deliver a good television show; both radio and television would kill me."[39]

While network and sponsors were fretting over Benny's nonappearance on television, his weekly radio show continued to garner kudos from critics and the public; the programs of these years are considered by fans to be his "golden era" of characters, situations, and performances. Highlights include one of Jimmy Stewart's rare radio appearances soon after Benny switched from NBC to CBS (January 9, 1949), a classic Benny the Shmo episode, in which he joined Stewart at a table at the Brown Derby restaurant and proceeded to destroy everything at the table. In the next episode (January 16, 1949), Jack borrowed household items from his neighbors the Ronald Colmans. Jack walked down the street with an empty cup to borrow flour and suddenly a coin dropped in it (the footsteps and "clink" with no dialogue made a perfect radio "picture joke"). Subsequent weeks included sketches about the radio cast striking for higher wages and Jack holding them prisoner until they relented, Jack losing $4.75 at the racetrack, and the spiraling consequences of Jack giving a bum fifty cents.

Other notable radio episodes drew on such familiar themes such as Jack's birthday shakedown of his cast for gifts, the annual Christmas shopping episode, Professor LeBlanc's misery being Jack's violin teacher, Sheldon Leonard's tout giving Benny ludicrous advice, Frank Nelson's insults, Mary and Rochester's wickedly sharp puncturings of Jack's egotistical excesses, and Jack boiling over with frustrated aggravation and yelling "Wait a minute!" or "Now, cut that out!" Other than the one ill-considered revival of the "Rochester in Harlem" skit of 1940 that Benny and the writers fell back on while on a rushed trip to New York City, which drew sharp negative reaction from the African American community, Benny's radio programs of this period were sharp, fresh, and inventive, filled with both small talk and mayhem. Based on well-established themes, they were nevertheless lauded for their liveness, rollicking humor, and "looseness" in capitalizing on cast members' minor script fluffs.

On the fall 1950 radio season opener (September 10, 1950), Jack was frustrated to find that all the CBS radio studios were booked and were being used for TV broadcasting (an ironic comment on Benny's ambivalent situation). Jack asked CBS vice president Howard Meighan where he could locate space in which to perform his radio show, and Meighan suggested NBC. Jack threw a tantrum. To compound Benny's anxieties, Sunday night TV programs were eating into his East Coast radio audience base. His radio program also faced new competition on the airwaves in fall 1950, when NBC launched *The Big Show* from 6:30 to 8:00 P.M. on Sunday evenings, directly opposite the popular show NBC had lost to the rival network. It was an audaciously expensive and elaborate ninety-minute weekly radio spectacular, hosted by Tallulah Bankhead and featuring Fred Allen and many other A-list guest stars. Traditionally, top radio programs had never run opposite each other in the rival networks' schedules, as conservative sponsors wanted as large an audience as possible guaranteed for their shows. NBC created this last great radio extravaganza as a sustaining program (without commercial sponsorship), hoping to attract deep-pocketed advertisers to support it, to prove that primetime radio was still a top entertainment medium. If its success humbled Jack Benny, that traitor to NBC, all the better. The *Big Show*'s high quality was lauded by critics, yet despite a surfeit of expensive talent (reportedly NBC spent up to $100,000 an episode for star performers), *The Big Show* never attracted the sponsors that NBC sought, and its ratings remained meager.[40]

Whether or not Jack Benny was anxious to move from radio to television, social trends becoming apparent in 1950 were forcing his hand and adding to CBS and American Tobacco's urgency in pushing him toward the new medium. Articles in trade journals and the popular press in 1950 documented a startling trend—Americans across the country were turning off their radios, even when they did not yet own televisions. (They attended the movies much less often, as well.) In cities like Portland, Oregon, which had no TV station, the highest Hooper radio ratings were now 18–21 as opposed to the 31–35 of just a few years previously.[41] Economists, sociologists, and media historians have attributed the sharp postwar drop in American moviegoing to the Baby Boom and changing demographic trends, maintaining that families shifted money away from movie theater attendance and put larger shares of their time and money into having children, moving to suburban homes, purchasing expensive consumer goods, and taking up hobbies. These reasons explain why people would not travel downtown to the older movie theaters that had little parking for cars. But radios were already in their homes (and in an increasing number of cars). Critics suggested that the "sameness" of top radio programs, many of which had been on the air for fifteen years, also brought on audience boredom.[42] Those who had televisions, however, were watching them obsessively.

Studies now showed that families who had owned TV sets for eighteen months listened to very little radio after 6:00 P.M., and Jack Benny's previously high Sunday evening radio ratings were hit particularly hard. Another article noted that, "in the last 11 months, television's share of the total night time broadcast audience in New York City (both radio and television) had increased from 19 percent to 44. In Los Angeles it has moved up from 10.5 to 36 percent.... More people in New York City watched Milton Berle on television than listened to Jack Benny on radio." This was despite the fact that three times as many New York homes had radio sets as had TV sets.[43] Nationwide, *Sponsor* reported, Jack Benny's radio show was now heard in 9 million homes, while Milton Berle's TV show was viewed in 6.5 million residences. TV was growing even more rapidly in parity with radio than industry spokesmen had ever predicted.

BENNY'S FIRST TV PROGRAM, OCTOBER 28, 1950

Even as the growing ranks of TV journalists focused their attention on the brash new video comedians, when Jack Benny finally appeared on a special forty-five-minute live broadcast on Saturday, October 28, 1950, the event was one of the most anticipated in TV's young history. This first show preempted Ken Murray's hour-long Saturday night musical-comedy variety program, which was also sponsored by American Tobacco. Benny was joined in CBS's New York studios by several of his regular radio cast members—Eddie Anderson, Don Wilson, and Mel Blanc. Benny also brought his popular group the Sportsmen Quartet, to sing the slyly comic Lucky Strike commercials.

FIGURE 24. Local television program guides promoted Jack Benny's first TV program as a special event in October 1950. Note how Benny is associated with his wheezing, ancient Maxwell, whose sputtering engine was voiced on radio by Mel Blanc. Loyal audiences wanted to see their favorite humorous aural aspects of Benny's show made visual. Benny's great concern was the efficacy of trying to do that. *TV Forecast*, Chicago, October 28, 1950. Author's collection.

Publicity for the upcoming video filled Benny's radio programs for weeks beforehand, much as Benny had cross-promoted his films on the airwaves a decade earlier. The October 22, 1950, radio episode featured Jack and Rochester packing for their trip to New York. At the airport, Benny encountered the race track tout (Sheldon Leonard) who argued he should take oranges instead of apples for the trip, and the crazy flight announcer (Mel Blanc) and ticket agent (Frank Nelson) aggravated him before he boarded the plane. The show served as send-up of Benny's nervousness. On the October 29, 1950, radio show (which would be aired on the evening following his first TV program), Jack was interviewed by a reporter who asked how Jack had met Ronald and Benita Colman. Mary retold the story of the Jack Wellington dinner invitation fiasco. This program, with the Colmans reprising their original roles, re-created Benny's favorite and most highly praised radio episode, originally performed in December 1945. Benny was taking no chances in trying to have his programs serve as a one-two popularity punch in TV and radio that week.[44]

Benny, his writers, and his production staff had ambitiously planned several elaborate visual spectacles for his premiere television broadcast, such as a filmed scene inserted at the opener that was to show a city bus pulling up in front of Benny's Beverly Hills mansion and riders' surprise when Jack gets off, banging people in the head with his flailing violin case. This was abandoned for lack of time, and a ridiculous-looking cardboard cutout of a bus slid onto the small New York studio stage instead. Also planned in the script was a scene in Jack's living room (re-created onstage) in which Rochester, while busy cleaning and singing, would "reveal" his face by polishing a circle of glass wax off one of the windows (while hanging outside the frame to wash it) and smiling to the TV audience. This was also cut at the last minute.[45] Rochester nevertheless performed an intricate skit, in which he danced and sang while dusting the living room and conversed with Polly the parrot. The crash and clang of the unseen Maxwell wheezing up the driveway outside introduced Jack to the scene, and he proceeded to carry on a phone conversation with the guest star, singer Dinah Shore, with an attempt at re-creating a split-screen effect that came off as absurd because the two were merely separated by a cardboard wall. Next, in a skit that emulated a radio routine, a nervous-looking Benny talked from the front of a small stage (keeping his eyes on the studio audience rather than the camera lens), and Shore took up a big chunk of the show's time performing three songs (including the middle-of-the-program comedy commercial, singing with the antic, gesticulating Sportsmen).

In a final attempt at incorporating a visual joke into the episode, as Benny again stood on the small stage in front of the studio audience, he pulled out his violin to end the program with a concert. The three hundred members of the studio audience were supposed to rise and leave in a huff. The show ran out of time, however, and cut off abruptly, with just the front row of attendees beginning to get up. The end result was more choppy and low-keyed than Benny might have liked, but the skit nevertheless garnered a modicum of audience laughter. The TV program was the huge draw that CBS, the sponsor, and Benny had desired. Hooper's reports registered Benny's debut show at a rating of 41.5, with a 76.6 percent share of the American television audience (which now incorporated 107 stations in 63 cities with 3.9 million TV sets in use on the East Coast and Midwest, with a total of 8.7 million sets across the nation).[46]

Benny might have hoped to see the same laudatory reviews in the TV columns for his initial foray into the new medium that his radio show regularly earned, but he was disappointed. The majority of comments ranged from neutral to negative, illustrating how divided critics were over what performance and narrative qualities comedy television programs should emphasize. Should there be any holdover from radio, or did a new medium demand different characters, new forms of humor, and innovative ways of performing it? The *Chicago Herald American*'s reviewer loyally appreciated Benny's attempts to blend familiar aural elements with attempts at visual humor. Janet Kern termed it a "history making performance. For the first time I can recall, a radio comedian converted to TV without slipping out of character ... His program was the radio show come to life. That meant one of the best TV comedies ever."[47] Several reviewers measured Benny's program with faint praise against the perceived "errors" other comedians had committed on TV. The *San Francisco Examiner* critic asserted that Benny had succeeded in comparison to other TV comics because "he eliminated the pathetic pie in the face antics of TV's first king, Milton Berle. He had no truck with the harum scarum gyrations of the big variety shows."[48]

More ambivalent critics had hoped for a much more visually focused program and even a different comic persona. The *New York Times*'s Jack Gould expressed disappointment with the radio-flavored quality of Benny's program:

> [T]hough Jack's premiere had a number of diverting moments and unquestionably enjoyed novelty interest, the major part of the presentation was largely

a revival of one of Jack's favorite radio formats—the program devoted to telling how the program is going to be done... Jack is not going to achieve his end if he does not think much more in visual terms than he did on Saturday and develop a second joke that has nothing to do with penny pinching.[49]

Others took the opportunity to heap on negative comments about his lack of fast-paced visual comedy. "Jack Benny Premiere on Television Fizzle," declared Hartford Connecticut's *Sunday Herald* reviewer. "Jack Benny flunked his television debut last night," wrote the reviewer, who then called Benny "an ex-radio star stage-frozen by the new medium."[50] "Benny's long-awaited video bow suffered to some extent the same shortcomings which have marked the TV debuts of other long-established showbiz toppers, notably Fred Allen and Eddie Cantor," carped *Billboard*'s reviewer, criticizing Benny's and others' "reluctance to depart in any substantial measure from the pattern on their many and consistent triumphs in all other phases of entertainment, particularly radio."[51] Only the *New York Herald Tribune*'s John Crosby, while joining the chorus of those disappointed that the TV program was not an entirely new creation, picked up on a quiet new visual addition to Benny's comic repertoire that the others, in their demands for slapstick, had overlooked. "The Benny radio show was always noted for the skillful use of sound effects—footsteps, nickels clinking in Benny's palm, doors slamming. On television these have been replaced by sight gags—Mr. Benny employing a long, long look where he once used long, long pauses."[52]

Benny responded defensively to these reviewers' complaints, grumbling to a *Variety* reporter, "You can't win with these people, anyhow."[53] Radio performer and critic Goodman Ace defended the star against the journalists in his *Saturday Review of Literature* column. Ace rolled his eyes at the critics who insisted that Benny should create an entirely new character for the new medium and start throwing cream pies, chiding them for their new mantra "'it needs action—if there is no action, it's not television; its radio.'"[54]

TRY AND TRY AGAIN?

The negative reviews and his frustration with how best to create a television program rankled Benny throughout the rest of the year. At the last minute he canceled a December 1950 TV appearance because he and the sponsor could not agree on the length of the next episode. Benny had asked for forty-five minutes to allow the physical humor sufficient time to develop, but American

Tobacco demanded insertion of additional commercials. Finally, Benny agreed to squeeze his TV show into the half-hour block. Still uncertain of the best format to suit these East Coast audiences and critics, in his second TV program Benny tried to create a combination of nightclub and burlesque performance, incorporating sexually suggestive skits. It resembled a Las Vegas routine. Jack's monologue riffed on his cheap hotel room in New York (which came off as a tired reprise of jokes he'd been making for years on the radio). Guest star Frank Sinatra, along with crooning several songs, was given numerous opportunities to brag about his sexual prowess with women. He even demonstrated this expertise to Benny in an encounter with buxom television actress Faye Emerson, in the rehashing of a stage routine Benny had been doing for years, in which Jack's attempt to engage the woman in a love scene plays much more successfully when she repeats it with the handsome singer. The entire episode seemed desperate for bawdy adult laughter.[55]

Jack Benny had been performing this more risqué type of vaudeville skit for years during personal appearance tours, using showgirl Marilyn Maxwell and Phil Harris to show up Benny's lack of seductive skills. On the radio, Benny and his writers had also deployed the gag of Benny being bested by a more virile lover when he had guest stars Humphrey Bogart and Lauren Bacall on the radio show.[56] Nevertheless, none of those prior routines had carried the intimate visual impact of the close-ups of Sinatra and Faye's liplock, broadcast into conservative families' living rooms.

Outraged viewers protested to local newspaper critics that this Benny show had crossed the line. The kissing scene did not fit their expectations of what kind of entertainment Jack Benny would offer, and the skit's vulgar sensuality affronted them.[57] The *Chicago Tribune*'s reviewer judged, "That L-O-N-G TV kiss outlasted its welcome; viewers brand two minute buss bad taste.... [T]he Sinatra-Emerson encounter the longest ever seen on television, was clocked by the CBS timekeeper at two minutes ten seconds, far in excess of the maximum bussing permitted in the movies."[58]

A distraught Kentucky viewer wrote, "If friends of mine had acted that way in my living room, I would have handed them their hats and coats and told them to leave. I have thus given coat and hat to Jack Benny, Frank Sinatra and Faye Emerson. They are no longer welcome in my living room."[59] A Chicagoan griped, "The Jack Benny show was rotten and the Frank Sinatra-Faye Emerson kiss was so shocking we just sat here as though someone had hit us on the head ... What good does it do us to teach our children to conduct themselves properly and then to see such rot?"[60] Nevertheless, these complaints also drew retorts from more liberal viewers—"We burst into gales of laughter at our house during the Sinatra-Emerson kiss on the Benny show—and we're not exactly morons. You'll always find some biddies who will claim that this undermines the morals of our youth. I hope they have more programs like that one," wrote another, more amused Chicago viewer.[61]

With his third TV show, broadcast April 1, 1951, an anxious Jack Benny retreated from his use of vaudeville themes and returned to the familiarity of situation comedy, which at least had pleased the audiences and critics who had enjoyed his radio program. Although some reviewers continued to complain that his programs did not incorporate sufficient televisual elements, a growing number of critics began to reassess the show and acknowledged that the Benny program was becoming a proper television comedy. Increasingly, they focused on the addition of his long, injured stare out at the audience as a remarkably effective visual facet of Benny's comic timing.

Benny's third attempt at television was a remake of the skit (first performed on radio in 1941) in which Jack barged his way into an audition for a melodramatic play featuring prominent film actors Claudette Colbert and Basil Rathbone. This episode was framed entirely as a narrative situation; there was no onstage monologue, no break for a performer's songs. It was a surefire, time-tested bit of comedy (although the episode used none of Benny's regular radio cast), in which the Jack Benny character was at his most vainglorious and obnoxious. He was deservedly humiliated by everyone, from the theatrical director to the disgusted Hollywood stars to a disdainful butler. Benny had garnered positive reviews every time he used the routine (he had performed it at least half a dozen times over the years, most recently in a reprise with Colbert and Vincent Price on his own radio program on February 6, 1949). Benny's ability to persuade Colbert and Rathbone to repeat their roles, making rare New York TV appearances, certainly helped guarantee that this episode would go over well with audiences and critics. Nevertheless, some critics remained as negative as before.

Luckily for Benny and his production staff, the coaxial cable had finally traversed the Rocky Mountains to make coast-to-coast live broadcasts of prime-time network television possible, and Benny was able to transmit his first program of fall 1951, live from CBS studios in Los Angeles. For Benny it meant no more planes or train trips to New York to make television appearances and much more control over the program's production. This led to more confidence for the frustrated Benny, who explained to a Boston reporter that what was beginning to work for him on television was a melding of his vaudeville techniques of connecting to the audience with his radio characterization and situations, but with attention to the limitations of television:

> A lot of the things I'm doing on television are like what I used to on the stage—the frustration bits, the embarrassing situations, the master of ceremonies monologues. On TV I can look directly at the audience and get intimate with them. I can put over the expressions of frustration and embarrassment. Visual expression, without overdoing it, is a most important aspect of television comedy. In radio you have to make up for the lack of visual help. You go overboard and even get wild. When addressing a TV audience, I don't have to get that wild.[62]

By fall 1952, many of the early TV comic stars, from Milton Berle and Eddie Cantor to Dean Martin and Jerry Lewis, were complaining of overwork and exhaustion; their health problems and ratings declines spelled an end to their programs.[63] Jack Benny's work routines were not quite as frantic—his radio programs were still aired weekly, but his sponsor and network allowed him to prerecord a number of episodes. He appeared on TV only five or six times per season. As Benny persevered, and as the other more raucous live comedy programs were replaced by more sedate suburban-based sitcoms, television critics began modifying their evaluation criteria for what made successful televisual comedy; they became more appreciative of Benny's quieter TV efforts. *Variety* now declared, "His [video] show is at its strongest when the comic assumes that look that denotes exasperation and a myriad of other emotions. The longer he holds onto that pose, the funnier the show becomes."[64] *Billboard* praised, "[There is] visible evidence that Benny now has the medium well in hand, and that he has discovered the technique of transferring to the visual all the uproarious characteristics of his radio series. Benny, the master of the long take and the significant sound, has become, for TV, the king of the meaningful stare."[65] Benny's December 30, 1952, TV episode in which Jimmy Stewart guest-starred now garnered praise both for Benny's injured looks directed out at the audience and for the actors' physical hijinks:

> High spots of the evening were Miss [Sara] Berner's snuggling up to an embarrassed Stewart on the dance floor and loudly crooning the lyrics of "you belong to me" in a nasal Brooklynese and Benny's doing a sort of shmo shuffle around the room with the equally embarrassed Mrs. [Gloria] Stewart. The latter scene was the funniest spot on the show with Benny whirling the long-suffering Gloria into a spin away from him and seizing a passing water by

mistake. The comedian hardly moved a muscle for several seconds, but his frozen agony and humiliation as he realized his faux pas created the perfect illustration of a man desperately wishing he could sink through the floor. Jack Benny does more with a shamed silence or artful pause than any comedian in the business.[66]

Benny was also able to employ his long, questioning looks out at the audience to enhance his direction of the other actors' performances during live TV broadcasts. Live television production was significantly more complicated than radio practices, with directors having to manage not only cast members' performances but also camera placement and movement, lighting, and sound. Benny was more dependent in TV on the assistance of a producer/director (Ralph Levy) to put the entire program together, especially if Benny was in the middle of the scene performing. But Benny was just as concerned as previously about maintaining the deft, split-second comic timing of the acting ensemble for which his shows were famous. His cast members were not gathered around a microphone across the stage within his line of sight, but were scattered more widely across the set. With the cameras rolling, Benny could not gesticulate or nod to help pace them, and he did not want to clutter up the soundtrack with superfluous "hmmmms" and "wells" that might be muffled by audience laughter. But he could insist that the actors pay attention to his stares out into studio auditorium and wait until he had finished to begin their next line. Then every laugh could be milked out of each line of the script.

To sponsors and critics, loud, frequent audience laughter remained a key indicator of the success of a TV show, the same way it had been sponsors' means of judging how effectively a radio comedy program had gone over. Now Benny could use the physical and visual aspects of his injured stare to create extra laughs that did not exist in the scripted dialogue. A critic on studio set noted, "Very often Benny can take a line that's worthy of no more than a snicker and, by looking into the audience for just the proper length of time, build that snicker into an important laugh."[67]

Increasingly, instead of lambasting Benny, critics began to praise the comic's TV prowess. "More and more, Benny is using added sight gags and what you see is becoming as important as what you hear. He probably is the first of the standard comedians to breakaway almost completely from laughs dependent upon words."[68] Benny would never give up his focus on the radio-inflected banter and repartee of humorous characters bouncing off one another, but this was not an insignificant compliment to pay. Ultimately, Jack Benny was one of the most successful of the older radio/vaudeville

FIGURE 25. In the 1950s, the characters of Jack and Rochester became more closely entwined as an interracial "Odd Couple" in both Benny's radio and television programs, as more of the situation comedy involved their adventures together. This joke magazine reflects the inseparable nature of their bond, and Rochester's fearless criticism of the Boss's failings. *1000 Jokes*, March 1956. Author's collection.

comics to make the transition to television and to make good use of its visual opportunities.

THE END OF AN ERA: BENNY LEAVES RADIO

In 1952, Jack Benny finally began garnering praise for his eight-episodes-a-year television series, but he still faced the issue of radio—how long should he remain on a fading medium that was losing its mass audience? Listener numbers continued to decline across the nation, to less than half of what they had been in 1948. Nevertheless, that still represented ten million people, and sponsor American Tobacco considered these remaining listeners prime targets for their advertising message.[69] Cigarette sales were tremendously dependent on the constant boost of advertising to keep the product's name fresh in buyers' minds. American Tobacco was unlikely to attract large numbers of new and impressionable young smokers to Benny's show, which is why Luckies also sponsored the popular radio and TV music program *Your Hit Parade*. Sales of unfiltered cigarettes were also declining as younger consumers switched to the new brands. Nevertheless, the sponsor needed Benny's radio listeners to continue on as loyal Luckies smokers.[70] So American Tobacco executives pleaded throughout the first half of the decade to keep its radio as well as TV salesman on the job. The CBS radio network, too, depended on Benny's continued popularity to hold together the remnants of its primetime radio audiences. The trade papers in these years regularly featured headlines such as "Lucky Strike, CBS Beseech Benny to Continue in Radio."[71]

However, making it significantly more difficult to keep producing the radio show at his desired level of quality, in April 1952, American Tobacco slashed Benny's radio production budget for the upcoming year by 30 percent.[72] Benny regretfully had to let his longtime bandleader Phil Harris go, and replaced him with the less expensive but pleasantly bland Bob Crosby (Bing's younger brother). Benny cut back on the writers' input too, as increasingly, radio episodes were revamped from old scripts; more episodes were prerecorded, and fewer guest stars appeared on the show. Nevertheless, Benny and his radio crew still created some fine programs in these years of dwindling audiences. "As long as Jack Benny's re-entrenched in the Sunday at 7:00pm slot, radio's still riding the big time kilocycles," said *Variety* of Benny's opening program of the fall 1952 season. "For 30 minutes there wasn't the slightest evidence or suggestion that the TV ascendancy had rubbed off some of the glamor—and audience pull."[73] In late 1953, Benny reassured a *Los Angeles Times* reporter that he was still an outspoken advocate of radio:

> Two years ago I started to get a little worried about radio because everyone around the country only spoke to me about my TV show.... But last year the swing was back to radio talk again and I realize it was just the excitement and newness of television that made it the number one topic of conversation. After 22 years in radio, I still think it's one of the world's greatest mediums of entertainment.[74]

Despite Benny's insistence that he relied on the well-honed characters of his radio cast for the core of his TV humor, however, even after he was able to transfer TV program production back to California, Benny used his radio cast significantly less often on TV than might have been expected, even though his radio cast turned out to be excellent TV performers. With his extensive tutelage in the arts of vocalization and comic timing, Benny had developed them (Wilson, Harris, Day, Livingstone, Anderson, and Blanc) from being announcers, singers, band members, and special effects voice performers into true radio comedy stars. However, on Benny's 1950s TV shows, guest stars from the film world played a much larger role, while he relied heavily on his regular cast members for the weekly radio show. Don Wilson appeared on nearly every TV episode to do the commercials, but the Sportsmen Quartet appeared on TV only sporadically before 1954. Phil Harris was now absent from both the radio and TV programs. The narrative world of the popular Phil Harris/Alice Faye radio program continued to feature him as Jack's bandleader, cavorting with band members Frankie Remley and Charlie Bagby, and characters like Sheldon Leonard and Frank Nelson who also frequently appeared on Benny's radio program.

Mary Livingstone, who suffered from increasingly crippling mike fright, excused herself from radio broadcasts as much as possible, and was coaxed onto the television program only five times before fall 1955. She made semi-iregular appearances for the next two years, in episodes filmed at the studio, not in front of live audiences, and even then she insisted on brief cameo appearances. Benny's programs lost some of their deliciously snarky bite with Mary gone, because he did not replace her. Eddie Anderson's role as Rochester, however, expanded to fill the role of Benny's radio and TV partner. His lines were as smart and witty as ever, but Rochester was never allowed to skewer Jack's pretentions as sharply as Mary. As both the Benny radio and TV show developed more of a domestic situation comedy format, Rochester and Jack appeared together even more often. Anderson appeared on about half of the Benny TV programs through 1955, and then most of the subsequent shows after the radio series concluded. Even without their constant appearances on television, long-time Benny fans probably did not notice the absence of these familiar characters, as they had become permanent parts of Benny's narrative world. All they had to do was pop up occasionally, and fans would assume that they continued to be part of the story line. After all, many fans continued to think that Carmichael the polar bear (a fantasy character from 1939) still lurked in Benny's basement awaiting the visit of another gas man.

While in the late 1940s Benny's radio ratings had been in the range of 26–27 points, Benny's radio program in the 1953–1954 season program held a Neilsen rating of 8.2 (close to first place) and was number one on the air in the 1954–1955 season, with a rating of just 5.8 points.[75] The evening radio audience had shrunk so much that, from Benny's point of view, it was difficult to justify continuing on in the medium. Jack Hellman noted in early 1954 that, despite the pleading of CBS radio top brass, Benny

> seems to be losing his enthusiasm for radio. He knows he's not playing to nearly as many millions as in past years and that's an actors' normal reaction a full house always gets a better performance than half a house. Benny, however, as in the past, will go along with his sponsor's wishes. . . . TV is his first love now and he would rather give it all his time.[76]

Although *Variety* reported in March 1955 that Benny would continue to create a few new radio shows and rerun older episodes in the coming year, by the summer, Benny and American Tobacco decided to finally pull the plug on any newly produced radio broadcasts.[77]

By the mid-1950s, as televised humor moved past the pratfall and pie throwing of Milton Berle's frenetic comedy-variety and settled into more predictable and calmer formulas of suburban situation comedy, it increasingly returned emphasis to radio-like dialogue segments while visualizing domestic spaces. In his own TV efforts, Jack Benny still faced the challenge of balancing verbal comedy with visual comedy, struggling to please vexatious critics and audiences and creating comic performances that met his own standards for quality. That Benny succeeded in garnering high ratings through his third decade of broadcasting is a testament to both his skills and the great affection that the American public had for him. Although he broadcast on television only sporadically in the early 1950s and never more than twice a month over the rest of the decade (which makes his ratings somewhat difficult to generalize and compare with weekly programs), Benny's TV ratings were in the top ten through the latter half of the decade. Even after Lucky Strike relinquished its sponsorship of his television program in 1959, for four more years of the early 1960s Benny's TV show garnered respectable ratings.

Numerous traces of Benny's long radio career carried over into the television programs he created through 1964. Benny and his writers mined the years of successful radio skits, comic situations, characters, and places that were beloved by fans. Many skits and situations on Benny's TV programs were reworkings, adaptations, and embellishments of favorite radio routines. In 1955, critic Goodman Ace argued that reviewers should give verbal and aural elements of TV programs more credit for their aesthetic contributions instead of dismissing well-crafted dialogue as merely "talk-talk-talk" that lacked necessary action and movement onscreen. "I think the time has come to face the fact that television is radio with the added dimension of a little sight," Ace maintained.

> A recent TV show by the estimable Jack Benny could have been—and because I haven't been listening to radio much, for all I know it was—one of his delightful radio programs. It was the show where he was casting characters for a movie of the story of his life. Practically all of it took place in an office set and all we heard was some of that horrible stuff called "dialogue." It could all have been transplanted to radio, even to the big sight laugh where he was kissed by a luscious blonde.... The time has come for us to stop watching television and start listening to it.[78]

The foundation of Jack Benny's televised humor still relied on witty dialogue and verbal humor, from bad puns to bantering repartee, word pictures that created wild exaggerations, and elaborate unseen fantasies. However, Benny and his writers did continue to endeavor to integrate visual elements and sight gags into his television programs.

Sometimes Benny and his writers tried a little too hard to overcompensate for their reputation of creating radio humor. They would create elaborate visual physical jokes with complicated props, and in a program that moved so relatively slowly, their TV efforts could not reach the comic heights of what imagined fantasy had provided for radio listeners. The elaborately constructed re-creations of Jack's Maxwell, vault, vending machines, or booby traps set up in his bedroom to thwart burglars disappointed some critics, who felt that these gags should again be produced by unseen sound effects and left to viewers' imaginations. A San Diego television critic in 1956 recalled that reviewers and Benny himself in the late 1940s had so doubted that his most fantastical aural humor could be translated to the visual medium:

> Our concept of Benny's vault ... is still the concept that radio gave us. On this [TV] show, when the two workmen come to Benny's house to repair the vault, the jokes begin at once—and our imagination is put to the test immediately. Benny, first of all, must instruct the workmen on how to find their way down to the subterranean vault. "Turn right," Benny commands, "when you get to the barbed wire." (Barbed wire? The sight of barbed wire would be

gruesome. The sound of it is irresistibly funny.) Now the men are descending and Benny is wearing binoculars. "They're halfway down," Benny announces, peering. "When you get to the moat," he shouts, "watch for the draw bridge. And be careful of the alligator!" Later the workmen emerge from the vault—and they're actually wrestling with an alligator. This is the punch line of the sequence and for Benny, I'm afraid, a painful one because it is entirely too obvious for a comic of his high standards. The joke was much better when it remained a radio joke put to TV—a joke for the imagination rather than for the eye.[79]

Nevertheless, even the most aurally focused comedian could create one of the most memorable visual comedy acts of the decade. In March 1959, Benny appeared in a twice-per-season variety program, *The Jack Benny Hour*. In addition to Bob Hope and Mitzi Gaynor, Benny's guest performers were the Marquis Chimps. Jack appeared in a segment on stage joining the three Marquis Chimps, an animal act that had performed on the Ed Sullivan program. The animals wore human clothes, rode bicycles, and performed human-like tricks. In a skit that director Bud Yorkin luckily caught on film during rehearsal, a slow-moving Jack "in ribtickling deadpan style" engaged in a hilarious "chimprovized" skit with the monkeys on an empty stage. The chimps, who alternately imitated Benny, interacted with him, and mocked him, walked out on him when he began to play "Love in Bloom" on his violin. Jack (channeling Charlie Chaplin or Buster Keaton) seemed to naturally enter the monkeys' realm, as he sat in a child's chair on stage next to the monkeys, and became their bemused straight man, sharing his reactions silently with the audience. "The act hit a high mark in video comedy," claimed delighted reviewers, who ten years later were still fondly recalling the skit as one of the most memorable visual moments in TV history.[80]

Conclusion

Looking back over his twenty-three-year career in radio broadcasting, Jack Benny had so much of which to be proud. He had become one of the most familiar voices on the radio, America's first truly mass medium of communication, speaking weekly to thirty million or more listeners. In the preceding chapters, we have explored how brilliantly Benny moved between separate entertainment forms, combining aspects of vaudeville and film, radio and live performance. Benny created new styles of entertainment as he honed his career, from developing the master of ceremonies role—the modern, urban, polished, but self-deprecating figure who informally drew audiences and disparate acts together into a whole—to the lead character in a situation comedy—that new episodic form demanded by the needs of radio broadcasting's massive time demands and broad reach. Benny and his writer Harry Conn developed the iconic character of "Jack," the "Fall Guy," vain braggart, frustrated employer, disrespected media celebrity, the butt of every joke and insult slung by his workers.

Benny and his writers over the years not only created his own famous character, but in developing the sitcom they also honed a cast of delightful characters who melded crazy fictional characteristics with excellent performing skills of talented players—Mary Livingstone, and Eddie Anderson's Rochester Van Jones in particular. The Benny show humor frequently used these main characters to parody and impertinently tweak social norms of midcentury American society—that women should be quiet and obedient; that middle-class white men should be strong, virile leaders; that African Americans should never critique their employers. Benny and his production group developed a particularly effective form of aural humor, where the laughs came not from old jokes refreshed with new surroundings, but the

FIGURE 26. The biggest star in radio, when radio was the most prominent mass medium in the United States. *Radio Stars*, February, 1938. Author's collection.

humor of character, of sounds like the Maxwell, of silences such as Jack's exasperated humiliation, of surprises like Mary's sudden retorts. The Benny group managed even to make the often-dreaded commercial language sound hilarious. American audiences loyally listened to him, Sunday nights at 7 P.M., whether they were eating dinner, sitting around their sets, or driving in their cars. The Benny program was as familiar as family, even as its humor slyly questioned ideas about how relationships, power, and identity should work in modern society. Jack Benny was, and remained, an American institution.

He may have concluded his radio career in May 1955, but, far from retiring, sixty-one-year-old Jack Benny remained as active a performer as ever—appearing regularly on television, in live stand-up comedy shows, and in charity symphonic musical performances. The narrative and comic ideas of Benny's radio show remained at the core of his character and star persona, seamlessly woven into his humorous monologues and long lasting in the public memory.

Benny created and starred in his own half hour television program for fifteen years, from the broad variety programs of the first "golden age" of live broadcasting in the early 1950s, through the predominance of produced-on-tape sitcoms in the networks' weekly schedules in the mid-1960s. Benny's TV show often featured sketches directly adapted from the old radio show, and incorporated long-running radio characters Don Wilson, Eddie Anderson/Rochester, the Sportsmen Quartet, and Mel Blanc in his many guises, as well as the wheezing Maxwell and the underground vault. As they had in radio, the characters did not need to appear every week to remain a vital part of the Benny narrative—they were so well established in the audiences' minds that they could pop up every once in a while, so the occasional appearance of Frank Nelson's obnoxious sales clerk, Mary Livingstone, Dennis Day, the Beverly Hills Beavers scouting troupe, or put-upon Hollywood celebrities like Jimmy Stewart did not require elaborate introductions. Benny and his writers still took care, as they had always done, to keep changing up the mixture, adding new skits, occasional new characters (like Harlow, Don Wilson's son, the apprentice announcer), and special guests, to keep the show fresh and not completely tied to a situation comedy format.

Between 1954 and 1958, Jack Benny also regularly appeared on the CBS monthly *Shower of Stars* variety program, serving as emcee or doing a one-off comic or dramatic skit that amplified the narrative world of his regular show, or that reinforced Benny's larger star persona (as his film roles had done in the 1930s and 1940s). In a February 13, 1958, episode of *Shower of Stars*, "Jack Benny Celebrates His 40th Birthday," the show reunited notable performers from the comic's radio days, including early announcers Paul Douglas and George Hicks from 1932; orchestra leaders George Olsen, Don Bestor, Ted Weems, and Johnny Green from 1933; and even pinch-hitting tenor Larry Stevens from 1944. That Benny assumed members of the TV audience fondly remembered the unseen cast-mates from more than twenty-five years before is a testament to the long-lasting relationship he had with his fans. Benny and his radio cast also voiced an adorable Warner Bros. Looney Tunes cartoon produced for exhibition in movie theaters, which was based on his radio show, "The Mouse that Jack Built" (1959). As Mel Blanc was the most prolific and popular vocal artist in the Warner Bros. studio animation department, the short made for a perfect combination of nostalgic fun and transmedia adaptation of Benny's narrative world.

While incorporating references to his old radio world into many of his projects, Jack Benny's later career also continued to touch on the developments Benny had brought to American entertainment. Benny appeared in televised situation comedies, the episodic character-focused comic form that Benny's radio program had done so much to develop, back in 1932. Benny appeared occasionally, usually as "himself" and not a completely fictional character, in Danny Thomas's *Make Room for Daddy*, and Lucille Ball's *The Lucy Show*. Lucy had wanted to have Jack guest star on her program while creating *I Love Lucy* in the early 1950s, but at the time her recalcitrant sponsor, Philip Morris cigarettes, forbid a performer associated with another tobacco brand to appear on its program.[1]

In the 1950s and 1960s, Jack Benny became a popular attraction at the Las Vegas and Lake Tahoe casino resorts. He developed solo stand-up comedy routines, expanding the work he had done back in vaudeville, on the road in USO tours during World War II, and in the earliest of his TV shows. Adult-focused, sophisticated, nightclub stand-up performers really came into their own in the 1960s,[2] and Benny added some frank language to his basic Fall Guy routine, and did well in tours of British venues and a one-man show at the Ziegfeld Theater on Broadway in 1963. Benny took this solo routine as well to television, from guest shots on the Ed Sullivan show to cameo appearances on the hip programs aimed at younger primetime viewers such as *The Smothers Brothers Comedy Hour* and *Laugh In*, and in the Dean Martin celebrity roasts in the early 1970s.

Jack Benny made guest appearances on late night talk shows, a new television program form that had its roots in Benny's performance style. In fact, legendary talk show host Johnny Carson was a fervent Jack Benny fan and considered Benny a role model and mentor. As an undergraduate student at the University of Nebraska in the late 1940s, Carson was greatly influenced by the work of top radio comics, particularly Benny and Fred Allen. He wrote a smart and witty senior thesis, "How to Write Comedy for Radio," and submitted it in recorded form, which can be accessed online through the University of Nebraska's website.[3] Since Benny's vaudeville work in the 1920s as an emcee had an informal ease that connected him to the audience, him to the acts, and the self-contained acts to the audience, his performances were a prefiguring of talk shows he appeared on, such as Carson's and Dick Cavett's.

In this era, Benny also rediscovered his passion for the violin. He practiced at home four hours a day, his daughter Joan recalled.[4] He donated a tremendous amount of time and energy to give charity concerts to raise funds for struggling symphony orchestras around the United States in the 1960s and 1970s. Benny would state wistfully that he knew audiences flocked to the concerts to hear Jack massacre sonatas in comic fashion, but he longed to play as a serious musician.

Benny remained a potent symbol for promoting consumer goods, and in the 1960s he was active in commercial product advertising, pitching Texaco gasoline, insurance, television sets, and other products. Not only did Jack Benny always carry with him listener memories of the old radio show, but also audiences persistently associated him with Jell-O and Lucky Strikes. Advertising executives marveled at the longevity of that link and wished they could manufacture that alchemy of long-lasting positive identification. One remarked in 1962 that "Still, no performer today ... is as associated with a product. Maybe that is good, maybe it's a very rare combination to make something sugary or something deadly, so much fun."[5]

The rapid series of wrenching cultural changes in the 1960s made all the old established comedians seem behind the times, and out of touch with the hip culture of the younger generation. Benny fared better than some of the more purely nostalgic entertainers like Eddie Cantor and Bing Crosby, who seemed so wedded to their old musical choices. Benny continued to play "himself," the Jack character who was vain about his age, frustrated by the impertinence all around him. He didn't require the radio cast's presence and insults to enact who he was, and in doing solo bits, in my opinion, he was often funnier than on his TV show. It helped that Benny did not tell standard jokes as did Henny Youngman or Milton Berle, and that he kept his humor to cultural foibles as experienced through his own persona—if he had done political jokes like Bob Hope, the younger generation would have rejected him. Benny's best friend George Burns also aged well, reinventing himself as an ancient commentator. Despite his advancing age, Jack always managed to sound like he was in the present, instead of being merely an oldie-goldie act. Part of that genius is that Jack's cheap, Fall Guy character could continue to react to any new situation.

After his regular TV program was cancelled in 1965, Benny continued to front at least one Jack Benny special per year for NBC between 1966 and

FIGURE 27. Jack Benny attempted to build the market for fans to purchase recordings of his best radio comedy routines so that they could collect and savor examples of his humor when was not broadcasting live on air. *The Jack Benny Album,* 1947. Author's collection.

1974. In one of them, *Jack Benny's Bag* (NBC, November 16, 1968), he and Phyllis Diller performed a wicked parody of the hotel room seduction scene from the recent film *The Graduate,* the box office hit beloved of the younger generation. Benny in a black wig played young Benjamin Braddock being pursued by sex-hungry Mrs. Robinson (you have just got to watch this, hopefully it is on YouTube). Benny merges his classic character with a spot-on comment on the film, with a memorable sex-joke charm. (The accompanying renditions of the film's Simon and Garfunkel songs by young soul singer Lou Rawls and has-been Eddie Fisher adds to the bizarreness of the sketch.)

. . .

This is where I came in, as that twelve-year-old who wanted to learn more about Jack Benny's radio programs. Originally broadcast live, out into the ether, they had become orphaned entertainment, unsaved, ephemeral, and gone. How foolhardy of sponsors, radio networks, and performers, to consider all this material as useless as last week's newspaper. The fact that we have any historical broadcasts to listen to today is due to the efforts of hundreds of individual Jack Benny fans.

Jack Benny himself had attempted in 1947 to extend the ephemeral life of his live radio broadcasts by recording some of his best routines. Prominent radio performers had recorded a small collection of albums, the Top Ten series distributed by the Monitor label, which also included recordings of *Amos 'n' Andy*, Bergen and McCarthy, Burns and Allen, Cantor, *Duffy's Tavern*, and Fibber McGee. The series was, unfortunately, a commercial failure for the artists. Perhaps the series was not marketed well, as the records weren't released with the full promotional heft of CBS's Columbia records behind them. Perhaps radio audiences had not yet been educated to desire to collect and savor a library of comedy recordings. The market for comedy recordings did begin to flower in the United States in the late 1950s and early 1960s. Perhaps Benny was too far ahead of his time.

While in retrospect it seems foolish and wasteful for radio networks and sponsors not to have produced recordings of radio entertainment broadcasts, as broadcasting historian Eleanor Patterson notes, many factors militated against it. The ethos of network radio was liveness, and they discouraged the playing of records on the radio (musicians' unions supported these measures too, to keep workers employed). The quality of audio recording technology was very mediocre, prior to the development of magnetic tape recording processes in the post–World War II years. The material was considered topical and not worth archiving, and also tainted with its thorough commercialism. Network television continued these practices through the mid-1950s, as Derek Kompere documents.[6] Nevertheless, plenty of radio transcription disks were produced for sponsors and performers to keep records of their programs, and syndicated programs like "The Lone Ranger" were distributed to stations across the nation in recorded form.[7] Transcription disks, made of 16-inch thin platters of aluminum (glass during the war) reproduced broadcasts well, but were fragile to store, and could be replayed only a limited number of times. Network demands for liveness would only begin to change with the success of TV programs like *I Love Lucy* being produced on film and becoming available to fill the many extra hours of airtime as reruns, as Kompare describes.

In the 1960s and 1970s, fans of what was beginning to be called "Old Time Radio" (OTR) found ways to locate transcription disks, unearthing them from garbage dumpsters, and rescuing them from dusty old warehouses. They made sound tape recordings of the disks, many of which were very

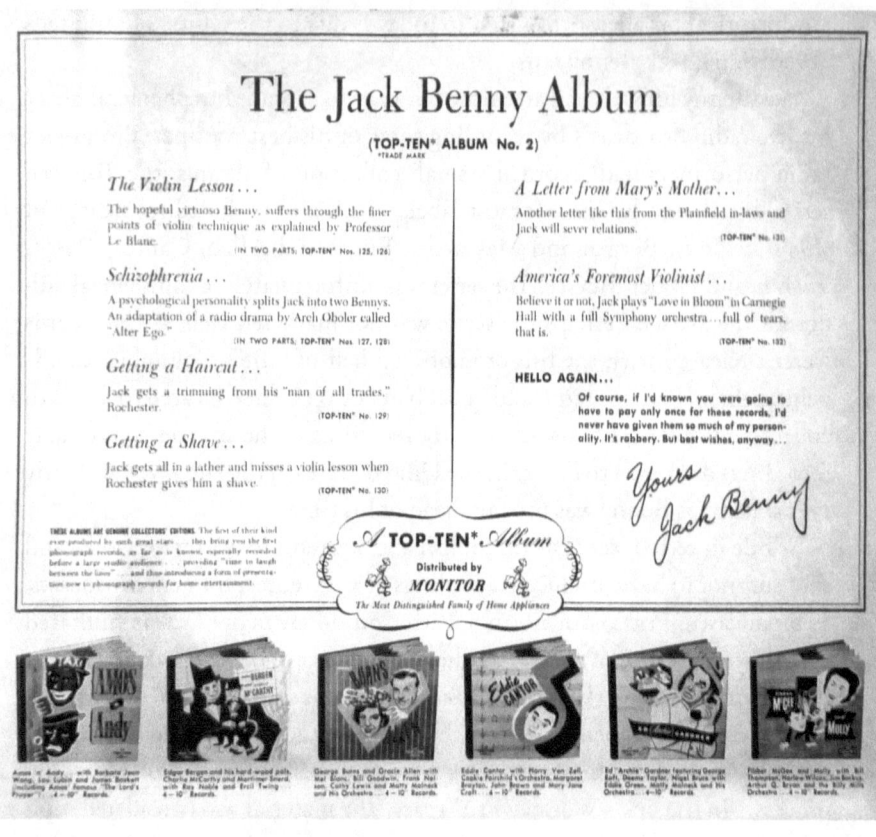

FIGURE 28. The "Top Ten" series of record album releases were early, unsuccessful attempts to provide consumers with permanent copies of ephemeral live broadcasts. In the 1950s, 1960s and 1970s, dedicated fans of "Old Time Radio" would collect, tape, organize and share the large collection of Jack Benny radio show broadcast recordings that we have available today. *The Jack Benny Album*, 1947. Author's collection.

scratched, damaged, and incomplete. Other broadcasts were culled from the recordings made by the Armed Forces Radio Service that had been sent to military bases overseas (these shows usually had had the commercials removed, further chopping up the original programs). OTR fans started to trade tapes with other fans, and began to build collections. Jack Benny had stored his old transcription disks in a hot Los Angeles storage unit, and those that he donated to UCLA when he gave them his collection of business papers, in the 1960s, were in bad shape, many so disintegrated that they were unplayable. Several entrepreneurial third party organizations commercially repackaged old radio programs for nostalgic enjoyment and sold sets of records and tapes.[8] Through fifty years of dedicated collecting, OTR devotees have amassed about 750 full or partial recordings of Benny's radio episodes. With digitized recordings, today we listeners can gain an appreciation for how past audiences, partaking of the Benny show in thirty-minute episodes aired weekly over many years, were rewarded with a long familiarity with the recurring characters, situations, repeated gags, and inside jokes that Benny and his writers wove into their episodes and could reference from years past. The website that I have created to accompany this book (www.jackbennyradio.com) also features material that audiences have not been able to hear since they were first broadcast in 1932 to 1936—excerpts from the scripts of Jack Benny's live programs for which no recordings survive. There are more than 250 episodes, and hopefully some contemporarily recorded re-creations of some of the best skits, will help bring new audiences, and critical appreciation, for the superb comedic work Benny and Harry Conn created in the first four years of the program.

A number of comedians from the 1950s onward have claimed Benny had a formative influence on them, from Carol Burnett and Bob Newhart to David Letterman, Phil Hartman, Kelsey Grammer, Harry Shearer (who played a Beverly Hills Beaver, back in the day), Albert Brooks, and Kevin Spacey. Hopefully Benny's legacy will continue, and the continued circulation of his radio programs as classics of American humor might be the way to do it. Ultimately, Jack Benny's accomplishments in radio and lasting legacy in American humor and cultural history are tremendous and long lasting, and hopefully will impact future generations.

NOTES

INTRODUCTION

1. Jack Benny and Joan Benny, *Sunday Nights at Seven: The Jack Benny Story* (New York: Warner Books, 1990), 1.
2. Benny and Benny, *Sunday Nights at Seven*, 6–15.
3. Susan Douglas, *Listening In: Radio and the American Imagination* (Minneapolis: University of Minnesota Press, 2004), 101.
4. Michele Hilmes, "Is There a Field Called Sound Culture Studies? And Does It Matter?" *American Quarterly* 57, no. 1 (2005): 251.
5. Andrew Crisell, *Understanding Radio*, 2nd ed. (London: Routledge, 2006), 22; Jack Gould, "How Comic Is Comic Radio?" *New York Times*, November 21, 1948, SM22.
6. John K Hutchens, "The Secret of a Good Radio Voice," *New York Times*, December 6, 1942, SM 26.
7. Hutchens, "The Secret of a Good Radio Voice"; see also discussion in Hilmes, "Is There a Field."
8. Hutchens, "The Secret of a Good Radio Voice," 27. Female performers with high-pitched voices had difficulties in radio, sounding artificial, but Mary Livingstone's lower tones would register clearly.
9. Larry Wilde, *The Great Comedians Talk About Comedy* (New York: Citadel, 1968), 39.
10. Joseph Julian quoted in Alan Havig, *Fred Allen's Radio Comedy* (Philadelphia: Temple University Press, 1992), 10; Joseph Julian, *This Was Radio: A Personal Memoir* (New York: Viking, 1975).
11. Erik Barnouw, *Handbook of Radio Writing: An Outline of Technique and Markets in Radio Writing in the United States* (Boston: Little, Brown, 1939), 57.
12. Art Hanley, *Radio Comedy: How to Write It* (New York: Humor Business [self-published by Hanley], 1948), Lesson 3, 15.
13. Hanley, *Radio Comedy*, 16.
14. Hanley, *Radio Comedy*, 24, 25.

15. Max Wylie, *Radio and Television Writing* (New York: Rinehart, 1939, 1950), 233.

16. Carroll Nye, "Air Comedian's Gags Metered for Laughs," *Los Angeles Times*, February 14, 1937, C10.

17. Milton Makaye, "Whiskers on the Wisecrack," *Saturday Evening Post*, August 17, 1935, 13, 50.

18. Tad Friend, "What's So Funny? Science Looks at Why Jokes Work," *New Yorker* 78, no. 34 (November 11, 2002), 78–93.

19. 'Benny the Man vs Benny the Radio Myth," c. 1945, in Benny scrapbook 1945, Benny Papers, American Heritage Center, University of Wyoming, Collection 8922, Box 116.

20. Hanley, *Radio Comedy*, 26–27.

21. Alan Dale terms it "verbal slapstick;" Dale, *Comedy Is a Man in Trouble: Slapstick in American Movies* (Minneapolis: University of Minnesota Press, 2007), 7.

22. Friend, "What's So Funny?"

23. Friend, "What's So Funny?" 80.

24. Friend, "What's So Funny?"

25. Hubbell Robinson and Ted Patrick, "Jack Benny," *Scribner's*, March 1938, 13.

26. John Morreale, "Philosophy of Humor," *Stanford Online Encyclopedia of Philosophy* http://plato.stanford.edu/entries/humor/ First published November 20, 2012.

27. Stephen Leacock, *Humor: Its Theory and Technique, with Examples and Samples* (New York: Dodd, Mead and Co. 1935).

28. Leacock, *Humor*, 15.

29. Leacock, *Humor*, 124–25.

30. Irving A. Fein, *Jack Benny: An Intimate Biography* (New York: G. P. Putnam's Sons, 1976); Milt Josefsberg, *The Jack Benny Show* (New York: Arlington House, 1977); Mary Livingstone Benny, Hilliard Marks, and Marcia Borie, *Jack Benny: A Biography* (New York: Doubleday, 1978); Benny and Benny, *Sunday Nights at Seven*; Arthur Frank Wertheim, *Radio Comedy* (New York: Oxford University Press, 1979); Havig, *Fred Allen's Radio Comedy*.

CHAPTER 1

1. Larry Wolters, "Olsen Recalls First Benny Show on Anniversary; Idea of Kidding Sponsor Was George's," *Chicago Tribune*, December 1, 1935, S6; "With Canada's Mounted," *Variety*, January 19, 1932, 58.

2. "Inside Stuff—Radio," *Variety*, June 7, 1932, 49; "Canadians Hear New Program by Canada Dry Ginger Ale," *Montreal Guardian*, May 5, 1932, 2.

3. *Canada Dry Program*, May 2, 1932; Advertisement, *Variety*, October 1, 1932, 16.

4. "Radio's Script Act Cycle," *Variety*, May 10, 1932, 55; Ben Bodec, "Radio in '32," *Variety*, January 3, 1933, 59.

5. Kathryn H. Fuller Seeley, "Dish Night at the Movies: Exhibitors and Female Audiences during the Great Depression," in *Looking Past the Screen: Case Studies in American Film History and Method*, edited by Jon Lewis and Eric Smoodin (Durham, NC: Duke University Press, 2007), 246–75; Alan Havig, *Fred Allen's Radio Comedy* (Philadelphia: Temple University Press, 19–21).

6. See Roland Marchand, *Advertising the American Dream: Making Way for Modernity 1920–1940* (Berkeley: University of California Press, 1985).

7. Larry Christopher, "Stars Shine Best When Polished," *Broadcasting and Television*, October 1956, 118–26.

8. Fuller Seeley, "Dish Night at the Movies."

9. Brett Mills, *Television Sitcom* (London: British Film Institute, 2005); Horace Newcomb, *Television: The Critical View* (Oxford: Oxford University Press, 2000).

10. "Annual Radio Poll," *New York World-Telegram* (February 1933), in Benny Scrapbook 1933, Jack Benny Papers, American Heritage Center, University of Wyoming) Collection 8922, Box 116; Lawrence E. Mintz, "Standup Comedy as Social and Cultural Mediation," *American Quarterly* 37, no. 1 (1985): 71–80.

11. Holly A. Pearse, "As Goyish as Lime Jell-O? Jack Benny and the American Construction of Jewishness," *Jewish Cultural Studies* 2008: 272–90.

12. Robert W. Snyder, *The Voice of the City: Vaudeville and Popular Culture in New York* (New York: Oxford University Press, 1989).

13. Robert J. Landry, "For Benny It Was Big Time or Nothing; He Wasn't for Coalminers," *Variety*, April 30, 1940, 24, 45.

14. "Majestic, Chicago," *Billboard*, September 27, 1920, 9; "Keith's, Cincinnati," *Billboard*, October 1, 1921, 11; "Orpheum, St. Louis," *Billboard*, October 31, 1925, 15.

15. "Palace, Chicago," *Billboard*, November 15, 1924, 14.

16. "Palace, New York," *Billboard*, April 18, 1925, 14. Another review specifically noted that that he used no Yiddish in his act. "Palace, New York," *Variety*, September 21, 1927, 26.

17. Abel Green, "The Big Band Cavalcade: A Study in Changing Sounds and Economics," *Variety*, January 3, 1968, 151.

18. Maurice Zolotow, "The Fiddler from Waukegan," *Cosmopolitan*, October 1947, 49–51, 137–38, 141–46; 142.

19. "Palace, New York," *Variety*, April 7, 1926, 26.

20. "Review of Vitaphone No 2997," *Variety*, August 29, 1928, 15.

21. "Frank Fay," *Los Angeles Times*, September 27, 1961, 1.

22. Frank Cullen, Florence Hackman, and Donald McNeilly, *Vaudeville Old and New: An Encyclopedia of Variety Performances in America*, vol. 1 (New York: Psychology Press, 2004), 370–71.

23. Robert Landry, "Frank Fay, One of Real Vaude Greats, Dies at 63," *Variety*, September 27, 1961, 2.

24. Maurice Zolotow, "Frank Fay: Mystical Ex-vaudevillian Teams with Invisible Rabbit to Make a Big Theatrical Comeback," *Life*, January 8, 1945, 55, 58, 60, 63; 58.

25. Landry, "Frank Fay," 2, 78; Cullen, Hackman, and McNeilly, *Vaudeville Old and New*, 369; S. D. Trav, *No Applause, Just Throw Money, Or, The Book That Made*

Vaudeville Famous: A High-Class, Refined Entertainment (New York: Macmillan, 2005), 184.

26. Cullen, Hackman, and McNeilly, *Vaudeville Old and New*, 21; P 21; Anthony Slide, *Encyclopedia of Vaudeville* (Oxford: University of Mississippi Press, 2012), 169.

27. Zolotow, "Fiddler from Waukegan," 142.

28. "Palace, New York," *Variety*, May 2, 1931, 26.

29. "Palace, New York," *Variety*, January 8, 1930, 103.

30. "New Palace, Chicago," *Variety*, December 7, 1929, 18.

31. "Palace, New York," *Variety*, November 24, 1928, 17.

32. *Variety*, January 1, 1930; "Hollywood Chatter," *Variety*, September 18, 1929, 4.

33. "Capitol Theater," *Billboard*, September, 1932, 11; "Film House Reviews," *Variety*, February 11, 1931, 52.

34. *Canada Dry Program*, May 2, 1932 script, Jack Benny Papers, Los Angeles, University of California at Los Angeles Special Collections, Collection 134, Radio Scripts Box 1, file 1.

35. *Canada Dry Program*, May 2, 1932 script, Benny Collection, UCLA.

36. "Were You Listening Last Night," *Pittsburgh Press*, May 10, 1932, 11.

37. *Canada Dry Program*, May 11, 1932, script, Benny Collection, UCLA.

38. Review of *Canada Dry Program*, *Variety*, May 10, 1932, 58.

39. "Canada Dry Program," *Billboard*, May 14, 1932, 17.

40. Christopher, "Stars Shine Best When Polished," *Broadcasting and Television*, October 1956, 122.

41. Jerome Beatty, "Unhappy Fiddler," *American Magazine*, December 1944, 142.

42. "Radio Its Own Menace," *Variety*, February 21, 1933, 59.

43. Jerald Manning, "Laughter by the Yard," *Radio Mirror* November 1938, 40.

44. "Radio Its Own Menace," *Variety*, February 21, 1933, 59.

45. Zolotow, "The Fiddler from Waukegan," 142.

46. Al Boasberg advertisement, *Variety*, March 1, 1932, 36; Sid Silvers advertisement, *Variety*, December 8, 1931, 30; "Boasberg Walks on B&A Over Difference in Stage-Air Royalty," *Variety*, May 10, 1932, 55; "Authors! Authors!" *Variety*, August 30, 1932, 57; "Percentage for 2," *Variety*, May 31, 1932, 1; "Fleishmann Hour Program," *Variety*, October 11, 1932, 58.

47. Al Boasberg advertisement, *Variety*, March 1, 1932, 36; "Air Getting Ex-Vaude Writers on Rebound," *Variety*, May 31, 1932, 56.

48. Fred Allen, *Treadmill to Oblivion* (Boston: Little Brown, 1954), 70; "Air Gag Writers Are Now Most Highly Paid Writing Contingent," *Variety*, May 16, 1933, 43. Milton Makaye, "Whiskers on the Wisecrack," *Saturday Evening Post*, August 17, 1935, 12, 13, 50, 52.

49. "Gag Writing: It's Big Business Now," *Literary Digest*, December 12, 1936, 24, 26.

50. "Air Gag Writers Are Now Mostly Highly Paid Writing Contingent," *Variety*, May 16, 1932, 43.

51. "Radio Its Own Menace," *Variety*, February 21, 1933, 59.

52. "Commission Curbs Contests on Radio," *Pittsburgh Press*, May 13, 1932, 24.

53. *Canada Dry Program*, May 11, 1932 script, Benny Collection, UCLA.
54. "Were You Listening Last Night," *Pittsburgh Press*, May 10, 1931, 11; May 17, 1932, 12.
55. *Canada Dry Program*, May 16, 1932 script, Benny Collection, UCLA.
56. "Were You Listening?" *Pittsburgh Press*, June 9, 1932, 20.
57. *Canada Dry Program*, May 23, 1932 script, Benny Collection, UCLA.
58. Ralph M. Blagden, "Laughter Around the Dial" *Christian Science Monitor*, April 22, 1939, 4, 12.
59. "Little Bits from the Air," *Variety*, August 23, 1932, 42.
60. "Little Bits from the Air," *Variety*, October 18, 1932, 42.
61. James Cannon, untitled, undated newspaper clipping, Benny Scrapbook 1932–1933, Jack Benny Papers, American Heritage Center, University of Wyoming, Box 90.
62. Bertha Brainard to John Royal, October 7, 1932, NBC Papers, Collection 17AF, Wisconsin Historical Society, Box 6, file 63.
63. Bertha Brainard to John Royal October 7, 1932, NBC Records, Wisconsin Historical Society.
64. *Canada Dry Program*, November 17, 1932 script, Benny Collection, UCLA.
65. "Canada Dry Program," *Canton OH Repository*, January 20, 1933, 24.
66. *Chevrolet Program*, March 17, 1933 script, Benny Collection, UCLA.
67. "Jack Benny Is Back," *Ottawa Citizen*, March 11, 1933, 7.
68. "Chicago Theater," *Variety*, July 4, 1933, 14.
69. Beatty, "Unhappy Fiddler," 143.
70. Beatty, "Unhappy Fiddler," 143.
71. O. O. McIntyre, "New York Day by Day," *Rochester (NY) Evening Journal*, September 26, 1934, 15.
72. "Jack Benny and Company," *Radio Guide*, March 2, 1935, 13.
73. Beatty, "Unhappy Fiddler," 143.
74. *Variety*, review of Benny show, October 2, 1935, 40.
75. *Variety*, March 13, 1935, 35.
76. Carroll Nye, "Benny Rates 'Tops' as Dialogue Reader," *Los Angeles Times*, May 12, 1935.
77. Carroll Nye, "Radio Writers Need New Type of Humor," *Los Angeles Times*, December 1, 1935, C12.
78. Lloyd C Greene, "Radio Broadcasts: Sad Faced Harry Conn, Radio's Little Known Mogul of Mirth," *Boston Globe*, July 14, 1935, A36.
79. Beatty, "Unhappy Fiddler," 143.
80. Larry Wolters, "News of the Radio Stations," *Chicago Tribune*, February 6, 1936, 14.
81. Larry Wolters, "More Listeners Give Views on Broadcast Fare," *Chicago Tribune*, February 16, 1936, SW 6.
82. *Variety*, March 11, 1936, 40.
83. Irving Fein, *Jack Benny: An Intimate Biography* (New York: G. P. Putnams' Sons, 1976), 67.

84. Fein, *Jack Benny*, 66.

85. Laura Leff, *39 Forever, Second Edition, Volume 1: Radio May 1932–May 1942* (North Charleston, SC: Book Surge, 2004), 232.

86. *Jell-O Program*, March 22, 1936 script, Benny Collection, UCLA. Jack Benny telegram to Harry Conn, March 24, 1936, Benny Collection, UCLA, Box 98, folder 21.

87. *Variety*, July 14, 1936, 10; "Wedlock, Snyder Arrive for Benny's Jell-O," *Variety*, September 18, 1936, 1.

88. Fein, *Jack Benny*, 67.

89. Harry Conn to Jack Benny, June 9, 1936, Benny Collection, UCLA, Box 98, folder 21.

90. Harry Conn to Jack Benny, June 9, 1936, Benny Collection, UCLA.

91. *Variety*, June 24, 1936, 57.

92. "Comedy Writer Lineup for Fall," *Variety*, August 19, 1936, 35; Jerald Manning, "Laughter by the Yard," *Radio Mirror*, November 1938, 41.

93. "Conn Dropped as Penner's Gag Composer," *Variety*, December 10, 1936, 1, 3.

94. "Harry Conn to Write for Jolson Show," *Variety*, January 22, 1937, 3.

95. *Variety*, March 2, 1937, 11.

96. "Earaches of 1938 Foil for C&S Hour," *Daily Variety*, November 23, 1937, 6.

97. "CBS Splurge on Conn Sustainer," *Billboard*, October 30, 1937, 9.

98. John H. Heiney, "Harry Conn in Earaches of 1938," *Washington Post*, November 21, 1937, TS5.

99. Review of "Earaches of 1938," *Billboard*, December 25, 1937, 8.

100. "Eddie Cantor Sued by Dave Freedman," *Variety*, April 3, 1935, 35.

101. "Conn Sues Benny," *Variety*, August 9, 1939, 31; August 12, 1940, P2.

102. Fein, *Jack Benny*, 67. Untitled Killgallen clipping, *New York Journal American*, November 17, 1958, no page, in *New York Journal American* Morgue archive collection, Briscoe Center for American History, University of Texas at Austin.

CHAPTER 2

1. *Lucky Strike Program*, April 27, 1947.

2. Mary Dalton and Laura Linder, eds., *The Sitcom Reader: America Viewed and Skewed* (Albany: State University of New York Press, 2005), 85, 101, 106.

3. Susan J. Douglas, *Listening In: Radio and the American Imagination* (Minneapolis: University of Minnesota Press, 2004), 109.

4. Kathleen Rowe, *The Unruly Woman: Gender and the Genres of Laughter* (Austin: University of Texas Press, 2011), 3–19.

5. Milt Josefsberg, *The Jack Benny Show* (New York: Crown, 1977), 253.

6. See Benny and Benny, *Sunday Nights at Seven*.

7. Harriet Menken, "Laughs from the Ladies," *Delineator*, August 1936, 64–65.

8. Orrin E. Dunlap, Jr., "Ladies of the Wavelengths," *New York Times*, March 13, 1938.

9. Sadie Marcowitz birth certificate, *Jack Benny Times* 31, no. 3–4 (May–August 2016): 9. The certificate indicates her name as Sadie, but she spelled it Sadye.

10. Mary Livingstone Benny, Hilliard Marks, and Marcia Borie, *Jack Benny: A Biography* (New York: Doubleday 1978), vii.

11. Livingstone, Marks, and Borie, *Jack Benny*, 39. Mary claimed she was thirteen when she and Benny met, but actually she was sixteen.

12. Josefsberg, *The Jack Benny Show*, 36.

13. Livingstone, Marks, and Borie, *Jack Benny*, 38.

14. "Marriages," *Variety*, January 19, 1927, 27.

15. Livingstone, Marks, and Borie, *Jack Benny*, 50, 54.

16. Livingstone, Marks, and Borie, *Jack Benny*, 49–50.

17. "Mary Livingstone," IMDB, http://www.imdb.com/title/tt2792434/?ref_=nm_flmg_act_8.

18. Fred Wilson, "She Couldn't Help Being a Radio Star," *Boston Globe*, June 30, 1935, 13.

19. Mary Benny, "Mary Benny Tells Why She Quit Show Biz," *Chicago Tribune*, June 19, 1965, A1.

20. *Canada Dry Program*, May 23, June 15, June 27, 1932 scripts, Jack Benny Papers, Los Angeles, University of California at Los Angeles Special Collections, Collection 134, Radio Scripts Box 1, file 1.

21. *Canada Dry Program*, July 27, 1932, script, WEAF Masterbooks, NBC Collection, Recorded Sound Division, Library of Congress.

22. *Canada Dry Program*, August 1, 1932 script, Benny Papers, UCLA.

23. Jack Benny with Charles Martel, "Never Try to Be Funny," *Tower Radio*, September 1934, 21.

24. *Canada Dry Program*, August 17, 1932 script, Jack Benny papers, UCLA..

25. *Canada Dry Program*, October 17, 1932, script, Jack Benny papers, UCLA.

26. *Canada Dry Program,* September 19, 1932, Jack Benny papers, UCLA.

27. Josefsberg, *The Jack Benny Show*, 68–69.

28. Shlepperman, and then Phil Harris and Dennis Day, would occasionally address Mary by the nickname "Livvy," which added an informal, flirtatious aspect to how the male cast members interacted with her.

29. *Canada Dry Program*, September 5, 1932 script(the script alternates between calling her Mary and Sadye), Jack Benny papers, UCLA.

30. *Chevrolet Program*, February 4, 1934 script, Benny Papers, UCLA..

31. Robert Heinl, "Radio Dial Flashes," *Washington Post*, November 21, 1932, 8.

32. *Canada Dry Program,* January 15, 1933 script, Benny Papers, UCLA.

33. "Benny, at $2750 Is Jolson's Successor; 2d Top Radio Salary," *Variety* February 28, 1933, 49.

34. June 1933 review of *Chevrolet Program*, Benny Scrapbook 1932–1933, Jack Benny Collection, American Heritage Center, University of Wyoming, Box 90.
35. *Variety*, January 2, 1934, 75.
36. Robert Heinl, "Radio Dial Flashes," *Washington Post*, April 11, 1933.
37. Robert Heinl, "Radio Dial Flashes," *Washington Post*, May 19, 1933, 9.9.
38. Thomas Doherty, review of Jill Watts, *Mae West: An Icon in Black and White* (Oxford 2001), *American Historical Review* (December 2002): 1576–77.
39. *Jell-O Program*, May 30, 1937.
40. Review of show at Palace, Chicago, *Variety*, July 4, 1933, 14.
41. Fred Wilson, "She Couldn't Help Being a Radio Star," *Boston Globe*, June 30, 1935, 13.
42. Larry Wolters, "How New Radio Season Looks to a Listener." *Chicago Tribune*, October 20, 1935, SW6.
43. "Write Comedy Verse! Fatten Your Purse," *Detroit Times*, May 4, 1936, Benny Scrapbook 1936, American Heritage Center, University of Wyoming, Box 90.
44. Untitled clipping, *Detroit Times*, May 5, 1936, Benny Scrapbook 1936, American Heritage Center, University of Wyoming, Box 90.
45. "Portland Hoffa, 80, Mrs. Fred Allen in Life and on Air,", *Boston Globe*, January 1, 1991, 17.
46. Leah Lowe, "'If the Country's Going Gracie, So Can You': Gender Representation in Gracie Allen's Radio Comedy," in *Communities of the Air: Radio Century, Radio Culture*, ed. Susan M. Squire (Duke 2003), 237–50.
47. Douglas, *Listening In*, 116.
48. Lowe, "'If the Country's Going Gracie,'" 38.
49. Lowe, "'If the Country's Going Gracie,'" 240.
50. George Burns, "Gracie Allen as I Know Her," *Independent Woman*, July 1940, 214, quoted in Shirley Staples, *Male-Female Comedy Teams in American Vaudeville 1965–1932* (Ann Arbor: UMI Research Press, 1984), 224.
51. Jim Cox, *The Great Radio Sitcoms* (Jefferson, NC: McFarland, 2007), 43.
52. Cynthia Clements and Sandra Weber, *George Burns and Gracie Allen: A Bio-Bibliography* (Westport, CT: Greenwood Press, 1996), 31.
53. Lowe, "'If the Country's Going Gracie,'" 248.
54. Lowe, "'If the Country's Going Gracie,'" 244. Gracie and Mary almost never interacted when Gracie guest-starred on the Benny program.
55. *General Tire Program*, June 15 1934 script, *Jell-O Program*, April 29, July 7, December 6, 1935, scripts, Benny Papers, UCLA.
56. Untitled article, *Detroit Times*, Sunday May 10, 1936, Benny Scrapbook 1936, Benny Collection, American Heritage Center, box 90.
57. Advertisement in *Modern Romances*, 7 (no date, ca. 1935), KFS clippings collection.
58. *Pittsburgh Post-Gazette*, March 18, 1941. Jennifer Hyland Wang has found fascinating parallels in the humor of Allen Prescott's daytime household hints radio program of the 1930s and 1940s. Wang, "Recipe for Laughs: Comedy While Cleaning

in the Wife Saver," *Journal of e-Media Studies* 4, no. 1 (2015), http://journals.dartmouth.edu/cgi-bin/WebObjects/Journals.woa/xmlpage/4/article/454.

59. "Jack Benny and His Gang," (undated, ca. 1939), [unknown source, in KFS clippings collection].

60. Edgar A Thompson, "Riding the Airwaves," *Milwaukee Journal*, May 30 1940, 2.

61. Edwin Schaller, "Jack Benny to Be Absent When Wife Debuts in Picture," *Los Angeles Times*, May 5, 1937, A10. "Mary to Star without Jack," *Washington Post*, May 30, 1937, T4.

62. Milt Josefsberg noted that she actually had two laughs—"a stage prop laugh which we'd have her use frequently on the air, and her real laugh, which is slightly heavier and heartier." Josefsberg, *The Jack Benny Show*, 184.

63. Carroll Nye, "Air Comedians Gags Metered for Laughs," *Los Angeles Times*, February 14, 1937, C10.

64. Livingstone, Marks, and Borie, *Jack Benny*, 66.

65. Erik Barnouw, *Handbook of Radio Writing: An Outline of Techniques and Markets in radio writing in the United States* (Boston: Little, Brown, 1939).

66. Barnouw, *Handbook of Radio Writing*, 57.

67. Karin Quimby, "Will & Grace: Negotiating (Gay) Marriage on Prime-Time Television." *Journal of Popular Culture* 38, no. 4 (2005): 713.

68. Rowe, *The Unruly Woman*, 3–19.

69. Gerard Jones, *Honey, I'm Home!: Sitcoms: Selling the American Dream* (New York: Macmillan, 1993), 196.

70. Rebecca Feasey, *Masculinity and Popular Television* (Edinburgh: Edinburgh University Press, 2008), 22, quoting Richard Zoglin, "Where Fathers and Mothers Know Best," *Time*, June 1, 1992, 33.

71. Jerome Neu, *Sticks and Stones: The Philosophy of Insults* (Oxford: Oxford University Press, 2007). 65.

72. Douglas, *Listening In*, 109, 114.

73. *Grape Nuts Flakes Program*, November 8, 1942.

74. Josefsberg, *The Jack Benny Show*, 70.

75. Hank Grant, untitled article in *Hollywood Reporter*, June 16, 1969, reprinted in Josefsberg, *The Jack Benny Show*, 137–9.

76. Josefsberg, *The Jack Benny Show*, 182–83.

77. Lucille Walker, "Mary Livingstone Is the Spark of Benny's Show," *St. Joseph (MO) News Press*, February 18, 1945, 1.

78. Jack Hellman "Chain Breaks," *Variety*, March 24, 1952, 44.

79. "It's Benny Two to One," *Newsweek*, March 31, 1947, 67.

80. Mary Benny, "Mary Benny Tells Why She Quit Show Biz," *Chicago Tribune*, June 19. 1965, A1. "Mary Livingstone Finally Decides to Work on TV," Fredericksburg, VA *Free Lance–Star*, October 27, 1952, 15.

81. Eve Arden interview with Check Schaden, recorded January 31, 1975, available at http://www.speakingofradio.com/interviews/eve-arden/.

82. Jack Hellman, "Light and Airy," *Variety*, November 9, 1970, 10.

CHAPTER 3

1. Carole S. Vance, "Social Construction Theory and Sexuality," in *Constructing Masculinity*, ed. Maurice Berger, Brian Wallis, Simon Watson, and Carrie Mae Weems (New York: Routledge, 1995), 40.

2. Margaret T. McFadden, "America's Boy Friend Who Can't Get a Date": Gender, Race, and the Cultural Work of the Jack Benny Program, 1932–1946, *Journal of American History* 80, no. 1 (June 1993): 113–34; Alexander Doty, *Making Things Perfectly Queer: Interpreting Mass Culture* (Minneapolis: University of Minnesota Press, 1993), 63–80, Scott Balcerzak, *Buffoon Men: Classic Hollywood Comedians and Queered Masculinity* (Detroit, MI: Wayne State University Press, 2013).

3. Douglas, *Listening In*, 117.

4. Gwenllian Jones, "Gender and Queerness," in *Television Studies*, ed. Toby Miller (London: BFI, 2002), 109–12. Michael Kimmel, "Masculinity as Homophobia: Fear, Shame and Silence in the Construction of Gender Identity," in *Feminism and Masculinities*, ed. Peter Murphy (Oxford: Oxford University Press, 2004), 182–99. Kenneth MacKinnon, *Representing Men: Maleness and Masculinity in the Media* (London: Arnold, 2003). Helene Shugart, "Reinventing Privilege: The New (Gay) Man in Contemporary Popular Media," *Critical Studies in Mass Communication* 20, no. 1 (2003): 67–91. Feasey, *Masculinity and Popular Television*.

5. Julie D'Acci, "Television, Representation and Gender," in *Popular Television Drama: Critical Perspectives*, ed. Jonahtan Bignell and Stephen Lacey (Manchester: Manchester University Press, 2005), 379, cited in Feasey, *Masculinity and Popular Television*, 2.

6. Feasey, *Masculinity and Popular Television*, 3.

7. Feasey, *Masculinity and Popular Television*, 3.

8. Feasey, *Masculinity and Popular Television*, 3, quoting Kimmel, "Masculinity as Homophobia," 185–86.

9. Arthur Asa Berger, *Jewish Jesters: A Study in American Popular Comedy* (Cresskill, NJ: Hampton Press, 2001), 3; Maurice Berger, Brian Wallis, Simon Watson, and Carrie Mae Weems, eds., *Constructing Masculinity* (New York: Routledge, 1995), 2.

10. Lori Kendall, "'Oh No! I'm a Nerd!' Hegemonic Masculinity on an Online Forum." *Gender and Society* 14, no. 2 (April 2000): 260.

11. Douglas, *Listening In*, 117.

12. Maurice Zolotow, "The Fiddler from Waukegan," *Cosmopolitan*, October 1947, 137.

13. Amiri Baraka, (as LeRoi Jones) *JELLO* (Chicago: Third World Press, 1970); the play was produced in New York City by the Black Arts Repertory Theatre in 1965.

14. *Lucky Strike Program*, November 26, 1950.

15. Elijah Wald, *The Dozens: A History of Rap's Mama* (Oxford: Oxford University Press, 2012), 8, 12–13.

16. Wald, *The Dozens*, 14.

17. Neu, *Sticks and Stones*, 73–74.

18. "The Mighty Benny-Allen Feud," *Radio Mirror*, July 1938, 16–17, 61+, in KFS clippings collection.

19. *Lucky Strike Program*, March 17, 1946; May 25, 1947; February 12, 1950.

20. Harriet Van Horne, "Allen Quips in as Jack Benny's Air Guest," *New York World-Telegram*, May 26, 1947, 17.

21. Review of Jack Benny at Roxy Theater, *Variety*, May 28, 1947, 49.

22. John Crosby, "A Salute to a Comic Who Was a Wit's Wit," *Washington Post*, March 21, 1956, 46.

23. Zolotov, "Fiddler from Waukegan," 51.

24. Leo Calvin Rosten, *The Joys of Yiddish* (New York: McGraw-Hill, 1968), 354.

25. Martina Kessel and Patrick Merziger, *The Politics of Humour: Laughter, Inclusion, and Exclusion in the Twentieth Century* (Toronto: Toronto University Press, 2012).

26. David Zurawik, *The Jews of Prime Time* (Hanover, NH: Brandeis/University Press of New England, 2003).

27. Pearse, "As Goyish as Lime Jell-O?"

28. Charles E. Silberman, *A Certain People: American Jews and Their Lives Today* (New York: Simon & Schuster, 1985); David Kaufman, *Jewhooing the Sixties: American Celebrity and Jewish Identity: Sandy Koufax, Lenny Bruce, Bob Dylan, and Barbra Streisand* (Waltham, MA: Brandeis University Press, 2012).

29. Lawrence J. Epstein, *The Haunted Smile: The Story of Jewish Comedians in America* (New York: Public Affairs, 2002).

30. Epstein, *The Haunted Smile*; Berger, *Jewish Jesters*; Whitfield, Stephen J. "The Distinctiveness of American Jewish Humor," *Modern Judaism* (1986): 245–60.

31. Whitfield, "The Distinctiveness of American Jewish Humor," 41, 43.

32. Christie Davies, "Exploring the Thesis of the Self-Deprecating Jewish Sense of Humor," *Humor: International Journal of Humor Research* 4 (1991): 189–209. Neu, *Sticks and Stones*, 219–20.

33. Anonymous letter to FBI, dated April 1, 1939, 20. https://vault.fbi.gov/Jack%20Benny/Jack%20Benny%20Part%201%20of%202/view.

34. Sam Levenson, "The Dialect Comedian Should Vanish," *Commentary* 13 (January 1952): 168.

35. Marjorie B. Garber, *Vested Interests: Cross-dressing and Cultural Anxiety* (New York: Psychology Press, 1997).

36. Richard Maltby, "New Cinema Histories," *Explorations in New Cinema History: Approaches and Case Studies* (2011): 3–40; Kathryn Fuller Seeley, "Shirley Temple: Dreams Come True," in *Glamour in a Golden Age: Movie Stars of the 1930s*, ed. Adrienne L. McLean (New Brunswick, NJ: Rutgers University Press, 2011), 44–65.

37. Quimby, "Will and Grace," 717–18.

38. Ramona Curry, *Too Much of a Good Thing: Mae West as Cultural Icon* (Minneapolis: University of Minnesota Press, 1996); Steve Craig, "Out of Eden: The

Legion of Decency, the FCC, and Mae West's 1937 Appearance on The Chase & Sanborn Hour," *Journal of Radio Studies* 13, no. 2 (2006): 232–48.

39. Samantha Allen, "Whither the Transvestite? Theorizing Male-to-Female Transvestism in Feminist and Queer Theory," *Feminist Theory* 15, no. 1 (2014): 51–52.

40. Samantha Allen, "Whither the Transvestite?" 52.

41. Susan Murray, *Hitch Your Antenna to the Stars: Early Television and Broadcast Stardom* (London: Routledge, 2013), 142.

42. Murray, *Hitch Your Antenna to the Stars*, 136.

43. George Chauncey, *Gay New York: Gender, Urban Culture, and the Making of the Gay Male World, 1890–1940* (New York: Basic Books, 1994), 357.

44. John Royal to Mary McDonough, January 28, 1935, NBC Papers, Wisconsin Historical Society, Box 38 file Jell-O 1935.

45. Tom Carey to NBC, undated copy, attached to Janet MacRorie to John Swallow, January 19, 1937, NBC Papers, Wisconsin Historical Society, Box 93, file 15.

46. "NBC War Clinic," March 17, 1942, NBC Papers, Wisconsin Historical Society, folder 646.

47. John Lear, "You Can't Say That on the Air," *Saturday Evening Post*, July 12, 1947, 119.

48. *Dubuque Buyers Guide*, September 19, 1941.

49. Doris Arden, "The Old Girl Is Well Preserved," *Chicago Times*, August 17, 1941. Jack Benny Papers, American Heritage Center, University of Wyoming.

50. Review of Charley's *Aunt*, *Family Circle*, September 12, 1941, Benny scrapbook 1941, Jack Benny Papers, American Heritage Center, University of Wyoming.

51. *Albany NY Knickerbocker News*, August 29, 1941, review; "Jack Benny's Funny Aunt at the Albee," *Brooklyn Eagle*, August 29, 1941; "Benny Likes the Girls but Finds He Has to Play Up to the Men to Keep from Being Detected," *San Francisco Monitor*, August 2, 1941; Leo Mishkin, "Screen Presents: CA with JB Is Comedy Success of the Season," *New York Telegraph*, August 2, 1941, all Benny scrapbook 1941, Jack Benny Papers, American Heritage Center, University of Wyoming.

52. Harrison Carroll, "Premiere of Jack Benny's Charley's Aunt Gay Affair; Comedian Is Clever Choice for Broad Farce," *Los Angeles Herald Express*, August 1, 1941.

53. Howard Barnes, "On the Screen," *New York Herald Tribune*, August 1, 1941.

54. Edwin Schoallert, "Charley's Aunt Merrily Lives Again on Screen," *Los Angeles Times*, August 1 1941.

55. Winston Archer, review of "Charley's Aunt," *New York Post*, August 1, 1941, Benny scrapbook 1941, Benny Papers, American Heritage Center, University of Wyoming.

56. Leo Mishkin, "Screen Presents: Charley's Aunt with Jack Benny Is Comedy Success of the Season," *New York Telegraph*, August 2, 1941.

57. *Berwick (PA) Enterprise*, August 1, 1941.

58. "Benny's Oscar," *Boston Globe*, March 8, 1942, b6.

59. "Things Overheard on the Radio," *Saturday Evening Post* September 5, 1942, 32.

60. *Lucky Strike Program*, March 28, 1948.

61. Feasey, *Masculinity and Popular Television*, 26–27.

62. *Lucky Strike Program*, March 26, 1950.

63. Feasey, *Masculinity and Popular Television*, 26–28, quoting Gwenllian Jones, "Gender and Queerness," 109; Ela Przybylo, "Crisis and Safety: The Asexual in Society," *Sexualities* 14, no. 4 (2011): 444–61.

64. John Crosby, "The Perfect Title," *New York Herald Tribune*, February 4, 1948.

65. "Show Folk Frolic Big," *Los Angeles Times*, April 18, 1949, B7.

66. "Meet Gracie (Benny)," *Radio and Television Best*, October 1949, 34–35.

67. Harry Harris, "Around the Dials," *Philadelphia Bulletin*, March 12, 1952.

68. *Variety*, March 24, 1952, 44.

69. C. Foster to Irving Fein, March 10, 1952, Benny Papers, American Heritage Center, University of Wyoming, Box 89.

70. Ben Gross printed a viewer response to his review: "Mrs. Clara Winston of Manhattan takes up the favorite pastime of socking the critic. She says I was "dead wrong" in writing that Jack Benny, dressed in woman's clothes last Sunday, didn't seem especially funny to me. 'What's the matter with a man wearing female clothing? She writes. It is better than looking at naked women. Some females look too shameful to be on television. I thought Jack Benny looked wonderful. He certainly made a better looking woman, from his head to his feet, than a lot of females I have seen. A little innocent fun and comedy never hurt anyone and we certainly need a lot of it these days. I think you are jealous." "Televiewing and Listening In: with Ben Gross," *New York Daily News*, March 17, 1952.

71. Harry Harris, "Around the Dials," *Philadelphia Bulletin*, March 12, 1952.

72. Janet Kern, "Benny 'Knockout' in Gracie Allen Role; Imitation Gives Jack Some of His Best Repartee of This Season," *Chicago Herald American*, March 10, 1952; Bob Francis, "Jacqueline Benny's Fem Stint with Burns and Allen One of His Best," *Billboard*, March 22, 1952, 3.

73. Jack Gould, "Jack Benny, in Impersonation of Gracie Allen, Shows His Mastery of Deadpan Comedy," *New York Times*, March 12, 1952.

74. John Lester, "Benny and Burns Fare Not So Well," no date or newspaper name. Benny scrapbook 1952, Benny Papers, American Heritage Center, University of Wyoming.

75. Andy Wilson, "Looking and Listening: Feminine Attire to Get Laughs Leaves Observer Slightly Cool," *Detroit Times*, March 14, 1952. Benny scrapbook 1952, Benny Papers, American Heritage Center, University of Wyoming.

76. *Kansas City Star*, March 26, 1952, clipping; *Washington (DC) Star*, March 11, 1952, Benny scrapbook 1952, Benny papers, American Heritage Center, University of Wyoming.

77. Roger Swift, "Comedian Benny on Target Again," *Boston Herald*, April 21, 1952.

78. Jack Hellman review, *Daily Variety*, April 12, 1954, 9.
79. "Durante Quip for Quip," *Boston American*, April 12, 1954.
80. "Benny in Skirts a Scream; "Plugged Nickel" Fizzles; Comedian Is Good in Gracie Takeoff," *Hollywood Reporter*, April 15, 1954.
81. December 12, 1954.

CHAPTER 4

1. Estelle Edmerson, "A Descriptive Study of the American Negro in United States Professional Radio 1922–1953" (MA thesis, University of California, Los Angeles, 1954), 32.
2. Melvin Ely, *The Adventures of Amos 'n' Andy: A Social History of an American Phenomenon*. (Charlottesville: University of Virginia Press, 1991).
3. Jack Benny and Joan Benny, *Sunday Nights at Seven: The Jack Benny Story* (New York: Warner Books, 1990), 100.
4. Christopher Lehman, *The Colored Cartoon: Black Presentation in American Animated Short Films, 1907–1954* (Amherst: University of Massachusetts Press, 2009).
5. Harold Jovien, "'Rochester' Was Jack of All Trades before Radio Debut," *Baltimore Afro American*, October 6, 1945, 10.
6. Michael Carter, "Jack Benny's Gravel Voiced Rochester Talks to AFRO," *Baltimore Afro American*, February 3, 1945, 5.
7. Hilmes, *Radio Voices*, 20–21.
8. Hilmes, *Radio Voices*, xvi.
9. Robert McG. Thomas, "Eddie Anderson, 71, Benny's Rochester," *New York Times*, March 1, 1977, 24.
10. David W. Kellum, "Another Complete Story on Rochester," *Defender*, July 8, 1939, 8; Eddie Anderson, "Meet Rochester, He's Star on the Jack Benny Sunday Radio Program," *Defender*, July 1, 1939, 20.
11. Harold Jovien, "'Rochester' Was Jack of All Trades before Radio Debut," *Baltimore Afro-American*, October 6, 1945, 10.
12. Obituary, *Chicago Defender*, August 7, 1948.
13. CBS press release, "Philosophical Pullman Porter Inspired Benny Writers and Rochester Was Born with Eddie Anderson in Role," December 13, 1948, Eddie Anderson file, Margaret Herrick Library, Academy of Motion Picture Arts and Sciences archives.
14. Frank del Olmo, "Eddie Anderson, Famed 'Rochester,' Dies at 72," *Los Angeles Times*, March 1, 1977, 3.
15. Florabel Muir, "What's That, Boss?" *Saturday Evening Post* June 19, 1943, 15.
16. David W. Kellum, "Another Complete Story on Rochester," *Defender*, July 8, 1939, 8.

17. Harold Jovien, "Rochester Was Jack of All Trades," *The Negro: A Review*, February 1, 1946, 4.

18. "Eddie 'Rochester' Anderson Has Had Colorful Career," *California Eagle*, June 29, 1939, 2. "Rochester by Way of Harlem," *New York Times*, July 2, 1939, 3.

19. "Eddie 'Rochester' Anderson Has Had Colorful Career," *California Eagle*, June 29, 1939, 2.

20. Ragtime Billy Tucker, "Cast Dope," *Chicago Defender*, November 17, 1923, 8.

21. Michael Carter, "Jack Benny's Gravel-Voiced Rochester Talks to AFRO," *Baltimore Afro-American*, February 3, 1945, 5.

22. Thomas, Anderson obituary, *New York Times*, March 1, 1977, quoting Muir, "What's That, Boss? *Saturday Evening Post*, 1943.

23. "Eddie Rochester Dies in Los Angeles at 71," *New York Amsterdam News*, March 5, 1977, A3; *Washington Post* obituary; George A. Mooney, "Benny Admirer No.1; Eddie (Rochester) Anderson Comes to New York and Thereby Hangs a Tale," *New York Times*, January 5, 1941, x10.

24. "Coast Calls Marshall, Ford and Harris," *Defender*, January 25, 1941, 21.

25. "Eddie 'Rochester' Anderson Has Had Colorful Career," *California Eagle*, June 29, 1939, 2.

26. David W. Kellum, "Another Complete Story on Rochester," *Defender*, July 8, 1939, 8.

27. *Defender*, August 29, 1925, 6. CBS, "Philosophical Pullman porter"; "Eddie 'Rochester' Anderson Has Had Colorful Career," *California Eagle*, June 29, 1939, 2.

28. David W. Kellum, "Another Complete Story on Rochester," *Defender*, July 8, 1939, 8.

29. Eddie (Rochester) Anderson, "Meet Rochester," *Defender*, July 1, 1939, 20.

30. *Defender*, August 16, 1930, 5; *Defender*, August 23, 1930, 5; "LA Night Clubs Feature Stars," *Defender*, April 15, 1933, 5; *Defender*, May 12, 1934, 9.

31. "Herman Hill Recalls Rochester," *Los Angeles Sentinel*, March 3, 1977, 1.

32. *Defender*, December 14, 1935, 8.

33. Eddie "Rochester" Anderson, filmography, http://www.imdb.com/name/nm0026655/.

34. Edmerson, "A Descriptive Study," 19–26.

35. Edmerson, "A Descriptive Study," 98.

36. Edmerson, "A Descriptive Study," 30–31.

37. Edmerson, "A Descriptive Study," 118, 355.

38. Lizabeth Cohen, *Making a New Deal: Industrial Workers in Chicago, 1919–1939* (Cambridge: Cambridge University Press, 1991); Brian Ward, *Radio and the Struggle for Civil Rights in the South*. University Press of Florida, 2004.

39. Amy M. Ware, "Will Roger's Radio: Race and Technology in the Cherokee Nation," *American Indian Quarterly* 33, no. 1 (Winter 2009): 62–97; "Race Still Dissatisfied: Gulf Co. Claims They Can't Censor Star," *Atlanta Daily World*, January 30, 1934, 1.

40. "NBC's First All-Negro Opens on Blue Web," *Variety*, April 2, 1937, 2.

41. *Pittsburgh Courier*, April 17, 1937, quoted in Henry T. Sampson, *Swingin' on the Ether Waves: A Chronological History of African Americans in Radio and Television Programming, 1925–1955*. Vol. 1 (Lanham, MD: Scarecrow Press, 2005), 225–26; *Variety*, April 14, 1937, quoted in Sampson, *Swingin' on the Ether Waves*, 222–23.

42. Laura Leff, *39 Forever, Second Edition, Volume 1: Radio May 1932–May 1942* (North Charleston, SC: Book Surge, 2004), 223, 225. *Jell-O Program*, January 19 and February 2, 1936.

43. Benny and Benny, *Sunday Nights at Seven*, 100.

44. Benny and Benny, *Sunday Nights at Seven*, 101.

45. George A. Mooney, "Benny Admirer No.1; Eddie (Rochester) Anderson Comes to New York and Thereby Hangs a Tale," *New York Times*, January 5, 1941, X10.

46. Michael Carter, "Jack Benny's Gravel Voiced Rochester Talks to AFRO," *Baltimore Afro-American*, February 3, 1945, 5.

47. Hal Humphrey, "That's Rochester Who's Back and Jack Benny's Got Him," *Chicago Tribune*, November 10, 1968, SC A2.

48. Jill Watts, *Hattie McDaniel: Black Ambition, White Hollywood* (New York: Harper Collins, 2007), 129.

49. Hal Humphrey, "That's Rochester Who's Back and Jack Benny's Got Him," *Chicago Tribune*, November 10, 1968, SC A2. Anderson also acknowledged that Benny copyrighted the name "and years later Jack sold it to Eddie for a dollar."

50. Benny and Benny, *Sunday Nights at Seven*, 101.

51. Orrin E Dunlap Jr., "Benny at Breakfast: Jack Tells How His Show Is Put Together, Casting of the Troupe Is Explained," *New York Times*, April 28, 1940, 128.

52. Michele Hilmes, *Radio Voices: American Broadcasting, 1922–1952* (Minneapolis: University of Minnesota Press, 1997).

53. *Jell-O Program*, October 16, 1938.

54. "As Benny's Heckling Radio Valet the Ebony Comedian Has All but Lost His Identity as Eddie Anderson," *New York Times*, July 2 1939.

55. David W. Kellum, "Another Complete Story on Rochester," *Defender*, July 8, 1939, 8.

56. "On the Air," *Kansas City Plain Dealer*, January 14, 1938, 5; *California Eagle*, December 30, 1937, 1.

57. Lou Layne, "Moon Over Harlem," *Atlanta Daily World*, March 5, 1938, 16.

58. "On the Air," *California Eagle*, April 21, 1938, 8.

59. "Very Important Member of Jack Benny's Show Is Eddie Anderson," *New York Amsterdam News*, April 2, 1938, 16.

60. "Rochester Drops Character for His Off-Stage Fans," *Baltimore Afro-American*, August 19, 1939, 11.

61. Eric Smoodin, *Regarding Frank Capra: Audience, Celebrity, and American Film Studies, 1930-1960* (Durham, NC: Duke University Press, 2004).

62. Thomas Pryor, "To Rochester by Way of Harlem," *New York Times*, July 2, 1939, X3.

63. "Radio's Famous 'Rochester,'" *Pittsburgh Courier*, November 12, 1938; *Atlanta Daily World*, November 14, 1938, 2; "Presenting Eddie Anderson, 'Rochester' to Benny," *California Eagle*, November 10, 1938, 2B.

64. Hilmes, *Radio Voices*, 21.

65. Michele Hilmes, "Invisible Men: Amos 'n' Andy and the Roots of Broadcast Discourse." *Critical Studies in Media Communication* 10, no. 4 (1993): 301.

66. John Crosby, "Amos 'n' Andy," *New York Herald Tribune*, December 24, 1947, 34.

67. Hilmes, "Invisible Men," 319.

68. *Jell-O Program*, June 25, 1939.

69. Benny and Benny, *Sunday Nights at Seven*, 107.

70. *Jell-O Program*, March 19, 1939.

71. Orrin E Dunlap Jr., "Benny at Breakfast: Jack Tells How His Show Is Put Together, Casting of the Troupe Is Explained," *New York Times*, April 28, 1940, 128.

72. David W. Kellum, "Another Complete Story on Rochester," *Defender*, July 8, 1939, 8.

73. *Los Angeles Times*, February 3, 1939.

74. *Man About Town* Press Book, June 1939, Paramount pressbook collection, Margaret Herrick Library, Academy of Motion Picture Arts and Sciences.

75. *Cue*, July 1, 1939, Mark Sandrich Papers, file 114, Margaret Herrick Library, Academy of Motion Picture Arts and Sciences.

76. Howard Barnes, "The Screen," *New York Herald Tribune*, July 2, 1939, Mark Sandrich Papers, Margaret Herrick Library, Academy of Motion Picture Arts and Sciences.

77. "Eddie 'Rochester' Anderson Has Had Colorful Career," *California Eagle*, June 29, 1939, 2.

78. "Honest Signal," *Variety*, October 10, 1939, 4.

79. *Buck Benny Rides Again* pressbook, March 1940. Paramount Pressbook collection, Margaret Herrick Library, Academy of Motion Picture Arts and Sciences.

80. Watts, *Hattie McDaniel*; Matthew Bernstein, "Selznick's March: *Gone With the Wind* Comes to White Atlanta," *Atlanta History* 43, no. 2 (1999): 7–33.

81. "*Buck Benny Rides Again* Will Have Premiere at Victoria," *New York Amsterdam News*, April 13, 1940, 21.

82. Maurice Dancer, "3,000 Crowd Streets to Cheer Film Star; Californian Hailed in Big Harlem Demonstration," *Chicago Defender*, April 27, 1940, 20.

83. Alvin Moses, "Footlight Flickers," *Atlanta Daily World*, May 13, 1940, 2.

84. Dan Burley, "Cops 'Ride Herd' at Rochester Premiere," *New York Amsterdam News*, April 27, 1940, 1.

85. *New York Motion Picture Herald*, April 27, 1940; *New York Showman's Trade Review*, April 27, 1940; Mark Sandrich Papers, Margaret Herrick Library, Academy of Motion Picture Arts and Sciences.

86. *New York Showman's Trade Review*, April 27, 1940.

87. Howard Barnes, review of *Buck Benny Rides Again*, *New York Herald Tribune*, April 28, 1940, Mark Sandrich Papers, Margaret Herrick Library, Academy of Motion Picture Arts and Sciences.

88. *Defender*, June 22, 1940, 14.

89. "Rochester Kidnapped on Way to Harvard; 8 Jailed as Riot Follows Snatch," *Baltimore Afro American*, May 11, 1940, 14. "Harvard Men 'Riot' after Tech Prank, 8 Arrested," *Boston Globe*, May 1, 1940, 1. "Harvard Students Riot as MIT Abducts Rochester," *Defender*, May 11, 1940, 21.

90. "Negro Population Hails Rochester on Arrival Here," *Boston Globe*, May 2, 1940, 8; "Harvard vs. MIT= $35; Seven Students Fined $5 for Riot Avenging Eddie Anderson," *New York Times*, May 2, 1940, 23.

91. "Rochester Winner of 1939 Film Award," *Chicago Defender*, December 30, 1939, 17; "What 1939 Meant to the Negro in Hollywood," *Pittsburgh Courier*, January 20, 1940, 13.

92. "NAACP Gives Academy Awards to Film Actors," *Baltimore Afro American*, August 3, 1940, 14.

93. Earl J. Morris, commentary in *Pittsburgh Courier*, August 29, 1940, quoted in Sampson, *Swingin' on the Ether Waves*, 331.

94. "Schomburg Citations of 1940 Cover Wide Field," *Defender*, February 15, 1941, 12.

95. *California Eagle*, April 24, 1941, 8.

CHAPTER 5

1. Estelle Edmerson, "A Descriptive Study of the American Negro in United States Professional Radio 1922–1953" (MA thesis, University of California, Los Angeles, 1954), 178; Thomas Cripps, "Amos 'n' Andy and the Debate over Racial Integration," in *American History/American Television: Interpreting the Video Past*, ed John E. O'Connor (New York: Frederick Ungar, 1983), 27.

2. R. J. Smith, *The Great Black Way: Los Angeles in the 1940s and the Lost African-American Renaissance* (New York: Public Affairs, 2006), 18–19.

3. Smith, *The Great Black Way*, 18.

4. Joseph Boskin, *Sambo: The Rise and Demise of an American Jester* (New York: Oxford 1986), 179.

5. Earl J. Morris, *Pittsburgh Courier*, August 29, 1940, quoted in Henry T. Sampson, *Swingin' on the Ether Waves: A Chronological History of African Americans in Radio and TV Programming, 1925–1955* (Lanham, MD: Scarecrow Press, 2005), 331.

6. "Improved Negro Press: Less Discrimination Than Ever Before by the Public Prints on Negro Photos, Puffs," *Billboard*, March 13, 1943, 4, 10.

7. Florabel Muir, "What's That, Boss?" *Saturday Evening Post*, June 19, 1943, 15; Kirtley Baskette, "Rochester Van Jones Rides High," *Radio Mirror*, January 1940, 31, 49.

8. Ruby Berkeley Goodwin, "Finds Hollywood Is Easing Pressure Against Negroes; More Race Actors Are Getting Roles," *Atlanta Daily World*, May 11, 1942, 2.

9. Earl J. Morris, *Pittsburgh Courier*, August 29, 1940, quoted in Sampson, *Swingin' on the Ether Waves*, 331.

10. "How Rochester Walked in on Benny," *New York Amsterdam News*, February 20, 1943, 14.

11. "How Rochester Walked in on Benny."

12. *Lucky Strike Program*, April 2, 1944. In a typical typed broadcast script, Rochester's lines are all printed in standard English, with no dialect (and neither is Artie Aurbach/Mr. Kitzel's accent noted in his dialogue). On the other hand, informal English spoken by Mary and Phil (wanna, hadda, yeah, Jack's own dialogue in the script includes "rarin'," "tootin'," "gotta," and "will ya?") is included.

13. Boskin, *Sambo*, 180.

14. In one of the last direct references to skin color on the program, on the *Lucky Strike Program*, February 20, 1944, episode, guest star Groucho Marx visited Jack at home. Once inside the front door, Groucho announced that he was colorblind, commenting that he gave his coat to Jack, and shook Rochester's hand. Jack responded. "That was me—I'd been in the sun at Palm Springs."

15. Harold Jovien, "Critic Names Year's Best Radio Programs," *Defender*, September 26, 1942, 9.

16. Review of *Duffy's Tavern*, *Pittsburgh Courier*, January 9, 1943, quoted in Sampson, *Swingin' on the Ether Waves*, 433; Edward Bennett, "*Duffy's Tavern* May Be Too Hot for Dixie Houses," *Baltimore Afro American*, May 5, 1945, 8; "The radio version [of *Duffy's Tavern*] makes listeners feel that Gardiner and Green are not boss and waiter, but that they are two friends, working in the same crummy joint for a living. With Green as the only one who is supposed to have any real education or good common sense. Green is always telling Archie what he thinks of his rattle brained ideas, or belittling him in some way or another."

17. Bosley Crowther, "Tales of Manhattan," *New York Times*, September 25, 1942, 25; Bosley Crowther, "Little by Little: *Tales of Manhattan* Boosts the Stock of the Short Story in Films," *New York Times*, October 4, 1942, 43. See also Miriam J. Petty, *Stealing the Show: African American Performers and Audiences in 1930s Hollywood* (Berkeley: University of California Press, 2016).

18. "Coast Citizens Picket House Using Film *Tales of Manhattan*," *Defender*, August 22, 1942, 22; participant Wendell Green recalled the picketing in "Weekly Kaleidoscope," *Los Angeles Sentinel*, November 2, 1961, A6.

19. John Kinlock "Uncle Tomdom Put Under Glass," *California Eagle*, August 7, 1941, 1.

20. Harry Levette, "Wires Hot as Actors Picket Coast Theatre," *Atlanta Daily World*, September 2, 1942, 2.

21. "Film Stars Answer Charges by Public Protesting Uncle Tom Roles," *Chicago Defender*, August 29, 1942, 7.

22. "Criticizes Actors," *Defender*, September 12, 1942, 14.

23. Jill Watts, *Hattie McDaniel: Black Ambition, White Hollywood* (New York: HarperCollins, 2005), 213–25.

24. Thomas Djya, *Walter White: The Dilemma of Black Identity in America* (Chicago: Ivan R. Dee, 2008), 159.

25. Levette, "Wires Hot as Actors Picket Coast Theatre."

26. Levette, "Wires Hot as Actors Picket Coast Theatre."

27. Ruby Berkeley Goodwin, "Defends Movie Colony against NAACP Critics; Says Liberal Spirit Hovers Over Film Lots," *Atlanta Daily World*, December 7, 1942, 2.

28. "Speech of the Week," *California Eagle*, April 10, 1941, 10A; Barbara Savage, *Broadcasting Freedom: Radio, War and the Politics of Race 1938–1948* (Chapel Hill: University of North Carolina Press, 1999), 161–62.

29. Lauren Rebecca Sklaroff, "Variety for the Servicemen: The Jubilee Show and the Paradox of Racializing Radio during World War II," *American Quarterly* 56, no. 4 (2004): 952–973.

30. Jill Watts, *Hattie McDaniel*, 208–14.

31. "Rochester Visits Tuskegee" *Los Angeles Tribune*, January 10, 1944, 15.

32. "Rochester Backs America's First Negro-Managed War Industry Plant," *Defender*, April 4, 1942, 4; Donald Bogle, *Bright Boulevards, Bold Dreams: The Story of Black Hollywood* (New York: Ballantine Books, 2005), 269–74.

33. "Rochester Signs for $125,000 for Five Movie Plays," *Kansas City Plain Dealer*, June 19, 1942, 6.

34. "*Stormy Weather*, Negro Musical with Bill Robinson, at the Roxy," *New York Times*, July 22 1943, 15.

35. Fred Stanley, "Hollywood Takes a Hint from Washington: Two Big Negro Musicals Are Under Way," *New York Times*, February 7, 1943, X3.

36. Bosley Crowther, "Cleaving the Color Line: A New Attitude toward Negroes Is Apparent in Some Recent Films," *New York Times*, June 6, 1943, X3.

37. Phil Carter, "Review Hollywood Offerings since White-Willkie Meeting," *Los Angeles Tribune*, November 15, 1943, 18. Rob Roy, "Critic Says Hollywood Caters to South in Pictures; Even Lena Horne Gets Red Light, He Writes," *Defender*, June 26, 1943, 10.

38. Smith, *The Great Black Way*, 86–89.

39. Dominic J. Capeci Jr. and Martha Wilkerson, "The Detroit Riots of 1943: A Reinterpretation," *Michigan Historical Review* 16, no. 1 (January 1990): 49–72.

40. "Salute Dignified Treatment of US Negroes in Film," *Variety*, June 30, 1943, 1, 27.

41. "Hollywood Holding Up Pix Releases in Which Whites, Negroes Mix" *Variety*, June 30, 1943, 27. "More Negro Scenes Cut Out in Dixie Set New Problem for Pix Producers," *Variety*, 1 July 12, 1944.

42. "Think Race Riots Hurt Negro Films," *Defender*, July 31, 1943, 18.

43. "Tenn. Mob of Whites Halts Showing of 'Cabin' Movie," *Defender*, August 7, 1943, 1.

44. Benny to McQueen, May 29, 1944, Jack Benny papers, University of California at Los Angeles, Special Collections, Box 97, file 21.

45. "Butterfly McQueen Case Is Proof There Is, After All, Something in a Name," *Defender*, December 7, 1946, 11.

46. "Radio and Race," *Ebony* 1, no. 3 (1946): 43.

47. "Two Radio Shows Receive Awards for Racial Amity," *Los Angeles Sentinel*, April 11, 1946, quoted in Sampson, *Swingin' on the Ether Waves*, 591.

48. Sklaroff, "Variety for the Servicemen"; Jacqueline Trescott, "Butterfly McQueen: In Prissy's Shadow," *Washington Post*, November 7, 1976, 55.

49. Ole Nosey, "Everybody Goes When the Wagon Comes," *Defender*, March 11, 1944, 10.

50. Ole Nosey, "Everybody Goes When the Wagon Comes," *Defender*, February 10, 1945, 8; Ole Nosey, "Everybody Goes When the Wagon Comes," *Defender*, March 24, 1945, 8.

51. Ramona Loew, "More Negroes in Radio Urged by Norman Corwin," *Defender*, February 17, 1945, 2.

52. *Pittsburgh Courier*, February 24, 1945, in Sampson, *Swingin' on the Ether Waves*, 537–38.

53. *California Eagle*, February 1, 1945, 14.

54. "Defends Rochester Crap Shooting," *Defender*, February 24, 1945, 10.

55. Carter, "Jack Benny's Gravel Voiced," *Baltimore Afro American*, February 1945.

56. *California Eagle* congratulated Benny for having Joe Louis in a guest appearance on the show in November 1945, quoted in Sampson, *Swingin' on the Ether Waves*, 572–74.

57. Ole Nosey, "Everybody Goes When the Wagon Comes," *Defender*, March 24, 1945, 18.

58. "Comedy Rich in Laughs," *Los Angeles Times*, March 9, 1945, 9.

59. "'Brewster's Millions' Is Barred in Memphis," *New York Times*, April 7, 1945, 19.

60. "Rochester Has Too Much Equality—Crump Bans Film," *Defender*, April 14, 1945, 1; "'Brewster's Millions' Is Barred in Memphis," *New York Times*, April 7, 1945, 19.

61. "Lillian Smith Lashes Pix over Rochester Case Page 1," *Variety*, May 24, 1945, 3.

62. "Rochester's USO Tour Stalled by a Curious Yen for Ofay Muskers," *Variety*, May 30, 1945, 2.

63. "Our GI's in S. Pacific Fiercely Resent 'Uncle Tom' Roles," *New York Amsterdam News*, September 1, 1945, 1A.

64. Watts, *Hattie McDaniel*, 235–36.

65. Abe Hill, "Stereotyped Comics Viewed as Drawback," *New Amsterdam News*, March 24, 1945, 22.

66. Jack Hellman, "Light and Airy," *Variety*, March 18, 1946, 6.

67. Samson, *Swingin' on the Ether Waves*, 705–13.

68. "Radio and Race," *Ebony* 1, no. 3 (1946): 41–43; Larry Wolters, "Radio Lauded for Improving Race Relations," *Chicago Daily Tribune*, January 29, 1946, 24.

69. John Dunning, *On the Air: The Encyclopedia of Old-Time Radio* (Oxford University Press, 1998).

70. "5-a-Week Airshow Looms for Rochester," *Variety*, February 10, 1950, 1.

71. "Rochester Will Spoof Whodunits on Own," *Variety*, February 15, 1950, 22; "No Lucky Approval on Rochester as Yet," *Variety*, February 17, 1950, 5.

72. "This Is Hollywood;" *Defender*, March 4, 1950, 21; "Hear Radio Show Awaits Rochester's Return to States," *Defender*, June 17, 1950, 21.

73. Milt Josefsberg, *The Jack Benny Show* (New York: Crown, 1977), 83–84.

74. Josefsberg, *The Jack Benny Show*, 85.

75. "Jack Benny Show Stirs Harlem's Ire," *Defender*, February 11, 1950, 1; Edmerson, "A Descriptive Study," 186–88.

76. "Protests Jack Benny Show Stereotypes," *Atlanta Daily World*, February 15, 1950, 4.

77. Lillian Scott, "Along Celebrity Row," *Defender*, February 18, 1950, 8; "Along Celebrity Row," *Defender*, March 25, 1950, 8.

78. Al Monroe, "Swinging the News," *Defender*, February 18, 1950, 20.

79. "Sorry, Benny Tells Us," *Pittsburgh Courier*, February 25, 1950, 1, quoted in Edmerson, "A Descriptive Study," 186–87.

80. "Editorial: When Racial Jokes Aren't Funny," *Defender*, February 25, 1950, 6.

81. "Jack Laid an Egg," *Los Angeles Sentinel*, March 9, 1950, A8, quoted in Edmerson, "A Descriptive Study," 186–88.

82. "Rochester a First," *Atlanta Daily World*, April 27, 1950, 1; *Los Angeles Sentinel*, April 27, 1950, B1.

83. *Liberty* cover, November 29, 1942; *Time* cover, September 22, 1947; *Quick*, April 22, 1950; *Life*, May 8, 1950.

84. Donald Bogle, *Primetime Blues: African Americans on Network Television* (New York: Farrar, Straus and Giroux, 2002), 55.

85. Rob Roy, "Out of Hearts of Stars Came TV and Radio Bids to Sepia Artists," *Defender*, January 2, 1954, 18.

86. Edmerson, "A Descriptive Study."

87. Edmerson, "A Descriptive Study," 61–62, 78.

88. Edmerson, "A Descriptive Study," 71–72.

89. Edmerson, "A Descriptive Study," 73.

90. Edmerson, "A Descriptive Study," 75, 355; Earl Brown, "Rochester Still Says Yassuh to Jack Benny," *New Amsterdam News*, August 4, 1951, 6.

91. Hal Humphrey, "That's Rochester Who's Back and Jack Benny's Got Him," *Chicago Tribune*, November 10, 1968, SC A2.

92. Gerald Weales, "What Were Blacks Doing in the Balcony? The Day LeRoi Jones Spoke on Penn Campus," *New York Times*, May 4, 1969, SM 38–40, 44, 54, 56, 58.

93. Hal Humphrey, "That's Rochester Who's Back, and Jack Benny's Got Him," *Chicago Tribune*, November 10, 1968, SC A2.

CHAPTER 6

1. Pat Weaver, "If I Were Running the Network Again," *Sponsor*, August 26, 1963, 26; "Star Salesman of the Airwaves," *Kiplinger's*, 1962.
2. *Sponsor*, September 2, 1963, 32.
3. Ralph Lewis Smith, *A Study of the Professional Criticism of Broadcasting in the US 1920–1955* (New York: Arno, 1979).
4. Josefsberg quoted in Larry Oakner, *And Now for a Few Laughs from Our Sponsor: The Best of Fifty Years of Radio Commercials* (New York: John Wiley & Sons, 2002).
5. Draper Daniels, "Humor in Advertising," in *Copywriter's Guide*, ed. Elbrun French (New York: Harper, 1959), 137; Oakner, *And Now for a Few Laughs*, xix.
6. Cynthia Meyers, *A Word from Our Sponsor: Admen, Advertising and the Golden Age of Radio* (New York: Fordham University Press, 2013); Roland Marchand, *Advertising the American Dream: Making Way for Modernity 1920–1940* (Berkeley: University of California Press, 1985); Stephen R. Fox, *The Mirror Makers: A History of American Advertising and Its Creators* (Urbana: University of Illinois Press, 1984).
7. Meyers, *A Word from Our Sponsor*.
8. Daniels, "Humor in Advertising," 147.
9. Daniels, "Humor in Advertising," 140.
10. Daniels, "Humor in Advertising," 137.
11. Pat Weaver, "If I Were Running the Network Again," *Sponsor*, August 26, 1963, 25–26.
12. Elbrun French, "To Integrate or Not Integrate," in *Copywriter's Guide*, ed. Elbrun French, 222.
13. See discussion in Marchand, *Advertising the American Dream*.
14. Curt Peterson to Bertha Brainard, "Canada Dry" memo, April 15, 1932, in NBC Papers, Wisconsin Historical Society, Box 6, file 63 "Jack Benny 1932."
15. Daniels, "Humor in Advertising," 140.
16. Jack Benny and Charles Martel, "Never Try to Be Funny," *Tower Radio*, September 1934, 20, 21+.
17. Larry Christopher, "Stars Shine Best When Polished," *Broadcasting and Television*, October 1956, 118–26.
18. Margaret McFadden, "Warning—Do Not Risk Federal Arrest by Looking Glum!": Ballyhoo Magazine and the Cultural Politics of Early 1930s Humor," *Journal of American Culture* 26, no. 1 (March 2003): 124–34. Marchand, *Advertising the American Dream*, 312–14.
19. "Now That It Has a Sponsor," *Printers' Ink Monthly*, January 1939, 15.
20. Ben Bodec, "Radio in '32," *Variety*, January 3, 1933, 58.
21. *Variety* review, August 30, 1932, 50.
22. *Lucky Strike Program*, December 3, 1950.
23. "Waring All Set with Old Gold, Benny Maybe," *Variety*, January 24, 1933, 32.

24. *Chevrolet Program*, March 3, 1933.

25. Ben Bodec, "Radio in '32," *Variety*, January 3, 1933, 17; June 1933 review of Chevrolet program, *Forum*, no page, in Benny Scrapbooks, Box 90, Press clips 1932–1933, Benny Papers, American Heritage Center, University of Wyoming.

26. *Chevrolet Program*, May 23, 1933 script, Benny Papers, UCLA Library Special Collections.

27. Benny show review, *Variety*, October 10, 1933, 37.

28. Beverly Kimes, *Chevrolet, a History from 1911* (Cherry Hill, NJ: Automobile Quarterly, 1986), 70.

29. *Variety*, January 9, 1934, 33; *Variety*, February 27, 1934, 1.

30. "When the New Prez Likes Soft Music, Brother, Its Soft Music or Else," *Variety*, February 27, 1934, 1. "Dropping Jack Benny as Sales at Height Irks Chevy Dealers," *Variety* March 13, 1934, 29.

31. "Kindergarten for Sponsors," *Sponsor*, June 18, 1951, 22–25, 56.

32. "Shortage of Comedians and Time Hits GM, Which Eyes Jack Benny," *Billboard*, August 11, 1934, 7.

33. Bertha Brainard to Niles Trammell, February 17, 1934, NBC papers, Wisconsin Historical Society, Box 24, folder 11.

34. "Air Briefs," *Billboard*, March 3, 1934, 13.

35. Letters to the editor, *Radio Mirror*, October 1934, 54. *General Tire Program*, April 27, 1934.

36. *General Tire Program*, September 28, 1934, script. Benny Papers, UCLA Special Collections.

37. Jim Ramsburg, *Network Radio Ratings 1932–1953* (Jefferson, NC: McFarland, 2012), 23.

38. "Let Them Eat Cake," *Fortune*, October 1934, v 10, 68–75, 122, 124, 126, 129–30, 132, 135, 137.

39. Meyers, *A Word from Our Sponsor*, 152–54.

40. "Let Them Eat Cake," *Fortune*.

41. Fox, *The Mirror Makers*, 157.

42. *Jell-O Program*, October 21, 1934 script, Benny Papers, UCLA Special Collections.

43. *Kiplinger's Personal Finance*, July 1962, 6.

44. *Fortnight*, November 12, 1951, 28, quoted in *Selected Radio and Television Criticism*, ed. Anthony Slide (Metuchen, NJ: Scarecrow, 1987), 98–99.

45. Don Wilson, "Introduction," *Modern Radio Advertising*, ed. Charles Wolfe (New York: Printer's Ink, 1953) 537–38.

46. *Jell-O Program*, March 8, 1936.

47. Wolfe, *Modern Radio Advertising*, 44.

48. *Jell-O Program*, April 16, 1939.

49. Marsha Cassidy, "Touch, Taste, Breath: Synesthesia and Sense Memory and the Selling of Cigarettes on Television, 1948–1971," in *Media Convergence History*, ed. Janet Staiger and Sabine Hake (New Brunswick, NJ: Rutgers University Press, 2009), 34–45; Bruce Lenthall, *Radio's America: The Great Depression and the Rise of*

Modern Mass Culture (Chicago: Chicago University Press, 2007). Jason Loviglio, "Sound Effects: Gender, Voice and Cultural Work of NPR," *Radio Journal* 5 (2007): 2–3, 67–81.

50. "Jack Benny's Vacation Broadcast," *Radio Mirror*, September 1937, 14.

51. "Medal Award for Excellence to Young & Rubicam," *Advertising and Selling*, vol. 30, February 15, 1940, 70.

52. Ad for *A Night at the Opera*, *Variety*, November 6, 1935, 45–46.

53. Review of Paramount Theater, *Billboard*, July 8, 1939, 24.

54. Bertha Brainard to Sidney Strotz, December 14, 1938, NBC Papers, Wisconsin Historical Society, Box 94, file 26.

55. "Should You Hitch Your Product to a Star," *Sales Management*, March 1, 1939.

56. "Thru Sugar's Domino," *Billboard*, April 4. 1936, 24.

57. "Ad Group Honored for Achievements," *New York Times*, February 25, 1937, 40.

58. "Town Hall of Air Chosen for Award," *New York Times*, May 5, 1938, 26; Also Warren Dygert, *Radio as an Advertising Medium* (New York: McGraw Hill, 1939).

59. "Medal Award for Excellence to Young & Rubicam," *Advertising and Selling*, vol. 30, February 15, 1940, 70.

60. Everhard Meade, "Future Role of the Adv. Agency in Radio and TV Programming," *Variety*, January 4, 1950, 102; John McDonough, "Y&R at 75," *Advertising Age* 68, no. 44 (November 2, 1998).

61. Weaver interview, *Sponsor*, September 2, 1963, 33.

62. *Town Hall Tonight*, December 30, 1936 script, 11–12, Fred Allen Papers, Boston Public Library.

63. S. I. Steinhauser, "Ben Bernie and Jack Benny Plan Two Gun Feud with Allen," *Pittsburgh Post-Gazette*, February 4, 1937, 71.

64. Fred Allen Papers, Boston Public Library.

65. S. I. Steinhauser, "Increased Popularity is Fred Allen Reward for Jack Benny Feud," *Pittsburgh Press*, March 7, 1937, 48; "Riding the Airwaves with BCL," *Milwaukee Journal*, March 18, 1937, 34.

66. "Benny Renewal Marred by Clash Over Production," *Billboard*, March 16, 1940, 9.

67. "Rising Radio Sales Help Meteor," *Literary Digest*, n.d., Benny 1937 scrapbook, Benny Papers, American Heritage Center, University of Wyoming, Box 110.

68. *Variety*, September 29, 1944.

69. Christopher, "Stars Shine Best When Polished."

70. "Battle of Agencies over Jack Benny," *Broadcasting*, March 10, 1941, 18.

71. "Benny-Smith Swap Products," *Variety*, March 4, 1942, 26.

72. "Why Sponsors Change Agencies," *Sponsor*, December 1947, 15–17, 47–49; "Rising Radio Sales Help Meteor," *Literary Digest*, March 1937; Benny 1937 scrapbook, Benny Papers, American Heritage Center, University of Wyoming, Box 110.

73. Christopher, "Stars Shine Best When Polished"; "Benny's Break with General Foods, Y&R, Laid to Bad Exploitation Job," *Variety*, March 1, 1944.

74. "Jack Benny Divorcing Grape Nuts for Pall Mall and $3,900,000 Deal?" *Variety*, February 23, 1944, 1, 23.

75. Contracts between Benny and American Tobacco Company, April 10, 1944, Benny Papers, University of California at Los Angeles, Box 88, file 1.

76. "George Washington Hill Dead; Great Exponent of Advertising," *Printers Ink* 216 (September 20, 1946) 49, 144.

77. Alan Havig, "Frederick Wakeman's *The Hucksters* and the Post War Debate over Commercial Radio," *Journal of Broadcasting* 28, no. 2 (Spring 1984): 192.

78. *Sponsor*, December 1946, 46.

79. "Hollywood Inside," *Variety*, August 27, 1947, 2.

80. "GW Hill Repeats as LS-MFT Slogan Builds into Top Laugh Gag," *Variety*, January 19, 1944, 45.

81. "GW Hill Switches from Big Spot Advertising," *Variety*, November 8, 1944.

82. "Luckies Reported Dropping Kyser," *Variety*, October 18, 1944, 1.

83. Jack Hellman, "Light and Airy," *Variety*, October 23, 1944, 4.

84. "LSMFT for Benny," *Variety*, August 24, 1944.

85. Richard W. Pollay, "Targeting Tactics in Selling Smoke: Youthful Aspects of 20th Century Cigarette Advertising," *Journal of Marketing Theory and Practice* (Winter 1995): 9.

86. Review of Benny program, *Variety*, October 4, 1944, 24; Christopher, "Stars Shine Best When Polished."

87. Review of Benny radio program, *Woman's Day*, January 1945, Benny scrapbook 1945, Benny Papers, American Heritage Center, University of Wyoming, Box 116.

88. George Washington Hill to Jack Benny, October 20, 1944, Benny Papers, University of California at Los Angeles, Special Collections, Box 98.

89. Jack Hellman, "Light and Airy," *Variety*, November 20, 1944, 4.

90. "Don Wilson, 81, Announcer Who Was Jack Benny's Foil," *New York Times*, April 27, 1982, B8.

91. Jack Hellman, "Light and Airy," *Variety*, October 11, 1946, 8.

92. Jack Hellman, "Light and Airy," *Variety*, October 11, 1946, 8.

93. "You Can't Say That!" *Sponsor*, July 1947, 45–46.

94. *Lucky Strike Program*, October 16, 1949.

95. *Lucky Strike Program*, May 16, 1952.

96. *Lucky Strike Program*, March 21, 1948; November 23, 1947; May 30, 1948; April 25, 1948; January 12, 1947.

CHAPTER 7

1. "Seven Wonders Named," n.d. [1937], Benny scrapbook 1937, Benny Papers, American Heritage Center, University of Wyoming; "Hollywood Inside," *Variety*, January 21, 1937, 2. Apparently, the book apparently was never published.

2. Philip K Scheuer, "Stars Reap Profit from Side Money; Commercial Plugs and Radio Acts Fill Coffers of Film Folk," *Los Angeles Times*, May 2, 1937, C1.

3. "There's a Difference: Movies and Radio Are Neatly Weighed by a Jester Who Approves of Both," *Detroit Free Press*, n.d. [1936], Benny scrapbook 1936, Benny Papers, American Heritage Center, University of Wyoming.

4. Caroll Nye, "Galaxy of Radio Stars Coming to Hollywood in Summer and Fall Series," *Los Angeles Times*, May 25, 1936, 14.

5. Michele Hilmes, *Hollywood and Broadcasting: From Radio to Cable* (Urbana: University of Illinois Press, 1990).

6. See Jonathan Gray, Judd Ethan Ruggill, "Convergence: Always Already, Already." *Cinema Journal* 48, no. 3 (Spring 2009): 105–6.

7. Hilmes, *Hollywood and Broadcasting*; Ruggill, "Convergence," 107.

8. Hilmes, *Hollywood and Broadcasting*, 1.

9. Rick Jewell, "Hollywood and Radio: Competition and Partnership in the 1930s." *Historical Journal of Film, Radio and Television* 4, no. 2 (1984): 125–41.

10. Kathryn Fuller-Seeley, "Dish Night at the Movies: Exhibitors and Female Audiences during the Great Depression," in *The American Film History Reader*, ed. Jon Lewis and Eric Smoodin (London: Routledge, 2014), 246–75.

11. Hilmes, *Radio Voices*.

12. Hilmes, *Hollywood and Broadcasting*.

13. Henry Jenkins, *What Made Pistachio Nuts? Early Sound Comedy and the Vaudeville Aesthetic* (New York: Columbia University Press, 1992).

14. Jack Jamison, "This Is the Life; Jack Benny Doesn't Laugh at Life—but He Lets Life Laugh at Him!" *Radio Guide*, July 10, 1937, 8–9.

15. Hilmes, *Radio Voices*, 49–77.

16. Laura Leff, "Do You Know," *Jack Benny Times* 27, no. 3-4 (May–August 2012): 6.

17. Weldon Melick, "Genius in a Fog," *Radio Mirror*, February 1937, 79.

18. *Canada Dry Program*, May 25, 1932, script in Benny Papers, UCLA Special Collections.

19. Hilmes, *Hollywood and Broadcasting*, 66–67.

20. *General Tire Program*, June 8, 1934, script in Benny Papers, UCLA Special Collections.

21. "All Jack Benny Needs Is More Time for Jobs," *San Francisco Call*, no date, Benny 1934/35 scrapbook, Benny Papers, American Heritage Center, University of Wyoming.

22. Hilmes, *Hollywood and Broadcasting*, 69.

23. Don Gilman to John Royal, January 26, 1937, report on conversation with Will Hays. NBC Papers, Wisconsin Historical Society Box 93, file 15.

24. Dan Wheeler, "The Curious Case of Radio's Hidden Censorship," *Radio Mirror*, March 1937, 34–35, 75.

25. Irving A. Fein, *Jack Benny: An Intimate Biography* (New York: G. P. Putnam's Sons, 1976), 182–83.

26. "To Sunny California" *New York Times*, December 22, 1935, xx, 1."California Beckons," *New York Times*, December 20, 1936, section xx, i, "California Southland" *New York Times*, May 2, 1939, section xx, 6;

27. "California Southland," *New York Times* May 2, 1939, section xx, 6.
28. Hilmes, *Radio Voices*, 4–5, 11, 13.
29. "Benny at Breakfast," *New York Times*, April 28, 1940, 128.
30. Hollywood: Tourists Accommodated," *New York Times*, March 22, 1936, X4; Joseph Taylor, "Film Lots Play Host," *New York Times*, April 10, 1938, I59.
31. *Los Angeles: A Guide to the City and Its Environs* (Works Progress Administration, NY: Hastings House, 1941).
32. Janet MacRorie to Lenox Lohr, December 26, 1937, NBC Papers, Wisconsin Historical Society, Box 92, file 43.
33. "California Southland."
34. "Main Street," *Albany(NY) Evening Recorder*, July 17, 1941, 4.
35. "Benny Broadcasts Create Furor," *Palm Springs Desert Sun*, February 21, 1941.
36. Hilmes, *Broadcasting and Radio*; Hilmes, *Radio Voices*; and Meyers *A Word from Our Sponsor*.
37. Alton Cook, "Rule Film Stars on Radio; Movie Companies to Take Full Charge of Their Stars' Activities on the Air," *New York World Telegram*, March 9, 1937.
38. "Pix-Air Tie Dubious: Harrington Predicts Star Sponsor Grief," *Variety*, October 30, 1936, 1, 5.
39. "Hollywood Challenges the East as Center of Radio," *New York Times*, October 1937. Orrin E. Dunlap Jr., "The Swing to California," *New York Times*, October 17, 1937, 190.
40. Hilmes, *Hollywood and Broadcasting*, 72–73.
41. Catherine Jurca, *Hollywood 1938: Motion Pictures' Greatest Year* (Berkeley: University of California Press, 2012).
42. Don Gilman to John Royal, January 26, 1937, NBC Papers, Wisconsin Historical Society, Box 93, file 15.
43. Keith Kiggins to John Royal, October 28, 1938, NBC Papers, Wisconsin Historical Society, Box 94, file 10.
44. Janet MacRorie, "Radio's Contributions to the Motion Picture Industry," December 1, 1938, NBC Papers, Wisconsin Historical Society, Box 94, file 10,
45. Jurca, *Hollywood 1938*.
46. "Directors Last Long in Filmland," *Los Angeles Times*, May 29, 1938; Joe Pearson, "Mark Sandrich," *Hollywood Motion Picture Review*, July 9, 1938, both in Sandrich scrapbook, Margaret Herrick Library, Academy of Motion Picture Arts and Sciences, Mark Sandrich Papers.
47. *Motion Picture Herald*, July 17, 1939.
48. "Bally Rings Bell," *Variety*, October 30, 1939, 204. "H'wood Junket-Minded for Its Big Pix," *Variety*, October 30, 1940, 8.
49. *Variety*, June 9, 1939, 2. "General Foods Pony Up, Saves Benny Deal Fete for Waukeganites," *Variety*, June 21, 1939, 8.
50. Bosley Crowther, "There's Nothing Like a Gala 'World Premiere'," *New York Times*, April 21, 1940. "Jack Benny Makes Good in His Old Home Town," *Variety*, June 26, 1939, 3.

51. *Man About Town*, Paramount Studios advertisement, n.d. [1939], in Sandrich scrapbooks, Margaret Herrick Library, Academy of Motion Picture Arts and Sciences, Mark Sandrich Papers; *Box Office Digest*, June 29, 1939.

52. Louise Barber, "Mark Sandrich," *Hollywood Motion Picture Review*, August 5, 1939.

53. Preview of *Man About Town*, *Variety*, June 8, 1939, 3.

54. *Picture Reports*, June 8, 1939, *Man About Town* script, June 24, 1939, Sandrich scrapbook f113, Margaret Herrick Library, Academy of Motion Picture Arts and Sciences, Mark Sandrich Papers.

55. *Motion Picture Herald*, July 17, 1939.

56. *Box Office*, June 17, 1939, 27.

57. Archer Winsten, review of *Man About Town*, *New York Post*, June 29, 1939, Benny scrapbook 1939, Benny Papers, American Heritage Center, University of Wyoming.

58. *Variety*, May 3, 1940, 2.

59. "Here Is What General Foods Is Doing," *Buck Benny Rides Again* pressbook, in Paramount pressbook collection, Margaret Herrick Library, Academy of Motion Picture Arts and Sciences.

60. "Wanger Strong Advocate of Radio as a Pre-selling Medium for New Pix; Cites Buck Benny, Singapore," *Variety*, September 18, 1940, 8.

61. "Benny Film New Tops at NY Paramount," *Box Office*, May 6, 1940; "Freeman Urges Exhibs. to Build Up Attendance," *Film Daily*, June 20, 1940, 1, 10.

62. Review of *Buck Benny Rides Again*, *Variety*, April 17, 1940, 13.

63. Jimmy Starr, *Buck Benny Rides Again* review, *Los Angeles Herald Express*, April 11, 1940; Nelson Bell, review of *Buck Benny Rides Again*, *Washington Post*, May 17, 1940, 13; Philip K Scheuer, "Jack Benny Comedy Hero in 'Western'," *Los Angeles Times*, April 26, 1940, A10.

64. *Box Office Digest*, April 15, 1940.

65. Kenneth McCaleb, "Screening a Radio Program," *New York Mirror*, April 21, 1940, 13.

66. B. R. Crisler, "The Screen: Buck Benny Rises Again (Through a Riot) at the Paramount," *New York Times*, April 25, 1940, 28.

67. *Variety*, November 13, 1940, 1, 56.

68. "Boy Meets Facts" *Time*, July 21, 1940; "Wanger Strong Advocate of Radio as a Pre-selling Medium for New Pix."

69. "Crosby, Benny, Colman Paramount's Male Tops," *Variety*, January 3, 1940, 29.

70. *Today's Cinema*, London, May 31, 1940; *Daily Film Renter*, London, June 3, 1940, Sandrich scrapbooks, Margaret Herrick Library, Academy of Motion Picture Arts and Sciences, Mark Sandrich Papers.

71. *Washington Times Herald*, May 7, 1940.

72. *Box Office Digest*, January 8, 1941. Sandrich scrapbooks, Margaret Herrick Library, Academy of Motion Picture Arts and Sciences, Mark Sandrich Papers.

73. *Love Thy Neighbor*, Paramount Pressbook Collection, Margaret Herrick library.

74. Review of *Love Thy Neighbor*, *Variety*, December 25, 1940, 16.
75. Bosley Crowther, "The Screen: *Love Thy Neighbor*," *New York Times*, December 18, 1940, 32.
76. Bosley Crowther, "Out of Thin Air," *New York Times*, December 22, 1940.
77. Crowther, "Out of Thin Air," 103.

CHAPTER 8

1. "King Benny," *Time*, February 12, 1940.
2. George Rosen, "1948 Peak Year for Radio," *Variety*, October 25, 1948, 155; See also Alan Havig, "Critic from Within: Fred Allen Views Radio," *Journal of Popular Culture* 12, no. 2 (1978): 328–40.
3. Ralph Lewis Smith, *A Study of the Professional Criticism of Broadcasting in the United States 1920–1955* (New York: Arno, 1979).
4. Amanda Lotz, "On 'Television Criticism': The Pursuit of the Critical Examination of a Popular Art," *Popular Communication* 6 (2008): 20.
5. Cleveland Amory, "Jack Benny's $400 Yaks," *Saturday Evening Post*, November 8, 1948, 25, 81, 82, 84, 86, 89.
6. "Radio, Vaudeville & Camps," *Time*, April 13, 1942.
7. "By Request," *Time*, February 11, 1946; "The Lower Globaler," *Time*, October 18, 1943; "Entertainers," *Time*, October 11, 1943.
8. "It's Benny Two to One," *Newsweek*, March 31, 1947, 66–68.
9. "Radio Must Train 'em to Solve Problem of Vanishing Writers," *Variety*, July 14, 1943.
10. "Benny, Sans Writers, Others to Go, May Quit Radio Work," *Variety*. June 17, 1943, 1, 7.
11. "Deny Benny Asks Leave from Air," *Variety*, June 23, 1943.
12. *Billboard* reported: "Four new writers have joined Jack Benny show: Cy Howard, Milt Josefberg, 'Tack' Tackaberry and George Balzer will handle scripting" (October 2, 1943). Cy lasted only about thirteen weeks before leaving, and Sam Perrin would become the fourth writer.
13. *Variety*, December 15, 1942, 3.
14. "Hollywood Inside," *Variety*, May 29, 1945, 2.
15. Jack Gould, "Kate and Jack," *New York Times*, October 15, 1944, X7.
16. "Hollywood Inside," *Variety*, April 12, 1945, 2.
17. "It's Benny Two to One," *Newsweek*, March 31, 1947, 66–68. Jack Hellman, "Light and Airy," *Variety*, November 1, 1945, 4.
18. "It's Benny Two to One," *Newsweek*, March 31, 1947, 66–68.
19. "One-Man Crowd," *Time*, February 18, 1946.
20. Laura Leff claims that the first time Mel Blanc did the Maxwell engine was March 2, 1947. *39 Forever, Second Edition, Volume 2, Radio October 1942–May 1955* (North Charleston, SC: Book Surge, 2006), 250.

21. Amory, "Jack Benny's $400 Yaks," 84.
22. Jack Hellman, "Light and Airy," *Variety*, December 3, 1945, 4.
23. "Mr. Benny Relaxes," *New York Times* May 26, 1946, x7.
24. Amory, "Jack Benny's $400 Yaks," 86.
25. Jack Hellman, "Light and Airy," *Variety*, December 6, 1945, 4.
26. Jack Hellman, "Light and Airy," *Variety*, December 13, 1945, 4.
27. *Lucky Strike Program*, February 3, 1946.
28. Jack Hellman, "Light and Airy," *Variety*, January 10, 1946, 6.
29. Jack Hellman, "Light and Airy," *Variety*, January 28, 1946, 6.
30. *Lucky Strike Program*, January 27, 1946, script in Jack Benny Papers, UCLA Special Collections, Box 30, folder 4.
31. George Rosen, "Dialers Sour on Free Sugar," *Variety*, February 6, 1946, 1.
32. "Mr. Benny Relaxes," *New York Times* May 26, 1946, x7.
33. "Most Improved Numbers over Last Season in Past Few Weeks," *Variety*, March 27, 1946, 8.
34. "It's Benny Two to One," *Newsweek*, March 31, 1947, 66–68.
35. Robert J. Landry, "Wanted: Radio Critics," *Public Opinion Quarterly* 4, no. 4 (December 1, 1940): 620–630.
36. Landry, "Wanted: Radio Critics," 625.
37. Landry, "Wanted: Radio Critics," 629.
38. Gerd Horten, *Radio Goes to War: The Cultural Politics of Propaganda during World War II* (Berkeley: University of California Press, 2002).
39. Robert J. Landry, "The Improbability of Radio Criticism," *Hollywood Quarterly* 2, no. 1 (October 1946): 66–70.
40. Ralph Lewis Smith, *A Study of the Professional Criticism of Broadcasting in the US 1920–1955* (New York: Arno, 1979).
41. "Critic on the Hearth," *Theatre Arts*, January 1951, 32–36.
42. Smith, *Study of the Professional Criticism of Broadcasting*, 32.
43. Review of *Maxwell House Coffee Time*, *Variety*, October 6, 1948, 30.
44. "Appraising the Radio Editors," *Variety*, January 23, 1946, 25.
45. Orrin Dunlap, "Altering the Acts Is a Trick; Radio's 1935–36 Line Up Follows Last Year's Show Almost to a 'T'." *New York Times*, September 8, 1935, XII.
46. George Rosen, "Radio Programming Deadened," *Variety*, August 15, 1945, 23.
47. "Let's Face It," *Variety*, March 13, 1946, 35.
48. *Variety*, March 1946, 25.
49. "Gags Have Grown Up," n.d. [1945], 9–11, Benny scrapbook 116, American Heritage Center, University of Wyoming, Jack Benny Papers.
50. Gilbert Seldes, "Notes and Queries," *Esquire*, March 1946, 78.
51. Jack Hellman, "Light and Airy," *Variety*, February 21, 1946, 6; Milt Josefsburg, *The Jack Benny Show* (New York: Arlington House, 1977), 205.
52. John Crosby, "The Art of the Insult," *New York Herald Tribune*, October 14, 1946, 27.
53. John Crosby, "The Art of the Insult."

54. Smith, *Study of the Professional Criticism of Broadcasting*, 238, quoting Jack Gould, "How Comic Is Radio Comedy," *New York Times*, Sunday magazine, November 21, 1948.

55. Gilbert Seldes, "Actor for a Night," *Esquire*, June 1946, 107–8.

56. Josefsburg, *The Jack Benny Show*, 206.

57. John Crosby, "In the Footsteps of Harold Lloyd," *New York Herald Tribune*, May 6, 1946; "Don Quinn vs. Sinclair Lewis," *New York Herald Tribune*, May 20, 1946.

58. "Inside Stuff—Radio," *Variety*, May 22, 1946, 38.

59. John Crosby, "Breakfast with Freddie and Tallulah," *New York Herald Tribune*, May 19, 1946.

60. *Variety*, May 15, 1946, 49.

61. Crosby, "Don Quinn vs. Sinclair Lewis."

62. John Crosby, "Fourteen Years of Jack Benny," *New York Herald Tribune*, May 30, 1946. The Benny show had been broadcast May 26, 1946.

63. "Crosby Column Spurs Newspapers Generally," *Variety*, August 21, 1946, 35.

64. *Variety*, August 21, 1946, 35.

65. "Reporter with a Hammer," *Newsweek*, vol. 28, September 16, 1946, 66, 69; "For Listeners Only," *Time*, August 5, 1946.

66. *Billboard*, October 12, 1946, 3.

67. John Crosby, "The King Is Dead! Long Live the Dean!" *New York Herald Tribune*, October 7, 1946.

68. John Crosby, "Burns and Allen," *New York Herald Tribune*, September 18, 1946.

69. John Crosby, "Twilight of the Gods," *New York Herald Tribune*, November 6, 1946; "Twilight of the Gods, Part 2," *New York Herald Tribune*, November 7, 1946.

70. Jack Hellman, "Light and Airy," *Variety*, October 31, 1946, 6.

71. John Crosby, "The Fall Fashions in Jokes," *New York Herald Tribune*, September 30, 1946.

72. John Crosby, "The Nelsons of Rogers Road," *New York Herald Tribune*, January 19, 1946.

73. *New York Herald Tribune*, December 30, 1946, 31.

74. "Crosby's First Anniversary," *Newsweek*, May 19, 1947, 66.

75. Gilbert Seldes, "Actor for a Night," 107.

76. Josefsburg, *The Jack Benny Show*, 206.

77. John Crosby, "The Jack Benny Mystery," *New York Herald Tribune*, January 6, 1947.

78. *Lucky Strike Program*, January 5, 1947.

79. John Crosby, "Innocents in Hollywood," *New York Herald Tribune*, February 19 and 20, 1947.

80. "Don't Look Now . . . But Your Radio's Static," *Variety*, October 8, 1947, 25.

81. John Crosby, "Radio and Who Makes It," *Atlantic Monthly*, January 1948, 23–29.

82. Crosby, "Radio and Who Makes It," 25.
83. Crosby, "Radio and Who Makes It," 26–27.
84. Jack Gould, "The Peabody Awards," *New York Times*, March 24, 1946; John E. Reid Jr., "Half Century of Peabody Radio: A Descriptive Analysis," *Journal of Radio Studies* (1992): 143–50.
85. Gould, "How Comic Is Radio Comedy."
86. Jack Benny, "Gentlemen of Depress," *Variety*, January 5, 1949, 8.
87. John Crosby, "Down with the Critics," *New York Herald Tribune*, January 7, 1949.
88. Crosby, "Radio and Who Makes It," 29.

CHAPTER 9

1. Kathryn H Fuller-Seeley, "Learning to Live with Television: Technology, Gender, and America's Early TV Audiences," in *The Columbia History of Television*, ed. Gary Edgerton (New York: Columbia University Press, 2007), 91–110.
2. John Crosby, *New York Herald Tribune*, November 26, 1948.
3. http://www.tvhistory.tv/Annual_TV_Households_50–78.JPG.
4. Harriet Van Horne, "TV's Unkind to Benny, on Third Try," *New York World Telegram and Sun*, April 2, 1951.
5. James L Baughman, "Nice Guys Last Fifteen Seasons: Jack Benny on Television, 1950–1965," *Film & History* 30, no. 2 (2000): 29–39. Jack Benny and Joan Benny, *Sunday Nights at Seven: The Jack Benny Story* (New York: Warner Books, 1990), 236–44; Ralph Lewis Smith, *A Study of the Professional Criticism of Broadcasting in the US 1920–1955* (New York: Arno, 1979), 249: Smith says it was painless; Irving A. Fein, *Jack Benny: An Intimate Biography* (New York: G. P. Putnam's Sons, 1976), 142–44.
6. George Rosen, "Appraising the Video Comics," *Variety*, November 8, 1950, 59.
7. Janet Kern, "Televiews," *Chicago Herald American* (no date but presumably May 21, 1951); "Benny May Go All TV Next Year," Variety, January 24, 1952, 1.
8. John Dunning, *On the Air: The Encyclopedia of Old-Time Radio* (Oxford: Oxford University Press, 1998).
9. Gerard Jones, *Honey, I'm Home!: Sitcoms: Selling the American Dream* (New York: Macmillan, 1993). 50; Dunning, *On the Air*.
10. Jack Gould, "Radio and Television: Case of Fred Allen, TV's Problem Child, Who Has Failed to Attain His Proper Niche, Discussed," *New York Times*, October 31, 1951, 34; *Variety*, February 25, 1954.
11. "'Show for Show's Sake' Slogan As High Cost Precludes Top Talent Programs," *Variety*, May 14, 1947, 39.
12. "'Show for Show's Sake,'" 39.
13. Ben Gross, "Looking and Listening: Benny Reveals Secret," *New York Daily News*, undated article [1947], in Benny scrapbook 88, Benny Papers, American Heritage Center, University of Wyoming.

14. Virginia MacPherson, "Benny Fears Advent of Television" *The News*, Tonawanda NY, September 25, 1947.

15. George Rosen, "1948 Peak Year for Radio," *Variety*, October 25, 1948, 155.

16. See Tom Kemper, *Hidden Talent: The Emergence of Hollywood Agents* (Berkeley: University of California Press, 2010).

17. "Television Raids Scare Radio," *Variety*, April 28, 1948, 1.

18. Benny also credits Irving Fein, whom he had hired to handle PR but who became an astute business manager. Benny and Benny, *Sunday Nights at Seven*, 238.

19. "NBC 'Buys' Jack Benny for 4 Million," *Variety*, November 10, 1948, 1. See Eric Hoyt. "Hollywood and the Income Tax, 1929–1955," *Film History: An International Journal* 22, no. 1 (2010): 5–21.

20. Jack Hellman, "Light and Airy," *Variety*, November 18, 1948, 8.

21. See Pat Weaver, "If I Were Running the Network Again," *Sponsor*, August 26, 1963, 25–26.

22. Larry Christopher, "Stars Shine Best When Polished," *Broadcasting and Television*, October 1956, 118–26.

23. Thanks to Richard Simon for this link: http://taxfoundation.org/article/us-federal-individual-income-tax-rates-history-1913-2013-nominal-and-inflation-adjusted-brackets.

24. Jack Hellman, "Light and Airy," *Variety*, January 6, 1949, 6.

25. Laura Leff, *39 Forever, Second Edition, Volume 2, Radio October 1942–May 1955* (North Charleston, SC: Book Surge, 2006), 24–26.

26. Jack Hellman, "Light and Airy," *Variety*, January 6, 1949, 6.

27. Christopher, "Stars Shine Best When Polished."

28. "Benny Heading into Video; Aims Show for Tele When It's Ready for Him," *Variety*, December 30, 1948, 6.

29. Special *Los Angeles Times* section, March 8, 1949, Benny scrapbook 118, Benny Papers, American Heritage Center, University of Wyoming.

30. Jack Hellman, "Light and Airy," *Variety*, March 10, 1949, 6.

31. Arthur Altschul, "Jack Benny Considers His Future," *New York Times*, April 10, 1949, x9.

32. Altschul, "Jack Benny Considers His Future."

33. Larry Wolters, "Jack Benny Set for One Video Show a Month; It Will Be Vaudeville—and Expensive," *Chicago Tribune*, May 6, 1949, B13.

34. Jack Gould, "Television Lesson; Shows Should Be Staged for the Home Audience," *New York Times*, October 15, 1950, x13.

35. "Benny Passes Up All but Live Television Shows," *Variety*, July 26, 1949, 1, 11.

36. Jack Hellman, "Light and Airy," *Variety*, August 22, 1949, 6.

37. BBDO memo, July 26, 1949, from Wick Crider to Jack Donove about the American Tobacco account and a potential Benny TV show, found by Cynthia Meyers in Bruce Barton papers, box 75, American Tobacco folder, Wisconsin Historical Society, NBC Records.

38. Joe McCartney, "What Do You Think of Television, Mr. Allen?" *Life*, July 4, 1949, 69. See also discussion in Alan Havig, *Fred Allen's Radio Comedy*

(Philadelphia: Temple University Press, 1992) and Arthur Frank Wertheim, *Radio Comedy* (New York: Oxford University Press, 1979).

39. Evelyn Bigsby, "Year of Decision; Jack Benny Knows That Television Is Breathing Heavily Down His Neck. It Is Not a Question of Whether He Will Do It, But When," *Radio-Television Life*, October 20, 1949, 33, in Benny scrapbook 1949, Benny Papers, American Heritage Center, University of Wyoming.

40. Review of "The Big Show," *Variety*, November 6, 1950.

41. "Hooper Inaugurates His 'Shift of Accent' Ratings," *Variety*, March 22, 1950, 24; Crosby, *New York Herald Tribune*, November 26, 1948.

42. Douglas Gomery, *Shared Pleasures: A History of Moviegoing in America* (Madison: University of Wisconsin Press, 1992); Richard A. Easterlin, "The American Baby Boom In Historical Perspective," in *Population, Labor Force, and Long Swings in Economic Growth: The American Experience* (New York: Columbia University Press, 1968), 76–110.

43. Wayne Oliver, "TV to Hit 5,000,000 Sets Soon; Keeping a Dizzy Pace," *Binghamton (NY) Sunday Press*, March 5, 1950, 10C; *Variety*, March 22, 1950, 24.

44. Christopher, "Stars Shine Best When Polished."

45. Benny TV program Oct 28 1950," script located in *Truth Tobacco Industry Documents*, https://industrydocuments.library.ucsf.edu/tobacco/docs/#id=kkgb0020.

46. "Big Numbers for First Broadcast," *Telecasting*, November 13, 1950, 68.

47. Janet Kern, "Televiews," *Chicago Herald American*, October 31, 1950. Jack Benny scrapbook 1950–52, Box 116. Jack Benny papers, American Heritage Center, University of Wyoming.

48. Dwight Newton, "Day and Night with Radio and Television," *San Francisco Examiner*, November 15, 1950, Jack Benny scrapbook 1950–52, Box 116, Jack Benny papers, American Heritage Center, University of Wyoming.

49. Jack Gould, "Jack Benny Show Has Video Debut," *New York Times*, October 30, 1950, 33.

50. Review of *Jack Benny Program*, *Bridgeport Herald*, November 1950, Jack Benny scrapbook 1950–52, Box 116. Jack Benny papers, American Heritage Center, University of Wyoming.

51. Review of *Jack Benny Program*, *Billboard*, November 4, 1950, 12.

52. John Crosby, "Jack Benny Makes His Bow," *New York Herald Tribune*, November 14, 1950, Jack Benny scrapbook 1950–52, Box 116. Jack Benny papers, American Heritage Center, University of Wyoming.

53. George Rosen, "A B C Ds of Video Comedy," *Variety*, December 13, 1950, 1, 43.

54. Goodman Ace, "TV and Radio: Big Bargain from Waukegan," *Saturday Review of Literature*, November 11, 1950, Jack Benny scrapbook 1950–52, Box 116. Jack Benny papers, American Heritage Center, University of Wyoming.

55. *Jack Benny Program*, January 28, 1951 script, in *Truth Tobacco Industry Documents*, https://industrydocuments.library.ucsf.edu/tobacco/docs/#id=kkgb0020.

56. *Lucky Strike Program*, January 5, 1947.

57. Mary Wood, "Benny's Turkey a Very, Very Sad Affair," *Cincinnati Post*, January 30, 1951, Jack Benny scrapbook 1950–52, Box 116, Jack Benny papers, American Heritage Center, University of Wyoming.

58. Larry Wolters, "That L-O-N-G TV Kiss Outlasted Its Welcome," *Chicago Tribune*, February 5, 1951, Jack Benny scrapbook 1950–52, Box 116. Jack Benny papers, American Heritage Center, University of Wyoming.

59. "Now Ladd Has Earned Critic's Purple Heart," *Louisville Courier Journal*, February 11, 1951, Jack Benny scrapbook 1950–52, Box 116. Jack Benny papers, American Heritage Center, University of Wyoming.

60. "A Reader Finds Women in Video Too Revealing," *Chicago Tribune*, February 11, 1951, N-A9.

61. "A Reader Finds Women in Video Too Revealing."

62. Anthony La Camera, "TV Easy Step for Jack Benny," *Boston Advertiser*, December 16, 1951.

63. Susan Murray, *Hitch Your Antenna to the Stars: Early Television and Broadcast Stardom* (London: Routledge, 2013), 95–99.

64. Review of *Jack Benny Program*, *Variety*, December 19, 1951, 27.

65. Review of *Jack Benny Program*, *Billboard*, October 18, 1952, Jack Benny scrapbook 1950–52, Box 116, Jack Benny papers, American Heritage Center, University of Wyoming.

66. Review of *Jack Benny Program*, *Billboard*, January 10, 1953, Jack Benny scrapbook 1952–59, Box 23, Jack Benny papers, American Heritage Center, University of Wyoming.

67. Arthur Marx, "No. 1 Master of Timing," *New York Times Magazine*, February 13, 1955, 207.

68. "Benny in Skirts Is a Scream," *Hollywood Reporter*, April 15, 1954, Jack Benny scrapbook 1952–59, Box 23, Jack Benny papers, American Heritage Center, University of Wyoming.

69. Jack Hellman, "Light and Airy," *Variety*, December 13, 1951, 8.

70. "Tobacco on the Air," *Sponsor*, September 1948, 227–29, 94–97.

71. "Lucky Strike, CBS Beseech Benny to Continue in Radio," *Variety*, February 18, 1952, 14; Jack Hellman, "Light and Airy," *Variety*, March 17, 1952, 6.

72. "Jack Benny Program Budget Cut to 18 G," *Variety*, April 4, 1952, 1.

73. "BBDO's Ben Duffy Pleads with Benny to Continue Radio," *Variety*, March 7, 1952, 9; Review of Benny show, *Variety*, September 17, 1952, 38.

74. Walter Ames, "Top Names Are Still on Radio," *Los Angeles Times*, November 22, 1953.

75. Laura Leff, *39 Forever: Volume 2, Radio October 1942–May 1955*, second edition (North Charleston SC: Book Surge, 2006)6, 24–26.

76. Ruth Elgutter, "Fireside Viewing," *Toledo (OH) Times*, March 11, 1952; Jack Hellman, "Light and Airy," *Variety*, January 18, 1954, 10; "In TV, Each Viewer's a Critic; Jack Benny Finds 'Strain' Mounting," *Variety*, January 26, 1954, 1.

77. Jack Hellman, "Light and Airy," *Variety*, March 31, 1955, 11; Goodman Ace, "TV and Radio: A Penny's Worth of Jelly Beans," *Saturday Review of Literature*,

January 8, 1955, in Benny scrapbook 1955, Benny Papers, American Heritage Center, University of Wyoming; Larry Wolters, "End of an Era—Jack Benny Is Quitting Radio," *Chicago Tribune*, August 27, 1955, C1.

78. Goodman Ace, "A Penny's Worth of Jelly Beans."

79. Donald Freeman, "Radio Still Holds Imprint of TV 1959," *San Diego Union*, September 30, 1956, np in Benny scrapbook 88, Benny Papers, American Heritage Center, University of Wyoming.

80. Review of *Jack Benny Hour*, *Variety*, March 20, 1959, 26; Review of *Jack Benny Hour*, *Variety*, March 25, 1959, 50; Cecil Smith, "Benny's Birthday Bash Was a Beaut," *Los Angeles Times*, February 18, 1969, F11.

CONCLUSION

1. Peter Kovacs, "Big Tobacco and Broadcasting, 1924–1960: An Interdisciplinary History," PhD diss., University of Texas at Austin, 2017.

2. Richard Zoglin, *Comedy at the Edge: How Stand-Up in the 1970s Changed America* (New York: Bloomsbury, 2009).

3. Johnny Carson's 1949 honors thesis, "How to Write Comedy for Radio," is available in digital form through the University of Nebraska's website: http://digitalcommons.unl.edu/theaterstudent/1/.

4. Jack Benny and Joan Benny, *Sunday Nights at Seven: The Jack Benny Story* (New York: Warner Books, 1990).

5. *Kiplinger's Personal Finance*, July 1962, 6, notes "Jell-O will again sponsor his banter after a 20-year lapse (though some people think he's never had any other sponsor."

6. Derek Kompere, *Rerun Nation: How Repeats Invented American Television* (London: Routledge, 2006).

7. Avi Santo, *Selling the Silver Bullet: The Lone Ranger and Transmedia Brand Licensing* (Austin: University of Texas Press, 2015).

8. Eleanor Patterson, "Radio Redux: The Persistence of Soundwork in the Post Network Era," PhD diss., University of Wisconsin, 2016.

BIBLIOGRAPHY

ARCHIVAL COLLECTIONS

American Heritage Center, University of Wyoming
    Jack Benny Papers
    Irving Fein Papers
University of California at Los Angeles, Special Collections
    Jack Benny Papers
Margaret Herrick Library, Academy of Motion Picture Arts and Sciences
    Mark Sandrich Papers
    Production Code Administration Papers
    Paramount Press Book Collection
Wisconsin Historical Society
    NBC Records
Library of Congress, Division of Recorded Sound
    NBC Records
Boston Public Library
    Fred Allen Papers

TRADE PUBLICATIONS

Billboard
Broadcasting
Film Daily
Fortune
Motion Picture Herald
Sponsor
Variety

FAN PUBLICATIONS

Radio and Television Best
Radio Guide
Radio Mirror
Radio Stars
Radioland
Screen
Tower Radio
Tune In

PERIODICALS

Atlanta Daily World
Baltimore Afro-American
Boston Globe
California Eagle
Chicago Defender
Chicago Tribune
Los Angeles Sentinel
Los Angeles Times
New Amsterdam News
New York Herald Tribune
New York Times
Pittsburgh Courier
Washington Post

MAGAZINES

Colliers
Ebony
Liberty
Life
Look
Newsweek
Pageant
Saturday Evening Post
Scribners
Time

BOOKS AND ARTICLES

Allen, Fred. *Treadmill to Oblivion*. Boston: Little Brown, 1954.

Allen, Samantha. "Whither the Transvestite? Theorizing Male-to-Female Transvestism in Feminist and Queer Theory." *Feminist Theory* 15, no. 1 (2014): 51–72.

Anthony Slide. *Encyclopedia of Vaudeville*. Oxford: University of Mississippi Press, 2012.

Balcerzak, Scott. *Buffoon Men: Classic Hollywood Comedians and Queered Masculinity*. Detroit, MI: Wayne State University Press, 2013.

Baraka, Amiri (as LeRoi Jones). *JELLO*. Chicago: Third World Press, 1970.

Barnouw, Erik. *Handbook of Radio Writing: An Outline of Techniques and Markets in Radio Writing in the United States*. Boston: Little, Brown, 1939.

Baughman, James L. "Nice Guys Last Fifteen Season: Jack Benny on Television, 1950–1965." *Film & History* 30, no. 2 (2000) 29–39.

Benny, Jack, and Joan Benny. *Sunday Nights at Seven: The Jack Benny Story*. New York: Warner Books, 1990.

Benny, Mary Livingstone, Hilliard Marks, and Marcia Borie. *Jack Benny: A Biography*. New York: Doubleday, 1978.

Berger, Arthur Asa. *Jewish Jesters: A Study in American Popular Comedy*. Cresskill, NJ: Hampton Press, 2001.

Berger, Maurice, Brian Wallis, Simon Watson, and Carrie Mae Weems, eds. *Constructing Masculinity*. New York: Routledge, 1995.

Bernstein, Matthew. "Selznick's March: *Gone With the Wind* Comes to White Atlanta." *Atlanta History* 43, no. 2 (1999): 7–33.

Bogle, Donald. *Bright Boulevards, Bold Dreams: The Story of Black Hollywood*. New York: Ballantine, 2005.

Bogle, Donald. *Primetime Blues: African Americans on Network Television*. New York: Farrar, Straus and Giroux, 2002.

Boskin, Joseph. *Sambo: The Rise and Demise of an American Jester*. New York: Oxford University Press, 1986.

Burns, George, and David Fisher. *All My Best Friends*. New York: Perigee, 1990.

Capeci, Dominic J. Jr., and Martha Wilkerson, "The Detroit Riots of 1943: A Reinterpretation." *Michigan Historical Review* 16, no. 1 (January 1990): 49–72.

Carson, John. "How to Write Comedy for Radio." Undergraduate thesis, University of Nebraska, 1949.

Cassidy, Marsha. "Touch, Taste, Breath: Synesthesia and Sense Memory and the Selling of Cigarettes on Television, 1948–1971." In *Media Convergence History*, edited by Janet Staiger and Sabine Hake, 34–45. New Brunswick, NJ: Rutgers University Press, 2009.

Chauncey, George. *Gay New York: Gender, Urban Culture, and the Making of the Gay Male World, 1890-1940*. New York: Basic Books, 1994.

Christopher, Larry. "Stars Shine Best When Polished," *Broadcasting and Television* (October 1956): 118–26.

Clements, Cynthia, and Sandra Weber. *George Burns and Gracie Allen: A Bio-Bibliography.* Westport, CT: Greenwood, 1996.

Cox, Jim. *The Great Radio Sitcoms.* Jefferson, NC: McFarland, 2007.

Craig, Steve. "Out of Eden: The Legion of Decency, the FCC, and Mae West's 1937 Appearance on The Chase & Sanborn Hour." *Journal of Radio Studies* 13, no. 2 (2006): 232–48.

Cripps, Thomas. "Amos 'n' Andy and the Debate over Racial Integration." In *American History/American Television: Interpreting the Video Past*, edited by John E. O'Connor, 33–54. New York: Frederick Ungar, 1983.

Crisell, Andrew. *Understanding Radio.* 2nd edition. London: Routledge, 2006.

Crosby, John. "Radio and Who Makes It." *Atlantic Monthly*, January 1948, 23–29.

Cullen, Frank, Florence Hackman, and Donald McNeilly. *Vaudeville Old and New: An Encyclopedia of Variety Performances in America*, volume 1 New York: Psychology Press, 2004.

Curry, Ramona. *Too Much of a Good Thing: Mae West as Cultural Icon.* Minneapolis: University of Minnesota Press, 1996.

Dale, Alan. *Comedy Is a Man in Trouble: Slapstick in American Movies.* Minneapolis: University of Minnesota Press, 2007.

Dalton, Mary and Laura Linder, eds. *The Sitcom Reader: America Viewed and Skewed.* Albany: State University of New York, 2005.

Davies, Christie. "Exploring the Thesis of the Self-Deprecating Jewish Sense of Humor." *Humor: International Journal of Humor Research* 4 (1991): 189–209.

Doherty, Thomas. Review of Jill Watts, *Mae West: An Icon in Black and White* (Oxford 2001) in *American Historical Review* (December 2002): 1576–77.

Doty, Alexander. *Making Things Perfectly Queer: Interpreting Mass Culture.* Minneapolis: University of Minnesota Press, 1993.

Douglas, Susan J. *Listening In: Radio and the American Imagination.* Minneapolis: University of Minnesota Press, 2004.

Dunning, John. *On the Air: The Encyclopedia of Old-Time Radio.* Oxford: Oxford University Press, 1998.

Dygert, Warren. *Radio as an Advertising Medium.* New York: McGraw Hill, 1939.

Dyja, Thomas. *Walter White: The Dilemma of Black Identity in America.* Chicago: Ivan R. Dee, 2008.

Easterlin, Richard A. "The American Baby Boom in Historical Perspective." In *Population, Labor Force, and Long Swings in Economic Growth: The American Experience*, 76–110. New York: Columbia University Press, 1968.

Edmerson, Estelle. "A Descriptive Study of the American Negro in United States Professional Radio 1922–1953." MA thesis, University of California, Los Angeles, 1954.

Ela Przybylo, "Crisis and Safety: The Asexual in Society." *Sexualities* 14, no. 4 (2011): 444–61.

Ely, Melvin Patrick. *The Adventures of Amos'n'Andy: A Social History of an American Phenomenon.* Charlottesville: University of Virginia Press, 1991.

Epstein, Lawrence J. *The Haunted Smile: The Story of Jewish Comedians in America.* New York: Public Affairs, 2002.

Feasey, Rebecca. *Masculinity and Popular Television*. Edinburgh: Edinburgh University Press, 2008.

Fein, Irving A. *Jack Benny: An Intimate Biography*. New York: G. P. Putnam's Sons, 1976.

Fox, Stephen R. *The Mirror Makers: A History of American Advertising and Its Creators*. Urbana: University of Illinois Press, 1984.

French, Elbrun, ed. *Copywriter's Guide*. New York: Harper, 1959.

Friend, Tad. "What's So Funny? A Scientific Attempt to Discover Why We Laugh." *New Yorker* 78, no. 34 (November 11, 2002): 78–93.

Fuller Seeley, Kathryn. "Dish Night at the Movies: Exhibitors and Female Audiences during the Great Depression." In *The American Film History Reader*, edited by Jon Lewis and Eric Smoodin, 246–75. London: Routledge, 2014.

Fuller Seeley, Kathryn. "Learning to Live with Television: Technology, Gender, and America's Early TV Audiences." In *The Columbia History of Television*, edited by Gary Edgerton, 91–110. New York: Columbia University Press, 2007.

Fuller Seeley, Kathryn. "Shirley Temple: Dreams Come True." In *Glamour in a Golden Age: Movie Stars of the 1930s*, edited by Adrienne L. McLean, 44–65. New Brunswick, NJ: Rutgers University Press, 2011.

Garber, Marjorie B. *Vested Interests: Cross-dressing and Cultural Anxiety*. New York: Psychology Press, 1997.

Gould, Jack. "How Comic Is Radio Comedy." *New York Times*, Sunday magazine, November 21, 1948, SM22, 64, 66, 67, 68.

Havig, Alan. "Frederick Wakeman's The Hucksters and the Post War Debate over Commercial Radio." *Journal of Broadcasting* 28, no. 2 (Spring 1984): 192.

Havig, Alan. *Fred Allen's Radio Comedy*. Philadelphia: Temple University Press, 1992.

Hilmes, Michele. "Invisible Men: Amos 'n' Andy and the Roots of Broadcast Discourse." *Critical Studies in Media Communication* 10, no. 4 (1993): 301–21.

Hilmes, Michele. "Is There a Field Called Sound Culture Studies? And Does It Matter?" *American Quarterly* 57, no. 1 (2005): 249–59.

Hilmes, Michele. *Hollywood and Broadcasting: From Radio to Cable*. Champaign: University of Illinois Press, 1999.

Hilmes, Michele. *Radio Voices: American Broadcasting, 1922–1952*. Minneapolis: University of Minnesota Press, 1997.

Horten, Gerd. *Radio Goes to War: The Cultural Politics of Propaganda during World War II*. Berkeley: University of California Press, 2002.

Hoyt, Eric. "Hollywood and the Income Tax, 1929–1955." *Film History: An International Journal* 22, no. 1 (2010): 5–21.

Jenkins, Henry. *What Made Pistachio Nuts? Early Sound Comedy and the Vaudeville Aesthetic*. New York: Columbia University Press, 1992.

Jewell, Richard B. "Hollywood and Radio: Competition and Partnership in the 1930s." *Historical Journal of Film, Radio and Television* 4, no. 2 (1984): 125–41.

Jones, Gerard. *Honey, I'm Home!: Sitcoms: Selling the American Dream*. New York: Macmillan, 1993.

Jones, Gwenllian. "Gender and Queerness." In *Television Studies*, edited by Toby Miller, 190–12. London: BFI, 2002.

Josefsberg, Milt. *The Jack Benny Show*. New York: Crown, 1977.

Jurca, Catherine. *Hollywood 1938: Motion Pictures' Greatest Year*. Berkeley: University of California Press, 2012.

Kaufman, David. *Jewhooing the Sixties: American Celebrity and Jewish Identity; Sandy Koufax, Lenny Bruce, Bob Dylan, and Barbra Streisand*. Waltham, MA: Brandeis University Press, 2012.

Kemper, Tom. *Hidden Talent: The Emergence of Hollywood Agents*. Berkeley: University of California Press, 2010.

Kendall, Lori. "'Oh No! I'm a Nerd!' Hegemonic Masculinity on an Online Forum." *Gender and Society* 14, no. 2 (April 2000): 256–74.

Kessel, Martina, and Patrick Merziger. *The Politics of Humour: Laughter, Inclusion, and Exclusion in the Twentieth Century*. Toronto: Toronto University Press, 2012.

Kimmel, Michael. "Masculinity as Homophobia: Fear, Shame and Silence in the Construction of Gender Identity." In *Feminism and Masculinities*, edited by Peter Murphy, 182–99. Oxford: Oxford University Press, 2004.

Kompare, Derek. *Rerun Nation: How Repeats Invented American Television*. London: Routledge, 2006.

Landry, Robert J. "The Improbability of Radio Criticism." *Hollywood Quarterly* 2, no. 1 (October 1946): 66–70.

Landry, Robert J. "Wanted: Radio Critics." *Public Opinion Quarterly* 4, no. 4 (December 1, 1940): P620–30.

Leacock, Stephen. *Humor: Its Theory and Technique, with Examples and Samples*. New York: Dodd, Mead and Co. 1935.

Leff, Laura. *39 Forever, Second Edition, Volume 1: Radio May 1932–May 1942*. North Charleston, SC: Book Surge, 2004.

Leff, Laura. *39 Forever, Second Edition, Volume 2, Radio October 1942–May 1955*. North Charleston, SC: Book Surge, 2006.

Lehman, Christopher. *The Colored Cartoon: Black Presentation in American Animated Short Films, 1907–1954*. Amherst: University of Massachusetts Press, 2009.

Lenthall, Bruce. *Radio's America: The Great Depression and the Rise of Modern Mass Culture*. Chicago: University of Chicago Press, 2007.

Lotz, Amanda. "On 'Television Criticism': The Pursuit of Critical Examination of a Popular Art." *Popular Communication* 6 (2008): 20–36.

Loviglio, Jason. "Sound Effects: Gender, Voice and Cultural Work of NPR." *Radio Journal* 5 (2007): 2–3, 67–81.

Lowe, Leah. "'If the Country's Going Gracie, So Can You': Gender Representation in Gracie Allen's Radio Comedy." In *Communities of the Air: Radio Century, Radio Culture*, edited by Susan M. Squire, 237–50. Durham, NC: Duke University Press, 2003.

MacKinnon, Kenneth. *Representing Men: Maleness and Masculinity in the Media*. London: Arnold, 2003.

Maltby, Richard. "New Cinema Histories." *Explorations in New Cinema History: Approaches and Case Studies* (2011): 3–40.

Marchand, Roland. *Advertising the American Dream: Making Way for Modernity 1920–1940.* Berkeley: University of California Press, 1985.

McFadden, Margaret T. "'America's Boy Friend Who Can't Get a Date': Gender, Race, and the Cultural Work of the Jack Benny Program, 1932-1946." *Journal of American History* 80, no. 1 (June 1993): 113–34.

McFadden, Margaret. "Warning–Do Not Risk Federal Arrest by Looking Glum!": Ballyhoo Magazine and the Cultural Politics of Early 1930s Humor." *Journal of American Culture* 26, no. 1 (March 2003): 124–34.

Mellencamp, Patricia. "Situation Comedy, Feminism, and Freud: Discourses of Gracie and Lucy." In Feminist Television Criticism, edited by Charlotte Brunsdon and Lynn Spigel, 60–73. Maidenhead: Open University Press, 2008.

Meyers, Cynthia. *A Word from Our Sponsor: Admen, Advertising and the Golden Age of Radio.* New York: Fordham University Press, 2013.

Mills, Brett. *Television Sitcom.* London: British Film Institute, 2005.

Mintz, Lawrence E. "Standup Comedy as Social and Cultural Mediation." *American Quarterly* 37, no. 1(1985): 71–80.

Morreall, John. "Philosophy of Humor." *The Stanford Encyclopedia of Philosophy.* Stanford: The Metaphysics Research Lab (2013).

Murray, Susan. *Hitch Your Antenna to the Stars: Early Television and Broadcast Stardom.* London: Routledge, 2013.

Neu, Jerome. *Sticks and Stones: The Philosophy of Insults.* Oxford: Oxford University Press, 2007.

Newcomb, Horace. *Television: The Critical View.* 6th edition. Oxford: Oxford University Press, 2000.

Oakner, Larry. *And Now for a Few Laughs from Our Sponsor: The Best of Fifty Years of Radio Commercials.* New York: John Wiley & Sons, 2002.

Patterson, Eleanor. "Radio Redux: The Persistence of Soundwork in the Post Network Era." PhD diss., University of Wisconsin, 2016.

Pearse, Holly A. "As Goyish as Lime Jell-O? Jack Benny and the American Construction of Jewishness." *Jewish Cultural Studies* (2008): 272–90.

Petty, Miriam J. *Stealing the Show: African American Performers and Audiences in 1930s Hollywood.* Berkeley: University of California Press, 2016.

Pollay, Richard W. "Targeting Tactics in Selling Smoke: Youthful Aspects of 20th Century Cigarette Advertising." *Journal of Marketing Theory and Practice* (Winter 1995): 9.

Quimby, Karin. "Will & Grace: Negotiating (Gay) Marriage on Prime-Time Television." *Journal of Popular Culture* 38, no. 4 (2005): 713–31.

Ramsburg, Jim. *Network Radio Ratings 1932–1953.* Jefferson, NC: McFarland, 2012.

Reid, John F Jr., "Half Century of Peabody Radio: A Descriptive Analysis." *Journal of Radio Studies* (1992): 143–50.

Rosten, Leo Calvin, and Leo Rosten. *The Joys of Yiddish.* New York: McGraw-Hill, 1968.

Rowe, Kathleen. *The Unruly Woman: Gender and the Genres of Laughter.* Austin: University of Texas Press, 2011.

Ruggill, Judd Ethan. "Convergence: Always Already, Already." *Cinema Journal* 48, no. 3 (Spring 2009): 105–10.

Sampson, Henry T. *Swingin' on the Ether Waves: A Chronological History of African Americans in Radio and Television Programming, 1925–1955.* Vol. 1. Lanham, MD: Scarecrow Press, 2005.

Santo, Avi. *Selling the Silver Bullet: The Lone Ranger and Transmedia Brand Licensing.* Austin: University of Texas Press, 2015.

Savage, Barbara. *Broadcasting Freedom: Radio, War and the Politics of Race 1938–1948.* Chapel Hill: University of North Carolina Press, 1999.

Seldes, Gilbert. "Actor for a Night." *Esquire*, June 1946, 107–8.

Shugart, Helene. "Reinventing Privilege: The New (Gay) Man in Contemporary Popular Media." *Critical Studies in Mass Communication* 20, no. 1 (2003): 67–91.

Silberman, Charles E. *A Certain People: American Jews and Their Lives Today.* New York: Simon & Schuster, 1985.

Sklaroff, Lauren Rebecca. "Variety for the Servicemen: The Jubilee Show and the Paradox of Racializing Radio during World War II." *American Quarterly* 56, no. 4 (2004): 945–73.

Slide, Anthony, ed. *Selected Radio and Television Criticism.* Metuchen, NJ: Scarecrow, 1987.

Smith, R. J. *The Great Black Way: Los Angeles in the 1940s and the Lost African-American Renaissance.* New York: Public Affairs, 2006.

Smith, Ralph Lewis. *A Study of the Professional Criticism of Broadcasting in the US 1920–1955.* New York: Arno, 1979.

Smoodin, Eric. *Regarding Frank Capra: Audience, Celebrity, and American Film Studies, 1930-1960.* Durham, NC: Duke University Press, 2004.

Snyder, Robert W. *The Voice of the City: Vaudeville and Popular Culture in New York.* New York: Oxford University Press, 1989.

Trav, S. D. *No Applause, Just Throw Money, Or, The Book that Made Vaudeville Famous: A High-class, Refined Entertainment.* New York: Macmillan, 2005.

Vance, Carole S. "Social Construction Theory and Sexuality." In *Constructing Masculinity*, edited by Maurice Berger, Brian Wallis, Simon Watson, and Carrie Mae Weems, 37–48. New York: Routledge, 1995.

Wald, Elijah. *The Dozens: A History of Rap's Mama.* Oxford: Oxford University Press, 2012.

Ware, Amy M. "Will Roger's Radio: Race and Technology in the Cherokee Nation." *American Indian Quarterly* 33, no.1 (Winter 2009): 62–97.

Watts, Jill. *Hattie McDaniel: Black Ambition, White Hollywood.* New York: Harper Collins, 2007.

Weaver, Pat. "If I Were Running the Network Again." *Sponsor*, August 26, 1963, 25–26.

Wertheim, Arthur Frank. *Radio Comedy.* New York: Oxford University Press, 1979.

Whitfield, Stephen J. "The Distinctiveness of American Jewish Humor." *Modern Judaism* (1986): 245–60.
Wilde, Larry. *The Great Comedians Talk about Comedy.* New York: Citadel, 1968.
Wylie, Max. *Radio and Television Writing.* New York: Rinehart, 1939, 1950.
Zoglin, Richard. *Comedy at the Edge: How Stand-Up in the 1970s Changed America.* New York: Bloomsbury, 2009.
Zolotow, Maurice. "The Fiddler from Waukegan," *Cosmopolitan*, October 1947, 49–51, 137–38, 141–46.
Zurawik, David. *The Jews of Prime Time.* Hanover, NH: Brandeis/University Press of New England, 2003.

INDEX

Ace, Goodman, 49, 298, 307
advertising, 4, 5, 18, 22, 32–34, 188–222; criticism of radio advertising, 188, 195, 200, 208, 214–217; hard sell, 190, 192, 214–221; integration into radio programming, 18, 32–34, 190–192, 193–222; soft sell, 191–214, 218–222; success in radio, 4, 22, 196, 203, 205–206, 208–209, 218. *See also* advertising agencies; Jack Benny radio program; sponsors
advertising agencies. *See* Ayer, N.W; Jack Benny radio program; Young & Rubicam
African-Americans, 17–18, 91, 120–187; played by white actors on radio, 120; as radio audiences, 17–18, 91, 181; radio representations of, 17–18, 120–187; television representations of, 184–185, 289–290, 294–296, 298–299, 303. *See also* Anderson, Eddie; Critics
Allen, Fred, xi, 10, 22, 25, 38, 48, 49, 69, 91–94, 97, 140, 145–146, 147, 148, 160, 210–212, 226, 241–242, 246–249, 259–260, 261, 265, 267, 269, 271, 276, 277, 278, 284, 285, 291–292, 293, 298, 313; "Allen's Alley" radio skit, 92, 97, 99, 102, 145, 146; appearances on Jack Benny program, 92–94; Benny's "feud" with, xi, 17, 91–94, 210–212
Allen, Gracie 22, 31, 48, 53, 57, 69–72, 102, 111–118, 271, 284. *See also Burns and Allen Program*; Burns, George

Amos 'n' Andy (radio program) and Charles Correll and Freeman Gosden, 22, 31, 37, 44, 68, 71, 120, 127, 128–129, 135–136, 172, 173, 177, 179, 184, 196, 269, 271–272, 287, 289, 315
Anderson, Eddie, 4, 5, 8, 14, 17–18, 118–119, 120–153, 151, 154–187, 158, 182, 289, 294, 309; African American critics disapproval of, 142, 160–161, 165, 170–173, 180–183, 185, 187; African American critics praise of, 133–134, 145, 147, 148–153, 165, 171–172, 174; in *Brewster's Millions* (film), 174–175; in *Buck Benny Rides Again,* (film), 145–150; in *Cabin in the Sky* (film), 155, 164–167; childhood, 123–124; film appearances, 6, 126, 133, 143–145, 239–242; first appearance on Jack Benny radio program, 120; in *Man About Town* (film), 143–145; in proposed radio program, 178–179; in relationship with Rochester character, 120–123, 133, 145–146, 160, 172–173, 185–186; stardom of, 120, 133, 145, 154–155, 156–157, 160, 177, 183, 239; in *Tales of Manhattan* (film), 155, 160–163; vaudeville career, 125–127; voice of, 124–125, 130–131, 134, 337n12. *See also* Jack Benny radio program; Jack Benny TV program; Rochester Van Jones character
Arden, Eve, 53, 71, 84

Armstrong, Louis, 126, 128, 148
Artists and Models Abroad (film), 100, 228, 238
Artists and Models (film), 228, 238
Audiences (radio) and imagination, 1–2, 5, 8, 19, 30, 87, 88–89, 97–118, 120, 281–294, 310; small town, 232, 261; Southern, 120, 128, 140–141, 146–147, 166–167, 174–175; studio, 1, 9, 223, 302; surveys of, 238, 244, 246
Aural humor in radio, 1, 5, 6, 7–12, 19, 98, 284, 307–308. *See also* audiences
Ayer, N. W. & Son advertising agency, 21, 38–39, 192, 193

Baker, Kenny, 3, 47, 50, 53, 74, 82, 89, 133, 134, 213, 238
Baldwin, Harry, 32, 59, 254–255
Baraka, Amiri and *JELLO* (play), 90, 187
Barnes, Howard, 105, 145, 148, 245
Barnouw, Erik, 9, 74–75
Beloin, Ed, 45, 49–52, 74, 129–130, 167, 211, 228, 241, 242, 254, 256
Benny, Jack: as advertising creator, 5, 29, 188–223, 313; and childhood as Benjamin Kubelsky, 2–3; comic timing, 1–2, 5, 8, 29, 50, 74–75, 82, 91, 262, 301–302, 308, 311–314; death of, 7; as "Fall Guy" character, 1, 11, 13, 16, 23, 41, 52, 74, 85, 86, 94, 108–109, 221, 249, 258, 262, 292, 309, 312, 313; as intermedia star, 5, 15, 18–19, 223–249, 281–303, 309; and Jewish identity, 2, 16, 24, 86, 94–97; marriage to Sadye Marks, 57; Midwestern characteristics of, 8, 16, 24, 95, 281; post-television series career, 7, 311, 312, 313–314; and smuggling scandal in, 1939 6, 96, 208; relationship with radio critics, 268–280; relationship with sponsors, 5, 6, 21–23, 29, 38–39, 188–223, 283–303; relationship with TV critics, 297–308; as script editor, 10, 13, 16, 45–52; service in World War I, 3; as showrunner/producer, 5, 40, 45, 188–223, 281–303; television career, 289–303; in USO tours during World War II, 6, 92, 167, 175, 253, 312; vaudeville career, 3, 5, 15–16, 21, 23–27, 29, 31, 57, 92–94, 95, 221, 290, 312. *See also* Jack Benny radio program; Jack Benny television program; Livingstone, Mary; Masculine gender and Jack Benny character
Benny, Joan, xii, 15, 83, 313
Batton, Barton, Durstine and Osborne advertising agency, 210, 291
Bergen, Edgar, and Charlie McCarthy, 51, 99, 100, 238, 252, 269, 271, 277, 278, 284, 287, 315
Berle, Milton, 19, 114, 117, 271, 282, 290, 294, 301, 305, 313
Bernie, Ben, 3, 24, 95, 193, 195
Bestor, Don, 41, 68, 199, 231, 311
Big Show (radio program), 293
Black, Frank, 196, 197, 202
Blanc, Mel, 5, 8, 91, 178, 251, 256–257, 281, 292, 294, 296, 312
Boasberg, Al, 31, 49
Brainard, Bertha, 21, 27, 39–40, 102, 193, 198, 199, 213, 215
Buck Benny Rides Again (film), 145–150, 214–245, 252
Burns, Bob, 223, 238, 271
Burns, George, 17, 22, 31, 48, 57, 69, 95, 111–118, 284, 313. *See also* Allen, Gracie; *Burns and Allen* program
Burns and Allen (radio program), 32, 69–70, 256, 264, 271, 284, 315

Canada Dry Ginger Ale Company, 18, 21–23, 38–40
California, radio's move to, 198–199, 222, 223, 233–236; tourism, 18–19, 223–225, 231–235
Cantor, Eddie, 7, 22, 31, 37, 48, 77, 78, 95, 97, 99, 102, 114, 160, 200, 202, 223, 226, 229, 271, 278, 284, 285, 298, 301, 313
Carmichael the polar bear character, 133, 139, 146, 233, 242, 257, 305
Carson, Johnny, 312–313
CBS (Columbia Broadcasting System), 2, 38–39, 83, 115, 230–231, 236, 279, 287–303
Censorship (radio), 14, 99–102, 110, 208
Charley's Aunt (film), 17, 88, 102–106
Chevrolet Company, 40, 197–198

Colbert, Claudette, 231, 249, 300
Colman, Ronald and Benita, 1, 5, 53, 231, 249, 251, 252, 257–258, 260, 281, 292, 296
Comedy in radio, principles of, 1–13
Conn, Harry W., 8, 14, 16, 22–23, 31–52, 45, 58–61, 64, 129, 189, 193, 194, 221, 227–228, 229, 254, 256, 309, 317; creative partnership with Benny, 8, 16, 22–23, 32–44, 189, 193–200; experimentation, 8, 32, 35–38; later career, 16, 50–51; tensions over authorship with Benny, 16, 23, 32, 44–50; use ethnic voices, 8, 37, 47, 50, 129; vaudeville career, 32
Contests, radio, 35, 59, 258–261
Continuity Acceptance. *See* censorship
Corwin, Norman, 171
critics: African-American, 14, 18, 90, 128, 133–134, 142, 145, 147, 148–153, 160–161, 165, 170–173, 174, 180–183, 185, 187; film, 19, 103–106, 144–145, 148–150, 241, 244–248; radio, 6, 19, 30, 38, 41, 43–44, 46–47, 65, 250–251, 255, 259–261, 263–280, 294; television, 114–118, 282–303. *See also* Crosby, John; Gould, Jack; Gross, Ben; Hellman, Jack; Seldes, Gilbert; Van Horne, Harriet
Crosby, Bing, 27, 210, 223, 226, 244, 246, 249, 313
Crosby, John, 19, 94, 110, 136, 250, 266, 267–280, 282, 298

Devine, Andy, 134, 140, 146, 231, 241
Daniels, Draper, 190–192, 193, 194
Day, Dennis, 3, 4, 89, 98, 106–107, 109, 139, 145, 178, 213, 241, 255, 262, 281, 288, 311
dialects on Jack Benny radio program; black, 90, 122, 127–129, 136–142, 169–173, 179–183, 185, 292–293; ethnic, 8, 37, 47, 50, 127–128, 129–130, 176–177; Jewish, 96–98, 127, 176–177, 178, 255, 262
Douglas, Susan J., xii, 5, 15, 77, 89
Duffy's Tavern (radio program), 71, 160, 271, 277, 315, 337n16

Edmerson, Estelle, 185–186

Fay, Frank, 3, 24–26
Fein, Irving, 15, 46, 48, 115, 182, 218
Feud, Benny-Allen, xi, 17, 91–94, 210–212
Fibber McGee and Molly (radio program), and Jim and Marian Jordan, 44, 72, 73, 268, 271, 284, 315
film industry: tensions with radio industry, 18–19, 22, 227–228, 230–231, 235–237, 242, 244–248

Garbo, Greta, 37, 59, 63, 81, 142, 227, 228, 229
gender. *See* masculine gender construction; women
General Foods Corporation (Jell-O), 3, 16, 18, 139, 210–214, 240, 243–244, 247, 252, 253, 258
Gould, Jack, 19, 115, 250, 255–256, 264, 266, 278, 297
Great Depression, 3, 17, 22, 191, 196, 199, 202, 231
Green, Johnny, 50, 311
Gross, Ben, 115, 250, 264, 285

Harrington, Tom, 49, 209, 213, 235, 254
Harris, Phil, 3, 8, 51, 82, 88, 89, 94, 98, 100, 108–109, 133, 134, 139, 143, 145, 178, 231, 239, 252, 253, 267, 287, 288, 304, 305
Hays, Will, 236–237
Hellman, Jack, 114, 218, 258, 259, 260, 261, 271, 276, 287, 288, 289, 306
Hill, George Washington, 192, 214–218
Hilmes, Michele, xii, 15, 97, 128, 135, 225, 227, 232
Hoffa, Portland 69, 210
Hollywood Revue of 1929 (film), 3, 26, 226
Hoover, Herbert, 36–37, 197
Hope, Bob, 71, 77, 100, 102, 106, 195, 238, 244, 249, 252, 253, 256, 272, 277, 278, 284, 308, 313
Horn Blows at Midnight (film), 256
Horne, Lena, 162, 165, 166, 174, 177

Information Please (radio program), 92, 215
International Jack Benny Fan Club (IJBFC), xii, 13

INDEX · 369

Jack Benny radio program: black voices in, 90, 122, 127–129, 136–142, 169–173, 179–183, 185, 292–293; *Canada Dry Program* May 1932–Jan 1933, 7, 21–23, 27–40, 59–67, 89, 101, 192–196, 228, 229; censorship and, 14, 99–102, 110, 208; characters developed in, 3, 5, 16, 23, 37–52, 58–85, 131–133, 152–153, 184, 199–200, 309; *Chevrolet Program* March 1933–April 1934. 40–41, 67–69, 196–197; commercials in, 3, 4, 5, 30, 32–34, 35, 36–37, 38, 43, 52, 60–61, 72, 78–79, 89, 101, 132, 139, 192–196, 200–213, 218–221, 251, 296, 305; ends radio program, 6, 303–306; ethnic voices in, 8, 37, 47, 50, 127–128, 129–130, 176–177; experimentation in, 19, 23, 32–38, 52, 62, 218–219, 250, 256–262; gender issues in, *See* masculine gender identity, and women; *General Tire Program* April 1934–September 1934, 41–43, 199–200, 205; gifted Sunday 7:00 pm time slot by NBC, 213; golden era of Benny radio program, 1946–1955 6, 19, 249, 250, 292, 304–305, 311–317; *Grape Nuts Program* October 1942–June 1943, 78–79, 214; I Can't Stand Jack Benny contest, 14, 96, 140, 251, 258–261; *Jell-O Program* October 1934–June 1942, 43–52, 74–78, 122, 129–153, 200–213, 222, 228, 253; Jewish voices in, 96–98, 127, 176–177, 178, 255, 262; Jewish humor in, 94–97; liveness in radio broadcasts, 10, 22, 31, 82, 91, 262; *Lucky Strike Radio Program* September 1943–May 1955, 82–85, 167–185, 214–221, 254–280, 281–306; motion picture–related aspects, 5, 6, 40, 42–43, 76, 102–106, 225–228, 232–235; movie parodies in, 3, 19, 50, 63, 98, 102–106, 138, 225, 229–231, 249; racial issues in, *See* Rochester Van Jones character; relationships with film; radio and television critics, *See* critics; relationships with sponsors, 5, 18, 23, 38–40, 101, 188–223, 282–303; situation comedy in, 23, 77–79, 132; sponsor character in, 5, 89–90, 210; World War II era, 6, 19, 78–79, 83, 106–107, 217, 249, 250–257; Your Money or Your Life skit, 1–2, 13, 80. *See also* Benny, Jack; Jack Benny television program

Jack Benny television program: early local Los Angeles broadcast, xxx; first episode, 6, 294–298; "Gracie Benny" TV episodes, 17, 114–118; *Lucky Strike Program* 1950–1959, 294–309; other television episodes, 289–290, 298–308; radio contributions to Benny's TV program, 19, 301, 302, 306–308, 311; relationships with sponsors, 289–290, 294–308; relationships with TV critics, 114–118, 282–303; as sitcom 300; use of vaudeville in, 199–300; use of visual comedy, 301–302, 308, 311–314

Jell-O Company. *See* General Foods Corporation

Jessel, George, 22, 25, 95, 267, 271

Jewish identity: anti-Semitism, 25, 96, 259; Benny's religious and ethnic background, 2, 16, 24, 86, 94–97; discrimination against, 259; radio representations of, 47, 94–97, 129, 176–177, 178, 262

Jolson, Al, 51, 159, 196, 226

Josefsberg, Milt, 15, 62, 80, 110, 179, 180, 189, 254, 273, 275–276

Kirsten, Dorothy, 80, 220

Kitzel character, 97, 176–177, 178, 262

Kubelsky, Benjamin. *See* Jack Benny

Leacock, Stephen, 12–13

Liveness of radio, 10, 31, 82, 91, 262

Livingstone, Mary, 4, 9, 12, 14, 15, 16, 37–38, 39–52, 53–85, 66, 70, 88, 89, 90, 91, 98, 100, 107, 108–109, 130–131, 132, 133, 134, 139, 140, 145, 146, 168, 203, 228, 231, 233, 241–242, 265–266, 275, 281, 292, 309, 311; adopting Mary Livingstone name, 62–63, 133; in battle of the sexes, 75–81, 84–85, 91; childhood as Sadye Marks, 56; compared to Gracie Allen 16, 53–54, 69–72; compared to Mae West 16, 54, 63, 67–68; as creative force and producer, 39, 65, 83; in cross-dressing roles, 97–98; in Dumb Dora roles, 57–65, 74; early radio performances, 16, 37–38, 39–52, 58–62; as heckler, 9, 16, 41, 53, 73–85, 88, 91–91; laughter, 16, 53, 54, 58–61, 71, 73–85, 88; leaping into conversations (Barnouw), 9, 61, 73–75; Mama character 55, 61, 71; marriage to Jack Benny 3, 16, 55, 72, 81, 91; Marks, Babe (sister), 55, 56, 71–72, 77, 88; Marks, Hilliard (brother) 56; as member of Benny program's male gang, 16, 67, 97–98; microphone fright, 55, 73, 82, 84, 91, 262; mistakes made in performing scripts, 82, 91, 262; poems, 46, 47, 64, 68–69, 81–82; private life and personality, 54, 55, 57, 84; retirement of, 54–55, 83, 284, 305; as singer, 57, 73; stardom of, 55, 66, 68–70, 73, 83, 84; on television, 83–87; in "Twink Family" skit, 78–80; as undomestic, 72, 81; as unruly woman, 16, 54, 65, 68, 75–85, 88; vaudeville performances, 56–57

Love Thy Neighbor (film), 246–249, 252

Lux Radio Theatre (radio program), 224, 230, 246

MacRorie, Janet, 99, 237
Man About Town (film), 143–145, 239–241, 252
Marchand, Roland, 190, 194
Marks, Sadye. *See* Livingstone, Mary
Marx, Groucho, 337n14
Marx, Zeppo, 56
Masculine gender identity and the Jack Benny character, 5, 6, 25, 41–43, 86–119; acting in a homosexual manner, 86, 87, 100, 102, 110;acting with fluid sexual identity, 86, 87, 88, 101; as asexual, 86, 101; as cross-dresser, 17, 86, 88, 97–118; as effeminate, 86, 87, 95, 97–118; as employer/patriarch, 5, 86, 89–91, 132, 218–221, 262; as female impersonator, 17, 86–87, 97–118; as heterosexual "Broadway Romeo," 25, 62–63, 86, 103, 226, 229, 314; as heterosexual, deficient, 41–43, 75–80, 86, 95, 228, 314; as insult thrower/player of "the dozens," 86, 91–94; as Jewish male, 94–97; in a racialized relationship with Rochester, 86, 90, 131–132, 135–153, 156, 158–160

Masculine gender identity represented on Benny program, 5, 16–17, 41–43, 75–80, 86–119; as effeminacy, 87, 97–118; as heterosexual dominance, 24–25, 86, 87, 88, 100; as heterosexual failure, 77–80, 86, 87, 88, 97–118; in homophobia, 102, 107–108, 110, 116; in homosexuality, 87, 98–100, 101, 102, 107–108, 195; as patriarchal authority, 86, 89–91; through queer/LGBTQ readings, 87, 88, 97–118.

master of ceremonies (emcee, m.c.), 3, 22, 23, 25–27, 126, 290, 313
Maxwell automobile, 5, 8, 19, 81, 173, 242, 257, 281, 288, 290, 295, 307, 310
Mays, Dr. Benjamin, 148–149
McDaniel, Hattie, 146–147, 155, 164, 176, 177, 186
McQueen, Butterfly, 83, 168–169, 255
Meyers, Cynthia, xii, 190, 202
Morrow, Bill, 45, 49–52, 74, 129–130, 167, 211, 228, 241, 242, 254, 256
Mouse that Jack Built (film), xi, 311–312
Murray, Ken, 114, 208, 294

NAACP (National Association for the Advancement of Colored People) and Walter White and leaders, 161–162, 163, 177, 180–181
NBC (National Broadcasting Company), 2, 21–23, 27, 102, 199, 227–228, 236–237, 279, 287–288, 293
Nelson, Frank, 5, 9, 88, 90, 110, 114, 220, 257, 292, 296, 305

Olsen, George, 21, 28, 29, 30, 34, 38–39, 58, 60, 62, 63, 65, 193, 229, 311
OTR (Old Time Radio), xi, 13, 314–317

Palace Theater (New York City), 3, 24, 25, 26, 29, 290
Paley, William, 287, 288
Paramount Studios, film production and marketing, 143–145, 228, 238–249
Parker, Frank, 41, 47, 74, 102, 197, 199, 234

Parsons, Louella, 157–158, 230
Pious, Minerva, 97, 255
Polly the Parrot character, 257, 296

racial issues. *See* Anderson, Eddie; Rochester Van Jones, character; World War II.
ratings of radio programs, 40, 271, 293, 306 of TV programs 297, 306
Rochester Van Jones, character, 1, 5, 14–15, 17–18, 77, 83, 88, 89, 94, 98, 100, 106, 114, 116, 118–119, 120, 121–123, 129–153, 154–187, 228, 253, 255, 257, 265–266, 273–275, 277, 281, 289, 292, 296, 305, 309; and African-American community in Los Angeles, 125–127, 150–153, 155, 178–179; on Benny TV program, 184–185, 289–290, 294–296, 298–299, 303; "blackness" made visible on radio, 122, 130, 135–140, 159, 337n14; and Interracial understanding fostered by, 134–153, 157–159, 187–188, 255; and minstrel show stereotypes, 122, 127, 134–135, 136–140, 141, 159–160, 177; named Rochester by Jack Benny, 132; and prejudiced southern audiences, 122, 140–141, 146–147, 166–167, 174–175; and racial stereotypes in radio, 90, 122, 127–129, 136–142, 169–173, 179–183, 185, 292–293; and racism in radio broadcasting, 127–128, 130, 138, 140–141, 156–157; relationship with Jack character, 89, 90, 100, 120, 122, 126, 130–153, 155–187, 303, 305; and Uncle Tom charges, 121, 130, 142, 154–155, 160–161, 176, 177. *See also* Anderson, Eddie; Jack Benny radio program; Jack Benny TV program
Rogers, Will, 128, 202, 226
Roosevelt, Franklin D., 2, 8, 36–37, 40, 196

Salisbury, Cora, 3
Sandrich, Mark, 15, 142–148, 222, 238–249
Seldes, Gilbert, 19, 250, 265–267, 272
Shlepperman character, 97–98, 129
Shutta, Ethel, 21, 28, 29, 30, 33–34, 38–39, 59, 60, 61, 63, 65, 229

silence in radio humor, 1–2, 9, 74–75, 310
Silvers, Sid, 31, 39–40, 65
Sinatra, Frank, 299–300
Skelton, Red, 77, 100, 102, 271, 278, 284
sponsors. *See* Canada Dry Company, General Foods Corporation, Jack Benny program
Sportsmen Quartet, 89, 90, 218–221, 251, 269, 296, 305
Stevens, Larry, 255, 311
Stewart, Jimmy, 231, 292, 301–302, 311

television, 281–317: networks' abandonmment of radio for, 281–293; postwar rise of, 281–293. *See also* Jack Benny television progam
Thorgerson, Ed, 30, 32
To Be or Not to Be (film), 224, 252
Trammel, Niles, 198, 199, 280
Transatlantic Merry Go Round (film), 42–43, 228

Vallee, Rudy, 22, 27
Van Horne, Harriet, 92, 115, 250, 283
Vault, underground, 5, 19, 257, 281, 288, 290, 307–308
Voices in radio performance, 1–2, 7–12, 37, 71, 88, 120–121, 127–128, 130–132, 134, 176–177, 192, 196, 203–206, 209, 309

Waters, Ethel, 148, 155, 160, 165, 166
Waukegan, Illinois, 2–3, 95, 144, 239–240, 268
Weaver, Pat, 49, 188, 191–192, 209, 210, 254
Weems, Ted, 38, 40, 311
Welles, Orson, 175–176
West, Mae, 32, 63, 99, 228
Wilson, Don, 3, 4, 41, 43, 47, 72, 75, 78, 80, 82, 89, 91, 98, 100, 106–107, 108, 114, 116, 132, 139, 145, 191, 199–200, 203–209, 218, 241, 266, 270, 281, 288, 294, 305, 311
Women: female gender identity on Benny's program, 5, 16, 53–85, 87, 88, 91–92, 309; lack of, in major radio roles, 69; relationships with men on Benny program, 55–56, 75–85, 141; as unruly women, 16, 53–55, 63, 69, 141. *See also*

Allen, Gracie; Livingstone, Mary; West; Mae

Woods, Lyman, 3

World War II: efforts to improve representation of African Americans during, 18, 123, 151–154, 163–164, 165; race riots during, 164–167; racial segregation in military, 175–176, 250–257, 263; radio programs broadcast from military camps, 250, 253, 254; radio's role in; 19, 78–79, 92, 106, 214, 215; working women in, "Twink Family skit," 78–80. *See also* Jack Benny radio program

Wynn, Ed, 7, 22, 31, 38, 100, 195, 229, 282, 284, 290–291

Young & Rubicam advertising agency, 4, 49, 144, 191, 202–214, 235, 239–240, 243, 247, 252, 253, 254

www.ingramcontent.com/pod-product-compliance
Lightning Source LLC
Chambersburg PA
CBHW020634230426
43665CB00008B/168